LIFE AFTER VIETNAM

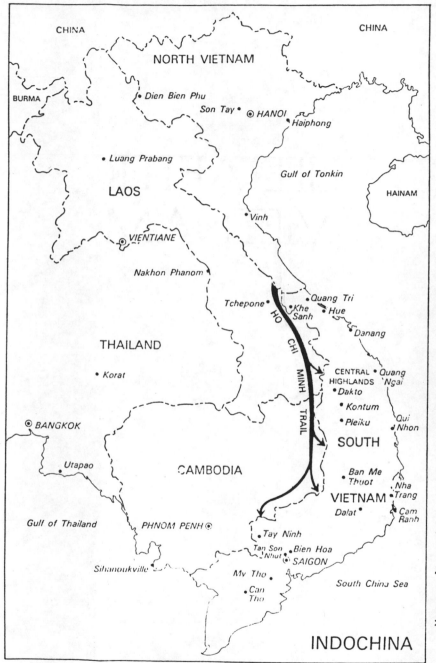

CHINA

NORTH VIETNAM

CHINA

BURMA

• Dien Bien Phu

Son Tay • ⊙ HANOI

Haiphong

• Luang Prabang

Gulf of Tonkin

HAINAM

LAOS

• Vinh

⊙ VIENTIANE

Nakhon Phanom

Tchepone • • Quang Tri
• Khe • Hue
Sanh

THAILAND

• Danang

CENTRAL • Quang
HIGHLANDS `Ngai
• Dakto

• Korat

• Kontum

• Pleiku

Qui
• Nhon

⊙ BANGKOK

SOUTH

• Utapao

CAMBODIA

• Ban Me
• Thuot

VIETNAM

Nha
• Trang

Gulf of Thailand

PHNOM PENH ⊙

Dalat •
• Cam
Ranh

• Tay Ninh

Tan Son • Bien Hoa
Nhut ⊙ SAIGON

Sihanoukville

Mv Tho

• Can
Tho

South China Sea

INDOCHINA

HO CHI MINH TRAIL

LIFE AFTER VIETNAM

*How Veterans and Their Loved Ones
Can Heal the Psychological
Wounds of War*

DELORES A. KUENNING

PARAGON HOUSE
90 Fifth Avenue, New York, N.Y. 10011

First edition, 1991

Published in the United States by

Paragon House Publishers
90 Fifth Avenue
New York, NY 10011

Library of Congress Cataloging-in-Publication data
Kuenning, Delores.
Life after Vietnam : how veterans and their loved ones can heal
the psychological wounds of war / by Delores A. Kuenning. — 1st ed.
p.   cm.
Includes bibliographical references (p.   ) and index.
ISBN 1-55778-231-8 (HC) : $22.95
1. Vietnamese Conflict, 1961–1975—Psychological aspects.
2. Vietnamese Conflict, 1961–1975—Veterans—United States.
3. Veterans—United States—Psychology.   I. Title.
DS559.8.P7K84   1990
248.8′6—dc20   90-19961
                                                                              CIP

LOVINGLY DEDICATED

to

All Vietnam Veterans,

both living and dead,

and those who love them

whose hearts still ache.

They've paid a terrible price.

Wars do not end when the shooting stops. They live on in the lives of those who are veterans of those wars. They live on in the lives of those who are the survivors and the dependents of those who lost their lives in war.

But, most of all, they live on and on, in the memories of those who have served, who have given their best for this country.

That is why this Nation should never forget, because the veteran never forgets.

—MAX CLELAND, Author of
Strong at the Broken Places

CONTENTS

PART I
UNDERSTANDING THE WAR IN VIETNAM

PART II
COPING WITH THE PAIN OF
WARTIME MEMORIES

Contents

PART III
SPIRITUAL HEALING

PART IV
OTHER THERAPY

APPENDIXES

ACKNOWLEDGMENTS

It is impossible to write a book of this nature without the assistance of many people. To all of you who allowed me to interview and record your story, I am indebted.

Many people were interviewed and gave me valuable historical background but their names and personal stories do not appear in this text. George Nicholas and Mike Matalik, a historian in his own right, are two such persons. David Missavage, Richard Rohlfs, Donna Johnson, and Gary Bjorkquist did so with slides. Team leaders Byron Coghlan, Gary Highfill, and James Dayton at the Quad Cities Vet Center, and Rodney Haug, Ph.D., Associate Regional Manager of Region V Veteran's Administration Vet Centers, have all been very supportive.

A special word of appreciation goes to members of Vietnam Veterans of America (VVA) Chapter #299 who have been helpful in so many ways. They welcomed me as an associate member and gave me much encouragement during the three years required to write this book. Bill Allen, President of the Illinois State Council of VVA, put me in touch with people who had valuable insights and information I needed. I'm sure at times some members may have felt uncomfortable having a "minister's wife" in their midst (we're stereotyped also), but if they did, I was never made to feel unwelcome. Those especially helpful were Robert Lintz, Gary Sawvell, Al Huber, David Missavage, and Larry Tschappat.

To the many professionals who gave of their valuable time for interviews, I am indebted. They are: Walter E. Bussey, Byron Coghlan, Sandra Davis, Frederick Downs, Congressman Lane Evans, Kevin Feather, Dr. Erle Fitz, Stephen Goose, Fred Gusman, Ira Hamburg, Jo Harris, Janine Lenger-Gvist, Edward Lundquist, Peter Kahn, Ph.D., Diana Keck, Rick Knowles, Jay Lintner, Judy O'Brien, Rev. Chuck Sampson, David Seamonds, Colleen Shine, Rev. John Steer, Sandy Strait, Fr. Mark Swanson, Laura Palmer, Ken Ruder, Phil Ross, Wanda Ruffins, Jan Scruggs, Carol Troescher, Ed.D., and Wayne Wilson.

My professional writer friends critiqued the manuscript and offered valuable reader reaction. They are: Judie Gulley, Barbara Foster, Connie Heckert, Sidney Seward, and Chris Walkowicz.

Perhaps the person most deserving of my gratitude is my husband, Ken, who sometimes had to wait for his white shirts to be ironed and who prepared meals while I was busy at the computer. He accompanied me to VVA meetings in Springfield; Galesburg Correctional Center; DeKalb, Illinois; and Des Moines, Iowa, so that I could conduct interviews or attend lectures. He also made it possible for me to do research in Washington, D.C., New York, Denver, and San Francisco. Any writer knows how valuable a supportive spouse is to any long-term writing project. A book project demands intense effort and concentration and one's life is planned around "the book" for many long months. This book required three years of intense work.

To editors Ken Stuart and Andy DeSalvo of Paragon House, and my agent, Ruth Wreschner, who made this all possible, go special thank yous.

The author is grateful for permission to reprint from the following:

"Tracing Procedures for Amerasians Searching for Their Fathers," International Notice Number #22, June 21, 1989. Courtesy of the American Red Cross.

"Wounds of War" by Don Baty. Used by permission of the *Missoulian*.

Vietnam Veterans: The Road to Recovery by Joel Osler Brende, M.D., and Erwin Randolph Parson, Ph.D. Copyright 1985. Used by permission of Plenum Publishing Corp. and the authors.

Before the Dawn by Mickey Block and Wm. R. Kimball. Copyright 1988 by Daring Books.

A Rumor of War by Philip Caputo. Copyright 1977. Used by permission of Henry Holt and Company, Inc.

Strong at the Broken Places by Max Cleland. Copyright 1980. Used by permission of Chosen Books/Fleming H. Revell Company.

Psalms of My Life by Joseph Bayly, 1987. Used by permission of David C. Cook Publishing Co.

"Chicago's Vietnam Veterans Parade—How One Weekend Healed a Million Old Wounds," by William Mullen. Copyright 1986, Chicago Tribune Company.

Nam Vet: Making Peace with Your Past by Chuck Dean with Bob Putnam. Copyright 1988.

War by Gwynne Dyer. Copyright 1985. Used by permission of Crown Publishers, Inc.

Vietnam: A History by Stanley Karnow. Copyright 1983 by WGBH Educational Foundation and Stanley Karnow. Reprinted by permission of Viking Penguin.

"Three Fathers Struggle to Reclaim Past in Vietnam" and "Amerasians Find Unlikely Allies in U.S. Women," by Ann Keegan. Copyright 1988, Chicago Tribune Company.

"Why the Pain Won't Stop and What the Family Can Do to Help," by Robert Marrs, *Post-Traumatic Stress Disorder and the War Veteran Patient*, William E. Kelly, ed. Reprinted by permission of Brunner/Mazel, and from the Vietnam Veterans Wives' Support Group, Macomb Community College, Mt. Clemens, Michigan, and Robert Marrs.

Born on the Fourth of July by Ron Kovic. Copyright 1976. Used by permission of McGraw-Hill Publishing Company.

Grief Recovery Handbook by John W. James and Frank Cherry. Copyright 1988. Used by permission of Harper & Row, Publishers, Inc.

Permissions

Dreams: A Way to Listen to God by Morton Kelsey. Copyright 1978. Used by permission of Paulist Press.

Vietnam: The Other Side of Glory by William R. Kimball. Copyright 1987. Used by permission of Daring Books.

Home from the War by Robert J. Lifton. Reprinted by permission of International Creative Management, Inc. Copyright 1973 by Robert J. Lifton.

Out of the Night: The Spiritual Journey of Vietnam Vets by William Mahedy. Copyright 1986 by William Mahedy. Reprinted by permission of Ballantine Books.

Map used courtesy of the University of Kentucky Press.

God Our Loving Enemy by Robert McClelland. Copyright 1969. Used by permission of Abingdon Press.

"Through a Glass Darkly: Vietnam, Alienation, and Passion," used by permission of *MINERVA: Quarterly Report on Women and the Military* (Vol. VI, No. 4, Winter 1988).

The Father Heart of God by Floyd McClung, Jr. Copyright 1985. Used by permission of the author.

An adapted version of "Nine Steps for Personal Growth" is used by permission of Conquerors Post-Abortion Support Group, a ministry of New Life Homes and Family Services, 3361 Republic Avenue, Minneapolis, MN, 55426.

The Psychosocial Milieu of Nurses in Vietnam and Its Effect on Vietnam Nurse Veterans by E. A. Paul and J. S. O'Neill. Copyright 1984. Unpublished manuscript, Northwestern State University of Louisiana, College of Nursing, Shreveport, LA.

Psalms/Now. Copyright 1973, Concordia Publishing House. Reprinted by permission of Concordia Publishing House.

Post-Traumatic Stress Disorders—A Handbook for Clinicians, Tom Williams, ed. Copyright 1987. "Readjustment Problems Among Vietnam Veterans," published by Disabled American Veterans, Washington, D.C., reprinted in this handbook.

"The Problems of Limited War," by Ernest Cuneo. Reprinted by permission, *The American Legion Magazine*. Copyright 1987.

"The Young Dead Soldiers" from *New and Collected Poems 1917–1982* by Archibald MacLeish. Copyright 1985 by the Estate of Archibald MacLeish. Reprinted by permission of Houghton Mifflin Company.

Scars and Stripes by Eugene B. McDaniel with James Johnson. Copyright 1975. Used by permission of Eugene McDaniel and Mrs. James Johnson.

Dreams: God's Forgotten Language by John A. Sanford. Copyright 1968 by John A. Sanford. Reprinted by permission of Harper & Row, Publishers, Inc.

The Healing Gifts of the Spirit by Agnes Sanford. Copyright 1966. Used by permission of Harper & Row, Publishers.

Shrapnel in the Heart by Laura Palmer. Copyright 1987. Used by permission of Random House, Inc.

"Welcome Home" by Laura Palmer. Reprinted by permission of International Creative Management, Inc. Copyright 1989 by Laura Palmer.

"U.S. Soviet Vets Share Grief of War" by Michael Parks. Copyright 1988, *Los Angeles Times.*

Permissions

Living the New Life by Gavin Reid. Copyright 1977. Used by permission of Abingdon Press.

Welcome Home, Davey by Dave Roever and Harold Fickett. Used by permission of WORD Incorporated. Copyright 1986.

In Love and War by Jim and Sybil Stockdale. Harper & Row, Publishers. Copyright 1984.

Vietnam: Curse or Blessing? by John Steer with Cliff Dudley. Copyright 1982. Used by permission of New Leaf Press, Inc.

Healing of Memories by David A. Seamonds. Copyright 1986. Used by permission of Victor Books.

"To Heal a Nation" by Joel L. Swerdlow. Used by permission of *National Geographic Magazine*, May 1985.

To Heal a Nation by Jan C. Scruggs and Joel L. Swerdlow. Harper & Row, 1985. Used by permission of the authors.

"Volunteers for America" by Mark Shields. Copyright August 4, 1987 by the *Washington Post*.

Comments by Steve Tice taken from videotape filmed at the University of Wisconsin, *A Program for Vietnam Veterans . . . and Everyone Else Who Should Care*, hosted by Charles Haid, a production of WTTW/Chicago. Copyright 1985.

Home Before Morning by Lynda Van DeVanter with Christopher Morgan. Used by permission of Beaufort/Kampman Books, Inc. Copyright 1983.

Veteran, the official publication of Vietnam Veterans of America, Washington, D.C.

Life Begins at Death by Leslie Weatherhead. Copyright 1969. Used by permission of Abingdon Press.

May I Hate God? by Pierre Wolff. Copyright 1979. Used by permission of Paulist Press.

Bill Moyers: A World of Ideas by Betty Sue Flowers. Copyright, 1989, Doubleday.

A Just Peace Church by Susan Thistlethwaite. Copyright 1986. United Church Press.

Vet Center Voice, ed. Gary Sorenson, 1985.

A People's History of the United States by Howard Zinn. Copyright 1980 by Howard Zinn. Reprinted by permission of Harper & Row, Publishers, Inc.

Verses marked "(TLB)" are taken from *The Living Bible* 1971. Used by permission of Tyndale House Publishers, Inc.

Scripture texts identified "(TEV)" are from the *Good News Bible*, the Bible in Today's English Version. Copyright American Bible Society, 1966, 1971, 1976.

Scripture texts identified "(RSV)" are from the *Revised Standard Version Bible*, copyright © 1946, 1952, 1971 by the Division of Christian Education of the National Council of Churches of Christ in the USA and used by permission.

Scripture quotations marked "(NIV)" are from the *Holy Bible, New International Version*. Copyright 1973, 1978, 1984 by the International Bible Society.

Scripture texts identified "(KJV)" are from the *King James Version*; "(NKJV)" are from the *New King James Version*, and "(NASB)" are from the *New American Standard Version* of the *Bible*.

FOREWORD

War is unmitigated evil. It lays waste not only the bodies of victims and perpetrators alike but their souls as well. Yet in the aftermath of war's terrible destruction there sometimes emerges a tender grace: an impulse, a drive toward healing and wholeness. Delores Kuenning has written a beautiful book that both describes this healing process and sets the course for those who undertake the journey.

Drawing upon her extensive knowledge of the social sciences and theology, the author integrates these disciplines in a sensitive and pastorally written guidebook for those afflicted with the psychic and spiritual scars of war. It is a book that should be read not only by veterans but by anyone who cares about healing the pain of soul that war inevitably produces.

Although she writes with the authority of one skilled in the art and science of clinical practice, her grasp of the religious dimension of healing is even more impressive. Clearly Delores Kuenning understands how the reconciling Gospel of Our Lord applies to those who still suffer the relentless spiritual pain of war. Her message is for all of us: veterans, family members, friends, church people. We would all do well to heed her words.

William P. Mahedy
Former Army chaplain, Vietnam veteran and author of
Out of the Night: The Spiritual Journey of Vietnam Vets

Introduction

Mike's letter from Vietnam in 1969 is one I will never forget. Mike was nineteen, barely out of high school, and had grown up in our Sunday School. He was a sensitive, intelligent young man.

"You'll never know what it's like to line up another human being in your gun sights for the first time," he wrote to my minister husband and me. His words were haunting.

I worried about Mike, not only for his physical safety but for the effect the war would have on his mind and spirit. For him, and millions of other young men like him, the rules of society had suddenly changed. The Judeo-Christian ethic, which shaped our Constitution and the laws of this land, reaffirms killing as an immoral, unlawful, and uncivilized act. Furthermore, Christians view all life as sacred and all people as children of God and brothers and sisters. Suddenly, those things didn't matter, and young men were being taught to "kill a Commie for Mommy!" Most Americans had never even heard of Vietnam.

My husband and I were opposed to the war because we thought it was wrong for our government to send young men into an *undeclared* war. We were against the war but never against the men who served in it. We agonized with those who lived with the uncertainty of having their lives "on hold" and never knowing when their induction notice might come. We agonized with those who could not conscientiously fight in the war and were forced to leave the country or become conscientious objectors. And we agonized for those young men and women serving in Vietnam.

It was not an easy time for young people coming of age or for their families who suffered with them in the painful decisions they had to make. Their options were to enlist, passively accept the draft notice and serve for one year, declare themselves conscientious objectors and serve as noncombatants, resist the draft and risk going to jail for three years, or go to Canada for life. *

I kept looking for glimpses of Mike on the evening news. The soldiers all looked so young. I felt the sharp contrast between the secure, comfortable lives we on the homefront enjoyed and those of the men and women who faced death every day in Vietnam. An unknown poet summed it up well:

> *For us it was the six o'clock news.*
> *For them it was reality.*
>
> *We called for pizza.*
> *They called for medics.*
>
> *We watched children play.*
> *They watched children die.*
>
> *We learned of life.*
> *They learned of death.*
>
> *We served dinner.*
> *They served their country.*
>
> *Our passion was success.*
> *Theirs was survival.*
>
> *We forget.*
> *They can't.*

Although injured twice, Mike survived the war.

Another young soldier came home from Vietnam while we were serving the same parish. Thank God my husband visited him, listened to him, and viewed his pictures with him. It was obvious to my husband the young man was emotionally shattered. Within a year after his return, he and his wife divorced.

Our small community was shocked when Ben Purcell, at age forty

---

* An estimated 40,000–60,000 fled to Canada or elsewhere; more than 7,000 were convicted for Selective Service violations, with nearly 40,000 under review in 1974; over 30,000 deserted.

the father of five, was reported missing in action. Six months into his tour, shortly after the Tet Offensive, the helicopter in which he was riding was shot down. For thirteen months his wife, Anne, didn't know whether Ben was dead or alive. We marveled at her staunch faith; she never gave up hope that Ben was alive. Years later, we learned that Col. Ben Purcell, the highest ranking U.S. Army returnee, had been imprisoned in various prisoner of war camps in North Vietnam. He was captured February 8, 1968, in South Vietnam and wasn't released until March 30, 1973.

The Vietnam War was only one of several conflicts in the sixties that tore at the very fabric of our American society. Added to the war were the racial revolution and race riots. The feminist movement was gaining momentum; women were seeking equality. There were the "hippies" and flower children. The generation gap widened. Parents and grandparents couldn't understand the beards, the dress, the lack of respect for traditional values. College campuses became centers of political activity and antiwar protest. Sexual mores were changing. The assassinations of President John F. Kennedy, the Reverend Martin Luther King, Jr., and Senator Robert Kennedy startled the whole world. And then there was Watergate, and public distrust of our government deepened.

Servicemen and women came home one by one, and we seldom thought much of it. Like most Americans, I simply wasn't aware of the wounds inflicted on their young lives by our apparent indifference and apathy. Some who were not apathetic were activists who couldn't separate the "warrior from the war" and chose to take their anger and frustration out on those returning from Vietnam. Others of us were not against the soldier; we simply felt the war was wrong and we wanted the killing and the war to end.

My interest in Vietnam veterans intensified during the six years of independent research I did for my book, *Helping People Through Grief*, especially when I read about what clinicians term "impacted" grief associated with Post-traumatic Stress Disorder. Shortly after finishing the manuscript for my grief book early in 1987, I went to the Vet Center in Moline, Illinois, to talk with Team Leader Byron Coghlan. "Is there a need for a book addressing the grief and spiritual issues of veterans?" I asked him. He assured me there was.

A counselor then invited me to accompany five veterans to the premiere showing of *Hamburger Hill*. Following the movie, Dennis

Osborne, Richard Rohlfs, Bill Tucker, Harvey Nelson, and one who prefers to be identified only as Larry—agreed to an interview. Thus began my research for this book and my deep involvement with veterans whom I have grown to love and respect.

During the viewing of *Hamburger Hill,* I realized that my thinking began to change from that of a civilian to one trying to see Vietnam from the soldier's viewpoint. I realized that once he stepped off the helicopter into a hot landing zone for the first time, all his options had vanished. It then became a matter of survival—of killing or being killed.

Until recently, there has been little understanding of the pain associated with wartime memories. One of the legacies of the Vietnam War is that we are finally gaining some understanding of that gut-wrenching, soul-shattering experience. The soldiers themselves are our teachers.

I feel it is important that civilians know the *pain and the price* some Vietnam veterans paid for serving their country. For most, the experience was terrifying, dehumanizing, and, on their return home, demoralizing.

It has taken nearly two decades for America to reach the point where it is acceptable to talk about Vietnam, and the veteran is free to grieve the many losses he or she experienced. But grieving is a social process; we cannot grieve alone. It requires support from others who care about our pain. We can all play a role in the healing process. All through the writing of this book, people have asked me repeatedly, "Were you in Vietnam?" or "Did you have a loved one in Vietnam?" Initially, I apologized and said, "No." It was apparent they were thinking that this woman doesn't have any business writing about this subject. Now when people ask me those questions, I boldly answer, "You don't have to be a veteran or have had a loved one in Vietnam to care about Vietnam vets!" Perhaps herein lies our hope—that persons like myself who have been sheltered from the harsh realities of war *will care* and take an interest in the unresolved issues of the war. Jan Scruggs, the veteran whose idea led to the building of the Vietnam Veterans Memorial in Washington, D.C., believes this also. He writes in his book, *To Heal a Nation,* "*Every* American, not just veterans and their families, is part of the healing and learning process which transcends Vietnam and its veterans and goes right to the heart of what America is and what it will be as a nation."[1]

Vietnam veteran and Pulitzer Prize–winning author, Philip Caputo, writes:

> If America wants its Vietnam veterans to be cleansed, it must give them . . . compassion for having been misused, dignity for having answered the call to arms and doing their duty as they saw it, [and] respect for having had the courage and the tenacity to survive.[2]

Generally, the churches of America have not acknowledged or even been aware of the soldiers' pain—now or then. One veteran told me that during his year-and-a-half hospitalization stateside as the result of war injuries, his home church sent him offering envelopes, but never once did he receive a get well card or letter from its members.

Another veteran relates how, shortly after returning home from Vietnam, he traveled all night on his motorcycle so he could attend Mass with his mother on Mother's Day. Because he had long hair and wore a leather jacket and looked like a "hippie," he was told by the church fathers his attire and appearance were unacceptable and he was not allowed to enter the church. He never again darkened the door of *any* church.

The parish my husband and I have served since mid-1969 sent cookies and made sure the church newsletter was sent to our service personnel. Our secretary's book is filled with thank-you notes from the men and women who let us know those gestures meant a lot to them. Generally, the local parishes have not been for the veteran "the healing place" that they were intended to be.

My hope is that this book will enlighten pastors and challenge churches throughout America to reach out to Vietnam veterans. We need to honor them for who they are today and the sacrifices they've made. They were victims of the war, too. A Veterans Day Service that my husband and I compiled and have used is included in Appendix D of this book.

Within these pages is the human story of what happened to some individuals who fought the war and how it has affected them and their loved ones. The veterans, spouses, mothers, and fathers of those missing and dead have personally shared their stories so that others might be helped and so that we might understand. By doing so, they have willingly laid bare their souls, disclosing their own confusion, bitterness, anger, sense of betrayal, and hurt that has been buried for too many years. For many, the pain is so intense it defies description. Those speaking choke up, their eyes fill with tears . . . the conversation lags while they regain their composure. Most apologize for their tears, the awkward pauses when the memories come rushing forth and are too painful to verbalize.

Many veterans, however, still choose not to talk about their experiences, especially with nonveterans, and one has to respect their right to silence. One can't impose discussions or understanding upon another person. We have to be sensitive to the need for such understanding or discussion. Other vets are eager and willing to speak to schools, churches, and other organizations. For them, healing comes through telling their story. Some speak out because they fear U.S. involvement in similar wars, and they don't want other young lives wasted.

Until recently, we have denied veterans an atmosphere in which they could grieve for the losses they have experienced. Too often, we have been guilty of telling them to "put the war behind them." Unfortunately, many veterans tried to do just that. Many have buried, denied, and repressed the enormous sadness that engulfs them. But buried grief doesn't go away.

This repressed grief has taken its toll on veterans' lives. Although no reliable statistics exist, counselors, and vets themselves, know that far too many of their buddies have died violent deaths since the war—many believed to be suicidal in nature. The *New England Journal of Medicine* published the results of a study in the late 1980s that estimated that as many as 59,000 Vietnam veterans may have killed themselves since returning from the war. The isolation and despair some vets feel is overwhelming to the point of desperation, driving them to seek an end to the pain by ending their own lives. There have been two suicides at the Memorial Wall in Washington, D.C.

It is important to remember, however, that the vast majority of Vietnam veterans are well adjusted and contributing members of society. But one can't ignore the fact that, according to studies done by the Research Triangle Institute released in 1988, *one in seven* veterans still has serious war-related problems.

Introduction

My reasons for writing this book are many.

Primarily, this book is for those still hurting from the war. The guidelines for doing the grief work, as well as some spiritual guidelines essential for healing and processing guilt, are intended to be suggestions for working through the "dark night of the soul," enabling the reader to emerge with some degree of healing and wholeness. There is a saying, *"The best way out is always through,"* and that is true for both grief and guilt. Much of the advice comes from veterans themselves as they discover the many doors to healing. Their stories of healing bring encouragement to us all.

Second, I have written *Life After Vietnam* to increase public understanding of the problems plaguing Vietnam veterans.

This book is also intended for spouses, family members and friends, co-workers, and the clergy, to enable them both to understand and to support the veteran. Guidelines to effective communication are offered to assist in this process.

I hope it will also help give vets a new perspective on faith issues. Many vets have reported to me on their loss of faith in God and belief in themselves as a good person. Wizened by war, the Vietnam veteran often speaks the language of the disenchanted and the disillusioned. All of the myths—all of the illusions—have been stripped away, including, on occasion, his or her faith in a good and loving God. They report that God seemed not only silent, but absent in Vietnam. Still others, especially prisoners of war, *relied* on prayer to survive. I believe it is important to explore these unanswered questions about God by asking: *Where was God in Vietnam?*

Based on my interviews with them, I believe combat vets have experienced life in its extremes, and only veterans of wars and those who have been victimized can fully comprehend the feelings inherent in seeing, participating in, or being a victim of the horrors of evil and "man's inhumanity to man."

My hope is that by exploring these unanswered questions about God, those who lost their faith can again begin to trust and find a source of healing and light that will warm and bring peace to the cold, aching, troubled corners of their hearts and minds.

I firmly believe that if veterans can push through the painful grief processes necessary for healing and sort through shattered belief structures, rebuilding a new and vital relationship with God, their emotional and spiritual journeys will lead to new strengths and new visions unique to our time. Chaplain William Mahedy, author of *Out of the Night: The Spiritual Journey of Vietnam Vets*, says it eloquently:

> Vietnam veterans went off to a distant jungle where they were pushed to the frontiers of faith. They came back home apparently broken, in despair, a "problem" to the nation. Now, in the maturity of early middle age, they have returned from nihilism and despair, seeking and finding answers to questions that have haunted them for years. Their quest is a story of immense beauty, one that will enrich America. It is a story of the most significant spiritual journey of our time.[3]

Delores A. Kuenning

How to Use This Book

Part I of this book is for those readers who wish to gain some understanding of the historical background of the war. Chapter 1 reveals how each presidential decision and the country's foreign policy led the United States deeper and deeper into a land war in Asia—a war that no president desired or intended. Chapter 2 points out how Vietnam differed from previous conflicts, both in fighting conditions and in the soldiers and women who served, and shows how these factors contributed to the psychological wounding of Vietnam veterans.

Part II presents the true stories of men and women Vietnam veterans, family members, or people closely connected to a vet, and the emotional wounding they live with as a result of the war's impact on their lives. Although there are both men and women veterans, there are many more men, so in many cases the veteran is referred to as "he." Read the stories to gain insight into thoughts, feelings, and the problems unique to PTSD, women veterans, living with a Vietnam vet, Agent Orange, losing a loved one in Vietnam, POWs/MIAs, and Amerasians. Each chapter gives an overview of the problem, lists books for additional reading, gives advice based on the wisdom of those who have struggled to grow from their experiences, and refers you to organizations that can be of help to you or serve as a channel through which you can become more deeply involved in veterans' issues.

Part III contains stories of the men and women who struggle with their moral and spiritual pain. *Where was God in Vietnam?* is a question unanswered for many. Perhaps you are still very angry with God. If you're still feeling guilty, then read the chapter on coming to terms with this guilt. Many of you have "unfinished business" from the war, and must do some grieving over lost friends. You will benefit by the steps outlined, not only by working through, but by growing as a result of facing this pain head on and doing something about it. Healing of memories is possible. Don't look at these unresolved issues in your life as impossible or insurmountable. Rather, look at them as an opportunity for growth and a way to remove the barriers that have restricted your life in so many ways.

I know that some of you reading this book are not of the Christian faith or members of a church. Hopefully, you too will learn a great deal about the war experience from the stories shared. Others of you are "turned off" to organized religion. Nonetheless, through cultural conditioning, if in no other manner, your conscience has been influenced by tenets of the faith. You pray to God, you feel guilt when doing something your conscience says is wrong, you attend Christian funerals and believe in heaven and hell. Some of you had religious training as a child. If all of these things are true about you, then you, too, can benefit by the sound principles of faith and healing found in this book.

Part IV is devoted to the healing power of the Vietnam Veterans Memorial Wall in Washington and delayed parades, which are both examples of public recognition. In the final chapter, I have provided the opportunity for you to hear from veterans how they want to be treated and to express their views about war. My hope is that their messages will "ring in your ears" for years to come.

Last but not least are the appendixes that you should consult for uplifting scriptures as well as a historical perspective of the church's involvement and stance on war. A "Word to the Church" and "Communication Guidelines for Pastors" are intended for the clergy and other church leaders. Churches need to become more involved and concerned about veterans and the pain they endure. A suggested Veterans Day Recognition Service is outlined, and guidelines for support of the POW/MIA issue are also included.

PART I

UNDERSTANDING THE WAR IN VIETNAM

Chapter 1

How and Why the United States Got Involved

The United States involvement in Vietnam didn't start in 1964. It dates back to World War II. The American Office of Strategic Services (OSS)—forerunner of the CIA—offered assistance to Vietnamese guerrillas headed by Ho Chi Minh in fighting the Japanese. Since 1941 Ho Chi Minh had led a small nationalist movement called the Viet Minh* in its struggle for Vietnam's independence and the fight against the Japanese. Japan had gained control of Indochina by diplomatic fiat shortly after the fall of France in 1940.

By 1941 the Japanese had bases in Indochina and control of the country's rice production, rubber, and transport industries. Proclaiming "Asia for the Asians," the Japanese overthrew the French administration in March 1945, killing or interning the French authorities. With the abrupt end of the war in August, the Japanese withdrew hastily, leaving a void in Hanoi.[1] Ho Chi Minh was ready to step in and fill that void.

Ho Chi Minh's efforts had been aimed at not only defeating the

---

* Also called the Revolutionary League for the Independence of Vietnam.

3

Japanese but ending colonial rule and establishing a new life for the peasants of Indochina who had been under French rule since 1887.

The Vietnamese had lodged these complaints against French colonialism:

> They have enforced inhuman laws. . . . They have built more prisons than schools. They have mercilessly slain our patriots, they have drowned uprisings in rivers of blood. They have fettered public opinion. . . . They have robbed us of our rice fields, our forests, and our raw materials. . . .
>
> They have invented numerous unjustifiable taxes and reduced our people, especially our peasantry, to a state of extreme poverty. . . .
>
> . . . [F]rom the end of the last year, to the beginning of this year . . . more than two million of our fellow citizens died of starvation. . . .
>
> The whole Vietnamese people, animated by a common purpose, are determined to fight to the bitter end against any attempt by the French colonialists to reconquer their country.[2]

As David Halberstam points out in his book, *Ho*:

> The French and the rest of the Western world read the daily dispatches telling of the noble struggle of the West against the Communists . . . but for the Vietnamese it was another war; it was the struggle not for Communism, but to throw the white colonist out. This was the heroic war for freedom. All those long-submerged and powerful Vietnamese aspirations were unleashed—and the Vietminh harnessed them to their revolution.[3]

WESTERN ALLIES DECIDE THE FATE OF VIETNAM

As World War II drew to a close, the Western Allies began planning the division of countries and shaping the world after the war. President Franklin Delano Roosevelt felt the French should be prevented from reestablishing Vietnam as their colony. Indochina had been "liberated by American aid and American troops," Roosevelt declared, and "should never simply be handed back to the French, to be milked by their imperialists."[4] But after Roosevelt's death in April 1945 his views were soon forgotten.

In August 1945, the Viet Minh declared Ho Chi Minh as the leader for all of Vietnam and the country as the Democratic Republic of Vietnam. Weeks later, the Viet Minh won most of the 400 seats in their National Assembly and Ho was proclaimed President. For a brief period after this election—a few weeks in September 1945— the Democratic Republic of Vietnam was free and united from north to south under Ho Chi Minh.

Between October 1945 and February 1946, Ho Chi Minh wrote eight letters to President Truman, reminding him of the self-determination promises of the Atlantic Charter. One of the letters was sent both to Truman and to the United Nations:

> I wish to invite attention of your Excellency for strictly humanitarian reasons to the following matter. Two million Vietnamese died of starvation during winter of 1944 and spring 1945 because of starvation policy of French who seized and stored until it rotted all available rice. . . . Three-fourths of cultivated land was flooded in summer 1945, which was followed by a severe drought; of normal harvest five-sixths was lost. . . . Many people are starving. . . . Unless great world powers and international relief organizations bring us immediate assistance we face imminent catastrophe. . . .[5]

Truman never replied.

Ho Chi Minh had made a similar appeal to Socialists at the Tours Congress in the early 1920s. The plight of the oppressed peasants in Vietnam, however, was met with indifference, although Ho had found the left-wing French Socialists sympathetic to his cause. But Ho wanted action and no action was forthcoming.[6]

Ho then turned to the teachings of Lenin. He viewed him as the "great patriot who liberated his compatriots" during the Bolshevik revolution in Russia. Ho is quoted as saying that gradually he came to believe that Socialism and Communism could liberate the oppressed nations and working people throughout the world from slavery.[7]

The aftermath of the long siege of colonial control in Vietnam was devastating to the country's people. There were few indigenous Vietnamese leaders to assume control; the French had denied them opportunities for leadership or training. Vietnamese citizens had not been permitted to purchase stocks and bonds nor were they permitted to own or participate in rubber plantation ownership.

After World War II, some historians claim the French colonists owned ninety percent of the country's industries.

And other forces were at work that would threaten their freedom.

At the Potsdam Conference (July 17–August 2, 1945) it was agreed by the Allies (United States, USSR, and Great Britain) that Chinese Nationalist troops under Chiang Kai-shek's China Command would occupy Vietnam.* Northern Chinese Nationalists did not challenge Ho Chi Minh's power. British Indian troops under another allied command were to take control of southern Vietnam; the French moved into Cochin China with their British allies. This was intended to be a temporary arrangement.

The Chinese Nationalists under the Potsdam agreements occupied northern Vietnam for seven months after the allied landings. After the agreed-upon time, England turned the southern part of Indochina back to the French, and Nationalist China did the same. Once again, Vietnam was under French control. The new government in Vietnam, however, demanded the withdrawal of the French from all of Indochina† and the independence of Vietnam. In March, 1946, as a compromise, the French and the Viet Minh agreed to French recognition of the Democratic Republic of Vietnam. Many of Ho's fellow countrymen felt he had sold out to the French.

But by December 1946, the French agreement with Ho had collapsed and the first Indochina War began in the northern and central regions. Ho based his government in the north in Hanoi; the French were based in south Vietnam in Saigon.

THE COLD WAR BEGINS

The Communist takeover of China in 1949 shocked the United States and helped persuade President Harry S. Truman to aid France in Indochina. On May 1, 1950, Truman initiated efforts to provide financial aid enabling the French to retain their hold on Vietnam. The United States looked beyond the Vietnamese insurgency in the north and perceived China as the ultimate Communist threat to be contained in Southeast Asia. The Cold War—the shift-

* Vietnam was composed of three regions—Tonkin in the north, with the capital at Hanoi; Annam in the center, capital, Hue; and Cochin China in the south, capital Saigon.
† French Indochina included Vietnam, Laos, and Cambodia.

ing struggle for power and prestige between the Western powers and the Communist bloc—prompted the United States to follow the general policy of containment, keeping the Communist states within their current boundaries. This philosophy later led to what became known as the "domino theory." This theory is based on the belief that if one country fell to Communism, others would fall also—one by one. The object was to prevent the first country from falling to Communism.

By 1954 the United States was financing 80 percent of the French war effort and had given them 300,000 small arms and machine guns, enough to equip the entire French army in Indochina.

General Bruce Palmer, Jr., says in his book, *The 25-Year War: America's Role in Vietnam*:

> In retrospect it seems clear that the Truman administration's decision to begin military aid for Indochina was taken in more or less instinctive support of the U.S. umbrella policy of containment everywhere in the world without much regard for the merits of each case and, in this instance, with little knowledge of the Indochina situation.[8]

From 1946 to 1953, the French, with allied Vietnamese units, fought the Viet Minh's well-armed, well-disciplined guerrilla forces who used combat methods following the teachings of Sun Tzu.[9]

On May 7, 1954, the Viet Minh's forces soundly defeated the French at Dien Bien Phu, thus initiating the demise of colonial rule in Indochina.

VIETNAM DIVIDED

At the Geneva Conference (April–July, 1954), during which an international assemblage met to come to terms with the struggle in Vietnam, it was agreed that the French would temporarily withdraw to the south, the Viet Minh would remain in the north, and an election to allow the Vietnamese to choose their own government would take place in two years. Therefore, the country was divided in two parts at the 17th parallel. Again, this division of *their* homeland was construed by Vietnamese nationalists as another betrayal by the French and the Communists.

For a brief period of time after division at the 17th parallel, the Vietnamese were free to choose which section of the country they wanted to live in—North or South Vietnam. More than one million persons, most of them Catholics, fled to the South. They were running away from Ho Chi Minh's oppressive regime, says Stephen Morris of the Institute of East Asian Studies at the University of California in Berkeley. He explains why:

> Violence was central to Ho's success. In 1950, Communists launched unprovoked military attacks against them [Catholics] despite the fact that the Catholics of North Vietnam were in alignment and fighting against the French. More than ten thousand Catholics were killed in less than a year.
>
> The core of Catholics who fled in 1955 did so, not because of religious doctrine, nor because they had collaborated with the French—although some of them had; nor because they were incited by CIA black propaganda as some claimed. They had acted independently of the Communists, and Ho could not accept that.[10]

In similar manner, Ho's agents had killed off rival non-communist national leaders in the mid-forties. The French had aided his efforts by turning over the files on the VNQDD (Viet Nam Quoc Dan Dang or Nationalist Party of Vietnam) and Dai Viets to him. A member of the VNQDD who escaped said nationalists were "hit on the head, sewn up in sacks, and dumped into rivers—literally hundreds and hundreds."[11]

UNITED STATES EXERTS ITS INFLUENCE

The United States wanted to give the Vietnamese an alternative to French and Communist rule, so American leaders moved quickly to prevent unification and to establish South Vietnam as an American sphere. A former Vietnamese official named Ngo Dinh Diem (who had been living in New Jersey) was set up in Saigon as head of the government and encouraged not to hold the scheduled elections for unification. The United States feared an election would ensure almost certain loss of Laos, Cambodia, and Vietnam to Communist control.

The Americans perceived Diem as being anti-Communist since

he had been out of the country during the Indochinese war. The Vietnamese, however, perceived Diem as being pro-French, a fact that would later lead to serious problems. Diem was a devout Catholic.

Diem came into power by a national referendum organized by the United States. The referendum had offered a choice between a monarchy under puppet Bao Dai or a republic with Diem as president. His brother, Ngo Dinh Nhu, also came into power and became head of the secret police.

UNITED STATES WITHDRAWS SUPPORT FROM THE FRENCH

In February 1954, during a news conference, President Eisenhower expressed these views: "I cannot conceive of a greater tragedy for America than to get heavily involved in an all-out war [in Indochina]." At that time, the French were begging for military troops to assist them in their war against the Viet Minh. Eisenhower remained firm; he would back the French with money, but not Marines. [12] A few months later—October 1954—President Eisenhower pledged support to Diem and South Vietnam. He broke with the French to favor the establishment and aid in the development of South Vietnam as an independent nation run by nationalists strong enough to resist the Communist invaders from Hanoi. American aid was no longer given through French authorities but directly to the South Vietnamese government.

Meanwhile, Viet Minh insurgents in the south became known as the Viet Cong (Viet Nam Cong San or Vietnamese Communists). The Communist-trained South Vietnamese rebels followed tactics of Vo Nguyen Giap who was a master of guerrilla warfare. The Viet Cong became a well-established political organization and were called "The National Liberation Front."

"U.S. leaders," says General Palmer, "failing to grasp the nature of the total threat, initially perceived the major threat to be an overt, across-the-border invasion by North Vietnamese or Chinese forces, and were slow in recognizing the serious threat posed by subversion, infiltration, and guerrilla warfare." [13]

In December 1954, the Eisenhower administration concluded a

formal agreement with France and South Vietnam to provide direct U.S. military assistance. The initial objective of the U.S. Military and Advisory Group was to create a conventional South Vietnamese army whose primary mission was to defend the country from external attack.[14]

According to the Geneva Accords, the United States was permitted to send 685 military advisers to South Vietnam; secretly, Eisenhower sent several thousand.[15,16]

Among the best known of these advisers or U.S. Special Forces were the Green Berets, responsible for developing and training the civilian irregular defense groups composed mostly of Montagnard tribesmen, who lived in the remote areas of Vietnam along the borders of Laos and Cambodia.

It became clear that American and French objectives in Vietnam were incompatible. Says Gen. Palmer, "The French wanted to preserve their special relationship with Vietnam, as well as with Laos and Cambodia, while the United States sought an independent, non-Communist Vietnam oriented toward the West. This basic contradiction led to the displacement of France in the region by the United States in 1955–56, which the French bitterly resented. To European countries, U.S. actions seemed hypocritical and they remained unwilling to support the United States in Vietnam throughout the war."[17]

By 1958 and 1959 armed terrorist activities had steadily increased. In early 1960 Diem, leader of South Vietnam, declared the country to be in a state of war against the Viet Cong, and asked for increased U.S. military assistance in both materials and training. The United States became involved in Vietnam because the South Vietnamese government, under the terms of the SEATO pact, asked for American help against armed aggression by a foreign power— North Vietnam.[18]

Not long after John F. Kennedy was inaugurated as President on January 20, 1961, he reaffirmed U.S. objectives. After relying on reports from General Edward G. Lansdale and General Maxwell D. Taylor, the Army's Chief of Staff during the previous administration, Kennedy directed a major expansion of the American military advisory effort—to almost seventeen thousand by the end of 1963. The President also authorized the commitment of U.S. Army helicopters in support of the Army of the Republic of Vietnam (ARVN).[19]

In May of 1963, Buddhist riots erupted in South Vietnam in protest of an edict forbidding the display of religious banners. The law had been enacted to disrupt the 2587th anniversary of Buddha's birth. What had angered Buddhists most was that a few days before, Catholics had marched with religious banners in Hue to celebrate the twenty-fifth anniversary of Thuc's elevation to bishop; Thuc was another Diem brother.[20]

Diem's own generals turned against him and Ngo Dinh Nhu. On November 2, 1963, just a few weeks before Kennedy was assassinated, Diem and his brother were murdered during a coup staged with Washington's knowledge. President-elect Lyndon B. Johnson felt it was the worst mistake ever made, for the ensuing series of corrupt governments and attempts to grab power created havoc in South Vietnam.[21]

By the end of 1963, American assistance to South Vietnam was costing $400 million annually.[22]

THE GULF OF TONKIN RESOLUTION

In early August 1964, a controversial event in the Gulf of Tonkin off the coast of North Vietnam changed the course of history. Lt. Gen. Phillip Davidson, in his book *Vietnam at War,* writes: "There has never been any doubt that North Vietnamese torpedo boats attacked the *Maddox* in international waters, but the controversy regarding this action turns around whether the United States provoked the attacks [August 2, 1964]."[23]

On August 4—just two days later—another alleged attack was made by North Vietnamese on the *Maddox* and the U.S.S. *C. Turner Joy.* An eyewitness on the scene was former Admiral James Stockdale who flew over the ships looking for enemy attack vessels. He was commander of an F-8 squadron off the U.S.S. *Ticonderoga* called in to strafe enemy boats. He saw no torpedo wakes, no boat gunfire . . . nor was any wreckage found the next day. The alert had been sounded, but Stockdale was convinced no enemy action transpired on the night of August 4.

Secretary of Defense Robert McNamara and President Johnson reported to the American public, however, that North Vietnamese torpedo boats had attacked two American destroyers—the *Maddox*

11

and the *C. Turner Joy*. President Johnson used this nebulous event, calling it "open aggression on the high seas," to order immediate air strikes.

Stockdale shares his feelings after learning about the Pentagon's decision to bomb North Vietnam:

> The bad portents of the moment were suffocating. We were about to launch a war under false pretenses, in the face of the on-scene military commander's advice to the contrary. This decision had to be driven from way up at the top. . . . It was all straight shot: Washington, Saigon, Ambassador Vientiane. On-scene naval officers couldn't turn that on or off any more than they could this thing now . . . it seemed to me important that the grounds for entering war be legitimate. I felt it was a bad portent that we seemed to be under the control of a mindless Washington bureaucracy, vain enough to pick their own legitimacies regardless of evidence.[24]

In *Love and War*, James Stockdale gives this account of what he thinks happened:

> As the only person in the world who had a good firsthand look at both the episode of the 2nd and the episode of the 4th, I cannot avoid the conclusion that McNamara wound up using August 2nd material when analyzing events of the 4th. I know this sounds like a simple and tragic way to commit a nation to war, but that's the way I read it. Recorded replays of PT boat–destroyer confrontation transmitted later, got into the August 4th file in the Pentagon. . . . Nobody was shooting at our destroyers or our airplanes that night. No aircraft "fell" and no ships were hit.[25]

Because of the Gulf of Tonkin incident, a Congressional resolution was passed, unanimously in the House and with only two dissenting votes in the Senate, giving Johnson the power to take military action as he saw fit in Southeast Asia. The Tonkin Resolution, or Southeast Asia Resolution, Public Law 88–408, was the only legislation that authorized involvement in Vietnam. A key paragraph in the Resolution read as follows:

> The Congress approves and supports the determination of the President, as Commander-in-Chief, to take all necessary measures to repel

any armed attack against the forces of the United States and to prevent further aggression.

The United States regards as vital to its national interest and to world peace the maintenance of international peace and security in Southeast Asia. Consonant with the Constitution, and in accordance with its obligations under the Southeast Asia Collective Defense Treaty, the United States is therefore prepared, as the President determines, to take all necessary steps, including the use of armed force, to assist any member or protocol state of the Southeast Asia Collective Defense Treaty requesting assistance in defense of its freedom.

The Tonkin resolution was broad enough to cover American operations in Thailand because of its membership in the Southeast Asia Collective Defense Treaty.[26] This resolution gave the President the power to initiate hostilities without the declaration of war by Congress that the Constitution requires.

In March 1965 Johnson sent the first American marines to Vietnam. Bombing of military and industrial targets continued systematically until March 1968, when raids were halted to promote peace negotiations. The number of American troops in Vietnam peaked at 543,000 in 1969.

Multinational forces from member countries of SEATO (formed in 1954 during the Eisenhower administration to halt Communist expansion in Asia) also fought in Vietnam. About sixty-nine thousand men from Australia, New Zealand, the Philippines, South Korea, and Thailand aided the South Vietnamese. Some thirty to forty thousand Canadian soldiers volunteered and served there also.

EACH PRESIDENT ADVANCED THE WAR

These decisions by each president, beginning with Truman, had moved the United States toward deeper and deeper involvement in Vietnam. In retrospect, General Palmer said of the war:

. . . the U.S. government, during the first stages of American involvement in the mid-1950s and early 1960s, was slow in recognizing the nature of the conflict in Southeast Asia and realistically evaluating the

13

situation in Vietnam. Although a few of our early American advisers had a good grasp of the situation, most lacked familiarity with the Vietnamese language and culture, and consequently did not understand or were misled by their Vietnamese counterparts. . . . Influenced by unreliable, overly optimistic assessments of progress and by the desire to look successful in the public eye, successive U.S. administrations seriously underestimated the situation in those crucial early years.[27]

Failing to realize the strengths of its enemies, the United States embarked on what was to become the longest war in U.S. history.

THE NO-WIN WAR ENDS

Public opinion on the home front ultimately forced American withdrawal from Vietnam. America's feelings toward the war changed dramatically in 1967. The war was dragging on and had no clear objectives. Americans had tired of sacrificing their sons and having their tax dollars spent on an aimless war. Because it was an undeclared war, there was a feeling that much of the killing was unjustified, and this made America turn against its own soldiers. By October 1969 a nationwide demonstration urging a moratorium against the war was staged.

Bitterness over the war forced President Johnson to withdraw from running for another term, and Richard Nixon was elected. On June 8, 1969, Nixon announced a new policy he called "Vietnamization" that included stepping up training programs for the South Vietnamese forces and the gradual withdrawal of U.S. troops, which began the following month.

In 1970 the invasion of Cambodia by the United States triggered more public protest on college campuses. The nation was shocked when National Guardsmen fired on a group of students at Kent State University in Ohio, killing four and wounding nine others. This event caused the Senate to take action by repealing the Gulf of Tonkin Resolution, a move designed by Congress to force withdrawal of troops from Cambodia.

On April 25, 1971, more than 300,000 protesters merged in the nation's capital to voice opposition to the war. It was the largest demonstration America had ever seen. William Wyman, a veteran who had lost both legs in Vietnam, was among those veterans who hurled down their medals and decorations on the steps of the Capitol in protest of the war.

Release of the "Pentagon Papers" to newspapers throughout the country in June 1971, revealing the secret government study of the war, deepened public distrust of the U.S. government. The "Pentagon Papers" raised questions about secret actions and decisions that had been made by the Pentagon. The papers also revealed that the government had deceived the American public through the information it released to the media—something the soldiers and women serving in Vietnam had known for some time. Many feel it was the distorted news coverage that had a cumulative effect on Congress.

An example of that distortion is the reporting of the Tet Offensive, says Reed Irvine, Chairman of Accuracy in Media. "The Tet Offensive was a turning point," says Irvine. "The fall of 1968, NBC news reported the Tet Offensive was a defeat for us, when in reality it was an outstanding military victory. Jack Burns [of NBC] knew it was wrong and called it to the attention of Executive Producer Robert Norshield. Rather than choosing to correct this perception, Norshield's response was, 'Tet was established in the minds of Americans as a defeat, therefore, it was an American defeat.' Think about that, a battle our soldiers won was transmuted into a defeat by our own news media."28

Nixon's successor, President Gerald R. Ford, asked Congress for $722 million in military aid for South Vietnam. Congress, now sensitive to public opinion about the war, granted only $300 million in emergency aid primarily for the purpose of evacuating Americans from Saigon.

Senator Steve Symms of Idaho says it was the Case Church Amendment that dealt the final blow. Terms of the Paris Peace accords that Nixon had signed clearly said the United States would lend support in enforcing the peace agreement.

"But the Case Church Amendment passed January 19, 1973, saying there would be 'no American activity in or over Southeast Asia' clearly telegraphed to the North Vietnamese we were not going to enforce the Paris Peace accords," says Symms. "The amendment cut further military aid to supply logistics and ammunition, and abolished U.S. air strikes if the North Vietnamese attacked. This is one of the most tragic stories in history; Cambodians, Laotians, and the Vietnamese lost their countries."[29]

A formal peace agreement was reached and signed by the United States, North Victnam, South Vietnam, and the NLF's provisional revolutionary government on January 27, 1973. The accord provided for the end of hostilities, the return of prisoners, the withdrawal of U.S. and allied troops, and the formation of a four-nation international control commission to ensure peace. The last of the U.S. ground forces left Vietnam on March 29, 1973. Without the U.S. military to back it, South Vietnam was invaded and Saigon fell. South Vietnam surrendered to North Vietnam on April 30, 1975. Saigon was then renamed Ho Chi Minh City.

PRESIDENT'S POWER LIMITED

The prolonged war in Vietnam stirred demand for checks on the president's war powers. As a result, the War Powers Act was enacted November 7, 1973, which requires the president, upon undertaking emergency military action in the absence of a declaration of war, to report the matter to Congress in writing within forty-eight hours. The combat action must end in sixty days, unless Congress authorizes the commitment. The sixty-day deadline can be extended for thirty days if the president certifies the extension's necessity for the forces' safe withdrawal. At any time Congress can order immediate removal of the forces by adopting a concurrent resolution, which is not subject to presidential veto.[30]

IN RETROSPECT

General Palmer, in the preface of his book, makes clear his feelings about America's servicemen who fought in Vietnam: *"No nation was ever blessed with more stouthearted men than the Americans who fought and died in Southeast Asia"* (emphasis added). "What is even more extraordinary is that the overwhelming majority remained loyal and continued to fight for months and even years after it was clear that our leaders and people at home were deeply divided."[31]

His critical remarks reflect more on top U.S. leaders, civilian and military, who made the key decisions affecting the direction and conduct of the war, as well as on commanders in the field.

The Vietnam Era is officially considered to date from August 4, 1964, to May 7, 1975. Legislation has been introduced, however, to change the definition of the "Vietnam Era" to the period beginning February 28, 1961. In 1990, there were 58,175 names of American men and women who died as a result of the war in Vietnam; new names are added occasionally as men die from war-related injuries.

More than 308,873 were wounded and approximately 75,000 were severely disabled; more than 2,300 are still unaccounted for and are considered to be missing in action or prisoners of war.

From 1965 to 1975, conservative estimates of the cost of the war was $143.8 billion dollars.[32] Other estimates run higher. Ford himself called the cost of the war—more than $180 billion—"staggering." And the price was destined to go higher: in the plight of hundreds of thousands of mentally and physically scarred veterans; in the prolonged anxiety of the families of MIAs; in a demoralized military establishment; in tens of thousands of political exiles, draft evaders, and deserters cut off from home; in a stagnant, inflation-ridden economy; and in the influx of nearly a million Indochinese refugees. As former Secretary of State Dean Rusk warned on April 30, 1975, "We haven't seen the final bill yet."[33]

THE COST TO VIETNAM

Historian Howard Zinn summarizes the devastation caused in Vietnam: "By the end of the Vietnam war, seven million tons of bombs had been dropped on Vietnam, more than twice the total bombs dropped on Europe and Asia in World War II—almost one 500-pound bomb for every human being in Vietnam. It was estimated there were 20 million bomb craters in the country. In addition, poisonous sprays were dropped by planes to destroy trees and any kind of growth; an area the size of the state of Massachusetts was covered with such poisons. Vietnamese mothers reported birth defects in their children."[34]

Recent statistics which come directly from the Department of International Relations of Vietnam seem to agree with a fact-finding

delegation from the Vietnam Veterans of America's (VVA) committee on POWs/MIAs that met with key personnel and Vietnamese
officials in 1989. The vice director of the department says . . . there
are ten million war victims: one million veteran victims; 300,000
invalids; and a total of 1.8 million family members that must be
cared for by the government. According to the ministry official,
Vietnam has 370,000 orphans under the age of 17, most of whom are
cared for by local communities, since care would overtax the central
government.[35]

Stanley Karnow, author of *Vietnam*, writes, "More than four million Vietnamese soldiers and civilians on both sides—roughly ten
percent of the entire population—were killed or wounded. In human terms at least, the war in Vietnam was a war that nobody won—
a struggle between victims. Its origins were complex, its lessons
disputed, its legacy still to be assessed by future generations. But
whether a valid venture or a misguided endeavor, it was a tragedy of
epic dimensions."[36]

What lessons have we learned from the Vietnam War? Bill
Moyers interviewed the Pulitzer Prize–winning historian, Barbara
Tuchman, for his PBS series, "A World of Ideas." They discussed this
very question.

Moyers points to this lesson:

I think in our collective wisdom the American people did learn from
the Vietnam experience not to let an American president take us into a
war unless he can present overwhelming evidence that our national
security is clearly at stake.

Tuchman replies:

. . . I think we have learned from that. I think it's also clear that when
you try to fight a prolonged war without national support, you lose.
You can't do it because the public just won't stand for it. It took a long
time for protest on Vietnam to make itself felt, but it did. We see the
phrase all the time, "We don't want another Vietnam."[37]

The facts shared here barely touch the surface. As author Douglas
Pike says in his excellent book, *War, Peace, and the Viet Cong*,
"Vietnam defies oversimplification." It is impossible to explore in
depth in a few pages this complex war. I have merely highlighted

the events and the presidential decisions that prompted and perpetuated United States involvement in the war.

The following are books you may wish to read for additional background.

ADDITIONAL READING

Austin, Anthony. *The President's War: The Story of the Tonkin Gulf Resolution and How the Nation was Trapped in Vietnam*. New York: J. B. Lippincott Company, 1971.

Bank, Col. Aaron. *From OSS to Green Berets*. New York: Columbia University Press, 1988.

Boettcher, Thomas D. *Vietnam: The Valor and the Sorrow*. Boston: Little, Brown and Co., 1985.

Davidson, Lt. Gen. Phillip B. (Ret.). *Vietnam at War: The History 1946–1975*. Novato, CA: Presidio, 1988.

Dawson, Alan. *55 Days: The Fall of South Vietnam*. Englewood Cliffs, NJ: Prentice-Hall, 1977.

Ellsberg, Daniel. *Papers on the War*. New York: Simon and Schuster, 1972.

Esper, George, and The Associated Press. *The Eyewitness History of the Vietnam War*. New York: Ballantine Books, 1983.

Giap, Vo Nguyen. *People's War, People's Army*. New York: Praeger, 1962.

————. *How We Won the War*. Philadelphia: Recon Publications, 1980.

Gibson, James William. *The Perfect War: The War We Couldn't Lose and How We Did*. New York: Random House, 1986.

Grinter, Lawrence, and Dunn, Peter M., eds. *The American War in Vietnam: Lessons, Legacies, and Implications for Future Conflicts*. New York: Praeger, 1986.

Hackworth, Col. David. *About Face*. New York: Simon & Schuster, 1989.

Halberstam, David. *Ho*. New York: Random House, 1971.

————. *The Best and the Brightest*. New York: Random House, 1969.

Herring, George. *America's Longest War: The United States and Vietnam, 1950–75*. Philadelphia: Temple University Press, 1986. (Copyright 1979, Random House)

Jennings, Patrick. *Battles of the Vietnam War*. New York: Bison Books, 1985.

Karnow, Stanley. *Vietnam: A History*. New York: Viking Press, 1983.

Kimball, Jeffrey P. *To Reason Why: The Debate About the Causes of U.S. Involvement in the Vietnam War*. New York: Knopf, 1989.

Krause, Patricia A., ed. *Anatomy of an Undeclared War: Congressional*

Conference on the Pentagon Papers. New York: International Universities Press, 1972.

Lacouture, Jean. *Ho Chi Minh: A Political Biography*. New York: Random House, 1968.

Maclear, Michael. *The Ten Thousand Day War*. New York: Avon, 1981.

Palmer, General Bruce, Jr. *The 25-Year War: America's Military Role in Vietnam*. New York: Simon and Schuster, 1985.

Parker, F. Charles, IV. *Vietnam: Strategy for a Stalemate*. New York: Paragon House, 1988.

Paterson, Thomas G. *Meeting the Communist Threat: Truman to Reagan*. New York: Oxford University Press, 1988.

Pike, Douglas. *War, Peace, and the Viet Cong*. Cambridge, MA: MIT Press, 1966.

Pratt, John Clark. *Vietnam Voices: Perspectives on the War Years 1941–1982*. New York: Penguin Books, 1984.

Rotter, Andrew J. *The Path to Vietnam*. Ithaca, NY: Cornell University Press, 1988.

Rusk, Dean. *As I See It*. New York: W. W. Norton, 1990.

Santoli, Al. *To Bear Any Burden*. New York: Ballantine Books, 1986.

Sheehan, Neil. *A Bright Shining Lie: John Paul Vann and America in Vietnam*. New York: Random House, 1988.

Stanton, Shelby L. *The Rise and Fall of an American Army: U.S. Ground Forces in Vietnam, 1965–1973*. New York: Dell, 1985.

Summers, Harry G., Jr. *On Strategy: A Critical Analysis of the Vietnam War*. Novato, CA: Presidio Press, 1982.

Turley, William S. *The Second Indochina War: A Short Political and Military History, 1954–1975*. New York: New American Library, 1986.

Chapter 2

WHY VIETNAM WAS A DIFFERENT WAR

It's hard for members of society, including veterans of other wars, to understand why Vietnam veterans have had more problematic readjustments to civilian life and have experienced more debilitating problems as a result of the war. Some unique differences exist, however, between the Vietnam conflict and World War II and the Korean War—the most recent wars in our collective memories. These factors have combined to create war-related problems that, in many cases, have totally disrupted all areas of the veteran's life, as well as the lives of his or her family.

Recently, while leading a seminar on the dynamics of grief, I mentioned that I was especially interested in Vietnam veterans and the fact that they've never been given permission to grieve the many losses they had experienced. A young woman in the first row spoke up loudly and said, "My brother was in Vietnam. *They were just boys!*"

THE SOLDIERS WERE YOUNGER

The average age of soldiers who served in World War II was twenty-six; for men sent to Vietnam, the average age was nineteen. Barely out of high school, these young men served in the military at a crucial stage in their emotional and spiritual development.

Dr. Joel Brende, coauthor of *Vietnam Veterans: The Road to Recovery* claims that the

> late teenage years are a time when young people are finding a spiritual value in their lives and are very open. . . . Some veterans' psychological development froze in late adolescence, causing continuing problems in areas like spiritual growth. Exposure to intense trauma at a formative age damaged normal spiritual evolution. Veterans whose spiritual development was cut short by war trauma must now go back and resolve value system development. [1]

Tom Williams, Psy.D., a Vietnam veteran and nationally recognized expert in PTSD treatment and training, adds this:

> . . . people in their late teens and early twenties hold to very high moral standards. They tend to see the world as black and white, but when they find themselves in a trauma situation such as war they soon learn that there are many gray areas. Nonetheless, they still judge themselves years later rather harshly because their moral development was frozen in time. . . . Adolescent idealism holds that life is fair, that good things should happen to good people, and bad things should happen to bad people. Clinging to this adolescent belief system obviously leads to a very self-punitive position. [2]

WORKING CLASS WARRIORS

"They were of the poor and working class," observed L. Fiedler in an article published by *Saturday Review* in 1972. "This was the first war fought for us by our servants," he added.

There were, of course, some from relatively comfortable or even well-to-do families. Mark Shields, writer for the *Washington Post*, elaborates:

. . . more than three out of four of the Americans killed there [in Vietnam] were enlisted men between the ages of 17 and 22 and under the rank of staff sergeant. And they came . . . disproportionately from the working-class neighborhoods of our nation.[3]

South Boston was just such a working-class neighborhood of approximately 2,000 draft-age young men during the 1960s. In Vietnam, 25 South Boston sons and brothers died in the service of their country. Between 1962 and 1972, Princeton graduated more than 8,000 men; six of them died in Vietnam. MIT graduated 8,998 during the same period, and two alumni were killed in Southeast Asia. Harvard graduated 12,595 men during those years and 12 of them were killed in the war.[4]

Selective service laws granted deferments to large numbers of college students. Marc Pilisuk, who in 1975 was with the School of Public Health at the University of California, explains what happened when the number of eligible draftees and volunteers declined:

When the well ran dry the army beneficently offered a second chance to its IY rejects (men unable to achieve minimum standards on mental abilities), and Project 100,000 sifted the ghetto ranks for soldiers. Other ghetto rejects were picked through again by such projects as the Pleasanton Job Corps Training Program which lured youngsters with job promises and then notified their draft boards when they were able to pass the literacy tests.[5]

Dr. Irving M. Allen, assistant psychiatrist at the Harvard University Health Service in Cambridge, Massachusetts, explains the impact of this on black youth:

Black Americans served in the Vietnam War in numbers proportionally equal to or even greater than their numbers in the general population. Although blacks served with distinction in all of the United States' prior wars, Vietnam was the first war for which they were massively recruited. Black youth responded to the call. The magnitude of black combat participation is demonstrated by noting that 5,711 blacks died in the war accounting for 12.5 percent of all American deaths.

According to Arthur Egendorf and associates' study of veterans' postwar adjustment—the Vietnam legacy study—blacks who enlisted sought economic and social advancement and viewed military life more favorably than did whites. Also in contrast to whites, black servicemen were better educated than their civilian peers.[6]

Although the men who were college graduates were fewer in number than those who came from the working class, the level of education of the men who went to Vietnam was higher than any of America's armies in the past. Of those who served, seventy-nine percent had a high school education—or better—when they entered military service. By comparison, sixty-three percent of Korean vets and forty-five percent of World War II vets had completed high school upon leaving military service.[7]

Native Americans, Mexican Americans, Asian Americans, Puerto Rican Americans—men from all ethnic backgrounds served in Vietnam.

WHY THEY WENT

Their reasons for enlisting or going to war were varied.

For some, it was a rite of passage. Serving in the military was a sacred duty, the example having been set by brothers, fathers, and grandfathers. It was a matter of honor and carrying on the family tradition. To refuse to serve one's country was out of the question.

Donna Ferron, sister of Gary Tousey, an American Indian who died in Vietnam, explains her brother's reasons: "Gary went for his country, his family, for us. He would rather go and fight Communism over there than have it come here, to us. Gary went with the view that he was going for us. He signed all his letters, 'Your protector, Gary.'"[8]

Some young men, though they may have had their own doubts and moral objections about serving in an unpopular, undeclared war, found it difficult to disregard the expectations of parents whose basis of comparison was other wars.

One by one the young men in our parish were being drafted. As a pastor, my husband felt it was important to point out to these young men and their families that there were legitimate alternatives. After Ken preached one morning about these alternatives, he was greeted at the door by irate fathers who in essence said, "How dare you plant these ideas in our sons' minds?" Soon, several wanted my husband fired. (Many pastors who spoke out for or against the war were fired and forced to leave their parishes.) He wasn't fired, because cooler heads prevailed, but that's how taboo the subject had become. What bothered us most was the unwillingness of parents to allow their sons the freedom to make their own decisions. It was an iron clad "my country right or wrong" mentality that allowed a young man little choice but to go to war to prove that he wasn't a coward—to his parents and society. Some parents seemed to project the attitude that they would rather have been proud of a dead son than ashamed of a living one who in conscience could not do what his country was asking him to do. For some, it was a disgrace to have a son who refused to serve his country as his father or grandfather had done in wars past. It was the patriotic thing to do.

My husband felt he could be supportive of either—those who chose to go to war, but also those who chose not to go to war—as long as it was a decision they personally had made. Novelist Tim O'Brien says it succinctly: "Very few guys go to war thinking of honor and glory and adventure. They go because they'd be embarrassed to look at their parents if they didn't."[9]

Many were lured into military service thinking they would gain vocational training. Dennis Osborne joined because he wanted to become a helicopter mechanic. He was a helicopter crew chief in Vietnam; today he can't stand to see or be near a helicopter, as they trigger too many bad memories. Some went for love of adventure. Many were inspired by John Wayne movies and visions of being another Audie Murphy. Murphy was the most decorated American hero of World War II, an infantryman who served in Southern Europe. He was wounded three times and was credited with killing 240 German soldiers.

Their reasons for going to Vietnam were varied and each veteran had his own reason. Many went because their country asked them to go, and in good faith, they responded.

A DIFFERENT TERM OF SERVICE

Psychological battlefield casualties have resulted from every war, but it wasn't until World War I that specific syndromes were associated with combat. Prior to that men were considered cowards or thought to lack discipline if they suffered from psychological problems. In the movie *Patton*, General Patton struck one such casualty while accusing him of cowardice, and sending him back into the battlefield. In Civil War days, this condition was called "soldier's heart"; after World War I, it was called shell shock. After World War II, it was known as combat fatigue or war neurosis, and at one point, all psychological casualties were labeled as cases of exhaustion.

James Goodwin, Psy.D., a Marine Corp veteran of Vietnam combat, did graduate work at the University of Denver's School of Professional Psychology after his military service. He wrote a paper that sheds much light on the conditions that gave rise to the evolution of Post-traumatic Stress Disorder (PTSD). He explains what lessons we learned from World War II and the Korean War:

> During the early years of World War II, psychiatric casualties had increased some 300 percent when compared with World War I, even though the preinduction psychiatric rejection rate was three to four times higher than World War I (Figley, 1978a). At one point in the war, the number of men being discharged from the service for psychiatric reasons exceeded the total number of men being newly drafted.

> During the Korean War, the approach to combat stress became even more pragmatic. Due to the work of Albert Glass (1954), individual breakdowns in combat effectiveness were dealt with in a very situational manner. Clinicians provided immediate onsite treatment to affected individuals, always with the expectation that the combatant would return to duty as soon as possible. The results were gratifying. During World War II, 23 percent of the evacuations were for psychiatric reasons. But in Korea, psychiatric evacuations dropped to only six percent (Bourne, 1970). It finally became clear that the situational stresses of the combatant were the primary factors leading to a psychological casualty.

> When direct American troop involvement in Vietnam became a reality, military planners looked to previous war experiences to help alleviate the problem of psychological disorder in combat. By then it was an understood fact that those combatants with the most combat exposure suffered the highest incidence of breakdown. In Korea this knowledge resulted in use, to some extent, of a "point system." After accumulating so many points, an individual was rotated home, regardless of the progress of the war. This was further refined in Vietnam,

the outcome being DEROS (date of expected return from overseas) system. Every individual serving in Vietnam, except general officers, knew before leaving the U.S. when he or she was scheduled to return. The tour lasted 12 months for everyone except the Marines, who, known for their one-upmanship, did a 13-month tour. DEROS promised the combatant a way out of the war other than as a physical or psychological casualty (Kormos, 1978.)[10]

The shortened term of service and DEROS date seemed, in the beginning, to have the positive effect of lessening the number of soldiers who had psychological breakdowns. An all-time low of only twelve breakdowns per one thousand soldiers occurred in Vietnam. Follow-up studies revealed a far different picture, however. In the early seventies large numbers of Vietnam veterans were complaining of symptoms similar to those of World War II veterans. DEROS created other problems. Unlike other wars, each man went to war alone and returned home alone. Each soldier retained only his or her perception of the war.

Byron Coghlan, former Team Leader of the Moline, Illinois, Quad City Veterans Center explains:

"In World Wars I and II and the Korean War, troops would go to the battle zones in troop transports. It would take them approximately a month to get there, and once there, soldiers would serve together. They would go into the front for about six weeks, then go to the rear for two weeks R & R. This continued during the two or three years they served. Then as a unit, the survivors would come back together and this would take another thirty days in the troop transport. For the married men, the military provided readjustment camps—usually in trailers—where the men could live with their spouses for about 30 days before returning home."[11]

Goodwin claims the value of men traveling in units meant that "these men had the closeness and emotional support of one another to rework the especially traumatic episodes they had experienced together. In battle, unit integrity acted as a buffer for the individual against the overwhelming stresses of combat."[12]

"For the Vietnam War, you went to El Toro Marine Air Station or Travis Air Force Base in California, flew to the entry port in Vietnam, and then were assigned to a unit as a replacement," Coghlan said. "The soldier would do his 365 days, and then return as an individual. He would come back alone and be home usually within three days.

"That to me was the greatest problem," said Coghlan. "The men came in as individuals and the war became individualized. When they came back there was no time to cry, to decompress, to work through the grieving process. They were simply plucked from the combat zone and set back into civilian life. And the people back here were not sensitive to these issues. You had these young men who were not old enough to vote or drink, but for the past year had risked their lives every day," said Coghlan. "Because of the nature of the war, the combat soldier had one goal: survival."

DEROS also created "short-timer's fever." New GIs were a liability when they first arrived in the battle zone; they were inexperienced and scared, sometimes too eager and apprehensive, but usually enthusiastic about the war. The soldier became effective when he could incorporate death and dying into his life on a daily basis, and had become numbed to it. This often occurred as a result of participating in the macabre ritual of stacking bodies for body counts. Soldiers were most effective in combat toward the ninth and tenth months of service. Near the end of his tour, the soldier was again fearful of being killed and once again became a liability to fellow soldiers, thus increasing stress levels.

THERE WERE NO FRONT LINES IN VIETNAM

Unlike World War II and the Korean War, there were no established battle lines in Vietnam, no identifiable front. It was guerrilla warfare—unlike any other war Americans have fought.

"Wherever you were, 365 days out of the year, the potential existed for you to be involved in conflict," Coghlan said. "There was no downtime except the two weeks of R & R."

"It was more of a policing action," he continued. "We didn't come in at the southern end of Vietnam and take real estate, then hold it. We came in at strategic locations [by helicopter], and tried to control the countryside from there. Many times we would take a village or a hill, then give it back. Basically, at times we had no real objective other than to just stay alive. Seeing his buddies killed on a hill, then losing the hill back to the enemy the next day, added to the soldier's sense of futility," said Coghlan.

"The enemy, except for the North Vietnamese Regulars, were not uniformed. So you had no idea who you were fighting. The enemy was not identifiable. The Viet Cong wired children with grenades and sent them into the midst of our soldiers. Or they would approach servicemen with a basket of eggs to sell; in the bottom of the basket was a grenade," adds Coghlan. "Sometimes in order to survive, you had to kill children, and that was hard to live with. The soldier soon learned he could trust no one.

"The enemy knew our cultural weaknesses," explains Coghlan. "They would have old men, women, and children walking down a road, and snipers would be on the other side shooting at us. The only way to protect ourselves was to kill innocent people."[13]

Because it was a guerrilla war, the very young, the aged, women—civilians of all ages were involved. The very people the U.S. soldier was sent to protect from Communist aggression served as workers among them by day, and at night often proved to be Viet Cong sympathizers.

Dr. Robert Jay Lifton in his testimony before a congressional hearing during the war said:

> In this guerrilla war, we are not up against men in uniform but against civilians. The enemy may be a farmer, or a woman or a child who holds a rifle that can be used to snipe. In this situation there is a belief that these people have killed and maimed so many men, and our soldiers have developed this habit or trait of viewing civilians as the enemy, and this is a dimension that has never happened in American military history.[14]

Danger was everywhere. Booby traps such as punji stakes, Claymore mines, the Bouncing Betty (a land mine that springs to waist high), medieval spikeballs, rocket attacks, and terrorist-style bombings were commonplace. Napalm, the jellied petroleum dropped from an airplane that bursts into flame upon impact, hit our own troops as well as the enemy.

Attacks by an unseen enemy were sporadic, usually at night. Often firefights consisted of shooting at blazing flashes from a treeline; less often it was hand-to-hand combat with the enemy. In some sections of the country, the enemy suddenly appeared, then disappeared into the complex underground tunnels like those at Cu Chi that stretched from Saigon [Ho Chi Minh City] to the border of Cambodia [Kampuchea]. Built in the forties and fifties to serve as hiding places for the Viet Minh as they fought the French, the tunnels served as a means to escape the overwhelming airstrikes by the U.S. B-52s and make surprise attacks on American forces.

Despite America's advanced technology and modern war equipment, its soldiers found themselves in a different kind of war. The U.S. Army's conventional thinking and training was no match for the jungle guerrilla warfare employed by the enemy in Vietnam.

John Steer, in an interview that appears in *Vietnam: The Other Side of Glory*, describes what it was like in the jungles of Vietnam:

> The jungles were awful places. There were snakes, mosquitos, malaria, and ringworm. There was bamboo poisoning on your arms, and it would be full of festering pus blisters. I mean ugly red pustules— not thin-skinned, but chunks of skin. We would have to take a stick and scrape them off as we gritted our teeth and watched the pus ooze out as we tried to wash it off.

> One time I was tromping through the jungle with diarrhea so bad I couldn't go a half hour without water running down my leg. These were all common occurrences out in the jungle. We were always wet; our feet were rotting, with big chunks of meat peeling off. We would wake up with leeches in our noses or any other place they decided to fasten themselves. Besides the never-ending fear of death, we had to endure a host of miseries: merciless humps through a sun-scorched landscape packing sixty pregnant pounds, brain-broiling heat,* hot-house humidity, dehydration, heat exhaustion, sunburn, red dust, torrential rains, boot-sucking mud . . . dysentery, razor-sharp elephant grass, bush sores, jungle rot . . . meals in green cans, armies of insects, fire ants, poisonous centipedes, flies, bush snakes, vipers, scorpions, rats, boredom, incoming fire, body bags, and a thousand more discomforts. [15]

Drs. Joel Brende and Erwin Parson in their book, *Vietnam Veterans: The Road to Recovery*, further elaborate on the types of diseases men succumbed to:

> . . . bubonic plague, cholera, fevers of unknown origins, melioidosis, internal parasites, rabies, tropical sprue, tuberculosis, leprosy, var-

ious strains of venereal diseases, and Japanese encephalitis (found mostly in Da Nang), in addition to malaria, the communicable disease that affected the largest number of American troops and accounted for a large proportion of man-hours lost on the battlefield. Another danger was being bitten by monkeys, who were always suspected of having rabies. [16]

UNCERTAIN OBJECTIVES AND DOUBT-RIDDEN MOTIVES

Military objectives were unclear in Vietnam and the American soldier found himself confused by the attitude of the South Vietnamese on whose behalf he was fighting. As Kit Bowen of Charlie Company wrote home to his father, "We are the unwilling working for the unqualified to do the unnecessary for the ungrateful. This is about as truthful as you can get."[17]

Contrast this with the statement made by Senator Yarborough, a World War II veteran, before a Senate Subcommittee on Veterans Affairs in 1970:

> We all knew that we were really fighting for the cause of liberty, for mankind, and there was a strong feeling that this was a crusade for justice and knowledge. It was a crusade of justice in which we knew that our survival was threatened by the brilliance of the German scientists and the fanaticism of the Japanese military. It was a matter of national survival and the terror of concentration camps, where millions of people were diabolically murdered, made it clear that we were fighting to save Western civilization. [18]

American soldiers resented, and justifiably so, the fact that some South Vietnamese (ARVN) soldiers fought poorly, and often American lives were endangered by the fact that the ARVN were not fighting as they should in their own defense.

While some American military leaders were excellent, others were insufficiently trained in jungle guerrilla warfare, often resulting in poor and ineffective leadership. Generally, officers served a one-year tour, just as the men they led, which contributed to inexperienced leadership. Some men wanted out from being "wasted"

---

* Temperatures sometimes reached 120 degrees F.

on search-and-destroy missions. A significant portion of the U.S. Army and Marine Corps began to attack their own leaders. Officers and sergeants, who either risked men's lives needlessly for their own career advancement or abused the privileges of higher rank, became targets. These attacks with the intent to kill or maim officers were called "fraggings."

James Gibson, author of *The Perfect War*, reports one such incident:

> One marine in an artillery unit tells how his fellow soldiers became enraged when their new commander began a contest with another unit on who had the most beautiful camp. Troops spent much time arranging the appearance of their cannons. "That f—— fool made us build him a porch outside his tent. And he had an umbrella sent from the States. He would sit there and sip drinks and stuff and overlook his domain. While the f—— guys would be out there killing themselves.[19]

Those under his command staged war calls during which everybody in the outfit at midnight started opening fire screaming "Gooks in the wire," meaning barbed-wire fences. During one staged attack, the commander's bunk was fired on with machine guns. He rolled out and escaped injury. Another attempt on the CO's life was made with a rigged booby trap in the captain's tent, but it blew the legs off the wrong man.

Official fragging statistics exist: 126 in 1969; 271 in 1970; 321 in 1971—for the Army alone. These figures are low. The official figures represent only those cases in which someone was caught or cases occurring in base areas far away from the enemy where it was clear that an American threw the grenade or pulled the trigger.[20]

SUCCESS WAS MEASURED BY BODY COUNTS

Diplomatic pressures on Hanoi and the bombing of North Vietnam in the early sixties had little effect in this unconventional war. Despite America's superior technology, success was hard to measure because the acquisition of territory changed day to day, often at the expense of young lives. This added to the soldier's sense of futility.

Leaders who headed the American Military Assistance Command concluded success could be measured by counting the bodies of the enemy dead. It became an officer's strategy of attrition. Promotion to the officer corps was based on his ability to produce a high body count. Rewards of beer or a hot meal were offered to soldiers whose units were successful. Philip Caputo in *A Rumor of War* explains how this affected soldiers:

> Our mission was not to win terrain or seize positions, but simply to kill: to kill Communists and to kill as many of them as possible. Stack 'em like cordwood. Victory was a high body count, a defeat, a low kill ratio, war a matter of arithmetic. The pressure on unit commanders to produce enemy corpses was intense, and they in turn communicated it to troops. This led to such practices as counting civilians as Viet Cong. "If it's dead and Vietnamese, it's VC" was a rule of thumb in the bush. It is not surprising, therefore, that some men acquired a contempt for human life and a predilection for taking it.[21]

A survivor of My Lai reported to Dr. Lifton that one of the attributing factors to the killing of civilians in that village was the desire for a high body count. Captain Medina, the company commander, had given the strong impression that "he wanted a big body count . . . [because] this was a chance to go out and really show the brigade that we're something."[22]

The My Lai massacre occurred on March 16, 1968, but was not disclosed until the autumn of 1969. Lt. William L. Calley's unit invaded the hamlet of My Lai, an alleged Viet Cong stronghold, and 347 unarmed civilians, including women and children, were shot to death.

ATROCITIES WERE COMMON

Evil unleashed produces an emotional numbness in men that allows them to do things to fellow human beings without feeling. Philip Caputo gives historical perspective to the atrocities in Vietnam:

> There has been a good deal of exaggeration about U.S. atrocities in Vietnam, exaggeration not about their extent but about their causes. The two most popularly held explanations for outrages like My Lai have been the racist theory, which proposes that the American soldier

found it easy to slaughter Asians because he did not regard them as human beings, and the frontier-heritage theory, which claims he was inherently violent and needed only the excuse of war to vent his homicidal instincts.

Like all generalizations, each contains an element of truth; yet both ignore the barbarous treatment the Viet Cong and ARVN often inflicted on their own people, and neither confront the crimes committed by the Korean division, probably the most bloody-minded in Vietnam, and by the French during the first Indochina war.

The evil was inherent not in the men—except in the sense a devil dwells in us all—but in the circumstances under which they had to live and fight. The conflict in Vietnam combined the two most bitter forms of warfare, civil war and revolution, to which was added the ferocity of jungle war.

Twenty years of terrorism and fratricide had obliterated most reference points from the country's moral map long before we arrived. Communists and government forces alike considered ruthlessness a necessity if not a virtue.

Whether committed in the name of principles or out of vengeance, atrocities were as common to the Vietnamese battlefields as shell craters and barbed wire. The marines in our brigade were not innately cruel, but on landing in Da Nang they learned rather quickly that Vietnam was not a place where a man could expect much mercy if, say, he was taken prisoner. And men who do not expect to receive mercy eventually lose their inclination to grant it.

At times, the comradeship that was the war's only redeeming quality caused some of its worst crimes—acts of retribution for friends who had been killed. Some men could not withstand the stress of guerrilla fighting: The hair-trigger alertness constantly demanded of them, the feeling that the enemy was everywhere, the inability to distinguish civilians from combatants created emotional pressures which built to such a point that a trivial provocation could make these men explode with the blind destructiveness of a mortar shell.[23]

A NATION DIVIDED

By the late sixties, the nation was deeply divided over military involvement in Southeast Asia. Congress vacillated in its funding of the war because of political divisiveness and public pressures to get out of Vietnam. The nation as a whole was not committed to the war in Vietnam, primarily because it was an undeclared war and many Americans disagreed with the "domino theory." Communist aggression ten thousand to twelve thousand miles away posed no threat to American soil. All of these factors had a devastating effect on the morale of its soldiers.

Men who served more than one tour were amazed to find that the morale changed from tour to tour. For example, from 1965 to 1967, the morale and cohesion of soldiers was good; 1968 through 1969 proved to be a transitional period of mixed cohesion and demoralization. From 1970 to 1972, there was a widespread breakdown in troop discipline.[24] Much of this reflected what was taking place back on the home front. Soldiers felt abandoned by their country.

Again, contrast this with the war efforts and sacrifices made during World War II. Women left the home and took jobs in ammunitions factories. Gasoline, shoes, and certain foods such as sugar, coffee, and meat were rationed. Travel was restricted because of limited fuel. Households saved lard and tin cans for recycling. Families bought war bonds to support the war. Soldiers returning from the war were treated as heroes and greeted with parades. The country was conditioned and made sensitive to the soldier's wartime memories and needs through movies such as *Home of the Brave*, *The Best Years of Our Lives*, *Pride of the Marines*, and *The Man in the Gray Flannel Suit*.

WHERE ARE THEY TODAY?

If one were to scan the country today in search of Vietnam veterans, you would find them in all walks of life. In 1987, there were forty-eight members of the House and Senate who were Vietnam-era veterans. Sandy and Jerry Straight, authors of a book about Vietnam war memorials,[25] said that while doing research for their book, they received letters from veterans who were city planners, mayors, doctors, lawyers, and executive directors of large corporations. Vietnam veterans are attending law school, coaching football, fixing car engines, programming computers, selling insurance, pastoring churches, and on and on. They have, like any group of people, risen to positions of importance and responsibility. Astronaut Captain Rick Hauck, a Vietnam combat veteran who served in the U.S. Navy, served as Mission Commander of the launching of the *Discovery* spaceship in September, 1988. You will find Vietnam veterans among your neighbors and friends.

The opposite is true also. Some soldiers returned so emotionally shattered that they have never been able to function in society. An estimated thirty percent of the homeless in this country are said to be veterans, and about half of those served in Vietnam. Forty percent of the jobless among the general population are said to be Vietnam veterans. More than 150,000 of these men have committed crimes and have been incarcerated since their return from war; another 200,000 are on parole. The government "programmed" young men to kill, but did nothing to help "deprogram" its soldiers. No counseling services were provided unless severe symptoms were exhibited before discharge or within one year after discharge. The Veterans Administration did not consider neuropsychiatric problems as service-connected after one year's discharge, so treatment from the Veterans Administration was very difficult to obtain (the Vet Centers did not open until 1979). The veteran returned home and found himself out of sync back in "The World."

To sum up, the war in Vietnam was an undeclared, limited warfare* with ineffective leadership and unclear objectives. Success was measured in body counts, not acquisition of territory. Although the United States had far superior technology, its fighting men were up against an ununiformed, unidentifiable, passive yet determined enemy who refused to fight on America's terms. Unlike World War II and the Korean War, most soldiers were given little information about the ideology of the war and the Vietnamese culture. Combat training consisted of indoctrination in dehumanization of the enemy; the enemy were "gooks" or "dinks." Civilians were viewed as the enemy. The soldier learned he could only trust another soldier, never the Vietnamese civilian. He found himself unwanted in the midst of an agrarian revolution. The South Vietnamese army was an unreliable, poorly trained ally. Strict rules of engagement limited

* Limited, undeclared wars are entered into by the Superpowers to avoid the threat of conflicts escalating into a nuclear holocaust. Unfortunately, most are fought in Third World countries who can least afford the devastating effects of war.

36

the soldiers' ability to fight to win or even defend themselves at times.

The DEROS rotation system, designed to alleviate mental stress, actually created different, more serious problems. Each soldier concentrated on survival. Although close with his friends, a lack of unit cohesion provided the soldier no time to grieve and work through his losses with other soldiers. With the exception of two weeks R & R, their lives were threatened 365 days straight. Even those in the rear echelons, some of whom called themselves "paper soldiers," were tainted by the war's peculiar stresses. Drug and alcohol use became a way for soldiers to further deaden their pain or relieve the boredom that went with some jobs.

The use of napalm, unique to this war, added to the horrific memories of grotesque scenes of charred bodies and massive destruction. The defoliants used to destroy the triple-canopy jungle, especially along the riverbanks, saved some American lives at the time of its use, but has caused serious—many times fatal—health problems for veterans since then.

Because of the hazy moral and political reasons for the war, the American public—and its soldiers—had doubts about our involvement. The full-scale organized protest movement among enlisted military personnel, as well as returning veterans, was also unique to this war. In April 1971, a large number of Vietnam veterans publicly protested the war by discarding their war medals. Trust in the U.S. government declined to an all-time low, especially after the release of the "Pentagon Papers," which clearly revealed that the government had deceived the American public.

Chaplains serving in the military had no clear moral directives for soldiers. Thus their authority as spiritual advisers and leaders was diminished.

The Vietnam conflict was a "living room war" viewed by Americans each day on the evening news. Upon return from Vietnam, the soldier saw the distortion of the news stories and realized that what took place in Vietnam was not being reported objectively. Our soldiers discovered the American public was more sympathetic to the Vietnamese than to the losses incurred by American troops. The war in Vietnam was the longest war America has ever fought and the only war America has ever lost.

The American soldier experienced a "bitter homecoming." For a year, he (or she) had dreamed of coming home. But many were met at airports by screaming protesters carrying signs that read "Baby Killer" or "War Monger." Emotionally shattered by his or her combat experiences, the veteran was stunned and hurt by this introduction back into American society. Many returned too young to vote. Some found themselves even too young to join veterans' organizations. Originally, veterans' organizations such as the VFW did not consider Vietnam a legitimate foreign war and Vietnam veterans were excluded from membership. Eventually, men were admitted, but women veterans were only allowed to join the auxiliary. In this way, they were rejected by the very groups they thought most likely to understand what they had been through.

Many soldiers, young as they were, had held positions of authority and were responsible for men, equipment, or aircraft worth a quarter of a million dollars or more, only to find themselves unqualified for good jobs back home.

"They were the first to be laid off if they did get a job because of a lack of seniority, so many could not succeed in even being bread winners for their families," said Coghlan. "These factors are cause for their rage. The soldier feels betrayed—like he was 'used,' then thrown away. They were made to feel unworthy in their churches, and yet they had this overwhelming moral question: 'What's going to happen when I die?' And parents told them to 'Put it behind them.'"

"All of these things began to eat away at the pride of the soldier," said Coghlan. "These men, most of whom are very sensitive, caring persons deep down, were given no gratitude or respect.[26]

Many veterans have reported to me they feel Vietnam was a war they were *not allowed* to win, and, because of the restrictions upon them, they had to fight the war with one hand tied behind their backs. This is a source of rage for many, for they were stigmatized for losing the war.

Wallace Terry, author of *Bloods*, writes, "There were no flags waving or drums beating upon the return of Vietnam veterans who were blamed by the right for losing the war, and by the left for being killers of the innocent.[27]

The Vietnam War—fought in the rice paddies, cities, jungles, highlands, and rough terrain in a country so beautiful it was often compared to Shangri-La—is still being fought in the minds of many soldiers who spent a year of their lives there.

For some vets, the invisible wounds from Vietnam have never healed.

PART II

COPING WITH THE PAIN OF WARTIME MEMORIES

Chapter 3

THEY CAME HOME CHANGED— WHAT IS POST-TRAUMATIC STRESS DISORDER?

A truck backfired and Bill spun around, his gun ready for firing at the enemy—only this was stateside and there were no VC. It happened at Fort Dix, New Jersey, after Bill Tucker* returned from Vietnam. GIs were laughing at him. At first he was embarrassed, then he told them, "I hope you guys never have to go through war." Bill meant it; he felt that he had just been to hell and back.

Bill found drugs and alcohol readily available on base, and he began drinking heavily. He didn't know why, but he stayed drunk. He even went on guard duty drunk. One night a soldier yelled jeeringly, "Hey, baby killer." Bill invited him into the guard tower, then proceeded to threaten the GI at gunpoint. Finally, he told him, "You're worthless. You're not worth killing and going to jail for."

---

* Bill Tucker was a sergeant in the U.S. Army serving with the 1st Americal Division. During his first tour in 1969–70, he was a military policeman and a noncombatant. His second tour (1970–71) in Vietnam was with the Americal Division in light observation helicopters on reconnaissance and hunter killer-teams.

Bill's first tour in Vietnam was similar to stateside duty and he was a noncombatant.* He had grown attached to Lam, a six-year-old Vietnamese boy and had initiated efforts to adopt the child he called "Louie." Lam was a tough little kid, a survivor, who thought it was more honorable to steal food than beg for it like the others. His clothes were mere rags that hung on his frail body. Bill cared for Lam and desperately wanted to give the child a home. Anything was better than the kind of existence the boy had on the streets.

Bill enlisted for a second tour giving him more time in Vietnam to complete the adoption process. Because he was unmarried, his request was ultimately denied, but before leaving 'Nam, Bill took the child to a Catholic orphanage in Trang Bang so he would be cared for.

His second tour was quite different from the first. He flew on light observation helicopters that hovered near the ground looking for camouflaged enemy camps. The first time he encountered enemy fire, it was an awakening unlike any he had ever known. Bill found that he had to be hyperalert every moment of every flight. The enemy was shooting at him, and if he wanted to stay alive, he would have to kill or be killed. He became quite good at what he had been trained to do. Too good. He came to view the enemy as nonhuman; he had no respect for human life or feelings for those he killed. Never had he felt such hate for the enemy; and on the other hand, never had he felt such love for his buddies, his crew mates. Minor disagreements didn't last long, for lives depended on how well you looked out for your fellow soldier. It wasn't until one day near the end of his second tour that he began to think about what he was doing.

"I had shot and killed a Vietnamese nurse disguised as a soldier wading in waist-high water along a canal. The next day, while going through her things, I learned with the aid of an interpreter that the letters she carried with her were love letters to her husband. She had come all the way from North Vietnam to serve wounded soldiers in South Vietnam," said Bill.

He began to question what he was doing. Questioning what one did could prove fatal; it made a soldier ineffective in battle.

"Just because we're Americans doesn't make us right. She believed in this war to the point she was willing to die for it. I knew I

44

was in trouble; I was thankful I had just a little time left." Stateside, his experiences began to take their toll on him:

"I felt people had to know what was going on, but no one would listen to me. Finally, I met a gal, a real nice gal, who finally said to me, 'There's something wrong with you, Bill.' She said it in such a way that it didn't embarrass me. I was coming to this realization also. I was having nightmares, waking up in a cold sweat. I thought I was losing my mind. One night I couldn't breathe and thought I was going to die. My vision was affected." This tall New Yorker with an athletic physique and gentlemanly ways was hurting and he felt that he was falling apart. He didn't know why.

"It was then I decided to do something. I insisted they take me to a hospital. My body and my mind just weren't working. People told me it was Vietnam but I couldn't understand why," said Bill. The doctor agreed. He told Bill he had a bad case of nerves and should be medically discharged. Bill felt he had to get out of the military. Shortly thereafter, he was discharged.

Since leaving, he has led what he calls a "gypsy lifestyle." He hasn't held a job longer than two years. "Everything is boring," says Bill. His quick temper and rage often led to trouble and bar brawls and scrapes with the law. At times he has contemplated suicide, but being Catholic, he fears going to hell. It wasn't until 1987 when he sought help at a Vet Center that he began to turn his life around.

* * *

Richard Rohlfs was twenty-four when he was drafted into the Army.* Dick says he was a "grunt," the lowest man on the totem pole. Grunts spent most of their time in the bush and jungles of Vietnam. The "humps" or long walks through the bush in search of the enemy, often near the Cambodian border, lasted as long as fifty days.

Dick had a Lutheran upbringing by caring, supportive parents on a farm in Iowa. He was and still is a quiet, sensitive man of principle who loves nature. Walks in the woods and the beauty of nature give him a sense of inner peace. What bothered him most about the war were the deaths of children. He had witnessed the aftermath of VC killings of children in an orphanage (see Chapter 13).

* Richard Rohlfs was a Spec. 4 in the Army, 11 Bravo, and spent most of his tour in 1967–68 in the Central Highlands. He fought on Hill 875 at Dak To.

Foreign investors owned large rubber and tea plantations in Vietnam, and these became safe havens for the Viet Cong. Because of the political and financial implications of bombing these plantations, our soldiers—though forced to fight the enemy on these grounds—would not be given air support because it would destroy the crop. Thus, the lives of American soldiers were considered more expendable than the money crops. Dick, like many soldiers, resented this. "This war was about money and politics," he said. "How do you justify all the killing?"

Upon his return home, his parents listened sympathetically and tried to understand, but there was so much that only one who had been there could comprehend. Dick was more fortunate than most veterans; he had a trade, and his job as a millwright was waiting for him. He describes the problems he experienced upon his return: "I would go to bed and sleep for twelve to fourteen hours but never feel rested. I went to a doctor who prescribed tranquilizers, but he had no understanding of my problems. So I turned into a workaholic—holding two jobs at times—and I did that for seventeen years. I burned myself out. Now I don't have a lot of drive. What do I do?"

Like many veterans, Dick has problems with authority, but the fact that he has an understanding supervisor has helped him keep his job. His boss, a Korean veteran, seems to sense when the pressure is building, and he helps Dick get through those difficult times.

Since the war, he has had nightmares. Sometimes in rage he has kicked out windows or thrown and broken things. His wife, Diane, is understanding, but after a brief separation, she gave Dick an ultimatum: Obtain help or else. It was that which prompted him to go to a Vet Center for help. His psychiatrist, comparing Dick to a "caged coyote," prescribed lithium for Dick to help him keep his emotions and depression under control.

Dick feels as if he left part of himself in Vietnam.

* * *

Dennis Osborne was the crew chief of an assault helicopter.* As such, he was extensively involved in dropping off and picking up the

---

* Dennis Osborne served with the Army's 1st Air Cavalry Division 229, B Company, in 1967–68.

Long Range Reconnaissance Patrols—called LRRP teams—that were usually comprised of five to seven men who would go deep into the jungle to observe enemy activity without initiating contact. His crew also medevaced the wounded.

The aftermath of the battle of Hill 875 is a memory which continues to haunt him some twenty years later. Dennis describes the scene:

"One morning after a long siege during which the soldiers had no support . . . nothing brought in, no bodies taken out . . . it was a sunrise morning; the air was very thick. We went to that hill to pull out wounded and dead. My first view was of charred bodies everywhere, pieces of bodies, and bodies that had grown stiff because people couldn't get to them. I can't describe it. To see frozen bodies that were charred and dismembered and with this horrible look of fear on their faces was devastating. The hill was blackened by mortars and rockets.

"The only person I saw alive was the person who was waving the helicopter down. I looked at him and he looked at me wanting some kind of response from me, some empathy . . . he had a haunted look, his face blackened with war grime; the only white skin to show through was that around his eyes. . . .

"It was very difficult for me. I had learned how to block all this out, just take it in stride and do my job and not be affected by it. If I started thinking about how I was feeling about all this, I couldn't do my job. I had to keep looking for the enemy or gun flashes and possible danger."

He says that was when the war really became real for him, and he became aware of the grotesqueness of it and the unnecessary loss of people—the slaughter. That night he went back to camp and smoked pot and drank beer. "It made life easier for me," he said. "It helped block out the pain."

Another vivid, haunting memory for Dennis involves a face-to-face encounter with the enemy. His was the "command" helicopter carrying the commanding officer as they attacked a village from the air hoping to flush out VC and NVA sympathizers. The enemy and civilians below him were in trenches. "We were shooting down into the open trenches. There were people with and without weapons. We were shooting everyone we could see. It was real bizarre; it was crazy. The commander was yelling, 'There's one over there, get that one.' There was one young VC wearing black trousers and white shirt and sandals carrying an AK-47. As we hovered, he dropped his gun and threw up his arms in surrender. The commander shouted at me, 'Shoot that S.O.B.' I did as I was told.

"I did what I was told, but I can't justify it. Commanders above had men below do the killing. This problem with authority has carried over into my job."

Dennis is serious in nature, clean cut, well educated, and very articulate. He has a degree in business and is successful in sales. Despite this fact, he has had nearly forty jobs. "As I get nearer to the top in management, I become more like the people I dislike," he said. "The lines of authority in business are much like those in the military," said Dennis.

But he has trouble concentrating, focusing his interests and committing himself to a career. Much of the time he feels like running, hoping a new environment will bring him some happiness, but it seldom does for long.

Dennis has gone through two divorces, and two other close relationships with women have ended. "I have not been able to communicate feelings or relate on a day-to-day basis. I had nothing to give them; I felt worthless in relationships. These were spiritually good women, and they were there for me, but I couldn't be there for them. I had trouble being a stepfather because my wife's children reminded me of the children in Vietnam. I have done so much blocking out; there are so many things I have to work through."

Knowing how sensitive the Vietnam issue was upon his return home, Dennis never attempted to talk about his Vietnam experiences with his wives or friends. He would not let himself be subjected to further ridicule or rejection. It wasn't until he went to a Vet Center and found a group of vets who had been through similar experiences that he could begin to talk about his pain. "It still hurts to talk about it," he said, "but talking always helps. The war was so unnecessary and so devastating."

He was able to stop drinking, but still experiences a generalized depression. His recurring dream is one of being dropped out of a helicopter and being surrounded by Vietnamese, some in uniform, some not. "Either I have a weapon that doesn't work, or none at all. It's real scary." He records these dreams in a journal and finds this is therapeutic also. Dennis is diligently working through his pain. He wants to be healed.

THE SIGNS AND SYMPTOMS OF PTSD

These men's lives reflect the symptoms of delayed stress reactions to war. In 1980, these problems were officially given a name by the American Psychiatric Association: Post-traumatic Stress Disorder (PTSD).* It should be remembered that it is *not* a mental illness; it *is* a reaction to the extreme stress these men and women suffered during and after the war in Southeast Asia. Similar symptoms have been found in victims of car accidents, sexual abuse, and child molestation, in women post-abortion, and in others who have been through natural disasters, personal trauma, or massive destruction. In other words, those who have had extremely stressful, traumatic experiences. PTSD can be acute, chronic, or delayed. The association further defines it as "the development of characteristic symptoms following a distressing event that is outside the range of usual human experience."[1] PTSD symptoms for Vietnam and other war veterans include:

- Depression
- Anger
- Anxiety
- Sleep disturbances
- Tendency to react under stress with survival tactics
- Psychic or emotional numbing
- Emotional constriction
- Loss of interest in work and activities
- Survivor guilt
- Hyper-alertness
- Avoidance of activities that arouse memories of traumas in war zone
- Suicidal feelings and thoughts
- Flashbacks to Vietnam

* American Psychiatric Association. (1980). *Diagnostic and Statistical Manual of Mental Disorders* (3rd ed.). Washington, D.C.: American Psychiatric Press Inc.

- Fantasies of retaliation and destruction
- Cynicism and distrust of government and authority
- Alienation
- Concern with humanistic values overlayed by hedonism
- Negative self image
- Memory impairment
- Hyper-sensitivity to justice
- Problems with intimate relationships
- Difficulty with authority figures
- Emotional distance from children, wife and others
- Self-deceiving and self-punishing patterns of behavior such as an inability to talk about war experiences, fear of losing others, and a tendency to fits of rage.[2]

The National Vietnam Veterans Readjustment Study released in 1988 by the Research Triangle Institute, a not-for-profit organization in Research Triangle Park, North Carolina, reported that over one in seven Vietnam Veterans—an estimated 480,000—suffers from PTSD. The study, headed by co-principal investigator Richard A. Kulka, points out the discrepancy between their figures and those released in a study done the same year by the Centers for Disease Control (CDC) in Atlanta, the agency officially designated by the government to conduct epidemiological research. CDC reported that only 2.2 percent of the veteran population had chronic PTSD *the month before examination.* Kulka's study indicates as many as 15.2 percent may have it. The major differences are in the criteria used for diagnosis and different methods of screening. It is important to point out, however, that "PTSD is a cyclical disorder and a vet could be symptom-free or free of certain symptoms at the time of or a month or two prior to the interview. What was revealing from our research" says Kulka, "was that our study indicates that sometime during their postwar lifetime, nearly half of the women and more than 50 percent of the male veterans have experienced PTSD or had significant symptoms of PTSD—that's 1.7 million veterans of the Vietnam war."[3]

A series of independent studies were done during the 1980s to determine whether those veterans who developed stress disorders were more vulnerable to the stress of war and war experiences by predisposing factors such as abusive childhoods, socioeconomic factors, or education, to name a few. Researchers also sought to determine if society's reaction to the discharged veterans was of sufficient intensity to have affected the veterans, independent of their prior history.

Results of the study done by Frye and Stockton (1982) revealed that the perceived helpfulness of the veteran's family upon his return was related significantly to his or her readjustment to civilian life. Those with supportive families fared best. On the other hand, it revealed that the veteran avoided discussing his experiences. Those who had experienced higher levels of combat were also more severely affected.

The results of the study done by Solkoff, Gray, and Keill (1986) were similar. They found that pre-service and early childhood experiences did not play a major role in development of PTSD. They concluded that PTSD sufferers had experienced more intense combat, had fewer contacts with other veterans after service, and felt they received little support from their families and spouses. The majority felt stigmatized and rejected by society and duped by the government.

These and similar studies confirmed two overall recurring themes: The stress factors that accounted for most of the variance of PTSD symptoms were the amount of exposure to death or injury and the amount of support they were given upon their return home.[4]

Again, CDC's report differs. It found that the disorder hit hardest among blacks, the underprivileged, and those who had had behavioral difficulties as children.[5]

"Being unable to do anything to stop the trauma makes it more likely that it will result in PTSD," reported Naomi Breslau, a psychiatrist at the Henry Ford Hospital in Detroit who studied 1,007 men and women who had gone through traumatic events. The study's 1990 report revealed that one out of four victims developed PTSD.[6]

Other researchers reported in 1990 that PTSD may be caused by altered brain chemistry resulting from catastrophic stress. Dr. Dennis Charney, director of clinical neuroscience at the National Center for Post-Traumatic Stress Disorder and psychiatrist at Yale University, says "Victims of a devastating trauma may never be the same biologically."[7] Some researchers believe, however, that *all* Vietnam veterans are affected.

Brian R. Alm, a corporate spokesman for Deere & Co. in Moline, Illinois, who served two tours with the navy in Vietnam, would agree. He challenges the armchair psychologists who tend to seek balance by dismissing as unimportant the lingering unrest of those who don't fit the stereotypes. His comments appeared in a column in the *Quad-City Times* in Davenport, Iowa:

> We're not all stressed-out, no, but we are not unaffected. Let it stand that we were, most of us, good people who went, came back, and took up our lives again. I haven't shot up a school or abandoned myself to drugs, but I do feel the things that others seem to be feeling, albeit less severely than those extreme cases that make for good Rather-esque drama.
>
> But as for the resentment resulting from the country's attitude toward us, the sense of separation from the United States during our absence, the guilt of survival (or even the relatively less agony of our service vis-à-vis that of others who had it a lot worse), the bewilderment about our intentions there at the time in view of target restrictions, the incredible and relentless exhaustion and frustration, the instant memory of choppers when the Army Reserve's Hueys fly overhead on weekend exercises, the horrible effects of war on the innocent, the absence of a parade or an acknowledgment back home, and other broad strokes of common experience, count me in when you tally up the PTSD-wounded. [8]

Denial has been the psychological mechanism veterans have used to cope with day-to-day living. Denial is the lid they use to "stuff" or repress the pain and troubling thoughts and emotions below the surface of the mind so that others may not see the craziness they feel. It is a defense mechanism. I know of one vet who never told his wife he was in Vietnam; another waited fourteen years before informing his wife. An estimated thirty percent of all Vietnam veterans still refuse to admit that they were ever in Vietnam. [9]

Alcohol and drugs help deaden the pain and reinforce denial. They are a form of self-medication many vets use to gain temporary relief from emotional and spiritual pain and a multitude of problems. Instead of helping, however, alcohol and drugs deepen depression.

The few studies that have been conducted on this problem show that combat veterans engage in more continuous and sustained drinking patterns than their peers. Veterans engage in binge drinking more frequently, and they appear to use alcohol as an anti-anxiety agent that induces a form of psychic numbing. Barbiturates, tranquilizers, stimulants, and opiates are sometimes substituted for alcohol, or are taken in combination with it. Thomas Brison and Vince Treanor are two experts who conduct workshops and seminars throughout the country and have taught a course at Rutgers University Summer School of Alcohol Studies on the correlation between PTSD and alcoholism. They cite a number of clinical studies that identify Vietnam veterans, especially those veterans who were involved in heavy combat, as being at high risk to develop alcohol or drug problems. They have also observed the vicious cycle: Drinking and drugs compound the symptoms of PTSD, which compound the symptoms of addiction, resulting in increasingly painful readjustment problems and progressively worse addiction. [10]

THE SENSES TRIGGER WARTIME MEMORIES

Denial works until something in the environment comes along that triggers memories. All of our sensations—sight, sound, touch, taste and smell—can evoke memory, but not all of them accomplish this with equal facility. For example, smell makes an immediate connection with the memory structures [of the brain]; hence its powerful effect in stimulating memory. [11]

Phil Ross, a psychiatric nurse who works in a Vet Center in Cedar Rapids, Iowa, shared this incident from his personal life. Because he is a nurse, he was once asked to assist in cleaning a neighbor's apartment after a teenage boy had committed suicide with a shotgun in his bedroom. Shortly after cleaning up the bloody mess, Phil heard a helicopter overhead. The sound of the rotor blades, combined with the sights and smells he had seen that day, triggered a flashback, and he was in Vietnam again. [12] Extreme heat and humidity . . . a green tree line . . . a path in the woods . . . the sight of Vietnamese refugees in this country are "triggers" that mentally transport veterans back to Vietnam. The smells of mildew, sulphur, urine, blood, or excrement, diesel fuel, gunpowder, or oriental food are reminders of war.

Jan Scruggs described for me an incident that happened near his home in Maryland. One evening he was called out by the local police to talk with a veteran who desperately needed help. The vet was a truck driver who had gone into a restaurant where oriental food was being served. The smell of oriental food triggered what Jan thought was a psychotic break. Jan talked at great length with the man and encouraged him to go to a Vet Center or counselor for help the next day. Jan believes there may be many such truck drivers— men choosing this form of isolation—who are walking time bombs because they have not decompressed their feelings. [13]

Some veterans report never feeling safe, so much so that many sleep with a gun or have weapons in their home—a learned survival tactic. Wives have learned never to touch their husbands while they're sleeping for fear of startling them, and finding themselves being attacked. These women are terrified by their husbands' dreams and nightmares and often report having to disentangle hands from around their throats. Many men feel comfortable only with their back to the wall in a room, never out in the open, unguarded.

Noises like popcorn popping or a car backfiring sound like gunfire. It is not uncommon for a vet to fall to the floor or take cover under a table upon hearing these noises. Medical scientists have developed some understanding of why PTSD sufferers startle so easily. "These people apparently have very high levels of norepinephrine," says Dr. Lawrence Kolb. Norepinephrine is a hormone that activates the adrenal gland. The implication, says the Columbia University psychiatrist, is that "the adrenal system is responding excessively to all sorts of things that other people don't respond to."[14]

Persons who have experienced uncontrollable stress are more sensitive to adrenaline surges, even decades later, scientists report. Dr. Matthew Friedman, executive director of the National Center for Post-Traumatic Stress Disorder, claims catastrophic stress alters three key brain systems, two of which produce hormones that mobilize the body in emergencies—catecholamines (produced by the locus ceruleus), and corticotrophin-releasing factor (CRF) produced by the hypothalamus. The third, the opioid system, is hyperactive and can blunt the feeling of pain that can account for emotional numbing. In PTSD, these systems can respond to situations that hold little or no threat and to emergencies that are not there in reality.

Dr. Friedman believes these findings may give rise to the development of drugs that can reverse the biological changes that occur in the body of PTSD sufferer, offering relief from recurrent nightmares, troubled sleep, frightening flashbacks, irritability and rage, and the host of symptoms accompanying the disorder. Several pharmaceutical companies are at work on developing drugs tailored to these specific brain imbalances.[15]

THE ROLE OF VET CENTERS IN TREATING PTSD

In the mid-1970s, the Disabled American Veterans (DAV) organization funded the Forgotten Warrior Project headed by John P. Wilson, Ph.D. That study led to outreach efforts to help Vietnam veterans. DAV opened seventy storefront offices across the country where volunteers from the mental health and counseling professions met with veterans. The "outreach" concept proved successful with veterans suffering from PTSD.

In 1977 psychologist Shad Mcshad, Chaplain William Mahedy, and Charles Figley, Ph.D., whose research and work among veterans with PTSD had become recognized nationally, were asked to put together a plan—a model program—they felt would work for veterans. This plan—very similar to DAV's storefront centers—was given to Max Cleland, the new head of the Veterans Administration. A VA committee refined the plan that was presented to Congress and, with support from Senator Alan Cranston and a senate committee, it was passed into legislation and funded in 1979.

In 1979, the first of the 196 "storefront" Vet Centers were opened throughout the country to offer free counseling services for Vietnam veterans suffering from PTSD. They emerged as the result of the concern by the Carter administration and the President's Commission on Mental Health, and through the efforts of Max Cleland, who insisted that the VA find a new approach to providing psychiatric services for these men. Vietnam veterans distrusted the government that had used, and then discarded them, and they wanted nothing to do with the standard medical models such as the hospitals and clinics VA offered.

The Vet Center is where healing begins for many. In an atmosphere of trust, acceptance, and caring in informal groups, veterans can discover they can talk about their pain and the feelings they have bottled up for many years.

For some of you, a Vet Center may provide the *first* opportunity that you will have to talk with others who truly understand what it was like to be in 'Nam. It becomes a closely knit support group. You can view educational videotapes that will help you understand PTSD. Trained professionals, many veterans themselves who specialize in guidance counseling, social work, and psychology, are there to offer their skills to help you cope with everyday problems.

"Unlike other forms of psychotherapy, the veteran usually experiences after his first counseling session an enormous sense of relief," said counselor Phil Ross.

Families of veterans are welcome also. Often it is the wife seeking treatment for her husband who makes the first contact. Living with a veteran whose rage is unpredictable can be frightening. Some wives are abused by their husbands. (Women partners can find additional help in Chapter 6.) Some Vet Centers have support groups for wives also. Counselors work with them and other family members to help ease tension in the family, hoping to create a more functional marriage and better atmosphere in the home.

Vocational guidance counselors and other employment specialists offer assistance to those seeking employment. The only requirements for eligibility for services at the Vet Centers is that you served on active duty between August 4, 1964, and May 7, 1975.

IS THERAPY EFFECTIVE?

Dr. Stephen Sonnenberg of the American Psychiatric Association reports that the treatment for PTSD is an intensive process. Sonnenberg says it is "a combination of group therapy, individual therapy, sometimes medication, sometimes family counseling. It really does require the full range of treatment in the armamentarium of the psychotherapists, and that's one of the problems. If you do not have well-trained psychotherapists you are not going to be able to treat it."[16] PTSD does respond to treatment. If not treated, it gets worse.

Fred Gusman, M.S.W., directs the Menlo Park Division of the Palo Alto VA Medical Center in California, and the Clinical Laboratory and Education Division of the new multi-site Center for the study of PTSD established by the Department of Veterans Affairs. Gusman says the Center's long-term studies and psychological data base show there is a high level of chronicity in PTSD. He explains: "If you have PTSD, that means you have some traumatic memories. The goal of treatment is to put those experiences into perspective and understand how they effect one's total self. There are times in one's life when those memories will come forward," says Gusman.

"If an individual developed a coping behavior to survive the experience, that becomes a way of life. No matter what kind of treatment one provides, these things can continue to come back periodically," he goes on. "That does not mean you can't live a marginal life; it just means you've got this chronic problem—just like a chronic cough. Even if you've worked it through, you are vulnerable to those memories. You cannot erase memories. That's a myth." Gusman tells therapists in training seminars that they are "doing the patient a disservice to give him or her the perception that therapy will make it okay."[17]

Opinions about the resolution of PTSD vary. A few believe it can be resolved. Dr. Charles Figley, long recognized for his work in PTSD, was asked if he believed that also. "Absolutely," he said. "There's no doubt about it. I mean if it's not curable, I would claim it's not PTSD."[18]

Dr. Joel Brende, presently at the Bradley Center in Columbus, Georgia, says that traditional psychotherapy has limits when veterans believe that a killer lurks deep in their soul. He feels that treatment strategies require going beyond traditional limits. Some therapists, he reports, are delving into spirituality, struggling to help veterans resolve mental pain. Belief structures, said Brende, change slowly. War has some veterans believing they are evil killers.

"You can't change it only with traditional psychotherapy methods, and you can't do it only as a spiritual problem either. You need both," claims Brende.[19]

In his work with veterans, Dr. Brende has explored in depth their belief structures and found that one-third were actively hoping to receive spiritual counseling as part of their treatment. For this reason he wrote, with veterans, a "Twelve Step Approach to PTSD" that is proving helpful to veterans. These appear at the end of this chapter.

Robert Erikson, Ph.D., Director of the Center for Stress Recovery at the Veterans Administration Medical Center in Brecksville, Ohio, also believes PTSD is curable.* He directs the Center's intensive seven-week inpatient treatment program, which is followed by six months of outpatient therapy, including both individual and group counseling. The Center's approach, called "Trauma Psychology," is based on the premise that recovery is an appropriate goal. "Therapists engaging clients in the belief that recovery is possible is at least half the battle," said Dr. Erikson.[20]

The Outward Bound program, a wilderness school to teach survival skills, has also proven effective in the treatment of PTSD. Bob Rheault, instructor and cofounder of the veterans' program, says that the Outward Bound program is "a deliberate recreation of the combat experience," a supervised journey back into the emotional realm of Vietnam with assigned gear, ground to cover, rations, maps and fear—but no guns. Thrown into a situation fraught with a familiar physical vulnerability, the men are called on to help with rudimentary survival chores and group planning. The hope is that, in the process of cooperation, they'll remember that they are not alone in the world.[21]

Inpatients at the Northampton VAMC in Massachusetts were the first to benefit by Outward Bound. Similar programs for veterans have been conducted in other states as well. There are those who would like to see such a program as an adjunct to all sixteen PTSD units throughout the country. Part of the problem, however, is cost: Thus far, the funds must be raised through private sources. They are not funded by VA.

A LIFE-CHANGING FAITH

There are some veterans who have found spiritual renewal through their faith. Chuck Dean, Mickey Block, and John Steer give testimony to that fact.

Chuck Dean, author of *Nam Vet—Making Peace with Your Past* and Executive Director of Point Man International (PMI), believes

* The views expressed by Dr. Erikson are his own and may not reflect the official views of the Veterans Administration.

PTSD can be overcome. Dean writes, "I now understand that a Christian is a person remade by God into a new, eternal, joyous being. PTSD is curable. Mine was cured almost three years ago. And I'm giving my time, strength and a good part of our family income to help brothers find release and final healing from this inner sickness."[22]

PMI is an international veterans-for-veterans agency operating out of its headquarters in Seattle with chapters in twenty-eight states, British Columbia, Ontario, and New Zealand. Point Man provides a support-group setting where Vietnam veterans can meet informally and let down their emotional barriers. A nonprofit organization, Point Man provides free counseling and emergency shelter and other services to veterans. If you believe you are suffering from PTSD, I highly recommend you read Dean's excellent book.

Veteran Mickey Block, a former Navy SEAL and president of Saved to Serve, Inc., a nonprofit outreach to hurting veterans and their families, in his book *Before the Dawn* writes:

The ultimate answer to the pain and grief lies not within ourselves. It doesn't come from secular institutions or man-made remedies. It comes from He who holds the copyright on reconciliation. The deliverance from guilt and rage and bitterness comes freely through Jesus Christ. My story is a witness to this reality. My body still bears the scars of child abuse and war—but I also bear His healing in my heart and soul. And I am not alone. Many across our nation have laid hold of this hope. Marriages are being put back together, memories healed, and men and women released from the bondage of drugs and alcoholism. They are finding forgiveness for the sins of yesterday, and learning how to forgive the injustices of the past. Multitudes who had long ago given up any hope of feeling can now love and live again. They have found this healing through Him who empathizes with the wounded and betrayed and misunderstood. He above all knows what it is to be mocked and spit upon and betrayed by an ungrateful nation which He loved and sacrificed Himself for. He suffered the same indignities. Yet, His love triumphs over all.[23]

John L. Steer travels throughout this country and abroad speaking to veterans. He is developing a retreat center for veterans and their families—Fort Steer—on his property in Charlotte, Arkansas. He writes:

To you that have problems, and to you who think you don't have any problems, I have the answer. It's a sellout to Jesus Christ. Some may say you have tried religion. I'm not talking about religion. I'm talking about a personal experience with Jesus Christ, the author and finisher of our faith.

When I went through jump school at Fort Benning, Ga., it took every fiber of my being to get through it, and it was the same with some of the training you took. If you would put half that much effort into seeking the Lord—I promise He will meet you. "Ask, and it shall be given you; seek and you shall find; and to him that knocks it shall be opened." I'm beginning to understand how God loved me so much He allowed me to go to Vietnam and to see and do all the terrible things I did and saw because He knew this is what it would take to break me and cause me to repent and serve Him. Jesus knew I would eventually serve Him. I praise Him for not letting me die out there and go to hell. . . . He has a perfect plan for your life. But until you decide to do it His way you are going to get scratched up. Listen for that still small voice beckoning you to accept Him and serve Him. Jesus is the ONLY answer.

Vietnam—was it curse or blessing? A little of both.[24]

As you read this chapter, you learned that the problems inherent in PTSD are many: alienation—from self, perhaps members of your family, from God—emotional numbing, moral and spiritual pain, and the unresolved grief many of you have succeeded in repressing for a very long time. Because of the multifaceted nature of the disorder, therapy for PTSD involves working on the physical, mental, and spiritual issues that require attention. Physical problems, of course, must be dealt with by appropriate medical doctors and/or psychotherapists. Hopefully, medications to blunt the devastating effects of exaggerated startle responses and nightmares will be available in the not-too-distant future.

But many of you do not live near a Vet Center where you or your family can take advantage of the counseling services provided for veterans. This book, therefore, is intended to be a self-help book you can use as an aid to healing. Guidelines for working through the grief aspects of PTSD are found in Chapter 13, "Unfinished Business and Steps Through Grief." The moral and spiritual pain of wartime memories are explored in Chapters 11, 12, and 14. Much can be gained by learning how others have dealt with the intense pain associated with wartime memories.

ADDITIONAL READING

Block, Mickey, and William Kimball, *Before the Dawn*. Canton, Ohio: Daring Books, 1988. (Can be ordered by writing: Mickey Block, P.O. Box 161262, Fort Worth, TX, 76161. Cost: $20.00.)

Brende, Joel Osler, M.D., and Erwin Randolph Parson, Ph.D., *Vietnam Veterans: The Road to Recovery*. New York: Plenum Press, 1985, Signet Book, 1986.

Burns, David C. *Feeling Good: The New Mood Therapy*. New York: William Morrow & Co., 1980.

Davis, George. *Coming Home*. Washington, D.C.: Howard University Press, 1971, 1989. (The Black experience.)

Dean, Chuck, with Bob Putnam, *Nam Vet: Making Peace with Your Past*. Mountlake Terrace, Wash.: Point Man International, 1988. (To order write: Point Man International, P.O. Box 440, Mountlake Terrace, WA 98043. Cost: $6.95.)

Egendorf, Arthur. *Healing from the War*. Boston: Shambhala, 1986.

Goldberg, Herb. *The Hazards of Being Male: Surviving the Myth of Masculine Privilege*. New York: Nash Publishing, 1976.

————. *The Inner Male: Overcoming Roadblocks to Intimacy*. New York: Nash Publishing, 1987.

Jacob, John. *Long Ride Back*. New York: Thunder's Mouth Press, 1988.

Kubey, Addlestone, O'Dell, Snyder, Stichman, and Vietnam Veterans of America. *The Viet Vet Survival Guide*. New York: Ballantine Books, 1985.

Roever, Dave, and Harold Fickett. *Welcome Home, Davey*. Waco, Tex.: Word Book, 1986. (Order from: Dave Roever Evangelistic Association, P.O. Box 10478, Ft. Worth, TX 76114. Cost: $15.00 hardcover; $8.00 paperback.)

Rogovin, Janice. *Let Me Tell You Where I've Been*. Jamaica Plain, Mass.: Stonybrook Press, 1989.

Steer, John, with Cliff Dudley. *Vietnam: Curse or Blessing*. Green Forest, Ark.: New Leaf Press, 1982. (To obtain, write: Living Word Ministries, 75 Holmes Road, Charlotte, AR 72522, Cost: $6.00.)

Van Blair, Reverend Bruce. *A Year to Remember*. Seattle, Wash.: Glen Abbey Books, 1988. (Written by a recovering alcoholic, it contains 52 contemplative messages on twelve-step recovery from a Christian viewpoint.)

TWELVE STEP APPROACH TO PTSD

1. **STEP ONE (POWER): Our first step is to accept the fact that we have become powerless to live meaningful lives.**
   "Even though we had the power to survive against the worst combat conditions, we must admit we have become powerless to win the battle against a new enemy—our memories, flashbacks and combat instincts. Some of us have become powerless over the continuing wish to gain revenge over those sudden impulses to hurt those who cross us or unsuspectingly annoy us. We even hurt those who try to love us, making it impossible to love and care for our friends and family. So, we isolate ourselves and cause others to avoid, dislike or even hate us. Our attempts to live meaningful lives and fight this psychological and emotional hell which imprisons us seems to be in vain. We now find ourselves powerless to change it."

2. **STEP TWO (SEEKING MEANING): Our next step is to seek meaning in having survived.**
   "If we are to survive this new battle, we seek meaning in having survived. We want to believe we have survived for a purpose. We would like to be free from nagging thoughts telling us we should never have left the battlefield alive—the place where our comrades gave their lives in war. We want to believe our lives will serve a better purpose if we are alive rather than dead. Thus, even though we often doubt that living is better than dying, we seek to find meaning in life rather than death, and hope to find life a privilege rather than a burden."

3. **STEP THREE (TRUST): Our third step is to begin to find relief by seeking help from God as we understand Him, and from persons we can learn to trust.**
   "If we are to find relief, we seek a source of help from person(s) whom we can learn to trust. Many of us also would like to trust God, as individually understood, and ask Him to show us the way out of our mental prisons, renewing our sensitivities to human emotions and spiritual qualities we fear we have lost."

4. **STEP FOUR (SELF-INVENTORY): We will make a searching, positive inventory of ourselves.**

"After taking the step of seeking and accepting help, we find ourselves aware of many negative qualities. In fact, although we might be willing to trust, we may fear that revealing ourselves to others will only be a negative experience. Thus, we ask a person we trust and a higher power to help us see our positive qualities. In that way, we can honestly evaluate the presence of both desirable and undesirable qualities."

5. **STEP FIVE (RAGE): We will admit to ourselves, to God, and to a person whom we trust, all our angry feelings and homicidal rage.**
"With an awareness that we are not alone, with improved self-esteem, and with a newfound desire to trust, we hope to understand the reason for our continuing rage. We will take the risk of revealing our angry feelings to a person we trust and God as individually understood. In so doing, we will discover that our anger is likely to be our only defense against helplessness and experiencing other emotions. Thus, this important step will help us to open the door to other painful memories and emotions."

6. **STEP SIX (FEAR): We will open the doors to the past and reveal to God and another person whom we trust our frightening, traumatic memories.**
"After beginning to realize that anger is often a defense against fear, we will now begin to understand the link between the two. In this way, we can begin to accept the fact that fear is normal and relief from fear may be found by facing it with the help of someone we trust and of God, as individually understood."

7. **STEP SEVEN (GUILT): We will ask forgiveness from God as we understand Him and recognize we are thus free from condemnation.**
"We ask for and accept forgiveness from God and a person(s) whom we trust for: committing, participating in, or knowing about acts committed which were unacceptable in our eyes, causing suffering and grief for other persons and now causing us to feel tormented with guilt and self-blame. After having accepted forgiveness from God and from another person(s), we can now forgive ourselves. But, we recognize that old habits of self-condemnation are difficult to break. Thus, self-forgiveness must be a daily matter."

8. **STEP EIGHT (GRIEF): We seek strength and support from God and another person to finally grieve for those whom we left behind.**

   "We seek strength to complete the grieving process for those who have died. We would like to finally be free, shedding tears without being lost in unending grief. This means also being able to understand the link between grief and all the feelings we have harbored for many years: anger at those who left us alone, guilt about surviving while others were killed, remorse for failing to save people who died, and yearnings to join those whose bodies have already been buried."

9. **STEP NINE (FORGIVENESS VS. SELF-CONDEMNATION): We reveal to ourselves, God, and those we trust all remaining suicidal or self-destructive wishes and make a commitment to living.**

   "We wish to expose and purge those negative forces within us which still may prevent us from making a complete commitment to life. Thus, after further self-evaluation, we reveal to ourselves, to God, and to those whom we trust all remaining suicidal wishes, and ask to be purged of the remaining, destructive, death forces which have hurt ourselves and others. Then, we seek and accept God's daily strength to make a daily commitment to living."

10. **STEP TEN (FORGIVENESS VS. REVENGE): We reveal to ourselves, God, and another person all remaining wishes for revenge and ask for God's strength to give these up.**

    "We seek and accept God's strength to give up our wishes for revenge toward those who hurt us and injured or killed our friends and loved ones so we can learn the full meaning of love of God, of others, and of ourselves."

11. **STEP ELEVEN (FINDING PURPOSE): We seek knowledge and direction from God for a renewed purpose for our lives.**

    "Having been freed from those burdens which have kept us from having meaningful and purposeful lives, we are ready to find a renewed purpose for our lives. Recognizing that God's power also can be a source of strength to live, we will daily seek freedom from old burdens or new problems through prayer, meditation, and a daily surrender to God. In this way, we can continue to find daily freedom from the past prison of rage, guilty memories, and impacted grief, and gain a knowledge of His purpose for our lives and the endurance to carry it out."

12. **STEP TWELVE (LOVING AND HELPING OTHERS): Having experienced spiritual rebirth, we seek God's strength to love others and help those who suffer as we have.** "Having had a spiritual awakening as a result of these steps, we seek to carry this message and to help all those who suffered as we have suffered."[25]

TRAINING SEMINARS

Training workshops for professionals and counselors on the Twelve Step PTSD Program, setting up Trauma Survivors Anonymous (TSA) groups, and Christian twelve-step groups are conducted periodically through The Bradley Center in Columbus, Georgia. The Bradley Center is a psychiatric center dedicated to emotional, physical, social, and spiritual healing.

Literature is available about each of the above programs by calling (404)576–9800, (404)576–6370, or by writing:

Joel Brende, M.D.
The Bradley Center
2000 Sixteenth Avenue
Columbus, GA 31993

Chapter 4

WOMEN—THE FORGOTTEN VETERANS

WAC Gloria Norfleet* was the last one to leave the field hospital. She had lingered to finish writing a letter for a GI from Champaign, Illinois. She quickened her pace to join the others who were waiting in the jeep. A small Vietnamese boy carrying a package passed her, entering the hospital just as she was leaving. And then it happened! An explosion threw her body ten meters, and her back and shoulders were riddled with shrapnel. The fifteen soldiers, three pregnant VC women, staff in the hospital—and the little boy—were killed. The child's package had contained a bomb.

Earlier that day, Gloria had been informed that her soldier husband, John, had been killed in combat.

Gloria enlisted in the Army in 1968 when she was eighteen. She signed up on a Wednesday and left the next day. She had been guaranteed in writing that she could train to become a physical therapist but her orders were lost, so the army decided she would be a medic. At Fort Sam Houston, she worked in personnel. In 'Nam she was assigned the role of operating room technician. Gloria

* The accounts of nurses are based on personal interviews.

66

became very good at teaching and at filling in wherever she was needed, and after a short while, was elected "WAC of the Year." She was assigned to the Bob Hope Tour and visited army installations around the world including those in Australia, Africa, and all over Europe. The bombing occurred during the world tour.

Gloria could not remember where or when she was injured; many details were still quite fuzzy in her memory. She was medevaced to a field hospital, and one of the nurses who cared for her was Lt. Sharon Lane* who was killed two months later in June, 1969.

One vivid, painful memory for Gloria happened on the way home. "When we landed in Hawaii, I deplaned on crutches and I was spat upon by protesters. I think all they did was stand out at the airport. They had signs that read, 'Baby killer.'" Emotionally vulnerable, Gloria was totally unprepared for this additional assault from *American citizens*. "That's why I shut up; I wouldn't talk about the war," said Gloria. In 1969, she had a nervous breakdown.

Gloria didn't talk about Vietnam until May, 1987. It was then that she joined the Central Illinois Chapter of ViêtNow—after much prompting from her friends. And it was then that healing began. Even her best friends had not known about her traumatic injuries or all that she had seen in Vietnam. No one knew the depth of her pain. At ViêtNow meetings, she learned that other veterans were hurting just as much as she.

"When you go into the meeting, you have to say your name, where you were at, and what you did. That's the first time I had ever said it. In our chapter there are kids that I went to high school with and they didn't know [about me]. After that, the vets really helped me," said Gloria. "We can talk about it. It's hard for them to talk about it, too, but together, it's really great."

She wishes more women would "come out." Gloria has a good friend in a veteran, John Dyson. "John and I can sit and cry together. He can think back about what he went through and he can tell me about it. And I can tell him what I can remember. So many details and names are still blocked out of my memory. It's just the idea that he was there. It's easier now because I know there are people out there; before I felt so alone."

* Lt. Sharon Lane is one of eight army nurses who were killed in Vietnam whose names are on the Wall. She was killed while caring for Viet Cong POWs at the 312th Evac Hospital at Chu Lai.

Gloria suffered from Post-traumatic Stress Disorder and had flashbacks. "You saw all kinds of things. They were kids—that's what the war was fought with. I remember guys in the hospital—shot, limbs missing, half a face missing. Those images never leave you," said Gloria, her voice breaking with emotion.

The Vietnam War had been a part of Gloria's life since she was fourteen years old. "The first time I was touched by Vietnam was when my girlfriend's brother was killed. My first husband was killed there; his brother was killed there also. And I watched a brother-in-law die from cancer as the result of exposure to Agent Orange."

When asked what the war did to her faith, she explained: "Before I went to Vietnam, I was a very religious person. I still believe in a Supreme Being, but I haven't really found Him since. I still believe in God, but I just don't understand [the war]."

She has been married four times; she married her last husband twice. Her eighteen-year-old daughter has been very supportive of her mother's ViêtNow activities. Gloria actively supported the building of the Vietnam Women's Memorial Project. Gloria worked hard, along with others, to bring unity rather than division among veterans by supporting the theme, *One Country, One Flag, and One Veteran.* "If it weren't for World War II vets, we wouldn't be here either," said Gloria.*

ONLY VOLUNTEERS GO TO VIETNAM!

Sue Procopio Cartwright, R.N., distinctly remembers the recruiter saying, "Nurses don't go to Vietnam; only those who volunteer." She was enrolled in nursing school in Vermont when recruiters came to her school and she joined the Army Student Nurse Program in her junior year. Upon completion of her State Boards, she reported to Fort Sam Houston in San Antonio, Texas, and then was assigned to California. In less than six months, her orders came for Vietnam. "Whenever you sign your name on the line, the army considers you a 'volunteer' and sends you where it wants to. I would like to get my hands on the recruiter who told me, 'Only volunteers go to Vietnam,'" said Sue.

*A few months after reviewing this chapter, Gloria Norfleet had back surgery after which complications developed. She is now comatose in a nursing home.

Sue panicked; she didn't want to go. After her thirty-day leave, she intentionally missed port call—the day of departure. The military told her she faked an "acute anxiety attack." Sue called it "gangplank fever."

"I found a lawyer. I told him I didn't want to go: 'I have brothers who are close to draft age, and I don't want to patch up young kids so they can go out and get killed.' I really was going to fight it," said Sue. She was considered a conscientious objector by the army and was required to see a psychiatrist and a chaplain. The psychiatrist told her she was immature and her reaction was nothing unusual. Lt. Col. Roy Peters, a Catholic chaplain, was called in to talk with Sue. She was in tears at their first meeting. Little did she know this would be the beginning of a lifelong friendship. She learned that Father Peters was an airborne military chaplain who served in battle with troops. During the course of their conversation he asked, "Have you ever stopped to think that this may be part of God's plan for your life and that you are needed over there?" She had to agree, there was need.

Sue was sent to the 71st Evacuation Hospital in Plciku. Her first assignment was to a forty-bed surgical ward comprised of twenty American patients and twenty Vietnamese Montagnards, the mountain people trained by American forces. Sixty days later, she was assigned to a medical ward where most of the men had diseases such as malaria or bubonic plague; some had poisonous snake bites. The nurses worked twelve-hour shifts—from 7 A.M. to 7 P.M. six days a week.

"The hardest part was not the long hours; it was being afraid all the time. You spent more time under your bed than in it," said Sue. "During an attack, we put our patients under their beds or laid mattresses over them to protect them. Every morning we'd have to go around and start all the I.V.s that had been yanked out during the attack.

"You lived differently over there. You lived one day at a time; there was always the threat of being killed. A lot of people were involved in relationships that I don't think they normally would have engaged in had it been any other situation," said Sue. "You partied as hard as you could off duty. Some drank. It was a necessary tension reliever. I smoked pot on occasion, but never before or during duty."

As she had not been under much of the extreme stress of nurses who worked in triage[1] or intensive care, she felt she was unaffected by her wartime experiences. But time proved otherwise.

Fifteen years later, during a period of high stress in her personal life—the death of a premature baby, her husband's retiring from the military, and the death of both of his parents—Sue was jittery and anxious. She remained tense all the time. Her job in public health was stressful, and it was her boss who finally suggested she go for counseling. Sue went to the Vet Center. The present-day stresses, added to unresolved stresses of her years in Vietnam, had to be dealt with. Reading the accounts of other nurses proved helpful for her; some of the books listed at the end of the chapter are about persons with whom she worked. Sue says she has no regrets for serving in Vietnam.

SOMEBODY HAS TO TAKE CARE OF THEM

"At least the army could have told us about the smothering heat and humidity," Donna thought to herself as she deboarded the plane in Saigon clad in a wool-blend, long-sleeved dress uniform appropriate for sunny California, but not Vietnam. Her feet were swollen, and she and others on board were having trouble getting their shoes on after the long, uncomfortable flight. It was the fall of 1966.

A bus met the plane. "It's too hot to wear these, but put your flak jacket between you and the side of the bus," the driver warned. The reality of being in a war zone quickly hit home.

Donna Perlinger Johnson, R.N., joined the Army Nurse Corp during training at St. Joseph's Nursing School in Omaha, Nebraska, in response to a recruiter's visit to the school the previous year.

"Despite how I felt about the politics of the war, I believed that if there had to be a war, and our men had to fight, then somebody had to be there to care for them," said Donna. She volunteered for Vietnam. She was assigned to the 12th Field Evacuation Hospital at Cu Chi, which was near the base camp for the 25th Infantry Division. For the duration of her tour, she worked in the emergency room that also functioned as admitting room and pre-op. She was the first to treat soldiers as they came in from the field.

"The wounded on stretchers were put on sawhorses as they came

70

in. We would cut off boots and clothing, insert an intravenous catheter, type and cross-match blood, stop the bleeding, put chest tubes in, debride burns—in other words get them ready for surgery if necessary. Most wounds were caused by mortars or shrapnel. Some were napalm burns," said Donna. Napalm, a jellied, flaming petroleum, clung to the skin and oozed into the pores causing deep burns. Donna was impressed with the excellent skilled surgeons and the quality of medical care given at her hospital.

"We had some soldiers who came in that were almost bled out from stepping into a pungi pit." The pits were approximately five feet deep camouflaged with a grass mat. At the bottom were dung-dipped bamboo sticks pointed upward, ranging from inches up to three feet long. "Often, the femoral artery in the groin was severed. It amazed me that we were able to save the majority of them," Donna said. "When our blood supply ran low, the staff gave blood.

"Some died as they came in, but the majority of our patients made it through pre-op, and we had the satisfaction of knowing that we had done our job. We never had time to get to know the fellas, or about their family or girl friends back home. In some ways, that was good," said Donna. "Those who got to know the soldiers on the wards may have had a harder time. If you let yourself think about what you had seen, you couldn't psychologically handle it. You had to do your job—become numb to it. There was no other way of dealing with it."

Donna was pleased that her nursing school had trained her well. "Never did I feel like I was unprepared or lacking in training for an emergency."

She marveled at the closeness that she felt with her friends. "You partied a lot to help you get through it," said Donna. "Often we would have to leave a party and go treat the incoming wounded."

Donna's philosophy of life helped her then, and has helped her since the war. "I did the best I could. I tell myself I'm human, too. I don't stew too long on past mistakes or decisions I've made. If it's not the right decision, I know it's not the end of the world. Life isn't going to be over if I make (or made) a wrong decision. A lot of people can't let go of guilt, but I realize we didn't have any control over some things. I just did the best I could, and I think that's what got me through."

Although Donna says Vietnam is constantly in the back of her mind, especially with all the publicity in recent years, she has experienced very few aftereffects. She has had some bad dreams after watching a movie about Vietnam but her adjustment to civilian life has been good.

Donna says that when she came home from the war, she appreciated not being quizzed about her experiences in Vietnam. "Mostly because anyone who hadn't been there just couldn't relate to it. There was no way I could describe it, so I just didn't want to talk about it. It was indescribable!"

Lynda Van Devanter, R.N., was among the first to attempt to explain what it was like for an army nurse in Vietnam. She describes the conditions under which the nurses at Pleiku worked in her moving book, *Home Before Morning*:

The fall monsoons brought our greatest number of casualties. It was a good time for the VC because they knew the country and were at home with its seasons. To our soldiers, the elements were merely another enemy which, in combination with the VC, proved unbeatable. If we at the 71st Evac had previously thought we were pushing ourselves to the limit, we were wrong. Before the monsoons, it would have seemed impossible for us to work any harder, but when the casualties increased, we kept going until we dropped. Then, after a couple of hours of sleep, we'd start back again. Overworked doctors, nurses, and technicians were falling into almost deathlike sleep at the operating tables. . . . We tried to sleep during every spare moment, taking our rest on floors, chairs, and even on empty gurneys. . . . As the weeks passed I began to feel like I needed a break or I would crack under the strain. But that break wouldn't come for a long time. Instead, we got more casualties and more rain.

We had cracks in the walls and floors of the O.R. The mud that poured down the hill would ooze through the cracks and mix with the blood in ways that were reminiscent of a fifties horror film. Most of the time we shoveled it over to the side and continued with surgery. Often, we found ourselves operating in an inch or more of mud. It was worse during the rocket attacks, when we had to lower the table and kneel in the muck. We tried to keep the rooms as clean as possible, but there was no way to stem the tide. When we had a lot of patients and constant rocket attacks, we knew that we could only handle the most important things. Mud on the floor was a low priority. . . .[2]

Hospitals were not immune to incoming mortars, rockets, or sniper attacks. Most hospitals were near an airport, making them easy targets for the enemy, and unarmed hospital staff were as vulnerable as the patients they cared for.

In an article that appeared in *Image: Journal of Nursing Scholarship*, Linda Spoonster Schwartz, R.N., M.S.N., explains:

> Because the Vietnam War was so different from other wars, the Geneva Convention provisions for noncombatants of medical facilities provided little protection. Hospitals often suffered heavy damages from rocket attacks, and some were overrun by the Viet Cong. In August 1979 the 6th Army Convalescent Center at Cam Ranh Bay was attacked by the Viet Cong. Enemy soldiers ran through the wards tossing homemade bombs and firing their automatic weapons at the unprotected patients, killing two and wounding ninety-nine (M. Green, personal communication, 1987). Nurses were wounded, injured and disabled as a result of these attacks.[3]

Eight female nurses died in Vietnam, as well as two male nurses.[4]

Rose Sandecki, R.N., a former army nurse, says that "even though vets in combat units saw much death and suffering in Vietnam, they did not deal with the numbers and recurrences of casualties on a daily basis seen by the people in the medical evacuation chain."[5]

To survive emotionally, medical staff members had to find ways of coping, often through emotional detachment, the same as soldiers did on the battlefield. A nurse (White, 1983) relates this horror story that dominates her Vietnam memories:

> . . . we were running out of supplies and didn't see how we would be able to take any more casualties that night. And then another chopper came in to the pad—it was about two in the morning—and they brought this guy off the chopper. We could hear him even above the noise of the rotor blades, screaming. . . . We could hear him coming in our direction on a stretcher, coming up the concrete ramp, up to the operating room. He had stepped on a land mine and had both arms and both legs blown off right at the trunk. His eyes had been blown away, but he was still alive and screaming all the way down the ramp. They wheeled him past us, put him down at the back and tried real hard to find a place to start an I.V., and to put him to sleep so they

could try to save him in some way. All the while he was screaming, "Let me die, let me die!" We listened to that for it seemed like thirty minutes until finally everything got real quiet and we knew he had died.

Somebody had a portable radio on a shelf. Bing Crosby was singing "Don't Fence Me In." After a little bit, everybody in the operating room started singing along. All of us in our cubicles were crying, the doctors and the nurses. Everybody up and down that place was just totally wiped out by the incident.

I think from that point on I just simply did not . . . [let myself feel]; it wasn't that I didn't care, but the only way I could deal with it was to simply shut everything out and not feel anything.[6]

THE FORGOTTEN MINORITY

Military records concerning the numbers of women who served in Vietnam are vague, for the government was not keeping close count. The fluctuating figures—ranging from five thousand to fifty-five thousand—were due to the integration of the service records during those years (enlisted men and women became "enlisted persons," obscuring the exact number of women). Women weren't supposed to be in dangerous war zones, so the military has also been somewhat guarded in its release of information about women.[7]

The most commonly accepted figures are that, of an estimated 250,000 women who served our country during the Vietnam era (1964–1975), 10,000 women, both military and civilian, are believed to have served in Vietnam. Ninety percent of the women who were there were nurses* in the U.S. Army, Navy, Air Force, and the United States Agency for International Development.[8] Others worked for government agencies such as the U.S. State Department, Information Services, the CIA, and Army Special Services.

But women served in many other capacities during the war. They were clerks, air traffic controllers, cartographers, entertainers, security personnel, intelligence officers, correspondents, and administrators. Some American Red Cross workers referred to themselves as "donut dollies"; their job was to serve coffee and doughnuts and

---

* Ten percent of the military nurse corps were male nurses.

talk to the soldiers. Many women were school and hospital workers for religious groups. An unknown number of women worked for civilian groups such as International Voluntary Services, Catholic Relief Services, the Mennonite agencies, the Tom Dooley Medical Foundation, and the USO. The American Friends Service Committee ran a day-care center for refugee children, provided rehabilitation services for amputees and handicapped civilians, and ran the VISA Program for young people, mostly American. Women worked for commercial airlines that flew in and out of the country, and civilian contractors employed women to work in various office-related jobs in Vietnam. Obviously, women played a vital role in Vietnam.

CERTAIN STRESSORS WERE UNIQUE TO WOMEN

Living and working in a combat zone produced some stresses for women that were similar to those soldiers experienced, others were markedly different, and some were gender-related.

Men in combat had to cope with sophisticated weaponry, guerrilla warfare for which they felt unprepared, an unidentifiable enemy, indistinguishable battle lines, unclear military objectives, and the political unpopularity of the war, which added to their sense of futility in fighting.

Most women who served in Vietnam had volunteered. Often older, most of these women had their schooling behind them. The average age of men was nineteen; for women, the average age was twenty-five.

Researchers have found that the most common stresses for women were those related to living in a war zone under life-threatening circumstances, caring for severely injured war casualties, and the negative reactions upon their return from Vietnam.

A study of 137 former Vietnam nurses reported in 1984 by the College of Nursing at the Northwestern State University in Shreveport, Louisiana, identified eight stressors that were significantly different for women:

Time in the military. Nurses who had served six months or less in the military had more difficulty coping. Because some of these nurses were recent graduates and also new to the military, adjusting to both of these factors in a war zone [and foreign culture] increased their stress.

Casualties. Much of the stress was due to the sights, sounds, odors, and emotional trauma experienced, resulting from large numbers of the severely wounded, very young casualties placed in their care.

Nurses' roles. Nurses who worked in emergency triage, operating rooms, and intensive care areas were subjected to very high levels of stress.

Supplies. Lack of certain supplies contributed to frustrations as nurses were unable to provide quality care and found their personal comfort limited.

Sexual harassment. Reported sexual harassment ranged from rape and assault to insults, unwanted attention, and sexist remarks.

Professional relationships. Nurses were not always valued by others in Vietnam, either as professionals or as persons of worth.

Survivor guilt. Even though nurses provided the best care possible, some of their patients died and the nurses experienced feelings of helplessness and guilt.

Threat to life. Women have reported memories of fear of personal harm or death; these fears were also evident in the descriptions of their dreams and flashbacks since returning from Vietnam.[9]

There were other stresses. After twelve-hour working days, women were invited and expected to attend off-duty social activities. Linda Schwartz explains:

Invitations to outside unit or squadron parties were extended through commanders to chief nurses, with the implied message that it was unpatriotic not to attend. For many women, this was intimidating; they believed that their participation was mandated. Some have reported that failure to comply, indeed attempts to "buck the system" on any issue, resulted in transfer to more dangerous locations, denial of "R and R" or changes in duty schedule.[10]

Some who failed to conform to these social expectations were labeled lesbians. Military women are stereotyped as masculine.

Women were also the victims of double standards. Nurse Lola McGourty reported in *Newsweek* that she and other nurses were restricted to the hospital compound for almost an entire year, ostensibly for their own protection. Doctors, by contrast, were free to roam; some, she recalls, flew model airplanes after their rounds while nurses remained constantly on call. [11]

Schwartz points out that the "Alice in Wonderland" quality of some situations defied understanding. For example, women have reported being guarded in their barbed wire compounds by patients in pajamas, flak jackets and helmets, sometimes with unloaded weapons; of being told to clean bloodstains off the grass outside the emergency room before an important general arrived; or of being blamed for the inadequacies and ineptitude of superior officers. [12]

Women were plagued with the added problem of conflicting roles. Schwartz points out that "servicemen came to regard them as mother, nurse, sister, girl next door, and girl friend, creating personal dilemmas for all concerned. In this emotionally charged atmosphere, some women said that they began to see changes in their personalities that were even harder to accept than the chaos of the war. The values that many women brought with them to Vietnam— to help, to heal, and to serve humanity—were incongruent with the objectives of the war—death, destruction, and devastation." [13] Many nurses volunteered their time in orphanages and villages helping civilians in the Medical Civil Action Program to restore some sense of normalcy to their lives.

Coming home was as devastating for women as it was for men. They were unprepared for the onslaught of airport arrivals where women in uniform were called "whores" and "baby killers." Former AF flight nurse Patricia Rumpza thought she had landed in the wrong country. Her comments appeared in an article in *California Nursing Review*:

"When I got off the airplane in LA, three people spit on me. I had literally just been saving the lives of their brothers, friends, and classmates and they were spitting on me!" Patricia hurriedly changed into civilian clothes in the airport bathroom. [14]

Readjustment to civilian life has been difficult. Relatives and friends expected these women to be the same as before the war, but they had changed. Lynda Van Devanter claims, "No one can see such things and remain unchanged."

Women, especially nurses, found it difficult to return to civilian nursing jobs. Caring for mass casualties had demanded every ounce of skill and energy they possessed. In the United States, veteran nurses were incensed at being required to take CPR courses, or being denied the right to hang blood. Van Devanter in her book, *Home Before Morning*, reports she had been trained by a surgeon in Vietnam to complete a spleenectomy so the physician could proceed to other patients. Stateside, jobs were meaningless and unchallenging. Many nurses became disillusioned with nursing and went back to school for more education. Women missed and longed for the bonds of comradeship experienced as an essential member of a skilled team in Vietnam.

WAR'S EMOTIONAL TOLL ON WOMEN VETERANS

The research done by O'Neill and Paul in the Louisiana Study identified fourteen adverse aftereffects on women as the result of their unforgettable year in Vietnam: recurring psychological problems, negative self-image, anxiety, depression, rage and anger, memory impairment, relationship problems on reentry, current relationship problems, substance abuse, flashbacks, hyperalertness, avoidance of activities that arouse memories (work-related), dreams and nightmares, and disturbed sleep patterns. [15]

Haunted by memories and unable to find or unwilling to seek help, an unknown number of women veterans have committed suicide since the war. Some women report they fear they "didn't do enough"; most can recall one particular soldier that "got to them" when he died. Some nurses built what they called "emotional walls that had been made impregnable." [16]

2nd Lt. Ellen Young said:

I quit looking at the faces of the ones who were going to die. I had his face embedded [a young soldier who had pleaded with her to not let him die] in my brain for the rest of my life . . . and I didn't need any

78

more. From then on, I coped, I survived. I learned how to take care of them and came to realize that if I could get through that year, I could do anything. . . . Nineteen years later, I still carry the young man's face, his words and my futility and rage against the carnage.[17]

Rose Sandecki explains: "This numbing, which helped her survive Vietnam, continues for many years upon her return home. *She is probably an expert at it today and, as a result, will not seek treatment for her PTSD.*[18]

Dr. John M. Boyle of Louis Harris and Associates believes "it's highly possible the women may have higher levels of stress and disorder than males."[19] The National Vietnam Veterans Readjustment Study revealed that those women exposed to high levels of war zone stress, such as exposure to the wounded and dead, have seven times the rate of current PTSD as those with low or moderate levels of exposure.[20]

Lynda Van Devanter, who admits it took years to untangle her life from Vietnam, recognizes the need for therapy and support groups. "Confronting trauma is easier said than done. It's a process that often involves nothing less than reliving the harrowing experiences of the war. Most veterans can't do it alone."[21]

Women have truly been the forgotten minority of the war. Initially, few counseling services were offered men; even fewer have been available for women veterans through the Veterans Administration. No comprehensive studies of women's readjustment or service-related health problems exist. Like male veterans, women have reported birth defects and health problems in their children and believe they, too, are also victims of Agent Orange (see Chapter 6). Currently, the New Jersey Commission on Agent Orange is conducting a study of the effects on women from exposure to dioxin-containing defoliants in Vietnam. The initial study focuses on problems of reproduction such as spontaneous abortions, still-births, infertility, birth defects, and early menopause.[22]

The Vietnam Veterans of America (VVA), headed by Mary Stout, a former army nurse, was the first organization to recognize the needs of women and include them in its membership. A poignant letter from a former Hospital Corps WAVE appeared anonymously in *Veteran*, the official publication of VVA. Addressing male veterans, the author expresses the needs of most women who served:

I am not trying to jump on a bandwagon to get recognition, I just need to get your support for serving you and my country in a part of the war zone that did not get hazardous duty pay. Our tour was not for one year, it was for the duration of our enlistment. Even more than that, most of us married vets, and we felt guilty for the pain we kept hidden. We felt unable to help you through yours.

My self-acceptance has been slow, and the highest time of my life was at a VVA reunion in Minnesota where I was hugged more than I have ever been before, and those were the most glorious hugs of acceptance.

And I can tell you this for sure—I am *proud* to be a Vietnam veteran, and I am honored to have served next to you. Thank you for being there when I needed you—then and now. [23]

THE WOMEN'S MEMORIAL PROJECT

Though delayed by their own denial and this country's lack of therapeutic support, the healing process has finally begun for some women. For former army nurse Lily Adams, it began at the dedication of the Vietnam Veterans Memorial in 1982. "A vet held out the flag to me. He said, 'Doesn't she feel good?' I started to cry. I was so angry with my country for treating us the way it had. We had been totally rejected. I remember touching that flag and, finally, forgiving."[24]

Former Navy nurse, Diane Carlson Evans, homemaker and mother of four from River Falls, Wisconsin, spearheaded the efforts to build a memorial that would recognize the valiant efforts of women. Diane's visit to The Wall in Washington, D.C., had been a turning point for her:

It made me cry, and that's what I needed, I was numb for so many years. I had never grieved, never cried. "The Wall" made me face reality. . . . I had always been fiercely proud of Vietnam veterans, but never felt it so strongly as I did in Washington [1982] those three days. We all needed to feel proud for so many years. [25]

In 1983, Diane shared her dream to build a memorial for women with Rodger M. Broden, a noted sculptor in Minnesota. Together they created a statue of a female Vietnam veteran. In 1984 Evans and Broden met with attorney Gerald C. Bender, a former marine who had been seriously injured in Vietnam, and Donna-Marie Boulay, R.N., J.D., a Minneapolis attorney and former nurse. Bender, Boulay, and Evans founded a not-for-profit corporation in Minnesota for the Vietnam Women's Memorial Project. The newly created corporation had three objectives: recognition, education, and research.

The project's office is now based in Washington, D.C., and is staffed. The organization's efforts are directed toward raising the money needed to erect the monument near the Vietnam Memorial, creating national public awareness and education about the women's role in Vietnam, and historical documentation of the numbers of women who served in Vietnam. All-out efforts are being made to locate these women.

Of the 110 monuments in Washington, D.C., not one depicts American military women. The present monuments are limited mostly to men, horses, and equipment. But women have served in all of America's wars. The statue of a nurse would be the first memorial honoring women.[26]

The Vietnam Women's Memorial Project has experienced a groundswell of support from many notable individuals and national organizations. Senate bill S. 2042 and House bill H.R. 4870 were introduced and passed in both Houses authorizing the building of the Women's Memorial. Mary Rose Oakar from Ohio functioned as the chairwoman of the Subcommittee on Libraries and Memorials and was instrumental in mustering the momentum needed to assure passage of legislation in the House authorizing the building of the memorial. Her moving testimony on September 23, 1988, appears in the *Congressional Record*:

To commemorate the dedication and sacrifice that so many women offered our nation is a noble and worthwhile cause. Over 10,000 women served in Vietnam, and through their efforts, our wounded were nursed back to health, our dying were comforted, and our soldiers' morale was kept high. There is little doubt that the wall of the Vietnam Veterans Memorial would list thousands of more names if these women had not chosen to serve. Their willingness to aid our nation in its time of need deserves to be recognized.

As coauthor of the bill, Sam Gejdenson (D-CT), testified:

> For so long we have forgotten to pay homage to the women who have made such a great effort in all our wars, from the Revolutionary War on. There comes a time when their recognition is long overdue. This is that time.[27]

On November 28, 1989, President George Bush signed legislation authorizing the Vietnam Women's Memorial Project to place a memorial honoring women veterans near the Vietnam Veterans Memorial in Washington. The project, chaired by Diane Carlson Evans, plans to work its way through the necessary federal agencies to determine the memorial's placement, develop a design selection process, mount a comprehensive $3 million fund-raising project, and hopes to build and dedicate the Women's Memorial by fall of 1992.

Like the Vietnam Veterans Memorial, the Women's Memorial will be a gathering place for veterans, both men and women, and for those who wish to pay their respects to the women who were there for them or their sons, husbands, and fathers. Unlike The Wall, it is a memorial dedicated to the *living* women who gave of themselves, often beyond the limits of physical endurance, only to emerge feeling guilty for not having been able to do more. This memorial, dedicated to all women veterans, will undoubtedly have the same healing effect as The Wall, for it will touch deeply the hearts of all who come, bringing to mind the sacrifice and love these women gave. For the women who served, it will be a source of pride and recognition. For the woman veteran who comes to the memorial, it will bring tears, stir emotions, and be a place of healing. Essential to healing is the need to know that you are loved and your efforts have been appreciated by others.

SOME ADVICE

Joan Craigwell, on staff at the Northern County Vet Center in Vista, California, says that most women veterans *fail to connect* the depression, the health problems they are having, and their anxieties to the Vietnam experience. Joan was a nurse in Vietnam during the Tet

Offensive. Today, she heads a task force of professionals who are preparing a special manual for Vet Centers so that counselors may better understand the problems unique to women Vietnam veterans.

If you are plagued by the symptoms of PTSD described in Chapter 3, it is important to listen to these symptoms and seek professional counseling in dealing with them. So often a woman, as the nurturer, tends to deny her own needs and problems. This may be especially true if you are married to a Vietnam veteran. Many women think the men had it so much worse, and so they discount their own needs. The Vet Centers are there for women veterans also. It may help you to read some of the books listed at the end of this chapter. Learning about the experience of others gives insight into our own story. Also, establishing contacts with other women and the network that can emerge from doing so will help relieve you of those feelings of isolation so inherent to PTSD. Sharing with those who have been there has special meaning.

ADDITIONAL READING

Campbell, D'Ann. *Women at War with America: Private Lives in a Patriotic Era.* Cambridge, Mass.: Harvard Press University, 1984.

Byrd, Barthy. *Home Front: Women in Vietnam.* Berkeley, Calif.: Shameless Hussy, 1986.

Elshtain, Jean Bethke. *Women and War.* New York: Basic Books, 1987.

Freedman, Dan, and Jacqueline Rhoads. *Nurses in Vietnam: The Forgotten Veterans.* Austin, Tex.: Texas Month Press, 1987.

Hampton, Lynn. *The Ace Tail-Gunner of the 91st!: Memoirs of a U.S. Army Combat Nurse in Vietnam.* Canton, Ohio: Daring Books, 1989.

Holm, Maj. Gen. Jeanne. *Women in the Military.* Novato, Calif.: Presidio Press, 1986.

Johnson, Louanne. *Making Waves: A Woman In a Man's Navy.* New York: St. Martin's Press, 1986.

MacDonald, et al; eds. *Images of Women in Peace and War: Cross-Cultural and Historical Perspectives.* Madison: University of Wisconsin Press, 1987.

Marshall, Kathryn. *In the Combat Zone: An Oral History of American Women in Vietnam.* Boston: Little, Brown, & Co., 1987.

Noel, Chris. *A Matter of Survival.* Boston, Mass.: Branden Press, 1987.

Norman, Elizabeth. *Women at War: The Story of Fifty Military Nurses*

Who Served in Vietnam. Philadelphia: University of Pennsylvania Press, 1990.

Roberts, Suzanne. *Vietnam Nurse*. New York: Ace, 1966.

Stiehm, Judith Hicks. *Arms and the Enlisted Woman*. Philadelphia: Temple University Press, 1989.

Van Devanter, Lynda, with Christopher Morgan. *Home Before Morning*. New York: Beaufort Books, 1983; Reprint ed. New York: Warner Books, 1984.

Van Devanter, Lynda, and Joan Furey. *Visions of War, Dreams of Peace: Writings of Women of the Vietnam War*. Anderson, Ind.: Warner Books, 1991.

Walker, Keith. *A Piece of My Heart: The Stories of Twenty-Six American Women Who Served in Vietnam*. New York: Ballantine Books, 1985.

Walsh, Patricia. *Forever Sad the Hearts*. New York: Avon Books, 1982.

Willenz, June A. *Women Veterans: America's Forgotten Heroines*. New York: Continuum, 1984.

PERIODICALS

For servicewomen or veterans, the MINERVA Center in Arlington, Va., headed by founder and coordinator Linda Grant DePauw, publishes two publications: *MINERVA: Quarterly Report on Women and the Military* and *Bulletin Board*. The *Quarterly Report* is a source for in-depth analysis, features, and history. The *Bulletin Board* is the only news magazine in the world to deal extensively and exclusively with items relating to women and the military. For more information write:

Dr. Linda Grant DePauw
The MINERVA Center
1101 South Arlington Ridge Road, #210
Arlington, VA 22202–9949
(703)892–4388

* * *

Lily Adams, R.N., writes and edits a national newsletter for military and civilian women. Cost is $8.00 for six issues for individuals; $15.00 for institutions. Write to:

Lily Adams, Editor
So Proudly We Hail!
P.O. Box 1703
Mill Valley, CA 94941

* * *

The National Women Veterans Conference publishes a newsletter called *THE NETWORKER*. Cost of the subscription is $12.00 per year. The Conference is committed to providing access to the publication and women veteran resources to as many women veterans as can be identified.

The National Women Veterans Conference, directed by Diana Danis, is a national organization based in Denver, Colorado. Each year it plans conferences of special interest to all women veterans evolving around the issues unique to them. For more information about the organization and acquiring the newsletter, write:

Diana Danis, National Chair/Director
National Women Veterans Conference
P.O. Box 12621
Denver, CO 80212
(303)433–2119

* * *

Contributions to the Vietnam Women's Memorial Project may be mailed to: 2001 S St. N.W., Suite 710, Washington, DC 20009; (202)328–7253.

VIDEOTAPE

The Invisible Force: Women in the Military. Focuses on episodes of racism, sexism, and struggles with Post-traumatic Stress Disorder in interviews with women veterans. Can be ordered from the William Joiner Center, University of Massachusetts at Boston, Harbor Campus, Boston, MA 92125 ($50.00 includes postage).

Chapter 5

OVERCOMING THE EMOTIONAL SCARS OF PHYSICAL WOUNDS

Jerrold Schroeder* enjoys splitting logs for firewood, but his wife, Pam, forbids him to use a chain saw. Jerry was blinded in Vietnam during a fire fight in 1971. He was twenty years old when it happened.

As an infantryman, he walked point for three months, then manned a machine gun for the next four. His six-man team had followed the NVA for three days through the jungle. They had set up ambushes and bedded down unknowingly only two hundred meters from the enemy's bunker complex. The next morning, Jerry was jolted awake by crossfire. If he could reach the machine gun across from him, he could counterattack the NVA. He safely made it to the gun, but was then hit. An A-K round slashed his face left to right across his eyes. Jerry was knocked unconscious by the blast. The team's medic, Mike Falbo, was soon by his side.

He awakened in the evacuation hospital at Long Binh, bandages

---

* Spec. 4 Jerrold Schroeder was in the U.S. Army, Co. C 1st of 7th, 1st Air Cav. Div. He served from 1970 to 1971. He takes pride in knowing this was Custer's unit during the Civil War.

covering his face. Nurses scolded him when he tried to remove them. "How are my eyes?" he asked them. Their voices were tense and they evaded his question. When they told him he would have to talk to the doctor, Jerry knew something was terribly wrong, but he still thought he could see.

His doctor answered in plain words: "You're blinded for the rest of your life, Jerrold." Disbelieving, he yelled, "Get away from me." As the reality set in, Jerry had no idea what the future would bring; his future seemed bleak. He was kept at Long Binh two weeks, sent to Clark Air Force Base for a few nights, and then transferred to Walter Reed Hospital for six weeks where he was taught braille.

"When I began learning braille, I realized I wouldn't have to spend the rest of my life sitting in a chair doing nothing," said Jerry.

He was hospitalized an additional six weeks at Hines Hospital in Chicago where he learned daily living skills at the school for the blind.

Having traveled on military flights with ambulances waiting, Jerry had come home in a bathrobe. Years later, when asked by other veterans to participate in parades, he had to admit he no longer owned a uniform. A local VFW group in his hometown of Morrison, Illinois, took up the challenge of finding one. A uniform was presented to him before a crowd of two hundred military personnel and friends at a special service at the Rock Island Arsenal on May 22, 1987. Among those friends was Mike Falbo, the medic who first tended his wounds in Vietnam and who now lives in Wisconsin. It was a tearful reunion.

Jerry was married to Pam in 1984. As a stepfather to her children—Amy, eighteen, Ann, seventeen, and Jeffrey, fourteen— he claims he feels as close as any father would his own children. He boasts of being a "tough disciplinarian." His wife chuckles when he says that. What is evident in their home is a deep respect for the man who plays ball with his son—a ball on a rope makes that possible. Jeffrey accompanies him in some parades and says he wants to be like his dad, and maybe go to the army some day. But Jerry doesn't encourage him; he doesn't want the same thing happening to Jeffrey.

Jerry helps with the garden and yard work, and all the housework, including washing windows. "She won't let me do the dusting, though. There are too many knickknacks I can break," says

Jerry, smiling as if happy to have an excuse. He walks six to ten miles a day. Living on the outskirts of town, he has learned to buy only whatever groceries he can carry home.

"The biggest difficulty I have is killing twenty-four hours a day," explains Jerry. There is no bitterness or anger in his voice. "Who should I be angry at? I volunteered to go."

"I've found that you shouldn't worry about what could have been; you have to go with what you can do. You have to take it a day at a time," says Jerry. "Any day you can put two feet on the floor is a good day."

Jerry was awarded a Purple Heart and Bronze Star for bravery under fire, but he downplays such commendations. "I don't feel like I did anything special. I was just like a million other guys that went there."

* * *

John Fulton* farms 920 acres despite the fact that he wears an artificial leg. Actually, the prosthesis gives him fewer problems than the leg that doctors saved in Vietnam. His left leg has nerve and muscle damage from the knee down, a stiff ankle, and no toe motion—his shattered leg and foot gave him so much pain surgeons had to fuse the ankle several months after the accident.

John stepped on a booby-trapped mortar round May 13, 1969. He remembers almost every detail to this day. He remembers his buddies yelling, "Doc stay off the trail. . . ." But it was too late.

"I remember yelling 'Oh, God, I've hit a mine!' I can still hear the click—the trigger mechanism of the mine—then I was hurled through the air. For a few seconds I was out. When I came to, I looked down and it was all red. My right leg was gone below the knee. The pain was terrible," said John. "Fortunately, I was wearing my flak jacket; that's what saved my life. The remaining leg and my right arm were riddled with shrapnel."

John was twenty years old when he was drafted into the army in 1968. He was engaged to his high school sweetheart, Loretta.

After surgery, John awakened with an army major standing over him and asking if he had any friends in Dong Tam, the site of the Third Surgical Hospital. Dick Krogman's name came to mind.

* Spec. 5 John Fulton was in Charlie Company, 3rd of the 47th Infantry, 9th Inf. Div., in 1968–69. He was based in the Mekong Delta.

"I'll track this young man down for you and ask him to come to see you," the officer told him. When Dick came to see John, he asked him to write to his parents describing his condition. To this day, John is thankful the major followed through as promised.

"Two hours after my parents were notified by an army telegram that I was injured," said John, "they received Dick's letter giving much more information and describing my injuries—but assuring them I would be all right. His letter really helped them."

Stateside, John was hospitalized at Fitzsimmons VAMC in Denver. Loretta and his mother came to see him his first week back. "I had my first and only five-minute crying spell when we saw each other. I weighed about one hundred pounds and they were stunned to see me for the first time. I believe my getting wounded hurt my father the worst, but he showed it to me the least," said John. He was released from Fitzsimmons on May 22, 1970, and on June 20, 1970, he and Loretta were married.

Today, John and Loretta engage in grain farming in northeastern Illinois. They have three living children—Monica, nineteen, Brad, fourteen, and Brent, six. Their oldest son died in 1976 of spinal meningitis. Like Jerry's, John's spirit is free of anger or bitterness. Both men, by realizing that blaming the war and others for their misfortune is futile, have overcome whatever anger or bitterness they may have felt.

"What does bitter get you? It gets you in more trouble." says John. "I feel the way I was raised by good, caring parents, and having a loving, supportive spouse has helped me through these tough times. Going to Vietnam, however, was nothing compared to losing our two-year-old son," claims John. "It was devastating."

Routinely, John puts on his leg at five o'clock each morning and wears it until night. During hot weather, he has to change stump socks more frequently to avoid creases that rub his stump raw. When that happens, he uses crutches. In February, 1989, he was fitted with a Seattle* foot that looks real and offers more flexibility, but which, he claims, required his learning to walk all over again.

"My kids don't think of me as a disabled person. I've never used it as an excuse, nor have I ever felt sorry for myself. I thank God for giving me the twenty years some guys never had. Every day is a

---

* Developed by orthopedic surgeon Dr. Ernest Burgess at the Seattle VAMC.

good day, but some are better than others," he claims. "I have this wonderful feeling that this [the farm] is where I belong and it is a good feeling. I say to myself, 'See what God can do for you!'

"Seeing and living with a lot of guys in the hospitals like myself—some triple amputees, some with eyes missing—helped me work through a lot of the grief before I got back home," he explained.

John says he questioned God in Vietnam: "I wondered why we seemed to lose all the good guys. While there, my faith took the form of prayer. I prayed all the time because I was afraid all the time. I would pray myself to sleep." John was cofounder of Kankakee Valley Chapter #52 of the countywide organization called the Center for Independent Living for the Disabled. By his drive and determination John inspires other disabled persons to live a normal and productive life.

* * *

Paul Rodgers' home in Garden Grove, California, is finished, but he says it almost killed him. "I hauled all the lumber and building supplies for the house from seven different lumberyards in my van. I broke my wheelchair three times. I'll build again, but next time, I'll pay someone else to haul the materials," says Paul.

Paul* is a quadriplegic. His neck was broken when an overloaded Chinook helicopter carrying nearly ninety ARVN and American soldiers crashed to the ground on May 6, 1969, near the Tay Ninh mountains. He landed on his back some fifty feet from the helicopter amidst a human pile of bodies, some dismembered. Paul saw one victim tearing cooked flesh from his face.

He couldn't move. The radio pack he wore on his back had caused his neck to snap when he landed. Mustering all of his strength, Paul rolled over onto his stomach and tried to crawl. He hooked his wrist around what he thought was a root or small tree trunk. Whatever he saw was loose and flimsy and unable to provide him any firm support in pulling himself forward. The intense effort only served to weaken him further. He found it difficult to breathe.

"A thousand things went through my mind," says Paul. "I knew

---

* Spec. 4 Paul Rodgers was with the U.S. Army, C Battery 6th Battalion in field artillery based near Phuoc Binh, 1968–69.

the immediate threat I faced was the helicopter's exploding any minute. It was filled with gas and hydraulic fluid since we had just loaded and little had been consumed.

"I pictured Jesus in the garden. . . . I kept praying, 'Not my will, but your's, Father . . . but I *want* to live!'" In the distance, Paul heard voices. Somehow he had to get the men's attention.

"Y-o-u g-o-t t-o h-e-l-p m-e . . . b-e-c-a-u-s-e t-h-e h-e-l-i-c-o-p-t-e-r is going to blow up!" he said gasping for breath.

Paul describes what happened next. "I couldn't take a normal breath because of my injuries. I knew my only chance for survival was with those two men. I went into a death act, flailing my arms from the elbow up, and I whispered that I was dying.

"I forced them through that death act to help me. Those guys just went nuts. . . . they went insane [with fear]. I knew I was acting, but I did what I had to do to get them to help me, jeopardizing their lives to save mine."[1]

Despite their fears, the two soldiers came forward, then hurriedly dragged Paul to safety, bumping his head on rocks and whatever lay in the path. They draped a tarpaulin over Paul to protect him from the blast. Only minutes later, the helicopter exploded, shooting flames ten stories high, Paul estimates. Fewer than ten men survived the crash.

Paul was hospitalized in Japan. Complications set in during transport to a stateside hospital; he developed pneumonia. His stomach muscles no longer assisted with breathing; the diaphragm had to compensate. Hypostatic pneumonia frequently threatens the life of a quadriplegic. (His level of nerve damage was at C-5, 6, and 7 (cervical vertebrae); his legs and the lower portion of his body were completely paralyzed and there was some paralysis of his arms and hands.) Miraculously, he recovered shortly after transfer to Fitzsimmons Hospital in Denver.

Today, Paul studies nutrition, the immune system and stress, biology, and the human anatomy. He carefully watches his diet so that bladder and bowel problems are minimal. Para- and quadriplegics are more subject to urinary tract infections because the bladder is spastic and fails to empty completely, thus harboring bacteria.

Paul shifts his weight frequently to avoid pressure sores. Poor circulation is another problem a paralyzed person experiences. Some develop decubitus ulcers and calcified joints. Paul takes care of his body and tries to prevent those problems through diet and exercise.

As we sat talking, his left ankle rested on his right knee and he looked quite casual. He showed me his hands. The palms of each of his hands is darkened with callouses from wheeling.

Paul has become very fast on wheels. In 1984, he participated in the fourth National Veterans Wheelchair Games and came in fourth in both the 400 and 1500 meter races, and second in ping pong. Again, in June, 1989, he participated, along with five hundred other veterans from all over the world, in the Long Beach Wheelchair Games held in Long Beach, California. He participated in the 800 and 1500 meter wheelchair races, weight lifting, ping pong, and billiards competitions. He won three third places, one fourth, and one fifth in his division in the events in which he was a participant. These games are growing every year and are sponsored by Veterans of Foreign Wars, Paralyzed Veterans of America, and various sponsors such as Rolls InvaCare of America.

There's an acceptance of his disability, which Paul says, stems in part from the fact that he was brought up around persons with disabilities. His mother is deaf. His grandfather founded a Rescue Mission, and many of the persons he met through the Mission had ' disabilities. Conditioned by these circumstances, his parents, he feels, may have had an easier time accepting his condition.

But sometimes, especially when he's feeling stressed, Paul gets angry: "In the beginning I wasn't bitter. But when I've got problems, I think of Nixon who was Commander-in-Chief and his dishonesty in the Watergate affair. I think of the Secretary of State in Illinois in the late sixties, who was believed to have been guilty of mismanagement of state funds. And I think of two local county sheriffs accused of wrongdoing. These people were supposed to be running our country, and they were dishonest. And I was over there fighting for this country. Yes, sometimes I feel angry and bitter." But Paul is not one to dwell on those thoughts for long. He prays and studies the Scriptures daily. His life is filled with activities and independent studies that broaden his interests and expand his horizons. He hasn't given up on the idea of getting married when the right gal comes along. Paul believes he'll walk some day. "It's just a simple matter of finding a way to get the nerves to regenerate," he explains.

* * *

Michael Morrow* had been on a bulldozer for months clearing jungle. While doing so, he was sprayed directly with Agent Orange. He welcomed a good hot shower in Quang Tri. Incoming mortars cut his shower short, and as he made a running dash for the bunkers, he fell on the slippery concrete slab dislocating his shoulder—and herniating several discs in his back. His right shoulder rested on his rib cage. The doctor who treated him misdiagnosed his condition and gave him a elpeau's bandage, then sent him back out for active duty with his arm in a sling. Michael was put into hostile country unable to carry a weapon. Frightened and unable to defend himself, he went back to the hospital. This time, he saw a different doctor who told him he needed surgery right away. The surgery he required could only be done in the States, so he was sent to Valley Forge Hospital where he remained hospitalized for nearly a year. Still, the three ruptured discs in his back were not diagnosed or treated. Other, more obvious injuries, had higher priority.

Being hospitalized beside GIs with limbs missing and more serious injuries made Michael feel guilty—he had fallen in a makeshift shower. "Why me? Why am I here?" he asked himself.

For the next twenty years, VA gave Michael physical therapy, arthrograms, and pain pills. Not until he went to a private physician was his back injury diagnosed. His injuries have greatly impacted on his employment opportunities and mental stress.

Michael has worked hard at overcoming adversity. He says, "You can't keep reverting back to all that was bad. It's self-destructive. It's time to move forward. We should understand and accept," he adds, "that no one owes us anything. What we get, we need to accomplish on our own."

For twenty years, Michael had numerous jobs but none as meaningful as the one he presently has helping other local veterans as a veterans employment representative with the Ohio Bureau of Em-

---

* Spec. 4 Michael Morrow was in the Army's 1st Infantry, 14th Combat Engineer's Battalion, I Corp, in May, 1969. He served side by side with his brother, James Morrow, of Newark, Ohio.

ployment Services in Lancaster, Ohio. He has found meaning for his life by "caring enough to make a difference."

VIETNAM INJURIES WERE PARTICULARLY SEVERE

The Vietnam War produced the most critically wounded soldiers ever to survive evacuation to mainland hospitals.[2] As a result of the United States' military involvement there, 308,873* men were wounded. A total of 75,000 are considered to be disabled. In Vietnam, soldiers experienced amputation or crippling wounds to the lower extremities at a rate 300% higher than in World War II. The rate of multiple amputations was 18.4% in comparison to World War II's 5.6% (U.S. Congressional Record, 1982). In December 1983, VA reported 587,032 Vietnam era veterans receiving service-connected compensation. Of these, 6,698 incurred anatomical loss of limbs and 10,839 the loss of use of limbs (VA Statistical Reviews and Analysis Division, 1983).[3]

Because of the weaponry used in Vietnam, injuries were severe: multiple mutilating wounds caused by high velocity bullets, mortars and rockets; shrapnel wounds caused by pieces of hot, flying metal, some large, some small; traumatic amputations from claymore mines or booby traps; deep penetrating wounds from pungi sticks, leading to gangrene and complications; massive smoldering burns from napalm or phosphorus incendiaries.

Despite this ghastly variety and the fact that medical professionals had to work under the worst possible conditions, less than two percent of the casualties treated during the war died as a result of their wounds. "The record of the Vietnam War in terms of saving the lives of the wounded was unparalleled in the history of warfare." (Holm, 1982)[4] The survival rate was 98.4 percent. Many men were saved who would have died in previous wars. This is due in part to the use of helicopter "dust-offs," which meant the wounded could be quickly taken to a medical unit. Advanced methods of trauma care saved lives, but neither of these advances would have meant much without the medical teams—the medics and corpsmen, lab and X-ray technicians, anesthesiologists, O.R. techs, nurses and

* *Data on Vietnam Era Veterans*, VA, April 1985, p. 12.

doctors—who often had to work beyond normal human endurance. Although more men came home from this war, they came home with more severe and permanent disabilities. The percentage of Vietnam soldiers who survived amputations or crippling wounds to the lower extremities was three hundred percent higher than in World War II and seventy percent higher than during Korea. The incidence of paraplegia was one thousand percent higher than in World War II and fifty percent higher than in Korea (Starr, 1972).

The Disabled American Veterans (DAV), a Washington-based, million-member, nonprofit organization claims there are currently 2.2 million disabled veterans in this country.

PEACETIME INDIFFERENCE

DAV claims history shows that the understanding of the American public and their elected representatives for the problems of disabled veterans fades as the memory of war grows weaker. This happened with alarming speed after the Vietnam War.[5] To make matters worse, the pressure to cut federal spending intensifies, and the temptation to economize at the expense of needed veterans' programs is more than many politicians can resist. Under such circumstances, a man or woman who was once injured in wartime hostility can again be injured by peacetime apathy. Over the past decade, for example, funding of VA medical programs has decreased substantially. As a result, facilities are deteriorating, and thousands of vets each month are without a source for the medical treatment they need. This occurs at a time of increasing demands for health care by an aging veteran population.[6]

DAV reports that disabled veterans are hardest hit in the areas of employment: "No matter how high the unemployment rate for the United States work force may go, the statistics for disabled veterans are always unacceptably higher. A 1986 Labor Department study revealed that one out of five disabled Vietnam veterans has dropped out of the labor force altogether. Of those still in the work force, Vietnam veterans with service-related impairments rated at thirty to fifty percent disabling suffered an unemployment rate of 16 percent, compared to 9.2 percent among all service-connected disabled veterans who served in Vietnam."

DAV asks: "Who deserves fulfilling employment more than men and women disabled in honorable, wartime military service to their country? No matter how well disabled veterans recover from illness or injury, no matter how well they adjust to and overcome their handicaps, they aren't participating fully in our society until they're working in jobs suited to their capabilities."[7]

POSITIVE CHANGES IN THE PHILOSOPHY OF HOSPITAL CARE

The medical management and care of the spinal cord injured (SCI) has changed a great deal since the end of World War II. For many years, para- and quadriplegics remained hospitalized in a safe hospital environment—"safe" meaning that patients can become very secure in a hospital setting where they are with other patients like themselves and staff members who need few explanations about what happened to them. Out in the real world, the "para" or "quad" has to face rude public stares, comments, and questions, insurmountable physical barriers in buildings and on the streets, and the psychosocial adjustments required for living in the family environments. In the hospital setting, for example, nurses assist with care for the patient's personal needs and body functions; in the home setting, someone has to be hired or a family member must assume the role of nurse and caregiver.

Frederick Downs, Director of Prosthetics and Sensory Aid Service for the Department of Veterans Affairs (formerly called Veterans Administration), explained what happened to change the approach to long-term hospitalization for the spinal cord injured.

"At the end of World War II, the life expectancy of the spinal cord injured soldier was five years. Often he died from urinary tract infections or other complications," says Downs. "Through advancements made by VA in care and infection control, now the SCI person presently has a life expectancy of only four or five years less than the average nondisabled person. Another process was the changing of philosophy regarding long-term hospitalization. If a SCI patient was going to live a normal life, then he had to leave the hospital.

"In the late sixties and early seventies," says Downs, "there were a number of activists among the spinal cord injured and they said:

'This is no way to be. You have to get these people out in society.'
In the mainstreaming process, the VA literally had to force some
patients out of the hospitals for their own good. Once outside,
however, they rediscovered life. Now we have an ongoing, ever-
growing, active disabled population. We are involved in those kinds
of devices that make one feel more at home in society. The idea is
not to allow patients to stay in the hospitals for long because it's not
healthy for them. We have whole systems designed to keep them in
the community.

"We [the department] provide those appliances that enable
someone to become independent again. That includes environmental control units, and all the mobility and functional aids that are
available to the disabled today," Downs explained.[8] All of his staff
are disabled Vietnam veterans, including himself.

Frederick Downs, author of *The Killing Zone* and *Aftermath*, lost
his left arm above the elbow, from stepping on a "Bouncing Betty"
mine in Vietnam. He feels it's important to have the disabled working with the disabled. "The people that I hire who represent Prosthetics and Sensory Aids Service in the medical centers are all
disabled. We not only talk prosthetics, we *are* prosthetics. If one of
the first persons the newly injured or disabled person sees is our
prosthetic rep who says, 'We're going to get you rolling,' and is
himself in a wheelchair or using some other prosthetic appliance, it
helps them feel less devastated. This is a way to begin the rehabilitation process."

Downs claims he and his employees are activists for the disabled
as well as being employees of the Department of Veterans Affairs:
"Because you are disabled yourself, you know what's possible and
fight within the system. The system really pulls for you; although
philosophically they're still very conservative, they still want you to
succeed. That's human nature.

"Despite what some veterans think of VA," says Downs, "the
reality is that there are changes and advances occurring that the
public has little knowledge of. . . . Flexible ball sockets for amputees, and all the lightweight prosthetic components available now
are just a small example. If you can save half a pound on your
prosthetic devise, it makes a world of difference."

Along with these advances, says Downs, are attitude changes
regarding the aging population and their losses. In the past, ampu-

tees, because of advanced age, were not considered candidates for prosthetics. "Some professionals used to think, 'He's too old, he just won't use it [a prosthetic],' " he claims.

"We've got people ninety-five years old wearing artificial limbs— and they are working. Some veterans that haven't walked for many years are now walking with a prosthesis! It's a matter of attitude change."

There is an excitement in Frederick Down's voice and manner as he shares these stories about bringing new hope and life to veterans of all ages.

HOMECOMINGS—SOME BAD, SOME GOOD

To add to their physical injuries, some Vietnam soldiers—even those with obvious, traumatic injuries—were subjected to verbal abuse and emotional wounding on their return.

Frederick Downs, in his book *The Killing Zone*, shares his story:

In the fall of 1968, as I stopped at a traffic light on my walk to class across the campus of the University of Denver, a man stepped up to me and said, "Hi."

Without waiting for my reply to his greeting, he pointed to the hook sticking out of my left sleeve. "Get that in Vietnam?"

I said, "Yeah, up near Tam Ky in I Corp."

"Serves you right."

As the man walked away, I stood rooted, too confused with hurt, shame, and anger to react.[9]

Downs goes on to say that even many years later, the same emotions still flood over him with the memory of that encounter.

The anticipation of "first encounters" with a spouse or girl friend and parents or siblings was terrifying for some, especially those with facial disfigurement. They feared rejection. One wishes they all could have been as tender and touching as the one Dave Roever experienced when he saw his wife, Brenda, for the first time.

A phosphorus grenade went off in Dave's hand in 'Nam and he had forty percent of his upper body and face eaten away by third-degree burns. Looking in the mirror for the first time devastated him and he feared how his young wife—not yet twenty—would react when seeing him.

Brenda Roever's response to her husband emanated from a pure and loving heart. Dave describes the scene:

> Brenda walked straight up to my bed, paused at the chart, and looked right at me. Showing not the slightest tremor of horror or shock, she bent down and kissed me on what was left of my face. Then she looked me in my good eye, smiled, and said, "Welcome home, Davey. I love you." To understand what that meant to me you have to know that's what she called me when we were most intimate; she would whisper "Davey" over and over in my ear. By calling me Davey, by invoking and embracing once more the intimacy of her knowledge of me, she said exactly what I needed to know. By using her term of endearment for me, she said, *You are my husband. You will always be my husband. You are still my man.* That word of tender intimacy was a creative word of perfect love which cast out my fears.
>
> All I could say was, "I want you to know I'm real sorry."
>
> She said, "Why are you sorry?"
>
> "Because I always wanted to look good for you. Now I can never look good for you again."
>
> She grinned and said, "Oh Davey, you never were good-looking anyway." And that was the beginning of the deep psychological and spiritual healing which eventually quenched the fire of my ordeal, at least enough for me to face the world again.[10]

Unfortunately, not all wives or loved ones could respond as appropriately as Brenda. Some partners walked away unable to say anything; others openly rejected and turned away from the injured veteran—if only for a moment—thus adding emotional injury to physical injury. Sometimes these bitter memories linger on for both veteran and partner.

* * *

The stories shared in this chapter are about men and their families who have adjusted well to living with their disabilities. The following is a summary of the lessons to be learned from them.

Advice to the Disabled Veteran:

- *Think in the present; take one step at a time.* Don't dwell on what could have been.
- *Be determined to live as normal a life as possible.* Never use your disability as an excuse for feeling sorry for yourself or for shirking responsibility.
- *Avoid reverting back to all that was bad.* Such thinking is self-destructive and results in bitterness that poisons the soul.
- *Accept the fact that people are curious about your disability if it is obvious.* Explaining will be less of a burden if you project an image of self-assurance and comfort within yourself. Once the unknown is dealt with, people are usually free to relate to you as a person from that point on.
- *Ask for help when you need it.* Friends and relatives (even strangers) are usually eager to help, but often need specific suggestions on how they may do so. Some refrain from offering for fear of offending you.
- *Try to keep your sense of humor.* It will help you over the rough spots and handle the absurdities that occur in life.
- *Rely on God as a source of strength for daily living.* God has promised to be with us regardless of what happens to us. Draw from His strength as you meet each new crisis. Believe that God understands your anger, fears, and frustrations.
- *Forgive those who may have hurt you.* Unless persons have been taught or have experienced working with the disabled or disfigured, they lack the social skills required to communicate effectively. Harboring resentment toward their insensitivity can only cause you more pain. If your spouse or parent was the offending party, it may help to go back in time and discuss these difficult moments, each of you sharing what you thought and felt at the time. Tell them you forgive them. Your loved one may have felt very guilty about hurting you.

Advice to the Nonveteran:

Perhaps you are wondering what the appropriate thing is to say to the veteran. The following may be helpful:

- *Tactfully ask what happened if not knowing prevents you from relating to a disabled or disfigured veteran.* Most persons would prefer your asking, rather than being avoided, stared at, or misunderstood. *Avoid* making comments about the war and how you felt about it. Instead, listen to the veteran if the individual chooses to talk about his or her Vietnam experience. If you must respond, do so with words of appreciation for service and sacrifice.
- *Don't think of the amputee, disabled, handicapped, or the disfigured person as an object of pity.* They don't want or need your pity. They want and need to be heard, to be respected as a person with a voice, and with rights the same as you.
- *Be willing to assist when it is obvious help is needed.* Barriers, such as heavy doors or other obstacles, prevent the disabled person's entry into a building. In some cases, it would be wise to ask how you can be of help.
- *Don't equate disability with sadness or mental incapacity.* Many veterans adjust quite well and have come to accept and enjoy life. Talk directly to the person; don't speak with someone else on his behalf.
- *Support those political candidates who are actively working on veterans' issues.*
- *Lend your efforts in eliminating physical barriers.* Many older church structures, city buildings, and movie theaters are still not accessible to the handicapped.[11]

ADDITIONAL READING

Block, Mickey, and William Kimball. *Before the Dawn.* Canton, Ohio: Daring Books, 1988.

Browne, Corinne. *Body Shop.* New York: Stein and Day, 1973.

Cleland, Max. *Strong at the Broken Places.* New York: Berkley Books, 1982.

Downs, Frederick. *Aftermath.* New York: Berkley Books, 1985.

_____. *The Killing Zone.* New York: Berkley Books, 1978.

Eilert, Rick. *For Self and Country.* New York: William Morrow, 1983.

Glasser, Ronald J. *365 Days.* New York: George Braziller, 1971, 1980.

Kovic, Ron. *Born on the Fourth of July.* New York: Pocket Books, 1977.

Roever, Dave, with Harold Fickett. *Welcome Home, Davey*. Waco, Tex.: Word Books, 1986.

Starr, Paul. *The Discarded Army: Veterans after Vietnam*. New York: Charterhouse, 1972.

ORGANIZATIONS

Disabled American Veterans (DAV) provides numerous services to disabled veterans and their families free of charge, i.e., counsels veterans and their families on veterans' benefits and services, acts as attorneys-in-fact and assists its clients file claims for disability compensation, death benefits, pension, and other benefits provided under federal, state, and local law. DAV requests hearings before government boards to present claims, and when needed, they review board decisions, advising veterans if appeals are warranted. DAV provides office-equipped vans called field service units, to bring services to its clients. When natural calamities such as floods, earthquakes or tornadoes strike, DAV has national service officers (NSO's) who go to the area to search out disabled veterans who need assistance.

The DAV also provides scholarships to children of disabled veterans who are unable to afford the cost of higher education.

DAV conducts seminars on job-seeking skills for disabled veterans and files formal complaints of job discrimination with proper government agencies whenever it is necessary to make equal employment opportunities a reality.

For more information about these and other services, call or write to:

Disabled American Veterans   Publishes the periodical:
807 Maine Avenue, S.W.   *DAV Magazine*
Washington, DC 20024
(202)554–3501

* * *

Paralyzed Veterans of America (PVA) National Veterans Benefits Department has a team of more than one hundred professionals nationwide to help veterans gain all the VA services and entitlements that are rightfully theirs as a result of military service to the United States. These services are free of charge.

The PVA is a veterans' service organization chartered by Congress but funded through private donations and neither seeks nor receives government funds.

PVA is a strong supporter of the National Veterans Wheelchair Games, Bowling, Tennis, and Ski Championships. On a community level, its chapters are actively involved in sports activities such as skiing, boating, archery, football, camping, kayaking, golf, hunting, tennis, hand-controlled flying, ultralight flying, swimming, scuba diving, racquetball, biking, basketball, table tennis, horseback riding, and weightlifting.

PVA's National Legislative and Advocacy Programs work to improve veterans' benefits and support the full civil rights of all of America's citizens with a handicap.

PVA's National Architecture and Barrier Free Design Program promotes accessibility to public buildings, housing, and other facilities for paralyzed veterans and other citizens with a disability or age-related impairment.

Paralyzed Veterans of America   Publishes the periodical:
801 18th Street, N.W.   *Paraplegia News*
Washington, DC 20006
(800)424–8200

* * *

Blinded Veterans Association (BVA), a nonprofit organization, was founded in 1945 by a group of veterans blinded in World War II. In 1958, the association was chartered by an act of Congress to represent blinded veterans officially. It is the only organization that seeks out blinded veterans where they live. The services of BVA are available to all blinded veterans whether or not they are members. BVA has regional offices across the country that carry out assistance programs at the state and local level. Field representatives assist veterans in obtaining benefits including disability compensation or pension, rehabilitation training, prosthetic equipment, and medical treatment.

Employment representatives, also blinded veterans, concentrate on finding satisfying careers, not just jobs for the visually-impaired. This may mean helping the veterans write resumes, preparing and filing job applications, and keeping them informed of potential job opportunities. Most importantly, employment representatives actively seek out, and in some cases create, potential job openings and then match up employers with the best qualified blinded veterans.

The BVA Bulletin, which is published six times a year, is the primary means of keeping blinded veterans informed. It is printed in large type and is available on recorded discs or in braille.

Blinded Veterans Association Publishes the periodical:
477 H Street, N.W. *The BVA Bulletin*
Washington, DC 20001
(202)223–3066

Take Charge: A Strategic Guide for Blind Job Seekers is available in print, braille, cassette, IBM disk, and VersaBraille II plus disk. Prepaid orders only: print edition, $23.95, includes shipping; all other editions, $19.95, shipped "Free Matter," for the blind, all others add $4 for postage. Write Braille Press, Inc., 88 St. Stephen St., Boston, MA 02115.

NEWSLETTER FOR THE DISABLED

A nationwide quarterly personals/dating/networking newsletter by and for disabled people and anyone wishing to meet disabled people is available by writing for more information or a free brochure or application. Write to: PEOPLENET, c/o Robert Mauro, P.O. Box 897, Levittown, NY 11756, (516)579–4043.

Chapter 6

WARRIORS' WOMEN—LIVING WITH A VIETNAM VETERAN

Mandy* says she buried her husband "a thousand times while he was in Vietnam. . . . I lived in constant fear of his being killed and mentally envisioned the nightmare of having to attend his funeral." She had friends who had had to do just that, and the thought terrified her.

Mandy and Greg were married for a little less than a year when he was drafted. They were young—Mandy was nineteen; Greg was twenty—too young to vote, but old enough to go fight a war that few Americans supported in 1969. Mandy's mother consoled her by saying, "When he comes home, they'll have a parade and dance in the streets like we did after World War II." She hung a blue service star in her window, the same one used when Mandy's dad served in the Pacific during that war.

"I watched the news to see if I could recognize Greg, thinking I might see him lying there wounded. Every night I put his picture

* Names of the women and their families, along with certain identifying factors, have been changed in some stories to protect privacy.

and letters under my pillow, and cried myself to sleep," says Mandy. Some twenty years later, Mandy still finds it painful to talk about that stress-filled year.

Greg was an infantryman, a "boonie rat," with the 101st Airborne surviving in the jungles that at night belonged to the Viet Cong. Knowing he had a good marriage to come home to kept Greg going; he clung to that, says Mandy. He was thrust into leadership as a squad leader early in his tour and Mandy says he felt very responsible for his men. Once, he turned down the Silver Star; he would not accept an award unless his men received one, too. It was this sense of duty that made it hard when his best friend, Mike, was killed soon after Greg left Vietnam. Mike was a fellow Iowan, a blond-haired, "prince of a fellow," whom Greg had grown especially fond and protective of. A less seasoned squad leader had taken Greg's command when he left 'Nam, and as a result of his inexperience, Mike was killed. Greg feels "if only" he had extended his tour, Mike might not have been killed. "If only" I hadn't wanted my husband home so bad, Mike might be alive today, thinks Mandy. Though Mandy never personally met Mike, she knew his family and wrote to him often. She loved him, too. She remembers fondly that she sent him brownies on his nineteenth birthday, the last one he would ever celebrate. Both Mandy and Greg still mourn Mike's death and the loss of years they should have shared in his friendship.

"When my husband returned from Vietnam, he was so appreciative of everything," says Mandy, "but he would make disturbing comments when things didn't go well, like, 'just go blow it up' when his car wouldn't start." She knew he was still combat ready. He warned Mandy, "Don't ever let me hit anybody."

"He looked terrible . . . his eyes were large and he had dark rings under them. He was thin and haggard looking. I knew my husband had been through a lot."

Mandy's mother had been wrong. There was no parade and no one danced in the streets for Vietnam veterans. The local newspaper wouldn't even do a story about his return.

Nothing could have prepared either of them for the barrage of probing questions asked by an insensitive landlady when the couple applied for housing. When she asked where they had been the prior year, Greg replied truthfully that he had served in Vietnam.

"Did you kill anybody? How many people did you kill? How did you kill them?" and on and on.

Mandy remembers Greg just standing there, stunned, unable to answer. She angrily replied, "It was a matter of survival and my husband is lucky to be alive." For the next ten years, Greg never again talked about Vietnam.

But the ten years of silence in their household ended when their baby was born with a rare birth defect. Greg was furious when he learned his daughter's condition could be related to his exposure to Agent Orange. He put his fist through a closet door; Mandy had never seen him so angry before.

"Greg has never cried about Vietnam; he won't allow himself to. I think he feels if he started crying, he'd never stop," says Mandy.

"Once during a siege of rage, I told him, 'Don't hit the wall, hit me. It's really me you're mad at.' A counselor later told me one should never do that. During this period, Mandy says that "everything was *my* fault. 'You're crazy' or 'you're nuts,' was his most common remark." Typically, her husband displaced his anger and felt he had no problems, a common reaction of denial.

Eventually, Mandy and Greg had counseling and both have become active in veterans' organizations. Together, they speak to organizations about Agent Orange and keep themselves abreast of veterans' issues and they have coauthored a book. Their daughter's mental capacities and physical abilities have far exceeded the doctor's original prognosis.

THE IMPORTANCE OF GETTING THE SPOUSE TO OPEN UP ABOUT VIETNAM EXPERIENCES

Cybil and Josh fell in love and were married shortly before Josh went to Vietnam. Josh was attentive, warm, and caring. Their lovemaking was gentle and mutually enjoyable. But the man who returned from the war after serving two tours in Vietnam was a different person. He was cold and unfeeling and Cybil soon learned he could be as cruel as he once had been kind. His explosive outbursts, and demeaning, cutting remarks often left her in tears and with bruises she hid under long-sleeved sweaters. Cybil had become "the enemy" in Josh's life. He drank heavily, and he became even more abusive as years went by. He demanded early in their marriage that she make sure there was always a case of beer in the refrigerator. Josh was controlling and manipulative. Cybil's life was unbearable during his dark moods, and still, she told no one.

After Josh's father died, he became increasingly moody. Cybil explained what happened then:

> During those months I learned what "doing the chicken" was. Josh would go into his moods and choke me until I passed out. Sometimes it would leave my face speckled in the morning. I tried to cover it up with makeup. When that didn't work, I told people that I had used a new soap that I was allergic to.

> After doing the chicken, Josh would wonder why I was moody. He never said he was sorry anymore. He told me I deserved it. The next day he would act like it never happened. He asked me if I tried to make him mad.

> Josh was especially cruel after Cybil lost her wished-for baby.

"You're lower than a gook! Even they can have babies. You can't even do that, you kill them!" he told her. She had a tumor that later required her having a hysterectomy. Cybil says:

> The worst thing was that I felt what Josh said was true. I was lower than an animal. It got so I began to think it was all me, that I wasn't good for anything. I began to gain weight. I munched on food all day even at work. I didn't care what the house looked like. After a big fight I tried to keep the house clean, but every day I got bawled out about something and I thought, "why put the effort into anything?"

Eventually, Cybil began to hate Josh, especially after the loss of the baby and the hysterectomy. Shortly after coming home from the hospital, something happened that caused Cybil to change:

> I had been home two days and had hung up the phone from talking to Karen [her good friend who was also married to a vet]. She had lifted my spirits and I was in a good mood. Josh walked up to me with his hands behind his back and a big grin on his face. I smiled back at him wondering what his surprise was. Quickly he put his hands to my face and stuffed pepper up my nose. I started sneezing violently. Every

time I sneezed my incision felt like it was ripping apart. I got to the bathroom and tried washing the pepper out. Still, the attack lasted for twenty minutes. Josh was laughing like a madman. "That's what you get for having your guts cut out!" he screamed.

I started building my own wall. In a way, I was glad that I could never have a baby. A child wouldn't know how to cope with the moods; even I didn't know how to cope with them part of the time. . . . I still loved him, but not as I had before or ever would again. . . . After this last episode I knew that I'd survive anything Josh threw my way. I was the one who had to take care of me, and Josh. I wouldn't ever again get any help, love, or understanding from Josh. No wonder Josh didn't care if he lived or died. You had to have some kind of emotion for that; his wall blocked out all emotion. I had to have just enough for both of us; however, I was learning I could be hard and callous, too.

I cried off and on for three days. Again, I couldn't tell anyone what had happened. I knew Josh needed help. . . . I wondered if all [Vietnam veterans] had trouble coping when a crisis arose. Did they all have that wall built up? The one where no one or nothing can penetrate. What had happened over there? Why wasn't there help for Josh and help for me? Vietnam did create a disease, a disease as deadly as cancer. How many times had Josh told me he should be dead? That he didn't care about anything or anybody.

Once she had found him in the living room with the loaded gun—the one he had slept with for years under his pillow. She then realized he wanted to die. Later, he laid the gun down and walked out of the house. The next morning he said, "Sometimes it seems as though there is a volcano inside of me, and I don't know what to do about it." He apologized for frightening her.

Cybil began to read about Vietnam; even if Josh didn't want to know about it, she did. Much to her surprise, he picked up her copy of *Charlie Company* and began reading. Slowly, she saw him begin to change and he began to talk about Vietnam. He was developing some self-awareness.

"Was I an alcoholic when I came home? Do I get 'dark' moods? Why have you stayed? Anyone else would have left," he said. This self-questioning brought forth some answers from Josh:

Do you remember the night I nearly choked you to death while I was sleeping? . . . I actually had to choke a gook to death. I was on watch and checking out a suspicious noise. The next thing I know this gook is sneaking up on me. I tried firing my weapon but it jammed. The gook was close enough, so I grabbed him by the throat and choked him to death.[1]

Long into the night Josh talked for the first time about what happened in Vietnam. She learned that he had wanted to reenlist, hoping that the third time would be the charm and he would die over there. Military officials refused to let him do so under those conditions. "They told me I had a death wish and that I was crazy," Josh admitted. "You know I really should be dead. In a way, I did die over there."

Cybil questions why the military did not offer Josh help and allowed him to walk into civilian life with that kind of attitude.

These incidents in Cybil's and Josh's lives have occurred over a period of nearly twenty years. Josh has weaned himself from the drinking habit, and the abuse has stopped, although his dark moods do recur from time to time.

When asked why she stayed with her husband, while many women married to Vietnam vets have not, her reply was, "If my husband had cancer or any other type illness, I would not have deserted him." At one point in her marriage, Cybil almost did walk out.

Living in a remote area, neither of them have had access to counseling at a Vet Center. But Josh has become more outgoing, and made a few friends with whom he can talk about his Vietnam experiences. At this point, he shuns getting involved in veterans' organizations. Josh cannot openly show or admit to loving her, but in little ways, he is becoming more thoughtful. For example, as a surprise, he gave her a cedar chest for Christmas, something she had always wanted. Cybil realizes that, in the past, his inability to show warmth stems from his believing, like many Vietnam vets learned, *if you don't care, you won't get hurt.* They have become active in a couples' motorcycle club, something they can enjoy together. Over the years, Cybil has been able to keep her sanity by having one good friend [Karen] with whom she could share, and having a good job and an understanding boss.

I asked Cybil if her faith helped her through this long ordeal. She replied, "It was something to hang on to. Even in the worst of times

I could still pray. I sat in my chair and cried and cried, and at the same time, prayed to God for strength to help me get through it."[2]

ACCEPTING VIETNAM'S ROLE IN HIS LIFE

Jane's first husband was a medic in Vietnam in 1967–68. Though he seldom talked about his experiences there, Jane knew her husband had seen horrible things: The nights betrayed his anguish. "During the night, he would wake up screaming, struggling, sweating . . . he'd go to the floor. If it ever started to rain, I woke him up and told him that it was raining and there might possibly be loud thunder. Loud noises startled him and sent him diving to the floor. He was one of three survivors out of his platoon," says Jane. "Otherwise, he seemed the same. But I was young and idealistic; I never looked for any problems. Vietnam was not real for me. No one wanted to know or cared about it. It was never an issue in our marriage. I had no way of knowing . . . this poor man had gone through all of this, and the American public didn't recognize his pain, nor did I." Jane and Jim's marriage lasted four years.

Several years later, Jane married another veteran, one who has fewer aftereffects and has become a leader among veterans. Unlike many veterans, Larry served in the army reserves after returning from 'Nam. He was able to talk about those experiences with other veterans in the reserves, and has since realized the value in having been able to do so. In 1986 he helped organize a chapter of Vietnam Veterans of America in his community. His involvement deepened in 1987 and he spent more time on the phone and at meetings, planning a "Welcome Home" parade.

"I thought I had *lost* a part of my husband," says Jane. "Vietnam was over twenty years ago. Why did I have to relive all this now? I was bitter."

But it was Jane whose face was bathed in tears the day of the parade. "When they came home there were no flags, no bands, no banners, no trumpets blowing . . . nothing. For the first time I realized we were family. I now accept the fact that Vietnam will always be a part of Larry's life, that we can't live like other people. Being involved with other wives and vets has helped me under-

111

stand. I don't resent his being on the phone with other vets any longer; I know they need to have a friend who will understand and care. Larry is a solid thinker and a wonderful person." Jane considers herself very fortunate.

FOR SOME COUPLES, RELIGION BRINGS HEALING

Maryln's husband was convinced his problems had nothing to do with Vietnam; if there were any problems, they were *hers*, not his. As the result of a telephone survey of vets conducted by the Lovelace Medical Center in Albuquerque, New Mexico, regarding PTSD, Harry became more aware of his problems. He was selected by the clinic for thorough tests at their expense. These were scheduled for September 24, 1985.

But prior to leaving, something happened that would forever change their lives. A run-in with an argumentative landlord prompted Harry to take his pistol from hiding. When the landlord attacked Maryln, Harry shot and killed him. Harry believed he shot him in self-defense, and so did Maryln. The county authorities considered it second degree murder and put Harry in jail for three months. During that time, a woman who read about their story in the newspapers wrote Harry a letter and called Maryln. Harry was planning suicide, he told his wife later. In her letter, the stranger described how he could receive Jesus Christ into his heart. Unknowingly, Maryln says she accepted the Lord the same night at a church service to which she had been invited by the same woman who had written Harry.

Later, a jury acquitted Harry in a 9–3 decision. But their state law requires a unanimous decision in murder trials, and, in a second trial two and a half years later, another jury found him guilty. Harry was incarcerated for murder. He is now serving a twelve-and-a-half-year term at MacNeil Island in Washington State.

As tragic as it may seem, Maryln says she and Harry have experienced incredible healing. "The *only* healing for us is Jesus," says Maryln. Harry will be heading an outpost [Point Man International Chapter] for incarcerated veterans.

"The Lord is doing incredible things through him. He's holding daily Bible Study groups. When he first went to prison, there were only two men going to chapel services; now fourteen attend.

"In my work as a mortgage broker–loan rep, I meet vets and their wives that I feel God sends to me. I don't have a group, but I'm out there. The very first thing I say to a vet is 'Welcome Home.' I plant seeds that God loves them." Maryln meets with and hopes to organize a support group for wives of incarcerated veterans.

"We've gone through so much together," she continues. "When Jesus is Number One in your life, your marriage is going to be blessed and bound by the love of God. Our marriage is stronger now than it ever was and the only reason is Jesus. Yes, there have been wounds and, yes, there have been healings, but the memory and the past are just that . . . it's yesterday. Today we're walking with the Lord and today it's a new day. It's important to keep moving forward and keep your eyes on Jesus. I write on Harry's letters, 'Keep looking up.' "[3]

Under the most adverse circumstances, Maryln and Harry found strength to cope with this tragedy through faith.

THE WAR'S TOLL ON MARRIAGES

From these stories, one can easily see that wartime memories and delayed stress have had a negative impact on the veterans' lives, and also on the lives of spouses, children, and others living with veterans. Statistics verify this reality.

Of those veterans who were married before going to Vietnam, thirty-eight percent were divorced within six months after returning from Southeast Asia (President's Commission on Mental Health, 1978).[4]

In the Congressionally mandated *National Vietnam Veterans Readjustment Study* released in 1988 by the Research Triangle Institute, the following statistics were gathered. Of those veterans participating in the study who have PTSD:

—One-fourth are currently separated or living with someone as though they were married.

—70 percent have been divorced (35 percent two or more times).

—49 percent have high levels of marital or relationship problems.

—55 percent have high levels of problems with parenting and half report poor levels of overall family functioning.

—One in four is very unhappy or dissatisfied with his life.[5]

—Exposure to high levels of war-zone stress was positively related to the number of divorces of female theater veterans.[6]

—Children of Vietnam veterans with PTSD tend to have more behavioral problems, including behavioral problems of clinical significance, than do children of Vietnam veterans without PTSD.[7]

PARTNER BURNOUT IS COMMON

In Aphrodite Matsakis's excellent book, *Vietnam Wives*, she says the Vietnam veteran's wife feels as though she is "walking on eggshells." Each word must be weighed before spoken, each action carefully planned. To fail to do so may evoke rage, sometimes abuse, from her partner. Unmerited blame is heaped upon her for the slightest of incidents. The veteran is often near crisis state with a low tolerance for frustration. Many times, wives say their husband does not remember explosive episodes or things done in the fit of rage.

The vet's emotional wall of denial and an inability to feel or express emotions can cause the spouse to feel emotionally abandoned. Matsakis equates this to "living with the ice man," a person with a cold, unfeeling heart. In some cases, she (or he) becomes the emotional nurturer for the entire family, including the veteran, causing many partners to experience "burnout" from the emotional overload and stresses associated with raising a family, sometimes being the sole wage earner if the veteran's employment record is unstable, having little energy left to care for herself. The veteran may be irresponsible in terms of helping with child care or household chores.

Some PTSD sufferers are controlling; others indecisive. Occasionally, a soldier had to make life or death decisions in combat that caused fatalities; thus, decision making in the everyday world is hard for him today.

Veterans want to be left alone and are often remote and isolated. Their wives feel even more alone. "The men have each other; the wife often has no one with whom she can share," one wife admitted. Her husband had become active in a veterans' organization and did not wish her to participate. Some veterans, on the other hand, tell me they wish their wives would become more involved. Some wives are weary of hearing about Vietnam; others wish their husband would share more.

Furthermore, wives report problems in the bedroom, ranging from the husband's being too demanding to seldom if ever having sex. Some report that lovemaking is often devoid of meaning and affection, thus further eroding the spouse's self-esteem.

In many instances, the wife will settle into a state of helplessness and despair. "Things always seem to get worse, never better," one woman told me. Seligman (1975) calls this state "learned helplessness" and says that this person has come to believe that responses will make little difference in the outcome of events. Learned helplessness becomes self-perpetuating.[8]

Candice Williams, Ph.D., claims that women, because of cultural conditioning, fall into the Compassion Trap. "Women have been traditionally conditioned—that is, reinforced by the social culture—to be dependent, passive, noncompetitive, interpersonally oriented, sensitive, subjective, nurturant, unable to risk, and emotionally labile. On the other hand, men are taught to be independent, aggressive, competitive, task-oriented, self-disciplined, objective, courageous, unsentimental, rational, confident, and in emotional control."[9]

A WOMAN HAS CHOICES

Janine Lenger-Gvist, M.S.W., former Vet Center counselor at Moline, Illinois, says the Number One problem she sees in working with Vietnam wives is that the woman doesn't realize she has choices. "The wife often feels that she doesn't have any power in the home environment. She is obsessed with her husband's PTSD and feels there is no way out," says Lenger-Gvist. "I try to help her realize she *does* have choices. She alone is responsible for her own happiness, and her happiness should not revolve around her husband and his emotions. I do not condone divorce, but letting her know that that *is* one option helps her feel less trapped in a situation. "It is comforting for a woman to learn that she can control her reactions to her husband's addiction, for example.

"Another common problem I've found in my work with wives are women who have phobias and anxieties. Some have anxiety attacks; others have a major depressive disorder. They're often smothered by a controlling man who runs a "tight ship" and relates in a *one-up/ one-down* type relationship. Many women have strong feelings of inadequacy, almost an inability to think because they have to "ask" their husband before doing things," she adds.

Lenger-Gvist has also observed that when the veteran does begin to get well, it can be upsetting for the spouse: "Having the husband change can create "fear of the unknown" for the wife and she begins to manifest various behavioral and physical symptoms. When the abnormal has become normal, because of their co-dependency, the equilibrium in the relationship has been disturbed, and subconsciously, the wife will then develop problems."[10]

WORKING THROUGH PTSD TOGETHER

Judy O'Brien, R.N., a volunteer counselor at a Chicago Vet Center, conducts sixteen-week, well-structured recovery programs for wives and partners of veterans. O'Brien believes, "If you live with a Vietnam veteran, you have your own PTSD." She believes that wives who waited by the phone, agonized while waiting for letters, and lived in constant fear, also have to work through their feelings of rage.

O'Brien challenges women to stop protecting their husbands. "Wives tend to mother them, to 'take over' for them. They deal with the phone company, IRS, and do all the book work. . . . Wives deny, too.

"The person with PTSD is no good to anyone until he (or she) takes responsibility for getting well. The spouse needs to have this attitude toward the veteran, 'This is your job and your problem. I will stand by you, and cry with you, but you have to help yourself.' "

Although O'Brien realizes some veterans do not always need a rap group, she feels the whole family recovers faster if all are involved in therapy. But, she admits, some men feel threatened because they don't want others to know what their home life is like: "Men are afraid their wives are going to make life hell at home for them, ask them questions, make them relive some experiences they'd rather forget."

Judy O'Brien speaks with the authority of one who has worked through her own PTSD and addiction. She had been a nurse in Vietnam, but became addicted to drugs for fifteen years after coming home from the war. She admits her marriage was falling apart. It was her husband's warning, "I'm leaving and I'm going to take the kid with me," that caused her to lock up the pills. She then realized she had to do something to straighten out her life. "I had to go back and feel all the things I hadn't felt," says O'Brien. "I learned you can't do it alone; you have to do it with massive support from others.

"Vets find that in group meetings, it is appropriate to let go of emotions. And they discover they're in some ways alike.

"In our wives' group, we learn ways to help [the veteran] and the wife, too. Without work, PTSD will stay the same," says O'Brien. "Groups are not formed to tell the wife to get out of her situation, unless there are extreme circumstances, but to help the couple stay together and make the marriage work."[11]

Psychiatrist Erle Fitz* has worked with Vietnam veterans since 1976. He helps wives understand what's going on with their husbands. "I try to help them understand the dynamics of 'impacted grief' and that it's not a reflection of the wife or the concerned other. In our culture, that's often the case. When things aren't going well between myself and someone else, until I learn better, I assume it's my fault and I do bad things to myself, which merely complicates the whole issue. And then both are relating in a 'partial sense,' " said Fitz.

"Marriage is tough enough at best, but when you're trying to relate to another person half covered over, it's almost impossible. If the wife is living in fear of her husband, she's relating out of a basis of fear, and withdraws from him. In like manner, of course, the husband can live in fear of his innermost secrets being discovered, and withdraws also. I think the symptoms of that type of relationship make the 'pathology' almost normal to what's going on," he concluded.[12]

* Dr. Erle Fitz is retired and living in Des Moines, Iowa.

117

Dr. Matsakis in her work with wives teaches the Al-Anon slogan "C-C-C": You didn't *Cause* it, you can't *Control* it, and you can't *Cure* it.[13] In doing so, she attempts to give wives added perspective to their husband's problems and not assume ownership of the husband's PTSD.

TAKING THE BIG STEP—ASKING FOR HELP

Christine Francis, the wife of a veteran who works in a Vet Center in Des Moines, Iowa, encourages wives to go for help even if their husbands refuse. "Forty to sixty percent of the wives contact the Vet Center first," says Christine. "The wives soon learn others are having similar problems; some will even say they could exchange husbands, their experiences are so similar."

Most wives report the hardest task they have is getting their husbands to a counselor or Vet Center. And counselors report vets have admitted to driving by the center for months, even years, before mustering the courage to go through the doors. Most often, it's the partner who calls for information. Some have threatened to leave their husbands if they don't go for help; others say this strategy would not work for them. Some do leave and seek a divorce; some *must* leave, at least temporarily, for their own protection or that of their children.

How common is abuse? In the survey of seventy-three Vet Centers polled by Matsakis, approximately one-fourth of the wives seen at the centers report not just mental, but physical abuse.[14] It should be pointed out, however, that no comprehensive study of veterans' spousal and child abuse has been done, so there is no way of knowing how this compares to nationwide statistics. An estimated 3 to 4 million American women are battered each year by their husbands or partners.[15] The rates of spousal assault and child abuse continually rise and most authorities claim abuse is underreported.

EFFECTIVE COMMUNICATION

Michelle Von Hotten's husband, Richard, lost both legs—one in Vietnam, the other after returning home—as the result of a helicopter crash in Vietnam. She and Richard have two lovely children.

118

From his wheelchair, Richard holds a good job and is an excellent father to his children, says Michelle. When they married, however, she learned she had to make her wishes known and take a direct approach to communication. Richard had been used to living alone.

"I think it's important to let your husband know what you want and that you need to have him listen to you, and that you want to listen to him," says Michelle. "I find it was helpful to say, 'These are the things I need. I need to feel like I am important to you, that it matters that I'm here. Enumerate the things you need. Be specific. Say, "I feel lonely," so that feelings are identified. Don't be accusatory.' Early in our marriage I told my husband, 'I love you and I want us to have a good life together.'" Michelle and Richard have a good life together and are active in veterans' organizations.

Based on my observations of functional marriages, those couples who do get actively involved together in either veterans' organizations (if the veteran has a strong need to do so) or some other shared activity fare the best.

Some veterans do not wish to identify closely with other veterans, however, and for various reasons choose to remain more closely identified with civilian status.

Obviously, communication with someone who has a deep reservoir of pain within can be difficult at best.

Robert Marrs, M.A., in his work with Vietnam veterans, their families, and friends, encouraged the development of communication guidelines for a variety of situations. We are indebted to Marrs and the Veterans Support Group at Center Campus, Macomb Community College, Mt. Clemens, Michigan, for sharing these situations with readers:

1. **Communication:**
   Communicating to him your concern for what he has been through.
   a) Indicate that *you care* and wish to hear if *he desires* to share his experiences and concerns with you. Is it necessary to know the specific war experiences, in order to understand your veteran?
2. **Listening:**
   His need to have a caring person or persons to hear and understand.

a) Attempt to understand his ideas as well as his feelings (i.e., "You're frustrated because you didn't get promoted.")

b) Be available and accepting.

c) Be more interested in expanding his beliefs and feelings.

3. **Comparing Experiences:**

All experiences are unique!

Do not compare your own war experiences or other heavy emotional experiences with those of the veteran even though they appear similar.

4. **Dreams and Nightmares:**

Most veterans experience dreams and nightmares directly related to their war experiences.

a) Dreams are an especially important release for the veteran. Dreams allow for feelings of guilt, fear and frustration to be lessened. (You might say, "It's OK, honey. I'm with you.")

b) Afterwards, ask if he would like to discuss the dream with you. Dreams are the mind's way of freeing itself from conflict.

5. **Loving Without Controlling:**

The need to express your love and concern for the veteran without controlling him.

a) Allow him the right to make *his own* mistakes.

b) Allow him to be himself without forcing on him your judgments or beliefs.

c) Be there, yet allow for distance at times that he requires it.

6. **Grief:**

a) To ask why him and not you is to ask an unanswerable and guilt-producing question. The simple answer "chance" has profound implications for anyone who has experienced war.

b) The pain and sorrow won't help either the lost person or you.

7. **Guilt:**

a) "I and the whole country share the responsibility for what you did."

b) "War is a terrible thing. Human beings are required to do inhuman acts against other human beings and the general population often denies this reality."

8. **Anger and/or Withdrawal:**

The hardest thing to do is not take it personally. The vet-

eran's anger is more than likely directed at himself and the
Hell that he has experienced.

    Establish ground rules of:

      1. No physical abuse.

      2. Agreement to talk when problems occur. What did I
do? What did you do? What could each of us have done
differently?

9. **Substance abuse:**

    Listen for repetitive "themes" of anger. Avoid arguing. Explore the "themes" when the person is straight (i.e., Say,
"When you are drinking, you repeat this concern with *anger*
and I'm worried that it just continues to torment you. I feel it
steals your potential.")[16]

HOMEFRONT CHAPTERS

The same effective approach used by Point Man International for
healing veterans suffering from PTSD has been extended to the
spouse of a veteran through *Project: Homefront.* Homefront Chapters are led by vet spouses, who have experienced the "war at
home." These women minister love, compassion, prayer support,
and the Word of God in small home groups on a weekly basis. By
doing so, these groups:

1) afford an opportunity for wives to know they are not alone;
2) facilitate understanding of PTSD and why the veteran responds as he or she does; and
3) help the partner focus on his or her own walk with God, which
can help the individual change the way he or she responds to
the vet through prayer and studying the Word of God.

    If you wish to receive a free newsletter for spouses called *R & R
News* or if you are interested in starting a Homefront Chapter,
write: The Homefront, P.O. Box 440, Mountlake Terrace, WA
98043, or call (206)486–5383.

ADVICE TO PARTNERS

Women often ask, "How do I get my husband to go to the Vet Center
for help?" Other women say, "I feel so helpless." The following is a

summary of suggestions gleaned from wives who are working—
some alone, others with their husbands—on PTSD-related problems:

- *Read to gain an understanding of PTSD and the war.* This will
  give you insight into your partner's Vietnam experience.
- *If your partner has not read about the war, encourage him to do
  so also.* Show interest by asking open-ended questions that
  invite discussion such as, "What was it like?" Then listen.
- *If your partner has PTSD symptoms that disrupt his life, your
  relationship, and family functioning, encourage him to go to a
  Vet Center or seek professional counseling.* Some wives have to
  give the spouse an ultimatum—go or else; for some that won't
  work. One wife physically transported her unwilling partner to
  a Vet Center and said, "Here he is; he needs help." You may
  have to use a variety of approaches. Reassure him that PTSD is
  a recognized disorder that can be treated.
- *Realize that your spouse must assume responsibility for getting
  well.* He has to help himself. You can stand by him and cry with
  him, but it is *his* problem.
- *Encourage your spouse to befriend other Vietnam veterans with
  whom he can discuss Vietnam experiences.* This is especially
  true if you are not located near a Vet Center. Having someone
  with whom he can discuss painful memories allows him to vent
  pent-up emotions. If your husband is chemically dependent on
  alcohol, this can become a problem if, during these contacts, his
  drinking increases. Treatment for chemical dependency is essential to recovery from PTSD.
- *Show interest in veteran-sponsored events; join in shared activities.*
- *Go to a Vet Center or seek counseling for yourself.* A support
  group for women and private counseling can be therapeutic and
  help you regain some sense of identity and control over your
  own life. If there is no Vet Center in your area, befriend another
  woman who lives with a Vietnam vet. Compare notes. This
  helps to lessen the feelings of isolation.
- *Understand that you are not to blame.* You didn't cause your
  partner's PTSD, you can't control it, and you can't cure it.
- *Take positive steps toward helping yourself overcome "learned*

helplessness." The books *Co-Dependent No More* and *Vietnam Wives* may be of special interest and help to you.

ADDITIONAL READING

Beattie, Melody. *Codependent No More.* New York: Harper/Hazeldon, 1987.

Mason, Patience. *Recovering From the War.* New York: Penguin, 1990.

Matsakis, Aphrodite. *Vietnam Wives.* Kensington, Md.: Woodbine House, 1988. Can be ordered by calling toll free 1–800–843–7323 or sending $18.70 per copy to Woodbine House, 10400 Connecticut Avenue, Kensington, MD 20895. Recommended reading for partners and former partners of Vietnam veterans and older children.

Norwood, Robin. *Women Who Love Too Much: When You Keep Wishing and Hoping He'll Change.* New York: St. Martin's Press, 1985; Reprint ed. New York: Pocket Books, 1986.

Palmer, Laura. *Shrapnel in the Heart.* New York: Random House, 1987.

Shedd, Charlie. *Talk to Me!* New York: Doubleday & Co., 1975, 1983.

Resources for Battered Women

Bowker, L.H. *Ending the Violence: A Guidebook Based on the Experiences of 1,000 Battered Women.* Holmes Beach, Fla.: Learning Publications, 1986.

Cantrell, L. *Into the Light: A Guide for Battered Women.* Edmonds, Wash.: The Chas. Franklin Press, 1986.

NiCarthy, G. *Getting Free: A Handbook for Women in Abusive Relationships.* Seattle, Wash.: The Seal Press, 1982.

————. *The Ones Who Got Away: Women Who Left Abusive Partners.* Seattle, Wash.: The Seal Press, 1987.

Savina, Lydia. *Help for the Battered Woman.* South Plainfield, N.J.: Bridge Publishers, 1987.

White, E. *Chain Chain Change: For Black Women Dealing with Physical and Emotional Abuse.* Seattle, Wash.: The Seal Press, 1985.

Zambrano, M. *Mejor Sola Que Mal Acompanada: Para La Mujer Golpeada/For the Latina in an Abusive Relationship* [Bilingual English/Spanish]. Seattle, Wash.: The Seal Press, 1985.

Chapter 7

THE ENDURING WOUNDS OF AGENT ORANGE

Mary Barton stood weeping at the end of the hospital corridor. Her husband's cries of pain could be heard over the entire floor and they tore at her heart. Eight nurses gently logrolled Wayne Barton to his side, but just the touch of their hands brought tears to his eyes and moans from his cancer-ridden body. Three more egg-sized tumors had erupted in the last three days, making a total of twenty-nine covering his entire body.

Mary couldn't stand to watch his misery.

How much longer, Lord? How much longer? Mary sobbed.

Wayne Barton died on April 2, 1987, less than six months after diagnosis. Lung cancer had spread rapidly throughout his body, involving almost every major organ and sixty percent of his bones. He was forty-three. His doctor believes his cancer was caused by exposure to Agent Orange* in Vietnam.

* Agent Orange, named after the color-coded orange stripe around fifty-five-gallon barrels in which it was stored, is a 1:1 combination of two commercial herbicides, 2,4-D and 2,4,5-T that has a highly toxic byproduct, dioxin. Herbicides were used in Vietnam, Laos, and Cambodia as defoliants to kill dense foliage along waterways, in triple-canopy jungle to deprive the enemy of concealed sanctuaries, around military installations, and to destroy the enemies' food supplies. Agents Blue, Purple, Pink, Green and White were also used. The sprayings began in 1961 and continued until 1971. Some scientists regard dioxin to be one of the most toxic chemicals known to man.

"We didn't start out believing it was Agent Orange," says Mary. "It was his physician, Dr. Ajaikumar, an oncology specialist, who first suspected it because Wayne was resistant to treatment."

Dr. B. S. Ajaikumar of Burlington, Iowa, explains:

> ... there is a trend in the patients who were exposed to Agent Orange: The cancer they develop is very resistant to any form of therapy. When people have cancer of the lung related to smoking only, at least initially, they have a fairly good response to the therapy. In my opinion it is possible that Agent Orange exposure has made the disease aggressive and resistant to therapy.[1]

"After Wayne found out that he had cancer, he would take our two adopted children in his arms and apologize for adopting them. He wanted to raise them," says Mary.

"Before Wayne died, he asked me and his doctor to do every test possible to find out what was causing his cancer. 'It won't help me, but it can help other vets,' he told me. I promised him I would do that."

An autopsy was performed at Iowa City Veterans Administration Medical Center and tissue samples were taken for further testing as Wayne had requested. The postmortem laboratory results confirmed what Dr. Ajaikumar had suspected: The adipose tissue test, performed by Dr. Michael Gross at the University of Nebraska, showed there were elevated levels—twelve parts per trillion of 2,3,7,8-TCDD dioxin—in Wayne Barton's body.[2] But the autopsy report, which stated that some farmers have reached levels of hundreds of parts per trillion, also raised the question as to whether the patient's exposure to herbicides occurred while living in the United States. In this country, herbicides containing dioxins have been sprayed along roadways, railroad tracks, and by crop dusters in farming areas to kill broadleaf weeds. In 1971, the U.S. Surgeon General banned the use of 2,4,5-T in homes, gardens, recreational areas, and aquatic sites.

Mary eagerly awaited other test results. Hoping to learn more, she called the VAMC. She was unprepared for their response. When pressing for information about the tissue samples and where they had been sent for testing, a VA official said to her: "It's none of your damned business." Mary was stunned and hurt by his words; it intensified her grief. After her initial reaction subsided, she was angry. She had always thought the purpose of the VA was to help veterans.

On behalf of Mary Barton, Iowa Senator Tom Harkin's office aided in the investigation of the VA's claim that Wayne Barton's dioxin level could have been due to environmental exposure. On February 9, 1988, Mary appeared before a VA hearing panel in Des Moines and stated her case. Testifying on her behalf were Wayne Wilson, Executive Director* of the New Jersey Commission on Agent Orange, and McRay Wood, a friend of her husband's who had served with him in Vietnam. Mr. Norman Ripperger of the Veterans of Foreign Wars was her accredited representative, along with a representative from Senator Harkin's office.

During his tour in Vietnam near Chu Lai in 1968–69, Wayne Barton worked nights as a radio operator. During the day when the sprayings occurred, he slept in an open, wire mesh–covered hooch. Upon investigation, it was revealed that, out of the 395 days during Wayne's tour, sprayings occurred on 337 days. Wayne Barton was in Vietnam thirteen months.

The HERBS** tapes kept by the air force give detailed information on 9,495 individual spray missions in Vietnam and dispersal of about 13.3 million gallons of herbicides.[3]

"Test me," Mary Barton told the appeal board. "Wayne was a truck driver and gone all day. I was the one home on the farm. I'm the one who should have elevated levels due to environmental exposure, not Wayne. He worked for Churchill Trucking Company for twenty and a half years, and although he occasionally handled herbicides for the trucking company, they were always in sealed drums."

Mr. Wilson pointed out at the hearing that the VA had failed to order additional tests—for a total of fourteen compounds—that would pinpoint whether a person's exposure was the result of service in Vietnam or the result of domestic exposure. After evaluating the cancer rates for the area where the Bartons lived and worked, Senator Harkin's office concluded the VA's claims were groundless.

Following the hearing, Wayne Wilson asked for the VA's policy regarding dioxin analysis on Vietnam veterans. He directed his

* Wayne Wilson resigned from the Commission in 1989.
** Computerized schedules of herbicide spraying missions.

question to Dr. Michael Gough, Chairman of the VA's Advisory Committee on Health-Related Effects of Herbicides, but his answer came from Dr. Lawrence Hobson, Acting Director of the VA's Agent Orange Projects in Washington, D.C., who, in essence, said at a public hearing, "The VA does not have a policy on actual analysis," and that *the analysis done on the veteran in Iowa was an error, a mistake.* (Emphasis added.)

A letter from Daniel Winship, M.D., Associate Deputy Chief Medical Director of the VA's Department of Medicine and Surgery, explained:

> VA Central Office is not approving requests to obtain blood or tissue for the purpose of TCDD analysis. We think that this position is well justified. Centers for Disease Control (CDC) research shows no significant increase of dioxin in ground troop veterans. Among Ranch Handers* there are elevated dioxin blood levels, but there is *no* correlation of the dioxin level with health status.

> Only CDC is capable of determining the blood levels for the VA. No other U.S. laboratories can make the delicate, complicated assays, and CDC has no capacity to do anything except research studies. Finally, current costs of the assays are high, approximately $1,000 or more per test.[4]

Ironically, the slogan "America is #1—Thanks to Our Veterans" appears at the bottom of the Veterans Administration letterhead on which Dr. Winship's letter was written.

Wayne Wilson of the New Jersey Commission explains the significance of Mary Barton's case:

> As far as we are able to ascertain at this point, Wayne Barton appears to have been the *only* Vietnam veteran that we can identify that the VA had performed, on a commercial basis, an analysis to see if dioxin was in his body. They did find what we consider to be four times the average that one would expect to find in an American who did not serve in Vietnam—his was twelve parts per trillion seventeen years after exposure. Recent studies done by the government reveal the half-life to be seven years; therefore, Wayne Barton could have been exposed to fifty parts per trillion or higher. That's a significant level of

* Ranch Handers were the servicemen who handled the chemicals. The project was called Operation Ranch Hand.

exposure. Given the fact that he died of a very aggressive form of lung cancer—a young man—one certainly has to view that with more than just suspicion. This case is representative of many other veterans. The federal government could give the benefit of the doubt—and the law says they can give the benefit of the doubt—on the side of the veteran.[5]

The question in this case is, why doesn't the government do the fair thing and give service-connected death benefits to Mary Barton and the children?

"If this case is representative, then we're talking about the people most in need. And if that's true, then the VA has failed miserably, because they have treated Mary Barton in the most callous, uncaring, insensitive way. The VA appears to have adopted a policy as the result of this case *after the fact*," contends Wilson.[6] (Emphasis added.)

The New Jersey Commission, founded in 1980, arranged for tissue samples to be sent to Umea, Sweden, for further analysis by Professor Christoffer Rappe, one of the world's leading dioxin chemists. Peter C. Kahn, Ph.D., Associate Professor of Biochemistry at Rutgers State University, interpreted those results for Mary. Wayne Barton's test results further showed unusually high levels of 2,3,7,8-TCDD and OCDD, better known as PCPs. Dr. Kahn explains the elevated levels:

It is well outside the normal range seen for men who served in Vietnam but whose Agent Orange exposure was minimal or zero. It is thus extremely unlikely that he acquired this much 2,3,7,8-TCDD by chance. Unless he was exposed to herbicides before going to Southeast Asia or since his return, which I gather is unlikely, exposure while in the military is the most probable explanation.

The other compound for which his level was high is OCDD. Here . . . he is well outside the normal range, which indicates a specific exposure. OCDD was not present in Agent Orange. It most frequently arose as a contaminant in the manufacture of pentachlorophenol,* which is often called "penta" or PCP.[7]

---

* Allegedly, there was extensive use of technical grade pentachlorophenol (PCP), a wood preservative and antifungal agent, during the years 1964–1973, when the United States was extensively involved in South Vietnam. (Schecter et al., "Chlorinated Dioxins and Dibenzofurans in Human Tissues from Vietnam, 1983–84").[8]

U.S. military records show many other toxic substances were mixed with the aforementioned herbicides and some have accused the government of spraying its own men with what critics call "toxic soup."

OTHER VICTIMS AND OTHER SURVIVORS

A year after her husband's death, Mary Barton was asked to testify at a congressional hearing before the House and Senate Veterans Affairs Committee regarding the Vietnam Veterans Agent Orange Disability Act of 1987.

On May 12, 1988, Mary and Judy Lewis testified. Four other women shared their stories through written testimonies. Each woman's father or husband had been exposed to spraying of herbicides in Vietnam, and each woman told her story of a young man suffering and dying long before his time.

Judy Lewis stated her father died from a "very, very rare form of cancer impervious to all treatment." Her younger brother (a post-Vietnam War baby) had almost died twice from a mysterious paralyzing disease.

Roslyn Hontz wrote of her thirty-nine-year-old husband living with non-Hodgkin's lymphoma. He had to quit his $35,000 job so he could be home for blood tests, doctors appointments, and other tests. Medications alone were costing $164 per month.

Judith Pugh described her husband's stormy life after Vietnam. He had been discharged with a heroin addiction, which led to a life of crime, which led to incarceration. Rehabilitation programs for detoxification and drug addiction were not available for vets following service. At age thirty-nine, he died of metastatic carcinoma of the adrenal gland, an extremely rare disease for a man this age. Judith told the panel, "He was able to salvage only *five* years out of his life through his belief in God in his sobriety."[9]

Admiral Elmo Zumwalt testified in Washington, D.C. on November 16, 1988, on Mary Barton's behalf before a Board of Veterans Appeals three months after his own son, Lt. Elmo Zumwalt III, who served in Vietnam, died from two rare forms of cancer. Admiral Zumwalt was Chief of Naval Operations in Vietnam, and during his command, ordered the spraying of herbicides, having been assured these chemicals were not harmful to humans. The Admiral's son died August 13, 1988, after a five-and-one-half-year battle with two different forms of lymphoma. The lieutenant's son has a serious learning disability.

Admiral Zumwalt began by telling his story, then added: "I don't think there is any longer any doubt that it [Agent Orange] is recognized as poisonous to human beings and animals." He then cited the studies done on Kansas farmers and the U.S. Marine Corp study that showed that former ground troops in Vietnam have elevated levels of lung cancer and non-Hodgkin's lymphoma.[10]

The Admiral's testimony was critical of the VA:

> In my judgment, as a layman, the data is very, very significant to establish the linkage of Agent Orange and cancer in the human being, and the great lengths [that] have been gone to by the Government to date to nullify the significance of data would border on being jocular, if they were not so tragic. I do not, as someone who has had a lot of experience with the analytical method, understand how it is possible to disregard all of the data that the Deputy Director of the Veterans Administration was able to testify before the Senate Veterans Committee on May 12, that there is not a shred of evidence to establish the linkage. I believe there is overwhelming evidence of the probability and that the time has come for the Government to recognize that responsibility.[11]

THE AGENT ORANGE CONTROVERSY

America first became aware of Agent Orange when, on March 23, 1978, WBBM-TV in Chicago presented a one-hour special with newscaster Bill Kurtis alleging that Vietnam veterans in the Chicago area were suffering from 2,4,5-T poisoning. He reported the findings of Maude DeVictor, a VA benefits counselor in Chicago, who, in 1977 after learning from veterans and veteran's widows about the use of highly toxic dioxins in Vietnam, suspected a link between Agent Orange and health problems. She asked veterans about their exposure to herbicides in Vietnam. Word of her investigation spread and she was deluged with calls from veterans. They reported having hypertension, emotional problems, overwhelming fatigue, nervous disorders, numbness in the extremities, lack of sex drive, intolerance to alcohol, headaches, skin rashes or chloracne, and cancers of the liver, prostate, stomach, large intestines, and testicles. She also found that many veterans had fathered children with birth defects. Clinical symptoms also include photosensitivity, elevated blood triglycerides and cholesterol, vomiting and diarrhea, pains in limbs and joints, insomnia, abnormalities in liver function, and psychological and personality changes.

In Vietnam, men often experienced the immediate reactions of skin rashes, migraine headaches, vomiting, and "black depression" after the spraying of defoliants. The army assured soldiers the chemicals were harmless; some rubbed it over their bodies thinking it was a bug repellent. Servicemen in Vietnam were subjected to Agent Orange in several ways: ingestion of contaminated food; drinking and bathing in contaminated water; inhalation and skin exposure from spray drift; inhalation from burning brush (burning releases preformed dioxin and can lead to formation of additional dioxin); and, in some cases, even the use of discarded drums that originally contained Agent Orange for hibachi-like grills.[12]

Bill Lewis, Project Director for the New Jersey Commission, claims preliminary studies on twenty women who served in Vietnam strongly suggests their exposure to herbicides has had a very serious impact on their health, especially on their reproductive systems. Their medical histories revealed a high incidence of miscarriages, hysterectomies before age forty, precancerous growths, fibroids, and lupus.

The initial symptoms displayed after exposure often disappear, but dioxin is stored in the liver and other fatty parts of the body. Thus, once a person has been exposed, the victim will continue to carry the chemical with him indefinitely and, in effect, will be continuously exposed. A sudden weight loss causing a reduction in the amount of body fat may release dioxin into the bloodstream in amounts presumably adequate to produce new symptoms.[13]

A 1969 study conducted for the National Cancer Institute by Bionetics Laboratory revealed that 2,4,5-T caused deaths in laboratory animals and stillbirths among offspring of test animals. There are also many reports on human health effects gathered as a result of occupational exposures.[14] The adverse effects shown in lab animals include cancer, impairment of reproductive function, suppression of immunological defenses against disease, and liver dysfunction.

Human studies have associated TCDD with soft tissue sarcomas, possible stomach cancer, chloracne (skin condition), liver damage, and reproductive disorders.[15]

Dioxin is known to be an animal and human carcinogen and a suspected teratogenic (causing developmental malformations or monstrosities in fetuses). Some scientists believe dioxin is mutagenetic (an agent that causes mutation of genes) and fetotoxic (destroys fetuses). More and more studies indicate that dioxin may have similar effects on humans.

A CAUSE OF BIRTH DEFECTS?

As early as 1969, South Vietnamese newspapers reported an increased incidence of human birth defects in some parts of the country and implicated Agent Orange as the cause.

Journalist John Pilger reports in his book, *The Last Day*, that a Vietnamese doctor at Hung Vuong reported a "fetal catastrophe"; out of 5,870 births, forty-seven had produced deformities reminiscent of thalidomide. Pilger was shown two deformed newborn babies at Tu Duc hospital. Both mothers, the doctor said, drank contaminated water in a sprayed area.[16]

In 1979 Dr. Ton That Tung, Director of the Viet Duc Hospital in Hanoi, released a report on birth defects in Vietnam. His study showed that children born to North Vietnamese soldiers exposed to Agent Orange had a much higher incidence of birth defects than do children of Vietnamese soldiers not exposed or the nonexposed general population.

Some of the most common birth defects were: a condition called "anencephaly" (major part or all of the brain is missing); hydrocephalous and other brain and heart disorders; facial disfigurement such as a missing nose or ear; shortened neck; shortened arms and legs; protruding eyes; missing fingers; absence of an anus; abnormal placement of eyes.

In addition, the exposed fathers' group had a higher incidence of sterility, while some spouses of Vietnamese veterans had a higher incidence of spontaneous abortions and premature births.[17]

Vietnamese epidemiologists believe that liver cancer, hydatidiform mole, spontaneous abortions, and neural tube defects are caused by the dioxin in Agent Orange in their country.[18]

Wayne Wilson reports that recent unpublished studies done in Vietnam indicate that dioxin is, in fact, moving in the environment through waterways and the food chain. Vietnamese researchers show that a whole *new* generation of adults and children are being exposed. This is based on exposure levels of Northern Vietnamese people recently sent to the South to work with the government.

Scientists have the task of proving how birth defects can be transmitted through the father. A study conducted by Centers for Disease Control of Vietnam veterans exposed to Agent Orange revealed that these men had higher estimated risks of fathering babies with spina bifida, cleft lip with or without cleft palate, and a variety of other neoplasms (new or abnormal growths such as a tumor).[19]

In 1988 Dr. Johnny Roy, a urologist specializing in studies of male infertility at the Oklahoma City VAMC, came forth with a study showing that a high number of Vietnam veterans have seriously damaged chromosomes that could account for the higher rate of birth defects among their children.

Dr. J. Rodman Seely, Director of the Genetic Diagnostic Center at Oklahoma City's Presbyterian Hospital, said he noted there is evidence in the damaged chromosomes that suggests exposure to a clastogenic agent sometime in the past, implying contamination by a herbicide. Dr. Roy's study reported chromosome aberrations, abnormal semen, sterility, and birth-defected children.[20]

In March 1980, Senator Tom Daschle and Rep. David Bonior received an anonymous memorandum written on VA stationery that stated these reasons for birth defects:

chemical agents 2,4,5-T and 2,4-D commonly known as Agent Orange and Agent Blue, are mutagenic and teratogenic. This means they intercept the genetic DNA message processed to an unborn fetus, thereby resulting in deformed children being born. Therefore, the veteran would appear to have no ill effects from the exposure but he would produce deformed children due to this breakage in the genetic chain. . . . Agent Orange is 150,000 times more toxic than organic arsenic.[21]

More than sixty-four thousand Vietnam veterans and their families claim to have children born with birth defects that may have resulted from the fathers' exposure to dioxin-laden chemicals. Some of these children have birth defects and disorders that are repairable and/or reversible.

Ken Ruder, Professor of Communication Disorders at Southern Illinois University, is conducting a study with Vietnam veterans and their children. He discovered an unusually high number of the children he was testing for learning disabilities had one thing in common: Their fathers were Vietnam vets. Further investigation revealed the fathers had been exposed to toxic herbicides. "A pattern emerged," says Ruder. "It looks like these children have a brain dysfunction that makes it more difficult to process speech."[22]

Dr. William Rea, a toxicologist in Dallas, Texas, believes that aberrant behavior, often diagnosed as Post-traumatic Stress Disorder, can be a symptom of chemical poisoning. Dr. Rea believes that each veteran's reaction to the same chemical can be different because of each person's individuality and genetics, and that American servicemen have had their immune systems ravaged and are now extremely sensitive to a variety of everyday chemicals.[23]

The World Health Organization, International Agency for Research on Cancer, in August 1977, published neurological and psychiatric effects of chemicals on man:

> Polyneuropathies: a number of disease conditions of the nervous system. There may be polyneuritis, abdominal pain, and mental disturbance. Lower extremity weakness. Sensorial impairments—sight, hearing, smell, and taste.
>
> Depressive syndromes: a state of general debility, both physical and mental.[24]

THE LAWSUIT ON BEHALF OF AN ARMY

In 1971 Michael Ryan's wife, Maureen, gave birth to a daughter who had twenty-two birth defects including two cervixes, two vaginas, two uteruses, four ovaries and no rectum.

Almost twelve years after Michael returned from Vietnam, the Ryans, along with nineteen other couples, filed a class-action suit against the seven American chemical companies* on behalf of all 2.8 million veterans who served in South Vietnam. The suit was settled out of court for $180 million dollars on May 7, 1984, the day the trial was scheduled to begin. Tied up in litigation, the fund grew to $240 million before it was dispersed in 1989.

Mary Barton received $2,720 from that fund as a survivor.

The bulk of the money was allocated for veterans' widows and those veterans one hundred percent disabled. Fifty-two million of the settlement was labeled as the Agent Orange Class Assistance Fund to provide grants to organizations to help meet the service needs of the class, including children suffering from birth defects. Additional sums were set aside for Australia and New Zealand to satisfy claims by class members from these countries. More than 255,000 veterans filed claims.

Some veteran advocates feared that if settlement monies were included as part of the veteran's income, it could affect his or her eligibility for VA pensions or medical benefits. Legislation was introduced in the House and Senate to prevent this scenario.[25]

VA DENIAL EMBITTERS VETERANS

Loyal Olson** of Davenport, Iowa, is angry and bitter. He suffers from a disease called porphyria cutanea tarda (a liver and skin disease). More than one hundred cysts, many of which have had to be surgically removed, have erupted on his body. The repeated formation of large water blisters has pitted and scarred his skin. He is so sensitive to sunlight that sometimes going out to get the newspaper triggers nausea and vomiting. An expensive sun screen helps some, but most of the time, Loyal is confined to his home in which the shades are pulled down to keep out the sunlight. He's had diarrhea constantly since the onset of the disease, well over eight years ago. Loyal's symptoms, however, began in Vietnam with acne vulgaria and cysts.

Loyal and his wife Ramona pride themselves on both having three

* Manufacturers were Dow Chemical, Hercules, Monsanto, T.H. Agriculture and Nutrition, Thompson Chemicals, Diamond Shamrock, and Uniroyal.

** Loyal Olson was a machinist's mate in the U.S. Navy, 1964 to 1967, and stationed on the U.S.S. *Oakhill*.

generations of men who willingly served in the military. Loyal enlisted in the Navy and served from 1964 to 1967 in Vietnam. His job as a machinist repairman was to go in and retrieve or repair damaged gun boats along the dangerous waterways. He was stationed on the U.S.S. *Oakhill*.

After returning from Vietnam, he married Ramona, established a business, and was considered by others in his field to be an expert in refrigeration and air conditioning. In 1982, his illness forced him to give up his business. Now, Ramona works and Loyal has to rely on Social Security disability payments. He is only forty-two.

Loyal set a precedent; he was the first Vietnam veteran to be deemed disabled by Social Security for the condition he firmly believes resulted from repeated exposure to dioxin-laden chemicals. Although he is one hundred percent disabled, VA does not recognize this illness nor does he receive disability payments from them. He is eligible for long-term disability compensation from the lawsuit mentioned earlier. The average annual payments to disabled veterans has been estimated at $5,700, with a maximum of $12,800 over a period of ten years.

Some of Loyal's bitterness stems from his early treatment. The VA dealt with him initially as a psychiatric case, and prescribed twenty-four different medications. Loyal reports that he has been unable to obtain some of his military records because they are considered "classified." Originally, the burden of proof was on the veteran; he had to prove he was in an area that was sprayed. That has changed.

"What hurts most," says Loyal, "is what I believe to be the effects of Agent Orange exposure on our youngest of three daughters who was born with spina bifida and clawed feet. I went to Vietnam willingly, but it tears my heart out to see her become a victim of the war, too."

"Our daughter was more fortunate than most," says Ramona. "The opening was low on her spine and was surgically repaired. As a result, however, she has a neurogenic bowel and bladder requiring catheterization five times a day. Despite all this, she is able to walk, attend school and is very bright." Ramona says all three girls are extremely sensitive to sunlight.

Loyal is angered by the government's refusal to accept responsibility. One of his best friends, Dwayne Winkler, who was a Ranch Hander, died of cancer in 1988. Like many other veterans, Loyal worries about dying and leaving his family. Despite his anger with the government, Loyal loves this country; his patriotism has never wavered. He served in good faith and would serve his country again if asked and he were able.

Veterans' disability claims and widows claiming survivors' benefits have repeatedly been denied by the VA because it has over the years consistently maintained a "no health effect" stance (VA Memo circulated 18 May 1978, Wilcox, pp. 191–94).

The Agent Orange issue has deepened the bitterness veterans feel toward the federal government. It represents the *ultimate betrayal*. Veterans claim that not only did the government poison its own troops, but it has also failed to show good faith regarding the health and welfare of its veterans. One wonders if Fred Wilcox's book title, *Waiting for an Army to Die*, truly describes the seeming lack of compassion the VA has demonstrated. As of this writing, however, there appears to be a slight glimmer of hope for change.

VVA SUES THE VETERANS ADMINISTRATION

After the public furor caused by the 1978 release of information by the Chicago station, WBBM-TV, the VA reluctantly began to give Agent Orange health exams. Persons examined were entered onto an Agent Orange Registry. In 1979 Congress passed Public Law 96–151 mandating the VA to conduct an epidemiologic study of the long-term effects of dioxin exposure. To stiffen its mandate, in 1981 Congress again passed legislation, Public Law 97–71, which established the presumption that veterans were exposed to toxic herbicides. It permitted the VA to give care, but little change in VA's policies resulted. After little or no progress on the mandated study, the VA turned the study over to the Centers for Disease Control (CDC) in 1983.

In 1985 Congress passed the Veterans Dioxin and Radiation and Exposure Compensation Act (Public Law 98–524). If the veteran could prove exposure occurred, by law he or she would be eligible for compensation. VA recognized and treated *only* chloracne. Veterans found it almost impossible to prove exposure under VA's guidelines. Not a single veteran or dependent was receiving compensation from the VA based on exposure to Agent Orange.

Fed up and angered by VA's treatment of veterans, Vietnam Veterans of America (VVA) filed suit on October 31, 1986, in the U.S. District Court in San Francisco against the VA in an attempt to change the way it dealt with claims. VVA's lawsuit alleged that the VA violated major provisions of the Dioxin Act. The law had mandated the establishment of an advisory committee composed of prominent scientists and veterans to review scientific studies on Agent Orange. The VA then was to issue rules for compensating claims based on the committee's recommendation.

According to VVA, the advisory committee only looked at seven of the more than a thousand studies available when the VA issued its regulations that chloracne would be the *sole* condition for which VA would compensate the veteran. VVA also alleged that the committee ignored certain types of studies that may refute VA's position. Additionally, the suit claimed the VA regulations discriminate against veterans by requiring a direct cause-and-effect linkage between toxic herbicides and their health problems.[26]

In May 1989 the U.S. District Judge Thelton Henderson ruled in favor of Vietnam veterans by ruling that the VA was unfairly rigid in determining that more than 33,272 (all but five had been turned down) were not qualified for disability benefits. Judge Henderson ordered the VA to reconsider those claims using less stringent tests.

A few days after Judge Henderson's ruling was announced, Edward J. Derwinski, the Department of Veterans Affairs first secretary, announced the VA would not appeal the judge's decision.

This represented the first glimmer of hope for veterans who remain cautiously optimistic the new guidelines will provide compensation for non-Hodgkin's lymphoma and soft-tissue sarcomas, and eventually, other dioxin-related illnesses.

ABSOLUTE PROOF VERSUS KNOWING

In 1988 prominent epidemiologists Drs. Jeanne and Steven Stellman of Columbia University reported a veterans study, funded by the American Legion, that discredited the Vietnam Experience Study (VES) published in May 1988 by CDC (called the "validation" study). The Stellman study proved that military records *do* exist to link the soldier to the area in which he served. CDC had claimed this was not possible, nor could CDC find a sufficient number of veterans to do an accurate study. It is likely similar debates will continue well into the next century.

The New Jersey Commission on Agent Orange has been one of the most active state organizations involved in the Agent Orange controversy. One of its first major research projects resulted in some startling findings: Allan Falk, chairman of the advisory committee that dispersed lawsuit funds, reported those findings in a *For Veterans Only* telecast:

> In our Point Man I Project, we [New Jersey Commission] established clearly that there are Vietnam veterans who were heavily exposed to Agent Orange who have up to ten times the level of dioxin in their level of blood today than background levels. This established without any question we can prove Vietnam veterans did get large doses of dioxin, and even today, fifteen or twenty years later, that dioxin is in elevated levels in their blood, and we know further that dioxin has a half-life of seven years, so even those elevated levels today are half, and half again of what they were when they left Vietnam. The question is, how many Vietnam veterans have these high levels? And that's what we're attempting to find out because it's very difficult to conduct these tests.[27]

Meanwhile, in the veteran community, there remains little doubt about the cause of their problems. Lt. Elmo Zumwalt III, before he died, shared how certain he was:

> I am a lawyer, and I don't think I could prove in court, by the weight of the existing scientific evidence, that Agent Orange is the cause of all the medical problems—nervous disorders, cancer and skin problems—reported by Vietnam veterans, or of their children's serious birth defects. But I am convinced that it is.[28]

Dr. John Kasik, chief of staff at the VAMC in Iowa City, in a 1989 newspaper interview said:

"I wish it could be resolved . . . but right now, there is little evidence that large numbers have died. I don't mean to sound glib, but deaths are the best statistics. You can't fake deaths. . . ."[29]

Sandra Davis, Agent Orange Coordinator for the national office of ViêtNow, a Vietnam veterans organization founded in 1981 with national headquarters in DeKalb, Illinois, would argue with Dr. Kasik.

Sandra says she hates to hear the phone ring. "More and more, the calls are Vietnam veterans who say they're sick and need to know if their war experience could be the cause."

Or, she says, "They're women whose husbands have just died. Somebody's told them about Agent Orange, and they've never heard of it. So they call me. I've had calls from six widows I didn't know in the last month alone.

"I get the feeling of overwhelming helplessness dealing with death so often. Anyone who says the Agent Orange issue isn't a real one hasn't had the phone calls I get all the time."

Sandy and John Davis's second child, Randy, was born with serious birth defects. At age fourteen he must be dressed, fed, changed, and carried. Sandy says he smiles a lot, and makes gutteral sounds that resemble "ma" and "pa," but "mentally he's trapped in a body that can't respond."[30]

Vietnam veterans have few doubts that exposure to toxic herbicides caused their illnesses and the birth defects in their children. Most went to Vietnam with good health and returned with problems unheard of in men their ages. Their network of relationships with other veterans confirm the incidence of birth defects—and that their buddies are dying young.

THE GOVERNMENT'S DENIAL

Why has the federal government consistently held a "no health effect" stance, discounted the studies done by scientists linking Agent Orange to cancer and birth defects, and refused to pay disability compensation for service-connected illnesses?

One reason some say is the liability factor. To admit to these claims would make the United States liable for damages in Vietnam, for soldiers from other countries who fought there, as well as to our own men and women. Some estimate this would result in claims costing billions of dollars stretching well into the next century. Another factor is the admission of the use of toxic chemicals, a violation of the Geneva Protocol of 1925, which proposed a ban on

140

chemical warfare. Agent Orange was first developed by the U.S. Army as an instrument of chemical warfare at Fort Detrick, Maryland (Wilcox, 1983).

Congressman Lane Evans from Illinois, who sponsored the Veterans Agent Orange Disabilities Act of 1987 in the House of Representatives,* claims he doesn't understand the reluctance.

> I think it's hard for us as Americans to imagine our government experimenting with human lives and not forewarning them. It's fundamentally un-American for us to do such things, and because it did happen, there's a reluctance to admit it. It's also part of the whole way society has dealt with Vietnam veterans in general—a denial of their problems, a need to move on and not want to dwell on the problems Vietnam presented to us emotionally, psychologically, and physically. There's also the huge financial burden. We cannot scientifically prove that direct exposure to herbicides causes these results, but we have a strong suspicion that the probability is there. When you look at studies that show that the marines in the I Corp area of Vietnam that was heavily sprayed have fifty-eight percent higher cancer rates and 110 percent higher non-Hodgkin's lymphoma rates, you've got enough evidence for a reasonable government to say, 'Let's help these people.' These are mortality rates we're looking at. The question is, what is this country going to do? I think it would be horrible if we would err on the side of saving money when we have vets and their families suffering and dying.[31]

Congressman Evans is chairman of the House Veterans Affairs Subcommittee on Oversight and Investigations.

* * *

The emotional void left by the death of Wayne Barton cannot be measured. His teenage children are without a father; his wife Mary is left without a caring, loving companion. The family is left to survive on Social Security survivors' benefits. Mary sold their house in the country—one they had worked so hard for—and moved to town. Because of the possibility that Wayne's death was the result of service-connected causes, one insurance company refused to pay

---

* The Disabilities Act was sponsored in the Senate by Senator Tom Daschle (D-S.D.) and John Kerry (D-Mass.)

her death benefits. Her son wants to become a mechanic; her daughter wants to study law. Mary doesn't know how she will pay for college. It pains her to think about it. She is employed, but her income is much less than Wayne's was.

After testifying a number of times before Senate hearings hoping to have Wayne's death recognized as service-connected exposure to Agent Orange, Mary feels she is no further along today than she was three years ago. The battle she fights is one on behalf of all vets, not just Wayne. Still, she encounters indifference from Dr. Hobson and others who discount her claims as well as the significance of one man's life and his importance to his family. On one occasion her survivor benefits were withheld for a ten-month period. She wonders if such occurrences are related to her struggle with these government-funded agencies.

On August 7, 1990, she met with Department of Veterans Affairs officials in Des Moines, Iowa, to review Wayne's file. During this four-hour session, to Mary's astonishment, she discovered the 250 pages of HERBS tapes documenting the daily record of Agent Orange spraying missions specific to the area in which Wayne Barton served were missing from her husband's file. Also missing from his file were copies of twenty yearly health exams performed for his employer—the most recent had been done a month and a half before diagnosis—proving he had no history of health problems prior to his cancer. Also missing were the three death certificates of Wayne's hooch buddies. DVA officials could offer no explanation for the disappearance of these records. (The presence of these documents in his file was recorded in the minutes of hearings held in Washington.)

Mary closed her eyes in disbelief. She could envision in her mind's eye Wayne Barton's face, tears streaming down his cheeks. She reached for the release she was expected to sign closing Wayne's case. And she thought of other veterans and the promise she had made to her husband. She tore it up. "I will never sign this. Never . . . as long as I live," she told them.

* * *

In October 1989 Admiral Zumwalt was appointed as special assistant to Secretary Derwinski of the Department of Veterans Affairs.

His task was twofold: 1) to determine whether it is at least as likely as not that there is a statistical association between exposure to Agent Orange and a specific adverse health effect; and 2) to evaluate the numerous data relevant to these statistics.

In his comprehensive report to Secretary Derwinski dated May 5, 1990, Admiral Zumwalt identified the following adverse health effects related to exposure, according to two recent studies:

AS *LIKELY* AS *NOT* TO BE CAUSED BY EXPOSURE TO AGENT ORANGE
(VERY HIGH CONFIDENCE OR CONFIDENT)

Very High Confidence	*Confident*
autoimmune diseases/disorders	brain cancer
	colon cancer
birth defects	gastrointestinal diseases
bone cancer	kidney cancer
chloracne and other skin disorders/skin cancer	leukemia
	liver cancer/other liver disorders
hematopoetic diseases	
Hodgkin's disease	malignant melanoma
lip cancer	nasal/pharyngeal/ esophogeal cancer
lung cancer	
multiple myeloma	pancreatic cancer
neurologic defects	prostate cancer
non-Hodgkin's disease	psychosocial effects
porphyria cutanea tarda	stomach cancer
soft tissue sarcoma	testicular cancer

In his report to the secretary, Admiral Zumwalt reveals that CDC's studies reached faulty conclusions and were based on flawed methodology, and that members of the Advisory Committee were biased. He feels there is more than adequate evidence to give the exposed Vietnam veteran the benefit of the doubt. By doing so, Admiral Zumwalt believes "there is the opportunity finally to right a significant national wrong committed against our Vietnam veterans."[32]

Will his report be taken seriously? Time will tell.

* * *

If you are a Vietnam veteran and have had health problems that you now realize may be connected to Agent Orange exposure, various veterans' organizations suggest you do the following:

- *Take an Agent Orange screening test at a VA hospital or clinic.* The most common symptom of Agent Orange exposure is *chloracne.* You are permitted one free health exam by the VA. Although these tests are cursory at best and do not include adipose tissue or blood tests that determine dioxin levels, by undertaking VA's screening tests, your name will be placed on the Agent Orange Registry. In the event the government at some future date recognizes other illnesses—in addition to soft tissue sarcomas, non-Hodgkin's disease, and chloracne—to be service-related and connected to dioxin-bearing chemicals used in Vietnam, your name will be on the registry and this is important.
- *Educate yourself and your family about Agent Orange.* Write for current information from the Vietnam Veterans of America. Request the free publications "VVA on Agent Orange" and "How to Submit a Claim." Other things you can do and other publications you can purchase are listed in this publication. Address your inquiry to:

  Vietnam Veterans of America
  1224 M St. N.W.
  Washington, DC 20005
  (202)628–2700

- *Write for information regarding spraying missions in Vietnam.* You may request a map and areas sprayed by writing:

  New Jersey Commission on Agent Orange
  Suburban Plaza
  25 Scotch Road
  Ewing Township, NJ 08628
  (609)530–8162

  You may also request your name be put on a mailing list to receive a quarterly newsletter called *Agent Orange Review.*
- *Submit a claim.* If you are disabled and unable to work, and

believe your illness is related to Agent Orange exposure, you may call the Agent Orange and Veteran Payment Program for more information about how you may submit a claim. Phone 1–800–225–4712.

ADDITIONAL READING

Brown, Michael. *Laying Waste: The Poisoning of America by Toxic Chemicals.* New York: Pantheon, 1980.

Carson, Rachel. *Silent Spring.* New York: Fawcett, 1962.

Dux, John, and P. J. Young. *Agent Orange: The Bitter Harvest.* Sydney: Hodder and Stoughton, 1980.

Ensign, Todd, and Michael Uhl. *GI Guinea Pigs: How the Pentagon Exposed Our Troops to Dangers More Deadly Than War.* New York: Playboy Press, 1980.

Fuller, John G. *The Poison That Fell from the Sky.* New York: Random House, 1977.

Gough, Michael. *Dioxin, Agent Orange.* New York: Plenum Publishing, 1986.

Harnly, Caroline D. *Agent Orange and Vietnam: An Annotated Bibliography.* Metuchen, N.J.: Scarecrow Press, 1988.

Hay, Alistar. *The Chemical Scythe: Lessons of 2,4,5-T and Dioxin.* New York: Plenum Press, 1982.

Hersh, Seymour M. *Chemical and Biological Warfare: America's Hidden Arsenal.* Bobbs-Merrill, 1968.

Linedecker, Clifford. *Kerry: Agent Orange and an American Family.* New York: St. Martin's Press, 1982.

Mason, Bobbie Ann. *In Country.* New York: Harper & Row, 1985.

Neiland, J. B., et al. *Harvest of Death: Chemical Warfare in Vietnam and Cambodia.* New York: Free Press, 1972.

Severo, Richard, and Lewis Milford. *The Wages of War.* New York: Simon & Schuster, 1989.

Van Strum, Carol. *A Bitter Fog.* San Francisco: Sierra Club Books, 1983.

Westing, A.H., ed. *Herbicides in War: The Long-Term Ecological and Human Consequences.* London: Taylor & Francis, 1984.

Wilcox, Fred A. *Waiting for an Army to Die: The Tragedy of Agent Orange.* New York: Vintage, 1983.

Zumwalt, Admiral Elmo, Jr., and Zumwalt, Lt. Elmo III, with John Pekkanen. *My Father, My Son.* New York: Macmillan, 1986.

FILMS/VIDEOCASSETTES

Green Mountain Post Films has four excellent films/videos that can be rented for educational use:

War Shadows is a twenty-five-minute video documentary that tells the story of Paul Reutershan who brought national attention to the plight of Vietnam veterans exposed to Agent Orange. Paul died at 28.

The Secret Agent is a one-hour color film exposing the issues of chemical warfare and environmental pollution by tracing the historical development of Agent Orange and the experience of Vietnam veterans.

Vietnam Experience is a thirty-minute music video that captures the vivid horror of the war. It is a heartfelt journey that will help us come to grips with an era that has changed us forever.

Ecocide: A Strategy of War is a twenty-three-minute, color 16 mm or videotape that gives an eyewitness portrayal of the war against the trees and crops of Vietnam. This film vividly documents the results of unprecedented tactics and forcefully brings home the threat that a war strategy aimed at the ecology poses, both to the direct victims and the rest of humanity.

For a catalog and pricing information write or call:

Green Mountain Post Films
P.O. Box 229
Turners Falls, MA 01376
(413)863–4754, 863–8248

* * *

If you wish to acquire information on scientific studies, write or call:

George Claxton
4400 Stillwell
Lansing, MI 48911
(517)882–4331

* * *

In you wish to be in touch with a veteran survivor, write or call:

Joe Cole
International Agent Orange Survivors
P.O. Box 7665
Olympia, WA 98503
(206)459–7189

Chapter 8

WHEN LOVED ONES DID NOT COME HOME

Sandy Ditch Schmidt* had convinced herself it was all a mistake. Another GI had been wearing her brother's shirt bearing his name. She would go to the funeral home, and find someone else lying in the casket. Then she could prove to everyone it wasn't true. She felt as if the world caved in on her when she saw that it *was* Dave, and he was dead!

Six years her senior, her only sibling had been her "very best friend in the whole world." She loved him beyond measure. He had been the typical "big brother" who took care of his little sister. They had gone places and done things together. Theirs was a special relationship. She had assumed he would always be there for her. Dave was twenty-five when he was killed near Dau Tieng in Vietnam. Sandy was nineteen. It was March, 1968.

"People would come to the house and try to console us, and they would tell me, 'Sandy, you've got to be strong for your mom and dad.' I knew that was true, but I had nobody," she said.

* The stories in this chapter are based on interviews with a loved one or family member(s) of a soldier killed in the war.

Even the soldiers in her brother's battalion stopped writing to her after his death. Sandy wanted to support her brother, and others like him, in all ways possible. For that reason, and at her brother's prompting to boost the men's morale, she had corresponded with some of his friends. Her letters were filled with trivia and the small talk of back home, but it seemed to mean a lot to the guys. At least she thought it had. She told herself they didn't know what to say to her now that her brother was dead.

One of Dave's buddies, suffering from an injury and on leave stateside, had flown in for the funeral. His coming meant a lot to her family. Her mind was in such a fog Sandy says she can't remember to this day much about the ceremony.

She needed to talk about her brother's death. "If my brother had died of cancer or some other disease," says Sandy, "I could have talked about his death, but because Vietnam was such an unpopular war, people didn't want to hear about it." A friend whom she had been dating was undergoing therapy, and she wasn't free to burden him with her sorrow. After breaking up with him, she met a Vietnam vet who, she thought, would understand and allow her to talk about her brother. Later they married. "Now," thought Sandy, "there is someone I can relate to." She was dismayed when her husband informed her that he did not want to talk about Vietnam, nor would he listen to her pent-up grief. Sandy felt even more alone.

Sandy sought comfort in books. She began reading everything she could find about Vietnam. She wanted to know what her brother and other soldiers had gone through.

Sandy says, "I was almost like an alcoholic. I bought the books on Vietnam and I hid them—in my closet, under my bed, or in my cedar chest—I only read them after my husband went to bed. There were so many questions in my mind that begged for answers. Was my brother alone when he died? Did he suffer? Could he have been saved?" At the time of his death, his family had been told that her brother had been caught in an ambush.

Eventually, Sandy and her husband divorced.

Frequently, people told Sandy to forget and "put it all behind her" or "get on with her life." But it wasn't that easy.

It was a friend of her brother's who helped her find some answers. He had been reading excerpts of books in a Chicago newspaper when he came upon the account of the death of a soldier called

"Ditch." Promptly, the friend called Sandy. Reviewing old letters to match names, they learned that Point Man Herb Mock's account of her brother's death appeared in Al Santoli's book, *Everything We Had.*

Painfully, Sandy read, ". . . as Ditch and Doc came up the trail to help us, the machine guns opened up and cut them to pieces." Doc was the medic. It described the ambush, the thick jungle, the anguish of the men who had to leave the bodies, their determination to go back and find them. Herb Mock says:

> I had to find Ditch, I wasn't going to leave him there, because Ditch was the center pillar guy of the platoon. He was older than anybody else, he was twenty-five. . . . He was a very good soldier, the best, and he was everybody's older brother. He was as good a man as I'd ever known. [1]

Sandy also learned that three men were killed the next day retrieving her brother's and Doc's bodies. "It saddens me," says Sandy, "to think that three other families are suffering the same as we are because they thought so much of my brother and the medic who tried to save lives. It was comforting to know my brother died in a friend's arms—and not alone."

It wasn't until 1987—nineteen years after his death—that Sandy found a climate of warmth and acceptance in which she could actively mourn her brother's death. She was encouraged by a veteran to march in a parade sponsored by the Vietnam Veterans of America Chapter #299 in the Quad-Cities, Iowa-Illinois towns bordering the Mississippi River. To honor her brother's memory, Sandy marched with other families who lost loved ones. Later, she became an associate member of the chapter.

Meeting with Vietnam veterans opened a whole new world for Sandy. She now had friends who were willing to listen. "They didn't just listen, they cared. They were interested in me—and my brother."

Sandy recalls that up until then, she would tell someone, "See this book. It tells how my brother was killed." And then she would get a blank look in return, and the friend would begin telling her about a pair of shoes she bought at the mall. "People just didn't know what to say—so they didn't say anything," said Sandy.

In contrast, she found the understanding she needed from Vietnam veterans. "The vets welcomed me with open arms. I always feel real down in March, the month my brother died. My veteran friends know that and they're always there with a hug or a comforting thought, and it's just great. It feels so good and I feel so much more positive now." Sandy says she now has a channel for giving the support she had been wanting to give for so many years. She serves as the POW/MIA Chairman for the Chapter.

Sandy admits to harboring resentment. "I still feel bitter because I lost an important part of my life," says Sandy. "I see what it has done to my parents; they've never gotten over Dave's death. My three sons will never know their uncle. I see what the war has put vets through—physically and emotionally. I can't understand how our government could have done that to these nineteen-year-old boys. And I don't see how, as a country, we could have turned our backs on our fighting men, even though we didn't believe in the war. The guys went through pure hell over there, and they don't deserve that. They didn't start the war and most of them didn't want to be there!"

* * *

There aren't many friends who talk anymore with Helen Marchant, seventy-seven, about her son, Paul, who died on October 8, 1969. Helen dreads the long weekends now that her husband is gone, too. Most people are with their families on weekends, so there's no one she can pass the time with. Her older son lives several states away and he won't talk with her about his brother. So Helen is left alone with her memories of Paul. She misses him terribly. His loss leaves a void in her life.

Paul LaFontaine Marchant was twenty-one when he enlisted in the army. Helen cherishes the few essays he wrote; she believes he would have been a writer had he lived. Slight in stature, he had excelled in wrestling in the ninety-five-pound division in high school. Following the family tradition, he proudly joined the army, went to officers candidate school, and became a scout dog platoon leader. Like all other things, he excelled in this also. But five months into his tour in Vietnam, an explosion occurred as Paul destroyed excess ammunition as ordered. He was burned over forty-five percent of his body from the explosion. His condition critical, he was medevaced to Yokohama, Japan. The Marchants received telegrams daily regarding their son. After his condition stabilized, doctors decided they could chance flying him to the burn hospital in Houston, Texas. Helen and her husband made preparations to go to Houston to be with their son.

Helen remembers the day they learned of his death. It was a foggy, dreary day. She and her husband were getting ready to leave for the airport, when she saw a policeman looking at their car; shortly thereafter, an army car drove up and a man in uniform stepped out—and Helen knew Paul had died. It was the eleventh day post-burn and complications had set in. What bothered Helen most was the suffering her son endured and knowing that he died alone.

"At first, we were both so stunned we couldn't even cry," says Helen. "Paul was buried with full military honors; there wasn't a dry eye during the service. Paul would have been so pleased to know that his wrestling team members and teacher were present at his funeral."

"My husband had a way of putting things out of his mind, and when I needed to talk about Paul, he chose not to," said Helen. After some time, Helen said her husband was able to talk about Paul, but it was always hard. She's not sure she would have survived without her faith and the help of their pastor. She and her husband attended the dedication ceremony of The Wall in 1982, and has been there several times since, placing a flag below his name. "I'm so glad so many people still go to see it," she says.

She still asks *Why? Why Paul?*

She wishes more friends would remember him and talk with her about him.

* * *

John and Helen Danay remember Jerry's last letter and tears come to Helen's eyes. Jerry Danay, twenty-one, was stationed in the mountains in Vietnam and he wrote, "Mom, it's just like walking on the clouds, we're in the mountains." She thinks of heaven . . . and their son.

Helen had warned Jerry to keep his feet dry to avoid foot rot, to keep his helmet on to avoid getting hit, and not to get hooked on drugs. Jerry assured her when he was hit the first time that he had been wearing his helmet. But no amount of parental warnings could have saved him from the rocket grenade that took his life. Jerry Danay was killed on March 12, 1971.

His father, John, was a World War II vet and fully aware of the differences between his and his son's war, especially the shoddy treatment given returning GIs, even by the veterans' organizations to which John belongs. He's proud of Jerry.

At their son's funeral, Helen's heart was warmed when a classmate said, "Mrs. Danay, I just want you to know I remember Jerry and appreciate what he did for us."

Helen Danay would agree with Helen Marchant: It's good to know their sons are remembered.

At the dedication of the Memorial Wall in 1982, John and Helen joined thousands of other parents who searched for names, made rubbings, and cried for lost sons.

* * *

For a span of four years, 1966–1970, Rozari Brooks jumped every time she heard the phone ring. Three sons, a stepson, two nephews, and a brother—a civilian on assignment for the government—were all stationed in Vietnam.

Rozari was a pharmacist's mate in the navy during World War II from 1943 to 1945. The military life was not new to her, but serving is far different from having almost all of one's family there. She lived from one day to the next. Each time the death of a young man in Vietnam appeared in the local paper, she grieved for him and thought, "It's my turn next."

She remembers one particularly difficult time. Years before, the family had planted two apple trees in their yard. Because of their shape, one tree was named after her son, Ben, who was short and stocky, and one was named after son John, who was tall and slender. One day during those trying years, under the burden of yellow, juicy apples, one of the trees broke off twelve inches above the ground. "Oh, my God, that's John. Something has happened to John," thought Rozari. The dread induced by the power of suggestion and symbolic thinking was overwhelming. "Fortunately," says Rozari, "a friend pointed out there were new sprouts and some life left in the tree, which helped ease my mind." Still, she fretted until she heard from John. When he called, it was to tell her that he had

153

been hit with shrapnel in the arm while his buddy standing twenty feet from him was killed. The date and times coincided with the fallen tree!

Another terrifying moment occurred when two marines walked toward her in a public place on one occasion. This time she thought something had happened to Ben.

One of the happiest moments in her entire life was Christmas, 1970, when the family was reunited—all had come home without serious injury. Rozari realizes how fortunate she is to have had all of her family return.

She considers herself a veteran of the war in Vietnam, also.

* * *

Martha was angry when Mark volunteered for flying more missions than required of him. They were engaged and planned to be married when he came home. He was her first and only love. She was in college and twenty; Mark was twenty-six. The ominous feelings she had about those missions were not unfounded. Mark's plane was shot down over Laos on January 1, 1968, and he was reported missing in action.

"I'll never forget the year 1968," says Martha. "I'd like to take it off the books." Serious health problems plagued her during her teen years, and losing Mark was almost more than she could bear in her weakened state of health. Martha remembers, "I just wanted to go on a rampage. Nobody could comfort me. I just went to my bed and decided I would never eat again; I wanted to die." Imaginings and questions haunted her day and night. Was he alive and injured? Was he captured and being held as a prisoner of war? Not knowing was hell.

Two weeks after Martha received the news of Mark's downed plane, her grandfather took his own life. Shortly thereafter her grandmother died, and before the year would end, a young cousin would die also.

Martha sank into a deep depression for which she sought therapy. As she struggled to finish the school year, lacking in concentration and feeling as though she were going crazy, college classmates and teachers were afraid she would end her own life and kept a close eye on her. Later, she missed two semesters as she grieved for Mark, her grandfather . . . and for her shattered dreams.

Her brother decided against enlisting; he felt the family could not stand one more loss.

As her strength returned, the anger and rage she felt were channeled into political activity—against the war. She became a strong Eugene McCarthy advocate, campaigning on his behalf. "I just didn't want to see any more people die," said Martha.

Even her father, a career military man, had been against the war in Vietnam. He felt it was inappropriate for the United States not to declare war if, in fact, our troops were fighting and dying there.

It was harder for Martha when Mark's parents, six years after his being reported missing, had him declared dead. They had been empathetic and supportive of her, but felt the need to bring some sense of closure to their own pain.

A romance with a former prisoner of war ended in more heartache for Martha. They were not compatible and she knew it would never work.

"At the age of thirty," Martha said, "I felt my biological clock ticking and wondered if I would ever marry and have children. I even considered the thought of having a baby and raising the child alone."

As she reached her mid-thirties, the rheumatoid arthritis and violent allergies that she had battled as a teenager—and now, stomach ulcers—ravaged her body once again and she was bedridden and had high fevers. Then something totally surprising, almost frightening, occurred. A person of faith, Martha felt what she could only describe later as "a powerful hand reaching out to me," which she concluded was the hand of the risen Christ. "There was a sense of warmth and light," said Martha, "and the pulsating message conveyed to me was that I would be healed, but never entirely, and that it would take a long time." As a result of that experience, Martha felt called to Christian ministry.

As Martha's health gradually returned, her thoughts turned toward more education. She went on for her master's degree at Vanderbilt University in Nashville, and theological training at Garrett Seminary in Evanston, Illinois, culminating in ordination into the ministry in 1984. She presently serves two parishes in Illinois as a pastor in the United Church of Christ and is known fondly by her parishioners as "Pastor Martha."

The horrible grief that she has been able to overcome to some degree has helped Martha deal with people in an added dimension. She marvels at the special rapport she has with young people and is amazed at how much fun they can have together. She claims this special relationship helps satisfy her psychological and biological need to nurture. She has found that anger and hurt can become a passion for bringing health to other people who are feeling that no one understands.

In the back of her mind, she still wonders about Mark. Would he have come home so changed they would have nothing in common? She's so independent now. She dreams of his coming home as a stranger and in her dreams, he has not aged as she has. She destroyed pictures of Mark soon after he was lost; it was too painful for her to look at them. She has other nightmares of his plane going down. She wonders where his bones are. Will they ever be found? If only the family could give him a funeral with honor—and she would know for sure.

There are some things Martha admits she still cannot do. Programs and movies about Vietnam are off limits for her. She can't bring herself to watch them. Nor can she go to a high school class reunion where mutual friends of theirs would ask questions.

"I feel America lost its innocence in Vietnam. What I fear most is that our country has not learned the lessons of history and will make similar mistakes in the future," says Martha.

Though God has given her a plan and purpose for her life—and a fulfilling life—she is quick to admit, "It's [the pain] still always right there."

*   *   *

Tony Cordero, twenty-eight, was only four years old when his father, Capt. William E. Cordero, went down near the Laotian border in Vietnam on June 22, 1965, the day after Father's Day. His father was the navigator on a B-57 bomber, had made the air force his career, was the father of four children with another one on the way, and was what Tony describes as "one hundred percent Hispanic Catholic." His mother was one hundred percent Irish Catholic.

Tony says he has a lot of memories of his father, but they're so brief and so insignificant: a pair of silk pajamas from Tokyo his father had given him, visiting the officers' club, riding on the back of his dad's motorcycle through fields of sugar cane, then sucking on a stalk of cane his father had cut for him, the whale of a whipping his brother got when he burned down the playhouse—all of which occurred in the Philippines where his father was stationed. A month after the plane had gone down in inclement weather, his mother, expecting her fifth child, returned with the children to California. He remembers hearing his mother crying and sobbing many nights in her bedroom. Eventually, his mother remarried.

He remembers never discussing his father much with his siblings, but each night the childrens' prayers ended, "God bless Daddy *wherever he is.*" In school it was hard, too. When discussions of fathers emerged, as they always do, Tony never felt comfortable in announcing that his dad's plane went down in Vietnam. If his father had died in an accident or from a disease, that would have been an acceptable reason for not having a dad. But he shied away from telling his classmates how his father died.

In 1969, some four years later, the air force notified the Cordero family that his father's plane had been found along with the remains of two men. Awarded the commission of major posthumously, Major William E. Cordero was buried with full military honors in Arlington National Cemetery on May 1, 1969. Tony remembers hearing of his grandfather's refusal to go to the funeral. "It was a matter of pride; he couldn't stand to see his son's remains in a box placed in the ground," says Tony.

As the twentieth anniversary of his father's burial neared, Tony thought more and more about his father. "In less than two years," says Tony, "I will have outlived my Dad. It's scary. All the things he did . . . he accomplished so much. My father was the first in his family to acquire a college education. He was so brave, so heroic, and he was twenty-nine years and eleven months old when he died. How can I ever measure up to that?" For Tony, his dad will always be a hero.

As he and his wife, DeAnna, rear their own two beautiful daughters, Tony realizes how many things he missed with his father . . . fishing trips, ballgames, the sharing of little successes: "I get to do things with my kids that my father never had a chance to do with us. I love them to death; they are the peace in my life."

Tony reflects, "I often wonder in those brief tragic moments as his plane went down what my father thought about. Did he think about us? Did he have a message for us? What would it have been? Did he suffer? I would give my eye teeth to have a conversation with my dad," says Tony longingly.

When his grandfather died, Tony slipped a family picture of him and his brothers and sisters into his grandfather's coat pocket, believing that in heaven his dad might see it: "I know Dad would be so proud of all of us."

Tony appeared on NBC's *Today Show* on Fathers' Day and his story was told in journalist Laura Palmer's "Welcome Home" syndicated column in 1989.

As responses came from other children of soldiers who died in Vietnam, he recognized the need to network and talk with others who suffered a similar loss. He plans to continue to collect names. No one knows how many children are out there who need to talk. (His name and the address where inquiries may be mailed are listed at the end of this chapter.)

THE PAIN OF FORGOTTEN MOURNERS

Many times the needs of children—unlike the needs of the spouse or parents of the deceased—are overlooked or discounted by those extending condolences during the time of intense mourning over the death of a loved one. Often, the care for a child or children is passed to relatives or friends during the activities and rituals surrounding death, and no one takes the time to answer his or her questions or give comfort. An older sibling may be told to "be strong" for others or "be the man of the house now," placing an impossible burden on young shoulders, and his or her grief is discounted and goes unrecognized.

Sometimes a sibling is excluded from important ceremonies, as was Rick Dennis whose big brother died in Vietnam. Not recognized for his need to be included as a member of the family, Rick painfully recalls being a spectator when his parents were awarded his brother's Silver Star posthumously.

"That was the worst of all," says Rick. "To this day, that just hurts so bad, that I was just ignored, just totally ignored. To top it all off, my mom and dad received gold stars to wear on their lapels, and I got nothing. I keep coming back to that. I think I would be OK today if I'd been able to stand there and be part of the family." Rick Dennis was twelve when his brother, Corporal Dan M. Dennis, died in 1967.[2]

Wives of soldiers killed in Vietnam were stung by the same stigmas that affected soldiers when they returned. The country was unsympathetic toward veterans, and this mood carried over and undermined the grieving process for many families. In most cases, all loved ones could cling to was the pride they felt for the supreme sacrifice their son or daughter, husband, or father made for this country—a pride not shared by many, other than those in the immediate family.

Wanda Ruffins, an MIA* wife, found she had to harden herself against the crude remarks of strangers who thought that such a young and pretty woman must be trolling for a good time. She said she learned that "being an MIA wife was a living hell." Her husband, Lt. Cmdr. James Ruffin, was shot down off the coast of North Vietnam in 1966 and she was six months pregnant with their first child.[3]

Many young wives, like Wanda and Tony's mother, bore sole responsibility for children alone. The uncertainty of not knowing put them in a state of limbo. Dare they cling to hope that their husband was alive? Some MIA/POW wives became active in the National League of American Families; a few traveled to Paris to attempt to learn whether their husbands were among those being held as prisoners.

Not knowing whether their loved one was alive or dead kept loved ones on an emotional rollercoaster and made it extremely difficult to move through the normal grief process or come to any sense of closure. Wanda Ruffins says she was amazed at how much grief she still felt when, in 1983, the remains of her husband were buried in Arlington National Cemetery. "I hadn't really dealt with his death," said Wanda.

For those who could not view the body of their soldier husband or son or father, it was difficult to believe that death was real. When this occurs, often mourners will search in crowds for years hoping that someday their loved one will reappear. Seeing the body removes all doubt. Many caskets returned sealed and mourners were denied the opportunity of confirming this reality.

* MIA means Missing in Action.

As years passed, some women remarried, had children, then were haunted by thinking, "What if he is alive, comes back—and I'm remarried?"

Today, Wanda, who has her master's degree in grief counseling, works for the Friends of the Vietnam Veterans Memorial and has organized a program called "In Touch" so that families who lost soldiers can connect with veterans who might have served with and known their loved one.

The lack of communication skills so common in our society partially accounts for the "aloneness" most mourners feel at the time of the loss of a significant person in their lives. It is only natural, therefore, for some persons to find that it was difficult during the war years to go through the grief process. It was difficult to talk about the war, and it was difficult to talk about the suffering caused by the war. Some who have lost loved ones still want and need to deal with their feelings of loss and anger. And for some, the healing process may have only just begun.

* * *

If you are the parent, widow, child, or sibling of a soldier who died in Vietnam, you may find the following helpful:

- *Maintain or establish communication with your deceased loved one's friends if possible.* You may be able to learn about his or her death, thus answering many unanswered questions for you. Write to "In Touch."
- *If those close to you won't talk about Vietnam, seek out friends who will.* Join a local chapter of Vietnam Veterans of America as an associate member. Talk with vets. They'll listen and they'll understand your need to talk about your loved one.
- *Don't discount your need to talk about your loved one, especially if you were a younger sibling or the child of a soldier who died.* Your suffering was just as real but may have been overlooked or less evident because you were "just a child."
- *Understand that young children or adolescents generally have to resolve grief in adulthood.* Children usually lack the coping skills and often have not been given adequate emotional support to grieve fully. This unresolved grief carries over into adult

life. Time does not heal all wounds. This buried pain must be faced before it can be healed.

- *Understand that your grief was further complicated by the war's unpopularity.* The prevailing mood of the country was not conducive to grief resolution. The lack of sympathy toward soldiers may have made it difficult for you to feel the emotional support you needed to mourn this devastating loss.
- *Go to the Vietnam Veterans Memorial Wall, parades, and other events and allow yourself to feel.* Tears bring healing. See Chapter 11 for more information on grief resolution.
- *Don't exclude children from these activities.* Explain why you are sad. Tell the child about the deceased loved one. Children benefit from these experiences. You are teaching them how to grieve.

If you have a friend or relative who lost a loved one in Vietnam, the following suggestions may be helpful:

- *Don't be afraid to mention the deceased soldier's name.* Your friend will appreciate your remembering the loved one.
- *Call your friend or relative on the anniversary date of his or her death if you feel this would be appropriate.* Naturally, if a wife has remarried and has made the adjustment, it would be inappropriate. For parents, it helps to know someone remembers.
- *Never say, "I know how you feel" or "I know what you're going through."* Only those who have experienced a similar loss can say that and understand the depth of this pain. Each person's grief and pain is unique.
- *Encourage your church to remember the deceased soldiers and their families.* A special recognition service is included in Appendix D.

IN TOUCH

If you have experienced the loss of a loved one in Vietnam and care to be in touch with others who have had similar losses, you may reach Tony Cordero and Wanda Ruffins at the address listed below.

Children in Touch
c/o Tony Cordero

or

In Touch
c/o Wanda Ruffins
Friends of the Vietnam Veterans Memorial
1350 Connecticut Ave. N.W.
Suite 300
Washington, DC 20036
(202)296–1726

ADDITIONAL READING

Brandon, Heather. *Casualties*. New York: St. Martin's Press, 1984. Thirty-seven relatives and friends of sixteen KIAs speak and share their grief and anger, and struggle to make sense of the loss that the war brought to their lives.

Palmer, Laura. *Shrapnel in the Heart*. New York: Random House, 1987.

Chapter 9

POWs/MIAs—Then and Now

The sound of a single shot reverberated in Lt. Col. Ben Purcell's ears. His mind refused to believe the VC would end a young man's life simply because he couldn't keep up; he wanted to believe the enemy had allowed the private to linger behind to offer him medical care. The soldier killed, Pfc. James George, had severe burns covering his hands, arms, and face. His eyes had swollen shut and he could no longer see as the five prisoners were forced to trudge barefooted through rough terrain.

Ben and the burned soldier had shared a boat the night before; he could only assume they were being taken to a prison camp. As Ben was forced into the sampan, Pvt. George had asked, "Colonel, are you a Christian?" Astonished, Ben answered, "yes."

"Then let us pray," replied George.

Prayer had always been important to Ben Purcell; at that moment, he said it "became the glue that held the broken pieces of my life together."

Earlier in the day—February 8, 1968—the helicopter carrying six men hovered low over the coastline of South Vietnam. It had been shot down and burned. The pilot was wounded by the same

blast that downed the Huey. They crashed in a cemetery approximately six miles south of Quang Tri City near the DMZ. It was
shortly after the Tet Offensive.

In the crash, Pvt. George's clothing caught fire. Within minutes,
five of the Americans aboard were surrounded, captured, strip-
searched, and with their hands bound behind their backs. They
were forced to remove their boots. (The wounded pilot evaded
capture for twenty-four hours.)

Ben had broken ribs sustained during the crash and this pain
added to his agony. Uncertain of each step as they trudged through
dark and rough terrain, Ben uttered a plea to God. "Lord, I need a
light," he prayed. As if an answer to prayer, a VC soldier beamed a
flashlight toward Ben's feet illuminating the treacherous path.

Their journey into the mountains lasted four days. During those
tortuous days and nights, the captives hobbled, then crawled when
their blistered feet became so tender they could no longer stand
erect.

Ben Purcell spent his fortieth birthday—one of six birthdays he
would spend in captivity—soon after arriving at a cabin along the
way to a prisoner-of-war camp. Following interrogation, he was
forced to crawl into a hole hollowed out of the dirt for prisoners.
When allowed out of the hole to relieve himself, he found lying on
the ground a hen's egg, which he handed to his interrogator. Ben did
not get back in the hole; he sat down next to the other prisoner
sitting at an open fire. Sometime later, the Americans were told
supper was ready. During the six days in captivity, the men had
been given only a few handfuls of rice to eat and little to drink.
Much to his surprise, Ben was handed a small metal saucer containing the cooked egg.

"It is the custom of the Vietnamese people," said his captor, "to
remember the special days in the lives of guests in their home, and
though you're not a guest in this man's home, he knows it's your
birthday, and he wants to honor it with the only thing he has to offer
. . . here's an egg for your supper." So, in a manner of speaking, life
did begin at forty for Ben as he observed this compassionate act by a
stranger.

After several moves, Purcell was moved to a new prison compound north of Hanoi. He, along with the other men, were considered prisoners of the Provisional Revolutionary Government of

South Vietnam rather than the Hanoi government because they were captured in the South. Purcell found himself in the company of high-profile prisoners: one CIA man, two from the Department of Army Intelligence, a civilian who ran the radio station in Hue, one official of the U.S. State Department, and two German nurses, and himself—an army colonel. His captors, however, were uncertain of his rank. Ben "fibbed" so often to his interrogators that he had them confused. (When the lists of prisoners were eventually released to the U.S. Government in 1973, Ben Purcell was listed as a civilian.) The CIA man felt this group had been singled out as possible "trade material" for use after the war.

Ben Purcell escaped twice during his imprisonment—December 7, 1969, and March 18, 1972. As the result of his second escape, word reached the army that Purcell had been taken to North Vietnam following his capture, but there was no information about his health or even if he was still alive.

Of the sixty-two months Ben was a prisoner of war, he spent fifty-eight months in solitary confinement.* During this time he experienced some kindnesses. He remembers one guard in particular who passed notes for him to another American prisoner—three in one day—on one occasion. This same man would bring him fruit from a tree in the compound or candy from his home—all at great personal risk. Interrogators took Ben out of his cell once a month to see if he was still sane.

During solitary, Ben experienced a touching and unforgettable moment. Each prisoner was given a broom to sweep his cell. After sweeping, the pile of dirt was swept outside through the four-inch opening under the door. On one occasion, after sweeping the dirt outside, he was surprised to see it being swept back inside his cell. Hurriedly, he repeated the gesture, now somewhat irritated. He didn't want to get in trouble with the guards over this incident. Again the dirt returned, but this time, Ben knelt and grabbed the broom of the unknown "dirt sweeper" on the other side of the closed door. He guessed it was a South Vietnamese prisoner-trustee. After a brief moment, Ben let go of the broom to avoid causing trouble for the trustee. Suddenly, a hand appeared under the door. "Our hands met in a handshake," says Ben, "unlike any I

---

* He was one of four men to spend over four years in solitary.

had ever experienced. It was the first time I had touched another human being in three and one half years! Today, I greet each person I meet with a handshake, and I am reminded of this young man."

Two months before release—on January 27, 1973—Ben was taken to Hoa Lo Prison or what was commonly referred to as the "Hanoi Hilton" where he was reunited with other prisoners. By this time, the guards had eased restrictions on communication, and the men talked all night, all the next day, and into the next night just catching up.

"A man lives on courage, hope, faith, prayer, and patience—the intangible things in one's heart," said Ben. "I lived with the hope that each tomorrow would be the day I would be released. But when that didn't happen, I would tell myself, 'Well, tomorrow's another day.' I spent 1,875 days living on that hope."

* * *

After Ben was reported missing in action, Anne Purcell decided to move her family from Boonville, Missouri, where Ben had been teaching at Kemper Military School and College, to Columbus, Georgia. Georgia was their home state. The Purcells had five children ranging in age from thirteen years to twenty months. Their youngest, Joy, had no memories of her father.

During the Korean conflict when men were reported missing or prisoners, income and benefits stopped for wives. Fortunately, the army had corrected this policy, and Ben's income continued, as well as the increases and promotions he would have received.

It was thirteen months from the time of the shootdown before Anne learned Ben had survived the crash and was taken prisoner, but she never knew whether he was wounded or even if he was still alive. She, like other wives of POWs and MIAs, grew frustrated at the Pentagon's policy of not making known the plight of prisoners.

"You can only keep a woman quiet so long," says Anne. "By the late sixties America learned that this policy wasn't working." Anne and other wives began "going public" with their stories, distributing literature, and creating public awareness. It was this public awareness that ultimately put pressure on the North Vietnamese to stop the torture and inhumane treatment of prisoners. North Vietnam considered our men war criminals since we were fighting an undeclared war. Therefore, they felt no obligation to abide by the

Geneva Convention that established internationally accepted guidelines on how an enemy should treat its captives.

Her one and only letter from Ben was smuggled out by a German nurse, Monica Schwinn, who was released in early 1973. In the lining of a small carryon bag, she had stitched three letters from Ben—one to Anne, one to his mother, and one to Army Intelligence informing them of the poor health of a prisoner who needed to be released as soon as possible so that he might get medical care. Anne was asked by the Pentagon to keep this a secret to avoid jeopardizing the delicate diplomatic relations involved in the prisoners' release from North Vietnam. Anne had written Ben every month for almost four years; Ben was allowed to write once while in the Hanoi Hilton—neither were given these letters.

Col. Ben Purcell was among the 577 prisoners who came home during "Operation Homecoming." He was one of the last to leave North Vietnam, arriving at Clark Air Force Base in the Philippines on March 27, 1973. As the highest-ranking officer,* Ben was spokesperson for this group. His historic words to America were: "*Man's most precious possession—second only to life—is freedom.*"

Upon his return home, a huge sign greeted Ben and Anne. It read: "Determination to live, plus patience to wait equals a joyous reunion for the Purcell Family." Ben learned that a neighbor, Bob Whitt, had been sending up a special prayer: that Ben be cared for by kind guards. And so he was.

The Purcells met with the family of Pfc. James George living near Fort Worth, Texas, after Ben's return. "It was a tearful reunion," says Ben. "They were relieved to know that Pfc. George was thinking of his Lord shortly before his death. Knowing more about his final days has helped ease their mind and they can get on with their lives."

When asked about his adjustment to civilian life, Ben says, "We're still adjusting. At first, when I grew short-tempered, Anne remained very understanding, very patient, and very loving—that's just her nature. I'm certain that had she not been of that nature, it would have been very difficult and I would have had serious problems like many ex-POWs."

The bond that had developed between Anne and Joy, their youn-

---

* Reflects promotion from Lt. Col. to Col. He was the highest-ranking U.S. Army returnee.

gest, was very deep; the unusual circumstances had served to forge an extremely close relationship between mother and child. For mutual solace, Joy, only a toddler when her father left home, had slept with her mother. When Ben returned, she was seven years old.

During the years her father was in captivity, Joy had sensed her mother's inner turmoil. At age twelve, she wrote a brief story. Following are a few lines from the story she named "Captivity," which shows her deep thoughts:

> While the war was going on in Vietnam,
>> Another war was going on in America.
> It was the war in my mother's heart.

Their faith has kept Ben and Anne from becoming bitter about his years of captivity. He also attributes this lack of bitterness to his ability to think of each of his captors as human beings, although he did resent Vietnamese officials for not informing his family he was alive during his years of captivity.

Ben retired from the Army in 1980 and keeps himself busy on a Christmas tree farm in Georgia. His health remains good although the aftereffects of malnutrition have been damaging to his eyesight and teeth—nineteen have required caps. He speaks to groups about his POW experience and witnesses to his faith. "Both Anne and I were bound together in our love for each other and in Christ's love for both of us," says Ben.

With the help of Dick Vaughn, the Purcells have written their faith story called *Love and Duty*.

DETERMINED FAMILIES HAVE MADE AN IMPACT

A small group of POW/MIA wives in California, headed by Sybil Stockdale, organized in the late sixties what was first called the League of Wives of American Vietnam Prisoners of War. The League of determined wives disagreed with Washington's policy of silence. Sybil's husband, Jim, a navy fighter pilot, had informed the navy through coded letters to his wife that American prisoners were being kept in leg irons up to sixteen hours a day. Navy Capt.

Jeremiah Denton, in a propaganda film produced by Hanoi, blinked in morse code, "T-O-R-T-U-R-E," revealing the plight of men captured, especially during the early years, 1964 to 1968.

After returning home, prisoners reported they had lived under these conditions during those years:

—Prisoners were often beaten daily, permanently crippling many and, according to the testimony, killing others.

—Prisoners were deprived of food and sleep for days at a time to break their will.

—Prisoners were held for months and even years in complete isolation from fellow captives.

—Prisoners were shackled in heavy iron bars or chains, and forced to sit, stand, or lie down in unnatural positions. Some were roped and hung head-down from the ceiling of their cells.

—Prisoners were denied medical treatment or given treatment insufficient to heal injuries and wounds. [1]

This small group of women gained the support of other families of missing men throughout the country and made their presence felt and views known to American's policy makers. Ultimately, they proved that exposing North Vietnam's inhumane treatment of prisoners did make an impact. The first POW/MIA story was released and published in October 1968. Life improved significantly for the POWs after 1969, when the United States made them the subject of a massive international lobbying campaign. And when North Vietnam thought the end of the war was imminent, says Ben Purcell, they wanted prisoners to show no evidence of torture or maltreatment.

The league incorporated on May 28, 1970, in the District of Columbia and became known as the National League of Families of American Prisoners and Missing in Southeast Asia. Today, the league, comprised of nearly three thousand six hundred, actively works to create public awareness about those men who they believe are still being held captive, and to recover the remains of missing soldiers. Some two thousand five hundred men never came home from the war. Some two hundred forty remains have been returned by the Vietnamese; only one hundred of those have been identified; according to the League, two thousand three hundred Americans are still prisoner, missing, or unaccounted for.

POWS' RESISTANCE

The soldier captured by the enemy soon found that he was not only a prisoner *of* war but a prisoner *at* war. He was now engaged in a different kind of war. It was not only a battle for survival but one against psychological coercion, physical torture, boredom, humiliation, feelings of helplessness, and oftentimes extreme mental depression.[2] Feelings of intense shame and guilt plagued those who succumbed to the intense pain of the "ropes" during which the man's body was contorted into a ball, or when his shoulders were pulled back tightly and he felt that his rib cage would explode. Few could endure such pain for long but most prisoners, bound by a code of honor, resisted as long as they possibly could. The enemy coerced the men into writing incriminating statements that could be used for propaganda, producing propaganda tapes, press interviews, and written letters, or broadcasts over camp loudspeakers to demoralize fellow inmates. All of these actions were contrary to the U.S. Military Code of Conduct. In 1966, prisoners also were threatened with war crimes trials, adding to their stress.

Prisoners fought back with two weapons: a coded communication system and a strong POW military organization based upon seniority or rank. These two factors helped preserve a prisoner's sanity and provided a man with support and direction, both vital to surviving life under the most terrible conditions.

Each man's experience in captivity was different. Location and time of capture were significant factors. Those captured in the North underwent an entirely different experience than those captured in the South. Those who became POWs prior to 1969 were tortured far more than those captured after 1969.

Shortly after "Operation Homecoming" in 1973, the U.S. Army, Navy, and Marine Corps decided to cooperate in a long-term study of the effects of the POW experience and established the Center for Prisoner of War Studies based in San Diego, California. Though many former POWs seemed free of pathology immediately upon

170

release from captivity, previous studies of POWs have shown that the "extraordinary stresses of incarceration" give them a heightened vulnerability that explains the delay, sometimes as long as five to ten years, in the appearance of symptoms of delayed stress and other health problems.

Readjustment problems were unavoidable, and these problems greatly impacted on the POW's family. Edna Hunter, Ph.D. explains:

> When the men returned, the wives expected much change and found little. The husbands, on the other hand, expected little change in their wives and families, and found much. It is little wonder that a substantial part of the post-repatriation reintegration adjustment was staged within the family arena.[3]

During the soldiers' absence, wives were forced to become self-reliant and assume the dual role of mother and father for children. Some were forced to work to supplement income. During the formative years of the lives of their children, the father was absent. He came home a stranger to them. All of these factors created new stresses for both the family and the man returning home after long years of a survival existence.

ARE AMERICANS STILL HELD CAPTIVE?

Many believe American prisoners and the remains of servicemen were retained by Hanoi to use as "bargaining chips." Our government failed to give the Democratic Republic of Vietnam the $3.25 billion of grant aid President Nixon promised for postwar reconstruction. Nixon's involvement in Watergate hindered his efforts and diminished his influence, preventing him from keeping that promise.

In 1973, shortly after Operation Homecoming, President Nixon and Secretary of State Kissinger sent Robert McFarlane, Kissinger's aide at the Paris peace talks and former National Security Advisor, to North Vietnam to offer one hundred million dollars in medical aid for the return of *remaining* prisoners. Hanoi refused the offer, insisting on the $3.25 billion promised. Since the war, the United

States has not had diplomatic relations with Vietnam and refuses to normalize relations until there is full withdrawal of Vietnamese troops from Kampuchea (Cambodia), a central government is established, and internationally supervised free elections can be held.

It is not inconceivable that prisoners have been held all these years, for it has been the history of Communist countries to retain prisoners. Some former POWs remember the threats made by interrogators to ". . . keep you in prison forever. . . . There are still Frenchmen in our prisons who did not reform their mind," they added.[4] The Gulag Archipelago, the Soviet Union's forced labor camp system, is one that the few persons who have been released from it—persons such as Alexander Solzhenitsyn—say holds prisoners who may never be released and will die there.[5]

Former Marine Robert Garwood affirms this fact. Garwood was captured in September 1965, and spent fourteen years in Vietnam. After his return to America in 1979, he was courtmartialed and convicted of consorting with the North Vietnamese. Some consider him a traitor; others consider him a victim. In an interview in *Playboy*, he reported that he had talked with villagers who lived near a prison compound:

> I found out that this was the French prison camp from Dien Bien Phu and that the last French prisoners were not released until 1970—200 of them from that very camp . . . they'd been there since 1954 and not released until 1970—that's almost 20 years.[6]

Some doubt Garwood's credibility.

A more recent account from a source generally accepted as trustworthy is that of Stan Contrell, an American long-distance runner who was in Vietnam north of Hue in February 1988, while filming a motion picture about his "Friendship Run." He was in Vietnam at the invitation of the Communist government in Hanoi. Vietnamese officials were showing him a re-education camp (open to the press) where South Vietnamese officials and military officers have been imprisoned since the war. Suddenly, they came upon an area of heavily camouflaged tunnels. There Stan Contrell is certain he saw Americans, perhaps as many as twenty. Abruptly, guards and his escorts thrust Contrell into a van and they hurriedly left the area. It was obvious he had seen something he was not supposed to see.

In addition, an official, after too many drinks, told Contrell, "There are numbers [American prisoners] here, but we can't tell you where."[7]

POW SIGHTINGS

Pentagon spokesman U.S. Navy Lt. Com. Edward Lundquist says that since the end of the war, the Pentagon has had over ten thousand sighting reports. "Although we can't prove there are Americans still detained against their will, we continue to receive information that precludes we rule out that possibility. There are about one hundred reports a month and about ten of those are first-hand live sightings," says Lundquist. "We have people who go out to the refugee camps and ask them what they know; we ride the circuit. We expend a significant amount of time and effort in investigating and soliciting reports. We try to correlate those reports. Some reports prove to be fabrications; a refugee may hope to gain favorable immigration status. Occasionally, a dog tag is presented as proof of a live American. Upon further checking we find that the soldier returned from the war." Others, he says, bear further investigation. The U.S. Government will not offer reward money, explains Lundquist. "We explain to refugees that this is a humanitarian issue."[8]

But the Vietnamese immigrants who've been in re-education camps before coming to America have no reason to fabricate the truth—they are already free and out of the country. Betty Anderson, Director of Resettlement and Immigration with the Catholic Diocese in Davenport, Iowa, says the Vietnamese immigrants tell her there are live American prisoners in Vietnam.

In 1989 a Japanese monk released from a prison camp in Vietnam reported to his daughter that he had shared a room with three Americans while in prison and had seen "about ten" American POWs when first imprisoned in 1975. He told her this after the U.S. embassy in Tokyo had asked him for information about live Americans. And there were others, he said. Unfortunately, Iwanoba Yoshida's health deteriorated after his release and he was unable to further communicate with U.S. officials. Earlier, Yoshida described the three Americans to his daughter as forty to fifty years old and said that every day they were taken to work on a prison construction crew. Yoshida suffered a stroke three years ago and was unable to work, but he told his daughter he survived because the Americans brought him bananas they collected during work. Before his stroke, Yoshida also said that he had been held in several other prison camps where he saw Americans. "There are still lots of them," the man's daughter quoted her father as saying. U.S. officials cautioned that the account remains unconfirmed and lacking in detail. [9]

According to United States Senator Charles Grassley (R-Iowa), a Pentagon panel chaired by a former director of the Defense Intelligence Agency concluded in September 1986, after a five-month review of intelligence files, that American prisoners are still alive in Southeast Asia. Since then, says Grassley, information continues to come in from reliable sources indicating that nearly 160 servicemen are in Southeast Asia, and are still in captivity. [10]

Some believe men are still in captivity in Laos and Cambodia, as well as Vietnam. Servicemen shot down in Laos were not among those prisoners released in 1973. Negotiations with the Hanoi government did not include bargaining for Laotian prisoners.

Veterans' opinions differ on this issue. Many believe there are living POWs in Southeast Asia. Some say if there are Americans in Vietnam, it is by their own choice. One veteran I interviewed says he thinks some Americans may have stayed behind and are making big money in drugs. Some accept Vietnam's repeated denials that there are living prisoners in Vietnam. Some say, if there are live POWs, they are in Laos. And of course there are those veterans who, after hearing arguments on both sides, simply say they don't know what to believe.

CAN WE GET THEM OUT?

If there are living POWs in Southeast Asia, the "how to" of getting men back has become a highly politicized issue and the main source of controversy between interest groups. Some feel the campaign is dominated by the far right.

Former Green Beret "Bo" Gritz attempted a "Rambo type" raid in the eastern jungles of Laos in 1982. No prisoners were found. He claimed to have had the Pentagon's and CIA's backing; government sources disavow any connection with Gritz.[11] At one time, say government officials, as many as thirty veteran groups were planning rescue attempts.

Former Congressman Billy Hendon (R-North Carolina) and former POW Capt. "Red" McDaniel's American Defense Institute, as well as other POW/MIA interest groups, believe they can "buy" back live prisoners. In 1987, relatives of missing Americans dumped two thousand five hundred leaflets on the Mekong River in Thailand hoping their $2.4 million offer for the return of U.S. prisoners of war would reach the Laotian shore. Hendon, who acted as spokesman for the group, said their unorthodox action was prompted by the U.S. government's failure to verify reports of sightings of live Americans in Vietnam, Cambodia, and Laos.[12] Their hope is that a defector will bring out at least what Red McDaniel calls, "one skinny live American." Hendon wants the United States to offer defectors political asylum.

Billy Hendon reported on the *Donahue Show* June 23, 1989, that he made overtures in Karachi, Pakistan, to negotiate a trade of Soviet POWs, captured by the Mujahidin—the army of "freedom fighters" who fought the Communist government in Afghanistan—in exchange for American POWs held in Southeast Asia. The U.S. government gave supplies and aid to the freedom fighters in the bitter struggle in Afghanistan.

Skeptics of this "buy them out" approach ask these fund raisers for accountability. If no Americans have been returned through this means, where does the money go? they ask. The League of Families is attempting to block the fund-raising efforts of such groups who have their POW/MIA booths near the Vietnam Veterans Memorial:

> It has been publicly stated that over $50,000 was collected from the public in a three-month time frame using the POW/MIA issue. That's an income of at least $200,000 per year through the marketing of America's POW/MIAs. Additionally, no vendors solicit public support at any other memorial in the nation's capitol.[13]

Critics of the league say it has aligned itself too closely with the government. Colleen Shine, former public affairs coordinator for the organization, refutes that claim. Shine says, "The League *is not* in the pocket of the U.S. government. I don't think we'll ever lose our stance of being a watchdog on the government. If the government advocates something that is not supportive of what we feel is in the best interest of returning our men, we'll be the first to condemn those efforts, and loudly. It is the 'in thing,' " explains Shine, "to say there's been a conspiracy and a cover-up [by the government]. Five investigations into the charges of conspiracy and cover-up have been conducted and the charges have been found to be unsubstantiated. Much time, money, and personnel resources have already been expended. It's important that people focus on moving *forward* in the efforts to account for the missing."

The league believes the men will only be recovered through diplomatic channels. She has this to say about "buying" back our men: "It's too simplistic. Rewards were offered in the past; they never brought any results. Such offers have caused high-level Vietnamese officials to publicly deny live Americans are still there. The league is working to establish flexibility and not back the Vietnamese into a corner," Shine explains.

"The prisoners are not statistics; they are missing relatives and they can be killed if it's in the best interests of the Vietnamese," she adds. "We don't want to do things that will jeopardize the lives of men that are there. Many of these efforts have been harmful to negotiations. For example, she explains, the leaflets placed in the Mekong River caused problems. Laos and Thailand have an agreement that neither country uses the other's land for subversive reasons. As a result of the leaflet incident, Laos came out with a statement saying, 'The U.S. government is practicing psychological warfare against our country.' That's not helpful during negotiations."[14]

Colleen's father, Lt. Col. Anthony Shine, whose plane was shot down in 1972, is among the missing. She was eight years old when it happened.

Mary Stout, President of Vietnam Veterans of America, reports a similar incident:

Groups demanding action on prisoners of war and the missing in action dumped 'care packages' for the missing Americans on the lawn of the Laotian embassy in Washington. The Laotians, who had been working quietly with VVA and the U.S. government to arrange crash-site visits and excavations of remains, halted all negotiations. They were furious. . . . The POW and MIA groups were unfairly intruding themselves into the delicate work that needs to be done government to government.[15]

Col. Charles Shelton, USAF, is the only American serviceman the U.S. government still lists as a POW. This is for symbolic purposes as intelligence reports indicate that he died in captivity in the mid-sixties. Col. Shelton was in radio contact with nearby aircraft and indicated that he was in good condition on the ground, after having ejected from his disabled jet. A villager reported that he witnessed Shelton's April 1964 capture and subsequent reports substantiated that the air force officer was a prisoner.[16]

THE SEARCH FOR REMAINS

Since 1982, when Deputy Assistant Secretary of Defense Richard Armitage first visited Hanoi to discuss the POW/MIA issue, significant progress has resulted from ensuing talks.

Credible intelligence data, gathered in 1979 from a Vietnamese referred to as "the mortician," indicate that the remains of over four hundred U.S. military personnel lost in Southeast Asia are being warehoused in North Vietnam. Thus, negotiations have centered around the return of these remains and others found in excavation of known crash sites.

In 1987, President Ronald Reagan named former Chairman of the Joint Chiefs of Staff General John Vessey as Special Presidential Emissary to Hanoi on this issue. Hanoi agreed to a two-year plan for joint activities in field investigations, surveys and excavations, and cooperation in solving discrepancy cases (persons who were seen alive, but with no accounting of their whereabouts given to the United States by Hanoi). The United States agreed to send representatives to examine also the plight of war orphans and cripples, in return for that nation's pledge to accelerate efforts to locate missing Americans.

"We agreed that we would address humanitarian concerns and not link them to broader political issues, such as normalization of diplomatic relations, resumption of trade, or economic aid," said Vessey upon his return from talks in Vietnam in mid-1987.[17]

By June 1989, six joint crash-site investigations had been conducted. A month earlier, a U.S. humanitarian team met with Vietnamese officials in Hanoi to review efforts by U.S. nongovernmental organizations to address Vietnamese humanitarian concerns. Vietnam, Laos, and Kampuchea are in dire need of humanitarian aid.

A VVA fact-finding delegation comprised of VVA President Mary Stout, Gordon Lane, Gib Halverson, Randy Barnes, and Joe Bangert traveled to Vietnam and Kampuchea in February 1989. VVA's objective was to explore the POW/MIA issue. There they met with Col. James D. Spurgeon, team commander of the Joint Resolution Casualty Center in Bangkok. This official reported to them that most sites had been vandalized, "stripped" for metal. He added that it had been difficult initially to convince the Socialist Republic of Vietnam (SRV) to permit access to many of the crash sites because the SRV was concerned that the United States was interested in gaining military intelligence. After months of talks, he reports, Vietnam has now granted full access to the sites.

The VVA delegation was the first to visit and talk with government officials in Kampuchea about the POW/MIA issue. Concerning the issue of remains, one official told them, "It is difficult to identify remains. All the documents of that time have been destroyed. There are thousands, millions of remains; it is like finding a needle in a haystack." The delegation viewed "the killing fields" where twenty or thirty mass graves are reminiscent of the Pol Pot regime. An estimated one million Cambodians were killed during this genocide by the Khmer Rouge.

Seeking the cooperation of the Kampuchean government, Mary Stout addressed the problem of repatriating the remains of missing Americans. In response, the deputy foreign minister told the delegation that he wanted the U.S. government to send an official government-sanctioned delegation to discuss the problem. "We have the remains, but the Americans have not come," he said. "The U.S. government must come here to talk and to show they are interested in the remains."[18]

*   *   *

POW/MIA interest groups urge the passage of the Missing Persons Act of 1989 (H.R. 1730) that is designed to change the way the government is allowed to alter the status of a person from missing in action to killed in action. The government claims it has done this to allow families to claim death benefits, GI insurance, and social security.

Marian Shelton, the wife of Col. Charles Shelton, worries that her husband will be declared PFOD (Presumptive Finding of Death—based on lack of evidence, the soldier missing in action is presumed dead by the government). In 1980 a military board voted to ask the air force to change his status from POW to PFOD but Marian hired a lawyer to protest that action. She claims that if her husband remains on the POW list, the government will work harder to discover exactly what happened to him when he disappeared in Laos.

Dermot Foley, whose brother is among the missing, knows that taking his brother's file out of the "active" drawer in the casualty office and putting it into a warehouse in St. Louis would effectively end any chance of finding out about his brother.[19]

REMAINS BRING ANSWERS TO UNCERTAINTY

The torment of never knowing what happened to a loved one is hard. It leaves a family in limbo. For many of you it has meant years of loneliness and a constant nagging uncertainty. This uncertainty has left you on an emotional roller coaster, plunging from hope to despair. You never forget, and you never stop caring or wondering when or if you will ever learn the whereabouts of your loved one.

One mother, Mafaida DiTommaso, thought she was near the end of a twenty-two-year-long search for her son, Lt. Col. Robert DiTommaso—missing since 1966—when she was notified in 1988 that his remains were being returned. (The seventy-five-year-old mother had once flown to Thailand in search of her son.) Her hopes were dashed when she reached Honolulu and was told it was all a mistake. Officials later apologized.

A niece explained, "It's horrible. It's worse this way, to tell the family after twenty-two years his remains are found, then all you get back is an identification card."[20]

Sometimes the wrong remains are returned. In 1985, Ann Hart was given the remains "positively identified" as those of her husband, Capt. Thomas Hart III, missing in Laos. She sought a second opinion from a forensic anthropologist, which revealed that the handful of bone fragments were not her husband's and could not be related to any one individual.

Ann Hart won a lawsuit and was awarded $632,000 for pain and suffering resulting from fraudulent U.S. Army identification of remains. The army's Central Identification Lab in Hawaii rescinded its earlier report. Ann Hart believes, based on what she feels are reliable sources, that her husband survived and is alive in Laos.

For those of you still awaiting answers, coping with this uncertainty may be the hardest and most frustrating thing you have ever had to do. It may help you to know that a significant factor in your inability to bring closure to grief, even though you are reasonably sure he is dead, is not having seen the body. Those families who can bury identifiable remains find that—though the pain never goes away—they can say good-bye and begin grieving anew with some sense of finality and resolution. There is a finality in seeing and touching the body of a loved one, and this opportunity has been denied to you. You are still not sure. And this may never change. Answers heal, and in most cases, you were not given sufficient answers to your questions. Nevertheless, there are some positive things you can do to help yourself:

- *Become involved with other families.* There is strength in numbers. Belonging to the League of Families can help you feel less isolated. The organization seeks answers to your questions and continually works toward resolution of the problems between the United States and Vietnam.
- *Seek out friends who will listen; you need to talk.* Talking about your loved one is therapeutic. Don't isolate yourself. You need support from both within and outside your family.
- *Try to remember your loved one.* Others will tell you to forget, but good memories are very important.

Also, taking action that might help your missing loved one or others can be very therapeutic. Suggestions for increasing public awareness of the POW/MIA issue are listed in Appendix E.

If you are a member of the family or friend of someone whose loved one never returned from Vietnam, these suggestions may help you know what to do to be of comfort:

- *Avoid telling the grieving persons to "get over it" and "get on with their lives."* It's not that simple. They interpret this to mean to forget this very special person, and they can't.
- *Listen when there is a need for them to talk about their loved ones or the issue of POWs/MIAs.* So few people will take the time to listen to their pain.
- *Don't be afraid to mention the lost one's names.* Your friends will be pleased that you remember and want to talk about him.
- *Give your friends permission to grieve in your presence.* Though many years have passed, grief will come in waves. Each person's grief is unique.
- *Remember, words aren't always necessary.* A warm embrace, a squeeze of the hand, or an arm around the shoulder says you care.
- *Avoid saying, "I know how you feel."* No one can totally understand another's pain. Only those who have had a similar loss can begin to understand. Helpful statements are: *How can I be of help? It must be hard to accept. This must be very painful.* Statements to avoid are: *It's Gods will,* and *Time heals all things.*
- *Remember them on the holidays that can be particularly painful.*
- *Share with your friends a pleasant memory or words of admiration for the missing or deceased loved one.*

* * *

Fortunately, some families did have missing loved ones return to them after the war. But many former prisoners of war have had difficulties as a result of the deep psychological trauma they experienced. Most men who are former POWs *do not want* to talk about these experiences. Ann and Ben Purcell offer the following advice to wives and family members:

- *Be patient.* Some ex-POWs suffer deep anxieties and feel as if something is always going to happen. These feelings stem from past conditioning.
- *Listen when and if he wants to talk.* You may not wish to hear stories again and again, but if your loved one wants to share them with you, listen. It helps lessen the pain.

I would encourage both partners to go to a Vet Center or seek professional counseling if depression or other problems disrupt family living. There should never be any shame attached to seeking help from skilled counselors.

ADDITIONAL READING

About the POW Experience:

Blakey, Scott. *Prisoner at War: The Survival of Commander Richard A. Stratton.* Garden City, N.Y.: Anchor Press, 1978.

Brace, Ernest C. *A Code to Keep.* New York: St. Martin's Press, 1988.

Coffee, Gerald. *Beyond Survival.* New York: G.P. Putnam's Sons, 1990.

Denton, Jeremiah A., Jr., with Ed Brandt. *When Hell Was in Session.* New York: Reader's Digest Press, 1976.

Dremesi, John A. *Code of Honor.* New York: W.W. Norton, 1975.

Gaither, Ralph. *With God in a P.O.W. Camp.* Nashville, Tenn..: Broadman Press, 1973.

Grant, Zalin. *Survivors.* New York: W.W. Norton, 1975.

Hubbell, John G. *P.O.W.: A Definitive History of the American Prisoner-of-War Experience in Vietnam, 1964–1973.* New York: Reader's Digest Press, 1976.

McDaniel, Eugene B., with James Johnson. *Scars and Stripes.* Irving, Calif.: Harvest House, 1980.

Norman, Geoffrey. *Bouncing Back.* Boston, Mass.: Houghton Mifflin, 1990.

Purcell, Ben and Anne, with Dick Vaughn. *Love and Duty.* (Release date uncertain.)

Risner, Robinson. *The Passing of the Night: My Seven Years as a Prisoner of the North Vietnamese.* New York: Random House, 1974, 1979.

Rowan, Stephen A. *They Wouldn't Let Us Die.* Middle Village, N.Y.: Jonathan David Publishers, 1973.

Schwinn, Monika, and Bernhard Diehl. *We Came to Help.* New York: Harcourt Brace Jovanovich, 1976.

Segal, Julius, Ph.D. *Winning Life's Toughest Battles: Roots of Human Resilience.* New York: McGraw-Hill, 1986.

Stockdale, Jim and Sybil. *In Love and War.* New York: Harper & Row, 1984.

United States Department of Defense. *POW-MIA Fact Book.* July, 1987.

A Woman's Search for Her Missing Husband:

Keenan, Barbara Mullen. *Every Effort.* New York: St. Martin's Press, 1986.

* * *

For more information about the POW/MIA issue write the agencies listed below:

Vietnam Veterans of America
2001 S Street, NW, Suite 700
Washington, DC 20009

The National League of Families of American Prisoners and Missing in Southeast Asia
1001 Connecticut Ave., N.W.
Washington, DC 20036
(202)223–6846

The league offers a comprehensive overview of the POW/MIA issue on videotape, *Seeking Answers.* VHS copies are available at a cost of $10.00 each, subject to full refund upon return of the undamaged tape. Send check or money order to the league's national office. (20 minutes.)

To learn the latest developments in the POW/MIA search and current statistics, you may call the

National League Update Line: (202)659–0133 or the
U.S. Department of Defense Informational Update Line:
(202)695–0192

An organization comprised of former POWs:
NAM/POWs, Inc.
Capt. Robert Doremus, USN Ret.
Secretary/Treasurer
2757 Elm Avenue
Bexley, OH 43209

Chapter 10

Amerasians—A Legacy of War

Linh Da and Ke Vinh* remember their American father. Linh Da was six, Ke Vinh was five, when the head of a civilian engineering company left Vietnam to return to America. Their mother, Mai Linh, refused to leave her homeland and her relatives. The American and Mai Linh had lived together for five years. He wrote to her twice after leaving Vietnam telling her he wanted to bring them to this country. She would need a birth certificate, he said, so he could begin the paperwork, a process that would last many long years.

She still has his letters and his picture, along with her passport, and an American bankbook showing a balance of more than five thousand dollars she had earned and saved while in Vietnam. At that time, the Communist authorities would not recognize her right to claim the money, so she was left without any savings to care for her family.

When Saigon fell and the Americans left Vietnam, Mai Linh

* The stories of Amerasian young people and mothers living in Davenport, Iowa, are based on private interviews.

184

feared for her children's lives. She left Saigon. The year following American departure, many South Vietnamese were put in special camps called "re-education camps" to reform their minds. Some were killed. Mai Linh protected her children by moving into the villages. She thought of darkening their faces or altering their features. Fortunately, no harm came to them. All the while, Mai Linh was making plans to leave, and in 1984, she secured her passport. She and the children left Vietnam December 31, 1987, first going to Bangkok, Thailand, where they spent twelve days in a transition camp. "We had no money, no clothes, and thin soup with no meat,". says Mai Linh.

They were then transported to the Philippines for the six months' training at the Overseas Refugee Training site in Bataan. Here they were acquainted with American culture and English as a second language. They arrived in Davenport, Iowa, in July 1988, after a very long and arduous journey.

The children remember what it was like being an Amerasian in Vietnam. "The Vietnamese told me to follow my father, because I am half American," said Linh Da. "They told me they didn't like me because my father made war and bombed our people."

"They treated me like I was not a good lady, like I was a whore," said Mai Linh.

Both Linh Da and Ke Vinh would like to see their father again. Mai Linh doesn't want to bother him, although she does hope that he will read this, if only to know they are safe and made it to this country. She knows he probably has an American family.

*　*　*

Chinh Ngoc-Duyen Cao had seven years of schooling in Vietnam, more than most Amerasians, and she will graduate with her American classmates. She looks more American than Vietnamese but she finds it difficult to know what to say to these teenagers. Her mother is depending on her, and she is proud of Chinh's studies in American schools.

Chinh and her mother came to this country in 1985 from Saigon. Chinh has light brown hair and a light complexion, and by nature is soft-spoken and a bit shy. Her mother never talks about Chinh's father; he is nameless.

*　*　*

185

Tuyet Thi Nguyen knows that her father's name is Bob. The picture of her mother and Bob, the American GI, are mingled with other precious pictures of family members who were left behind in Vietnam. The pictures are among the few possessions they brought with them in 1986 when Tuyet, her two younger sisters, and her mother left Vietnam and came to the United States. Tuyet and her mother would like to see Bob at least once, but they know their chances of finding him are slim. They have no last name, no address, no Social Security number, or branch of service.

Her mother brought Tuyet, nineteen, and her two Vietnamese daughters, Loan, fourteen, and Huong, nine, to this country because she, like most mothers of Amerasian children, wants her children to have a future. And that future, she knows, depends on getting an education. Tuyet had only three years of schooling in Vietnam. Despite that, she will graduate from high school, hopes to get a job, then in turn help her mother and younger sisters. Tuyet is a striking girl, with long black hair, dark eyes, and a pleasant, warm personality, a daughter any parent would be proud of.

In Vietnam, Amerasian children are denied good jobs and the right to go to college, or become professionals or work for the government.

But Tuyet's mother is lonely. She misses her relatives. It's harder for her because her English is limited. Although there are new and different struggles for survival in this country, this mother takes comfort in knowing her family has enough to eat. In Vietnam, there often wasn't enough food to feed her family adequately.

Loan is younger and is adapting faster and easier. She is a straight "A" student. Her English is good and she finds herself interpreting from English to Vietnamese, and vice versa, for others. Loan likes this country because she has more time to study; in Vietnam, most of her efforts, and those of her mother and sisters, had to be aimed toward earning enough to buy food and clothes and have a place to live. "Here," says Loan, "we have a good place to live and enough to eat, and I can study more." Loan's chances of going to college are better than her older sister's because she will have had more English, know math skills, and be familiar with the American educational system.

Once the youngest child is in school full-time, the mother is forced to get a job. The government requires it. The family has one year to become self-supporting.

STRANGERS IN A FOREIGN LAND

As Director of Resettlement and Immigration for the Catholic Diocese in Davenport, Iowa, Betty Anderson assists young Amerasians and their family members in settling in the community. Prior to their arrival, Betty asked the Vietnamese immigrants previously settled in the area if they would be supportive of the Amerasians. Amerasian children have been shunned in Vietnam because of their mixed blood.

Having won the support of the Vietnamese immigrants, Betty saw the wisdom in creating an "Amerasian Cluster," so the newcomers would have the support of other Vietnamese, as well as a sufficient number of persons like themselves, thus helping to ease the isolation many immigrants experience when they come to this land.

"They come expecting nothing, but find here a very warm, accepting, nonjudgmental community that welcomes them—and it's overwhelming for them to find such acceptance—something they've seldom felt before," Anderson explains. There are approximately fifty designated cluster sites throughout the United States. Sponsorship of Amerasian cases is by church congregations and agencies; in the unique case of Iowa, the state has assumed the sponsorship role.

"Almost every Amerasian's first hope is to meet his or her father," says Anderson. "Some only know their father's first name. Others may have a name but an outdated address. Much of their desire to meet their father stems from their search for identity. Many say they want to meet him just once.

"After the family gets settled, we begin to discuss the possibilities of what that meeting might mean for them. It could mean rejection or disrupting a family. The Vietnamese women understand these men probably have families now," says Anderson. "Many of them were not women of the street. Some were married to GIs. Some were clerical workers, interpreters, or housekeepers. . . . For some, these liaisons generated income for their families. Nonetheless, these mothers seem to have very little hatred or animosity toward the Americans who fathered their children. Some GIs sent money for their support after returning to America—at least for a while. And many GIs never knew they fathered a child," says Anderson.

The agency provides the family with a place to live including furnishings, food for the first two weeks, plus emergency food stamps, and medical care. Common health problems are tuberculosis and tooth cavities, stemming from poor nutrition and lack of professional medical or dental care.

During the first ninety-day period, agency representative Randy Le matches the able-bodied with suitable jobs. With the cooperation of several local employers, some Amerasian men are working in meat-packing jobs. The women often find work in the dressmaking industry. Their hands are small, and speed makes them efficient workers. Once employed, the families—ranging in size from two to thirteen—soon become self-supporting. The state requires the family to have somebody in the family working within ninety days unless the mother has small children at home and is the sole caregiver.

"Anything that was a problem in Vietnam becomes two times as great here with the added stress on the family," explains Anderson. "Although shunned by society in Vietnam, the Amerasian child may have had special privileges within the family or have been protected because he or she was the 'ticket out' of Vietnam.

"The Amerasian child may or may not be the oldest child in the family," she adds. "Birth order usually is not a viable tool in working with these families. As the sibling's attitude changes toward the 'Amerasian(s)' in the family, latent problems surface and the family dynamics change, leaving the Amerasian very confused. Sometimes these differences cannot be reconciled."

Anderson says another problem stems from the fact that the birth mother may not have raised the child in Vietnam, and the Amerasian child misses the person who cared for him or her. The mother whom they're living with may seem like a stranger. There have also been cases where an Amerasian child has been sold, and some have been abused.

"Our American school system accelerates their problems also," she adds. "At the present time, we're getting so many older Amer-asian adolescents who've only had two to four years of schooling before the Vietnamese forced them out of school. For them to go into our system is a very difficult situation for the teachers because most of these kids will not graduate," says Anderson. "They come in without the basic knowledge they need in order to graduate."

She reports there is some conversation going on in the school system about whether they should accept young adults over nine-teen who will not graduate. Anderson raises this concern: "My reasoning has been that, if the kids could at least get one year in our school system, they would get some idea what it is like. Then they would not be afraid of it, and they would also learn how to behave in it and how to deal with it. Later on, I know they're going to have to have more education. If they're encouraged to go for their G.E.D., they won't be so frightened because they know what the system is all about. So that's why we're encouraging the system to continue to allow them to enter.

"Our problem with a twenty-year-old is that they want to go to work. We are finding that a number of them are resistant to going to school, so we are having to place them in jobs. Looking at the world we live in twenty years down the road, those kids are going to be in very serious straits for jobs unless they acquire more education."[1]

Randy Le fled South Vietnam in 1975. Fluent in English, he assists Betty Anderson in job placement and settlement of the Amerasians in the Davenport Amerasian cluster site. "They leave to give their children a future." says Randy. "That's why we say the parents love their children very much, but when the children grow up they never look back. Children become independent at seven-teen or eighteen in the United States. In our country, whether you are twenty-one, thirty, or forty, you always listen to the parent. In this country, it is very different. Usually, the parent is very unhappy in the United States. They miss their holidays, their families. . . . They feel very isolated. The things they want to do, they cannot do any more. They will take any job—whether high or low pay—to earn money for their children's education. That is their one goal in life: to give their children a future. They know that when they die, there is nobody else to help their children.

"A car is almost essential in this country to maintain a job," explains Le, "but a car is very expensive. Having Amerasians live near each other allows them to help each other with transportation, learn English, and learn more about this culture," he adds.

Randy Le takes pride in knowing that about three hundred Amerasian and Vietnamese students are enrolled at the University of Iowa in Iowa City. To each family, he stresses the importance of working hard and making the most of the few years of high school training open to the students. He worries most about those Amerasians with limited or no English language skills who are too old to go to school and are forced to get jobs.

Le realizes the importance of placing each person in a job that he or she can do, and will enjoy as much as possible. "If I recommend someone for a job, and that person doesn't like the job or doesn't do good work," says Le, "the employer isn't likely to want to hire the next man or woman I recommend to them." Betty Anderson says she marvels at how good Randy is at placing the right person in the right job.

SURVIVOR SKILLS ARE STRENGTHS

Service providers have observed some obvious strengths in Amerasians. Donald Ranard and Douglas Gilzow in their report on *The Amerasians* published in 1989 by the Refugee Service Center, Center for Applied Linguistics, list these strengths and positive qualities that Amerasians brings to the resettlement experience:

—They have remarkable survival skills, and are not as dependent as other refugees—if kicked out of the house, they can find another place.

—They are more open and say how they feel. They tell you when they're angry or lonely. They'll cry. They do better in counseling.

—They have a lot of motivation. Also, it is comparatively easy to find good sponsors for them. Americans are very sympathetic to the plight of the Amerasians.

—Most are eager to work. They are used to working in Vietnam, and they don't resent it here.[2]

GETTING THEM OUT WASN'T EASY

After Saigon fell in 1975, thousands of Southeast Asians sought to escape Communist rule and persecution. Many drowned as they fled in flimsy, unseaworthy vessels. Often, pirates boarded the boats, raping and murdering the ships' passengers after robbing them of gold or any other possessions of worth. Some countries turned these refugees away and refused to help. The Orderly Departure Program (ODP) was created in 1979 under the United Nation's High Commission on Refugees as an alternative to the mass exodus of "Boat People." Under the auspices of ODP, the United Nations allowed qualified Vietnamese nationals to depart for permanent resettlement abroad. But the dozens of American soldiers who wanted to bring their children to America were unable to do so.

Because of increased pressure from GI fathers, media coverage, and Congressional interest, Vietnam began to say publicly that Amerasians were America's responsibility and the United States could have all these children if it wanted them. Thus, Congress, spearheaded by former POW Senator Jeremiah Denton (R-Alabama) and the late Congressman Stewart McKinney (R-Connecticut), passed a law in 1982 that permitted Amerasians born after 1950 in Korea, Thailand, and the countries of Indochina to enter the United States as immigrants.[3] But the 1982 law presented a major roadblock: It did not include the Amerasian's Vietnamese mother or siblings, and few mothers were willing to let go of their children. The child had to emigrate alone and be irrevocably released by his or her mother or guardian. Some nine thousand children did emigrate as a result of this legislation, but no resources had been allocated to assist Amerasians in adjusting to the United States.

Disagreements between the countries and delays in processing twenty-two thousand ODP applicants, plus a host of other problems with the program, led to its breakdown in 1986 and resulted in Vietnam suspending the processing of new cases. In 1987 Amerasian departures for the United States slowed to fewer than three hundred.

THE AMERASIAN HOMECOMING ACT

Le Van Minh lived on the streets in Ho Chi Minh City for most of his young life. Orphaned at age ten, he was the subject of cruel taunts and harsh treatment because of his mixed ancestry, and because of his appearance. A crippling and degenerative spinal condition left him wobbling on weak, matchstick legs that refused to support him for walking. His torso hangs low from his pelvis and his arms support and balance his upper body. His mother married a Vietnamese and had Vietnamese children. Minh was a painful reminder of her past, so she turned him out of the house to survive as best he could—or die. He slept in doorways. A fellow waif carried him each day to the streets where he sold paper flowers he fashioned himself. Minh's winsome smile overshadowed his soulful eyes; his mop of brown hair and freckles revealed a clear resemblance to his American father.

In 1985, Minh's infectious smile caught the eye of New York photographer Audrey Tiernan and, shortly thereafter, his picture and story appeared in American newspapers and touched many hearts throughout the country. Although famous, Minh was just as hungry and just as poor and still living on the streets of Ho Chi Minh City.

Minh's plight struck a chord in the hearts of Huntington High School students on Long Island who collectively decided to contact Congressman Robert Mrazek and tell him of their plans to bring Minh to America for medical treatment. Despite Mrazek's warnings of the possible diplomatic pitfalls, the students sent a special request to the Vietnamese Government appealing to its humanitarian interests. More than twenty-seven thousand students from Long Island signed a petition and pledged their support of the project. Their goal changed from wanting only to give Minh medical treatment to bringing him to the United States and finding him a foster home.

Eighteen months after Minh's picture had appeared in *Newsday*, a Long Island daily, Congressman Mrazek found himself en route to Hanoi to claim Minh. Today, Minh lives with a foster family near his beloved *Ba*, the name he gave the congressman—the Vietnamese word for Daddy. His deep involvement with Minh prompted Congressman Robert Mrazek (R-New York) and Congressman Thomas Ridge (R-Pennsylvania), two Vietnam era veterans, to introduce H. R. 3568 that addressed the major objections raised by Vietnam and yet preserved those elements most vital to the United States.

On December 22, 1987, the Amerasian Homecoming Act was signed into law. The legislation appropriated $5 million for fiscal year 1988 to move the families and give them language and cultural training before resettling them in the United States. The Amerasian Homecoming Act, also known as the Mrazek Act, allows Amerasians desiring to emigrate from Vietnam to leave by March 21, 1990.

The law provided that Amerasians, and their close family members, be admitted as immigrants but receive refugee benefits. These benefits include twenty weeks of English as a Second Language, Cultural Orientation, and Work Orientation courses in the Philippines, and resettlement assistance through private voluntary agencies when they reach the United States. An estimated one thousand two hundred people had to come out of Vietnam each month in order for the estimated eight thousand to twelve thousand Amerasians (a total of approximately thirty thousand persons if family members are included) to arrive in America during the specified two-year period. During the 1989 fiscal year, 9,683 persons emigrated. The State Department's goal for FY 1990 was fifteen thousand. An appropriations bill allocating additional funding for resettlement was introduced to make it possible to extend the deadline, possibly until September, 1991, in the hope that by that time another fifteen thousand could come and all Amerasians wanting to immigrate would have had the opportunity to do so.

Marta Brenden, program consultant for Lutheran Immigration and Refugee Service, says, "The Vietnamese believe it is only logical for the Amerasian to be in the father's homeland. Very likely the deadline will be extended and their government will be agreeable to that extension."[4]

OVERCOMING STEREOTYPES

As journalists became aware of the Amerasian children in Vietnam, most accounts depicted the homeless, abandoned, abused children of the streets. The term *bui doi*—dust of life—was frequently used to describe them. In Vietnamese, however, this term is used to describe any homeless person. Most thought it was a racial slur meaning "half-breed." Contrary to common belief, most mothers managed to keep their families together.[5] The conditions of Amerasians in Vietnam vary widely, making generalization difficult. According to a 1988 report by *Indochina Issues*, "Some have lived in abject poverty, on the very margins of society; others are accustomed to a standard of living significantly above that of the average Vietnamese citizen." Most lived somewhere in between—closer to poverty than prosperity, certainly, but not without at least the basic necessities of shelter, food, and clothing.[6]

Other issues are factors in discrimination against Amerasians and their mothers in Vietnam. Bill Herod, director of the Washington-based Indochina Project, says: "The amount of discrimination Amerasians and their mothers experienced depended in part on where they lived in Vietnam. If they lived in areas controlled by northerners, they were more likely to have problems than in places like Saigon, where the population was southern and people were used to Americans and Amerasians.

"Another factor," says Herod, "was the social background of the mother." Nguyen Ngoc Bich, a multicultural program coordinator in Arlington, Virginia, claims that discrimination in Vietnam against Amerasians and their mothers is more a question of class than race. He says, "It all depends on the social background of the mother—if she's upper class, people will feel a lot differently about her and her child than if they think the mother is a prostitute."[7] If one compares this to America, you might agree the same discrimination exists in some cases.

Few would disagree, however, that black Amerasians were treated even worse than white Amerasians in Vietnam. According to a study done in 1985 by the United States Catholic Conference (USCC), in almost all accounts, black Amerasians have had a greater number of problems in Vietnam. The study found that nearly one-third of black Amerasians had no schooling in Vietnam, compared to thirteen percent of white Amerasians. They were more than twice as likely to claim "unfair" treatment in school. In the research done by Dartmouth psychologist J. Kirk Felsman, he states that black Amerasians were more likely to have been in fights in Vietnam. The fighting was generally in response to racial taunts.[8]

Statistics collected by the Joint Voluntary Agency in the Philippines Refugee Processing Center estimate that around seven percent of Amerasians at the center have had no previous schooling. Most Amerasians report about six years of education, says the agency.[9]

FATHERS LOOKING FOR THEIR CHILDREN

When the French left Vietnam in 1954, arrangements were made by the French government for the resettlement of thousands of French-Vietnamese children. Our government made no such provisions. It was left up to the individual American soldier to legitimize and obtain visas for his Vietnamese child.

Through the years, several agencies such as the Pearl S. Buck Foundation based in Perkasie, Pennsylvania, and the American Red Cross have helped fathers search for and claim their Vietnamese children. In addition, the U.S. Department of State, Bureau of Refugee Programs, maintains a computerized file of men seeking a reunion with their offspring.

In the past, legal entanglements between the countries were a major cause of the delay. The U.S. State Department insisted on having birth certificates. Vietnam used the children as political pawns in their dealings with the United States over the MIA issue and its involvement in Cambodia.

American fathers were not permitted to visit their children in Vietnam until 1988. Then in an unprecedented visit, three fathers had tearful reunions with their children. Each man had gone to Vietnam hoping to return to America with his child. Carl Barefield of San Francisco was among them. Carl was reunited with his son, Thanh Hung, whom he hadn't seen since 1975. Barefield was a former civilian contractor who worked in Vietnam during the war. He couldn't believe it when his own government wouldn't permit him to leave with his son for America. An ODP official, after close scrutiny, was not convinced Thanh was an Amerasian child. Carl had to leave Ho Chi Minh City without his son.

The Homecoming Act has eased those restrictions. The United States no longer requires a birth certificate for each child. "Anyone who looks like an American is accepted," says ODP interviewer

John Jones. "Only a very small percentage of those wanting to come are rejected."[10]

Don Benson of Puyallup, Washington, was one of the three fathers who returned to Vietnam in March, 1988, to reclaim his daughter, Hanh Dung, now twenty-one. Don and his Vietnamese wife had left her behind with a grandmother. Before they could complete the paperwork to bring her out, Saigon fell. Hanh arrived in this country in May 1988 and fell into the arms of her father, a retired Special Forces sergeant. "I told you I would never give up trying," he whispered to her.[11]

The third father attempting to reclaim his child was Don Berges of Los Angeles. Berges is a former adviser with the U.S. Agency for International Development. His daughter, Dan Thao, thanked her father for coming to get her, but her feelings were mixed. All her life she had lived without her father. Now, if she chose to come to America, she would have to live without her mother. Berges promised to bring her mother to the United States as well. Dan's mother only asked that Berges love their daughter. For him that was no problem. "I will love her and I always have," he replied.[12]

* * *

In 1987, Vietnam veterans Bruce Burns, an attorney in San Jose, California, and Jim Barker, a counselor at the San Jose Vet Center, formed the Amerasian Registry. The registry is a nonprofit service supported by concerned veterans and members of the Vietnamese community. Its goal is reuniting vets with their Amerasian children. Mr. Burns claims approximately two hundred veterans have asked the registry for help.[13]

In spite of the Homecoming Act and services like the Amerasian Registry, only a small percentage of Amerasians are reunited with their fathers—less than two percent. Felsman's research indicates that only thirty-two percent had "a little" information about their fathers, and about fifty-five percent had none.[14]

The strong need that motivates the Amerasian to find his or her U.S. father is the need of "acknowledgment and identity," says Anh, a young woman who appeared on *The Oprah Winfrey Show* on January 27, 1988. Anh's father was contacted by phone. "Are you sure that's all she wants, just to meet me? She doesn't want any money or anything?" he had asked. "That's all," replied Anh. "I don't want anything from him. . . . For twenty years I lived without him, no money or nothing—I survive; why would I want it now? And it's just—it hurts," said Anh.[15]

How do U.S. women feel about Amerasian children coming into their lives? Bruce Burns says he's getting calls from wives who say their husbands have admitted having Amerasian children, and the wives are asking Burns how they can find the child. Daniella Sapriel, a Los Angeles lawyer whose husband fathered a daughter in Vietnam, explains:

> The baggage of emotion that goes with a child you have and can't find makes it very hard for these men to do anything.
>
> My husband would sit down to write a letter to her, and there was so much to say and so much to write, he sat there for hours unable to write anything. Because I care for my husband, I care for this little girl too.[16]

Burns says it is the women who are coming around. "I think there are many men who have been afraid for years to tell their wives, and when they finally do, the wife says, 'Stop being a jerk. Let's do something about it.'"[17]

Those agencies handling the search process for Amerasians and American veterans are very sensitive to the critical issues this raises for either party. Therefore, each agency has strict guidelines they must follow. For example, the American Red Cross, in a 1989 *International Notice* clearly states:

> Contact with the father must be made in accordance with the principle of confidentiality in such a way as not to jeopardize his privacy or threaten his present living situation and family members.
>
> If the father is identified and located, he will be asked if he will release his address to the inquirer. It will be entirely his decision regarding any contact with his child. Under no circumstances will the American Red Cross release the father's address without his *written* permission.
>
> If the father does not wish to release his address, he is asked to indicate what he wants the inquirer to be told: that the search was unsuccessful or that the sought person declined to release his address.[18]

Should the father acknowledge an interest in the child, he will need to think the matter through (and possibly to talk with a trained professional) in order to help him clarify his feelings and plans about future contact. Staff members of the agencies are prepared to make appropriate and necessary referrals. Exploration takes place with the father as to what kind of contact he would be willing and able to accept. Even if, at the point of initial discussion, he is not willing to have direct contact with this child, he may be willing to share important medical and/or family background information.[19]

ADDITIONAL READING

Santoli, Al. *New Americans, An Oral History: Immigrants and Refugees in the U.S. Today.* New York: Crown, 1988.

AGENCIES

Requests from Fathers:

If you are interested in tracing your Amerasian child, send a letter to the Orderly Departure Program. Information needed includes the mother's name, places where you served in Vietnam, places where mother/child resided in Vietnam, and the birth date of the child or approximate date. Any other information concerning the relationship can be useful. Send this information to:

Ms. Ricki Gold
Orderly Departure Program
Bureau for Refugee Programs, Room 5824
(Southeast Asia Office-SA-1)
Department of State
Washington, DC 20520
(202)663–1073

The following agencies may also be of assistance:

1.) Your regional office of the Veterans Administration. Sometimes Amerasian children will seek to identify their natural fathers through the VA or other government record sources.

2.) Your local chapter of the American Red Cross, or:

198

American Red Cross
International Social Services
17th and D Sts. NW
Washington, DC 20006
(202)639–3308

Bruce W. Burns, Esq.
American Registry
95 South Market Street
Suite 300
San Jose, CA 95113
(408)292–6683

The Pearl S. Buck Foundation
Greenhill Farms
Box 181
Perkasie, PA 18944
(215)249–0100

Ron Podlaski, Vice President
Vietnam Veterans of America Foundation
2100 M St. NW
Suite 407
Washington, DC 20037
(202)828–2630

Adoption and Foster Parenthood:

Amerasians' family situations range from orphaned adolescents to adults
with spouses and children of their own. Very few Amerasian minors are
available for adoption because few are without family members. Minors
who do depart Vietnam alone are placed in foster homes. The following
organizations work in the various states to arrange foster care for Amerasian children:

Lutheran Immigration and Refugee Service
360 Park Avenue South
New York, NY 10010
(212)532–6350

U.S. Catholic Conference
902 Broadway-8th Fl.
New York, NY 10010
(212)460–8077

If you wish to assist in the resettlement of Amerasians and their families, write to the following address for the names of the resettlement agencies:

Interaction
200 Park Ave. South
New York, NY 10003

PART III

SPIRITUAL HEALING

Chapter 11

WHERE WAS GOD IN VIETNAM?

Where was God in Vietnam? is a question that remains unanswered for many veterans. Angrily, they protest, "If God is good, why did He allow such things to happen?" Others ask, "Why didn't He stop it?"

Men in combat often talked about God. "God was a regular topic of [our] conversation," said Robert L. Peragallo in *Vietnam—The Other Side of Glory.* "Often, our casual raps drifted into questions about why God allowed wars, why innocent people suffered, or why God's dealings seemed so unjust."[1]

Robert Marr, who leads sensitivity groups for Vietnam veterans in Mt. Clemens, Michigan, says, "Veterans have cursed God as the result of some horror they have had to witness or be part of, believing that God should have stopped this terrible evil."[2]

Dennis Johnson remembers being terrified in an M-16 bunker in Da Nang under heavy fire, and cussing God out.

" 'If you're God, why in the hell don't you stop this? You're not good!' I said shaking my fist at God. At that moment, I felt there was nothing good about God," said Dennis.

These same questions haunted victims of the Holocaust. Devastating tragedies have occurred throughout history, and these questions emerge from believers and nonbelievers alike. Like deadly darts aimed at God's indifferent, uncaring silence in the midst of horrendous evil, these questions beg for answers and linger on unanswered.

It reflects the same feeling of abandonment Jesus uttered as he hung on the cross, "My God, my God, why have you forsaken me?" (Matt. 27:46, KJV). And people have asked through the ages, *Where was God when Christ was crucified?*

"I saw no evidence of God in Vietnam," said Dennis Osborne, a Roman Catholic from birth, who is still overwhelmed by the power of evil encountered in Vietnam. For him, it manifests itself as darkness in his soul. It's only now, some twenty years after Vietnam, that Dennis is searching for answers and attempting to rebuild his faith.

Many veterans lost what faith they had and have found little they could identify with in the Church in society today. "Losing their religion" was yet another one of the many losses some Vietnam veterans claim they experienced. Many are "turned off" to God and organized religion.

And yet, some soldiers found God in the midst of the hell they were enduring. William Kimball's book, *Vietnam—The Other Side of Glory*, gives testimonies of men and women who experienced spiritual rebirth, some in the midst of battle, others after coming home, as well as those whose perception of God's love never failed or faltered. Eugene "Red" McDaniel, a U.S. Navy Lieutenant Commander imprisoned and tortured in the Hanoi Hilton prison camp for six long years, is one such person.

Death seemed certain for Eugene. After six days of torture, he felt his seventh day would be his last. It was then he gave himself totally to God. "As I knelt crumpled on the floor in my own blood and wastes, I found myself yielding control to God . . . surrendering my fate to Him unconditionally. . . . God knew my breaking point. He knew exactly when the torture had to stop. Kneeling there, empty before God, I was overwhelmed by the sheer awesomeness of His presence and profound awareness that He was forging a deeper dimension of faith and commitment in my life to glorify Him in the years ahead. . . ."[3]

Back home, Eugene wondered, "Will I be able to share, in some small way, the sure and certain knowledge, developed in the darkest hours of a prison cell, that the love of God follows us wherever we go and protects us in all circumstances?"[4]

WAR'S DEVASTATION OF THE SOUL
AND EMOTIONAL WOUNDS

"I felt after my Vietnam experience that I was scarred, that my soul had been burned to a crisp," said Dennis Osborne. "I was raised in the Catholic Church and I knew the commandments by heart. In Vietnam, I had violated all those commandments . . . sleeping with Vietnamese women . . . killing people and supporting the killing of people . . . drinking to excess. I felt really dirty when I came back, and I didn't see any way I was ever going to get clean again. There's so much guilt that I had to process," said Dennis.

Upon their return home, Vietnam veterans were subjected to more emotional wounding—by protesters, by unsympathetic, unknowing acquaintances, even by family and friends. Few realized how devastating the war had been for these boy soldiers, these young men who had come from a "nation with the soul of a church."[5]

Ron Kovic, in his book *Born on the Fourth of July*, describes one such incident. Thinking they were shooting at Viet Cong, his friend Molina and other members of his unit had fired into a hut that housed old men and children:

> Molina turned the beam of his flashlight into the hut. "Oh God," he said. "Oh Jesus Christ." He started to cry. "We just shot up a bunch of kids!" The floor of the small hut was covered with them, screaming and thrashing their arms back and forth, lying in pools of blood, crying wildly, screaming again and again. They were shot in the face, in the chest, in the legs, moaning and crying. . . . He felt crazy and weak as he stood there staring at them with the rest of the men, staring down onto the floor like it was a nightmare, like it was some kind of dream and it really wasn't happening.

> And then he could no longer stand watching. They were people, he thought, children and old men, people, people like himself, and he had to do something, he had to move, he had to help. He jerked the green medical bag off his back, ripping it open and grabbing for bandages. . . .

"It's gonna be okay," he tried to say, but he was crying now, crying and still trying to bandage them up. He moved from body to body searching in the dark with his fingers for the holes the bullets had made. . . .

Afterwards, the men were not moving and some of them were crying now, dropping their rifles and sitting down on the wet ground. They were weeping now with their hands against their faces. "Oh Jesus, oh God, forgive us."

"Forgive us for what we've done!" he heard Molina cry.[6]

Richard Rohlf's feelings reflect the attitudes of many soldiers. He tells of an incident that occurred during the Tet offensive at Ban Me Thuot. The Viet Cong had butchered all the children, as well as the priests and Catholic nurses, in an orphanage that he had visited many times. "People are people, regardless of color," said Richard. "For adults to be killed, that's one thing, but kids are innocent, and they've got no control over the situation. That really got me . . . that really got me."

DOING EVIL TO ACCOMPLISH GOOD

All wars—whether fought for ideological, political, racial, economic reasons, or religious conflicts—cause peaceable citizens to do evil to accomplish good, or at least what their nation or cause perceives to be good. And all wars inflict human suffering on the innocent as well as on those actively engaged in fighting.

But the Vietnam War, unlike any other war in this nation's history, gave reason for the soldiers themselves to question the morality of the war. Many veterans came home and protested the war, and many formed the Vietnam Veterans Against the War (VVAW), which made its presence felt at both the Republican and Democratic Conventions in 1968.

William Mahedy in *Out of the Night* says it succinctly: "To believe [the notion] that war brings peace is a delusion. To act upon that delusion is the final corruption of the human spirit."[7]

The faulty thinking of the war mentality is evident in a statement made by an air force major who said after the destruction of Ben Tre in February 1968, "It became necessary to destroy the town in order to save it."

Soldiers themselves saw the folly of fighting a senseless war that had unclear objectives. It added to their sense of futility, especially when they saw their friends' lives wasted.

Some envied veterans of World War II. The objective had been clear: Stop Hitler! This nation supported, loved, admired, and sacrificed for its soldiers during what some are now calling the last "Great War." Vietnam was different in all these respects. Doing evil to accomplish good seemed pointless.

WAS GOD ABSENT IN VIETNAM?

Some were able to answer for themselves the question, *Where was God in Vietnam?*

Mahedy, who served as a chaplain in Vietnam, states that after one of his seminars with Vietnam veterans, a vet suggested this explanation: "God checked out of 'Nam because of what was goin' down there."[8] Mahedy refers to this seemingly apparent void and absence as "God's backside."

At such times, God has become the adversary, the One whom author Robert McClelland has fondly named: Our Loving Enemy. To enter into this abyss, this spiritual desert, is to learn that *God is both kind and severe* (Rom. 11:22, TLB). It is one thing for God to allow war to happen, but it is quite a different thing to expect him to approve of the things we do in the name of war.

Gavin Reid, author of *Living the New Life*, writes:

The father in Jesus' story [of the Prodigal Son*] keeps away from his son and therefore keeps away from all that his son does.

This is what is meant by God's judgment. We often think of judgment as if it were God coming in with a big stick. The truth is that God is love, and his way of judging is usually to keep his loving, protecting, helpful self away from us when we are in the wrong. St. Paul in his letter to the Christians at Rome uses the words: "God has given them over" (1:24, 26, 28). What he means is that God shows his anger by standing back and letting us go ahead with the mess that we are all making.[9]

* Luke 15: 11–32.

Robert Peragallo adds, "Back in the world, it was convenient to pass the buck and blame natural disasters on 'acts of God,' but war was another matter. After all, whether we were willing to admit it or not, even in the most vulnerable sessions of bar talk, we were the ones killing and being killed, and we didn't seem to need any help from above. Deep down inside, I think we all knew this."[10] His observations reflect a deeper truth.

WARS ARE MAN-MADE

The causes of war are numerous. Wars are power struggles. They are the result of man's unwillingness to sit down and resolve differences over the peace table and reliance on force to settle differences. Wars are many times the result of man's unwillingness to share this world's resources and wealth. Wars happen when one nation exploits or oppresses another. Wars happen when one nation becomes the aggressor and the other nation must defend itself. Wars and revolutions happen when a people's unquenchable desire for freedom surpasses their concern for their own personal safety. Wars are man-made and waged by governments as well as those struggling to be free.

The question of "why wars happen" cannot be answered apart from some understanding of the forces of evil in this world and how they oppose God's will—and some understanding of human nature. "What causes wars, and what causes fightings among you? Is it not your passions that are at war in your members? You desire and do not have; so you kill. And you covet and cannot obtain; so you fight and wage war" (James 4:1-2, RSV).

GOD WAS A SOURCE OF STRENGTH

For some soldiers, their faith in God became a source of strength and comfort in the midst of Hell, especially men subjected to severe torture as prisoners of war. Men like Jeremiah Denton, Eugene McDaniel, James Stockdale, Ben Purcell, and many many others have written their personal accounts of those experiences. Their stories reflect that "God is within" each man, and theirs was a tenacious faith that sustained them through starvation, serious injuries, extreme torture, and excruciating pain. And yet they kept the faith and did not blame God for their circumstances.

FAITH DIED FOR SOME

But for those who lost faith in God's goodness, as well as their own goodness, God seemed absent. Loss of faith generates sadness that can be compared to the sunflowers that grew on my father's farm in Ohio. Each morning, the large golden blossoms would lift their faces and follow the sun across the sky until nightfall. After sunset, the blossoms hung lifeless facing the ground. The day the soldier ceased to believe in God was the day he ceased to believe the sun was still shining, and he would no longer lift his head toward the heavens for sustenance and life-giving warmth. The sun still shone, but he no longer believed it was shining. Faith is like that. It can be lost and it can die. And when it dies, an emptiness invades the spirit, and one enters a spiritual darkness resulting in despair and cynicism.

THE PARADOX OF FREE WILL

Most of the time, we feel in control of our own lives. We control where we go, how we spend our money, the friends we associate with. But when catastrophic things suddenly happen and we feel out of control, we often tend to believe that God has caused the tragedy. In other words, God gets the blame.

And when face-to-face with unspeakable evil, we humans want God to intervene and stop the evil actions of others. The truth we find hard to accept in war is that God made man free. "Essential to humanity is the ability to make free choices," says Mahedy:

The paradox endures for all time. The all-powerful Creator gives to His own creation the power to disobey, to reject him and to destroy each other. This is a power that is never rescinded. . . . In Vietnam we were simply living out in vivid terms the consequences of human freedom. We were doing it to ourselves. This is the story of all wars

209

and genocides throughout history. To demand a coercive presence of God restricting our freedom to sin, no matter how horrendously evil the sin might be, is to misunderstand the creation story.[11]

Iona Henry, a woman whose husband and son were killed in a tragic car-train accident, reminds us that it is *human* planning and *human* decision that bring a car and locomotive to a certain spot at a certain time. She compares it to war.

It's like a soldier being killed in battle. If man creates the battle and the war, and places himself deliberately out where the bullets are flying, then he creates the possibility of being struck by one of the bullets. He has no right to expect God to stop the bullet, once man has pulled the trigger! What a confused madhouse life would be, if God were to interfere like that.[12]

WHAT DOES GOD WILL?

God intends for humankind to live in peace with one another, and each one of us to respect the sanctity of human life and the rights of all other living beings. Giving the Ten Commandments was God's way of saying, "Live by these rules, and you will have an uncomplicated life and live at peace with one another." These Commandments became the very fabric of a free society. To violate them is to violate one's self and jeopardize future peace of mind. Chuck Dean in his book, *Nam Vet* says, "Many of us went to Vietnam trained to kill the enemy. But few of us were mentally prepared for the reality of that action and its ensuing consequences."[13]

John Sanford, author of *Dreams: God's Forgotten Language*, states:

Some things are wrong, not because society says so, but because they contradict our deepest truest nature. Religious morality, such as the Ten Commandments, is a projection or externalization of our own inner truth (or voice of God). Moral commandments have validity, not because they are absolutely right in themselves, but because they are generalizations of what the voice of God within tells every man about his own life. . . . [T]he law of the soul is every bit as demanding as the law of man.[14]

Much of the tragedy of the Vietnam experience was that, having been taught to hate and kill the enemy, the soldier discovered after the fact that he was filled with *self-hate*, and had in reality mortally wounded the God-part of his own soul, for God is present in the depths of man's inner being.

Life, however, doesn't always give us easy choices. Sometimes circumstances force us to make difficult choices that throw us into a cauldron of violence not of our own making:

> For man also does not know his time: Like fish taken in a cruel net, like birds caught in a snare, so the sons of men are snared in an evil time, when it falls suddenly upon them (Eccles. 9:12, NKJV).

When that happens, it is especially important to remember: Wars are man-made.* Wars are started by men and they must be ended by men. The problem is that wars are much easier to start than they are to finish, as was so clearly evident in Vietnam.

BLAMING GOD

One reason persons feel cut off from God is their anger toward Him. It stems from having felt abandoned.

"This is the source of our anger at God," explains author Kenneth Zanca in *Mourning: The Healing Journey.* "We feel that we are left alone to face our troubles. God is unable or unwilling to intervene. . . . We blame ourselves for a lack of faith and that convicts us in our poor self-image even more. God's silence is deafening and we resent it."[15]

Anger is a common reaction to loss, but the question is, "Should we blame God for the war, the killing, and the inhumane acts and atrocities?" Is this not a case of misplacing blame? The danger and consequence of misplacing blame and staying angry at God is that it contributes to feelings of alienation and disharmony within the soul. Being angry at God creates a barrier that shuts one off from the Source of healing so vital for the wounded spirit and shattered emotions so typical of the Vietnam experience. Warren Wiersbe

---

* See Appendix A for The Church's Historical Approach to War.

warns, "Bitterness only makes suffering worse and closes the spiritual channels through which God can pour his grace."[16]

BUT GOD *ALLOWED* IT TO HAPPEN

Many persons justify tragedies by saying, "Well, it must have been God's will because He allowed it to happen."

When referring to God's seeming unwillingness to act, by using the word "allow," we project an image of an uncaring, detached God who shows a "careless disregard" for humankind. I believe the word "allow" is a poor choice of words and calls for a broader understanding of our concept of God's controlling all that happens.

Dr. Richard Rice, author of *God's Foreknowledge and Man's Free Will,* challenges the age-old belief that God is in total control. Rice believes that "God maintains ultimate sovereignty over history. But He does not exercise absolute control."[17] More simply stated, God does control the final outcome of history, but on earth—by allowing human beings freedom—His control is not absolute. Rice also believes that "God is not responsible for suffering. Suffering owes its existence to factors that oppose His will.[18]

". . . God affirms our sense of outrage at what has happened. Some things are simply wrong. He appreciates to the fullest our loss, our grief, and our pain at the very time we suffer it. His own sense of pain and loss far surpasses ours.[19]

I believe it was the God-part of the soldier's soul that wept when friends were killed, the God-part of the soul that was repulsed by the nightmarish war . . . the God within each person that was and is angered by the injustices still taking place. God is a God of suffering, who knows and shares in our torment.

But it was also the God-part of the soldier's soul that loved a fellow soldier with a purity and intensity of love never felt before or since. It was the God-part of some soldiers that caused them to risk their own lives to retrieve the body of a dead soldier. It was and is the God-part of a man [or woman] that reaches out to other veterans in need today. For you, this Scripture has special meaning: "Greater love hath no man than this, that a man lay down his life for his friends" (John 15:13, KJV).

GENTLE JESUS VERSUS SUFFERING SERVANT

Much of the teaching about the personality of Jesus Christ in our churches and Sunday schools emphasizes the tender, peace-loving spirit of the man. Such teaching shapes our image of him as the "gentle Jesus." On occasion, we hear from our pulpits some reference to Jesus' angry outbursts and demonstrations against the money changers in the Temple, but, by and large, the images of Jesus that we have passed down from generation to generation tend to paint a mental picture of Him as being a man of principle but so meek and mild he fails, in our minds, to know the depths of human passion and emotion. I make this point because I think, in part, this "gentle Jesus" image in the jungles of Vietnam may not have been sufficient to sustain one through the difficult faith crises faced in battle.

A more helpful and more accurate image of Christ is that of the "suffering servant," for it parallels in many ways the experience of the soldier.

Jesus knew what it was like to be faced with enemies. "Charlie" for him were the religionists of his day. Contrary to our image of him, he was not above name-calling. On one occasion he accused the Pharisees of being, "hypocrites." On another, he said to them, "You snakes, you brood of vipers" (Matt. 23:33, NIV). Those were fighting words even in his day. He fought his own private war with powerful forces that ultimately had him killed. He knew what it felt like to be betrayed. One day he was ushered into the city of Jerusalem by cheering crowds where he was to confront his enemies, knowing full well the dangers involved. One week later he was sentenced to death by an angry mob that sealed his fate by shouting, "Crucify him." Bodily, Jesus was destroyed by the forces of evil. He was the victim of an atrocity, hands and feet pierced with nails, and he hung on a cross to die an agonizing, slow death. And he was young, too. Far too young to die. Because he was more than man—the Son of God—He was the "point man" of our faith—he was out front, alone, leading the way—conquering sin and death for all time, and herein lies our hope. It was through Jesus' death that God made known his presence in the hearts of believers as "The

213

Comforter." Undoubtedly, Jesus Christ is the one person—the brother—who can understand the pain and hurt you are experiencing, for he has been there.

AMONG THE ASHES, A BURNING COAL

Among the ruins of a fire that has raged destroying persons, places, and things, are live coals. Though anger at God exists in the hearts of many, it is evidence of a relationship that begs for reconciliation and growth in understanding. The "live coal" of faith still exists.

McClelland says in his book, *God Our Loving Enemy*, that he believes that rage is an *appropriate* response. He refers to some of the Psalms as "swearing set to music":

> *My God, my God, why have you forsaken me?*
> *Why are you so far from saving me,*
> *so far from the words of my groaning?*
> *O my God, I cry out by day, but*
> *you do not answer,*
> *by night, and am not silent.*

> (Ps. 22:1,2 NIV)

McClelland believes that:

> Cursing God is as much an affirmation of faith in God for the person who hurts as is singing the Doxology for the person who is happy.[20]

> When we stand before God, there are times when rage is the only appropriate response.[21]

The author believes that "rage is a normal part of our encounter with God," as evidenced in the Book of Job.[22] He views rage as a gift, a gift of God. McClelland affirms that "the Christian faith gives us permission to be angry with God when we sense, as we often do, God's indifference. . . ."[23]

But he warns:

> Rage that goes no farther than mere blasphemy soon becomes cynical. To curse God and die, as Job's wife suggested, is the tragic waste of a

gift. Ernest Hemingway could not stand the fact that he could not control life and live it on his terms, so in a fit of rage, he committed suicide. What a senseless waste! A much better way is to direct our rage—not against life—but against God.[24]

It is far better to vent our anger at God who "knows the secret of every heart" (Ps. 44:21, TLB) than to vent it on a loved one such as a spouse or child, or the persons who irritate us. Pierre Wolff in his excellent book, *May I Hate God?*, compares this experience of venting our anger with God to human friendships:

> When I can freely show anger to my friend, I also show, paradoxically, that I believe his love is able to take it. If I cannot be myself with my friend, exactly as I am right now, for better or for worse, with whom can I be myself? Beneath my anger my behavior says this: At least with you I can reveal myself as I am. It is also taken for granted that my friend discerns that the root of my feelings is the love which was injured, or which I thought was injured: A love as deep as my violence is great; a love crying out its inability to live divided and its desire for reconciliation in justice. . . . Great love underlies the risk of such an encounter.[25]

Kenneth Zanca, speaking from his own personal experience in overcoming anger with God, writes:

> One way I overcame my hostility toward God was to express it. In time, I heard myself talk and realized how foolish I sounded. I got tired of being angry. I began to think of God as one who suffered a loss along with me. My loss was his loss too. Death is God's enemy too. Realizing this made me feel close to him. As St. Paul said: . . . and the last of the enemies to be destroyed is death (I Cor. 15:25).

> Hope, mine and God's, relieved anger. The power of faith in the resurrection is the center of true hope and peace. Without that hope, we are sad and indeed the most pitiable of people.[26]

The point Wolff and Zanca are making is this: Share your anger with God; He can take it. His love for you is deep and abiding. The God of the universe is also the God of the person. The important thing to remember, however, is that anger is a destructive emotion unless channeled into creative purposes. The ideal state of relationship with God is one of friendship. Good mental health is harmony between our soul and God. The means of achieving that harmony are dealt with in Chapter 12.

A NEW GOD, A DEEPER FAITH

Dennis Johnson, a pastor serving a church in Missouri, though cursing God in Vietnam, has come to know God in a new dimension:

"I grew up with a fairy-tale idea of God, but it was a God I couldn't reach. I called Him the 'God of the stained-glass window.' In Vietnam that image had to die.

"I know now there is a God," said Dennis, "but not the one I thought I knew. Going through the wilderness journey, like Jesus, I discovered that when I began to ask, *Why have you deserted me?* is when I found that I began to know God.

"He's elusive, but the God I know now has more depth than the one about whom I had been taught. He's not the hocus-pocus God. He's the real God who cares and weeps for us," explained Dennis.

WILL I GO TO HEAVEN?

When I asked about how he felt about heaven, one veteran replied, "I know I've broken the Commandments, and I'm so far gone I don't even let myself think about that anymore."

One cannot disregard the biblical evidence that one day, there will be a reckoning for what we do and how we live our lives. "And just as it is appointed for men to die once, and after that comes judgment . . ."* (Heb. 9:27, RSV). That final test is one *all* human beings must face, and none of us are privileged to know how God judges the heart of man. Don Baker, in his booklet *Heaven*, says there will be three surprises in heaven. We will be surprised

> to find some we did not expect,
> to not find some we did expect, and
> to find ourselves in heaven. [27]

* For more about judgment, read 2 Thess. 1:7–9; 4:16–17.

I believe the compassionate words Jesus spoke to the man who hung on the cross beside him were direct from the heart of God.

As the three men hung on crosses, each in his own agony, the criminal on one side hurled insults at Jesus, saying, "If you're the Messiah, save yourself and us." But the other thief rebuked him and said, "Don't you fear God? You received the same sentence he did. Ours, however, is only right, because we are getting what we deserve for what we did, but he has done no wrong. And then he spoke to Jesus, "Remember me, Jesus, when you come as King."

Whether Jesus knew the full extent of the man's crimes, we don't know. All we know is that Jesus spoke words of hope to the man, and said, "I promise you that today you will be in Paradise with me." (Luke 23:40–43, TEV).

The world had condemned the man to death; Jesus promised him Paradise.

ADDITIONAL READING

Capps, Walter H. *The Unfinished War: Vietnam and the American Conscience.* Boston: Beacon Press, 1983.

Kimball, William R. *Vietnam: The Other Side of Glory.* Canton, Ohio: Daring Books, 1987.

Mahedy, William P. *Out of the Night: The Spiritual Journey of Vietnam Vets.* New York: Ballantine, 1986.

McClelland, Robert W. *God Our Loving Enemy.* Nashville, Tenn.: Abingdon, 1982.

Wolff, Pierre. *May I Hate God?* New York: Paulist Press, 1979.

RESOURCES FOR CHURCHES

If you are a pastor or priest, refer to Appendices C and D for reference materials such as books, films, videocassettes that can be used in local churches. In addition, a special recognition service for Vietnam veterans, the names and addresses of veterans involved in ministry who do public speaking, information about starting a veterans' support group in a local parish, and Communication Guidelines for Clergy are also provided in these sections.

Chapter 12

COMING TO TERMS WITH THE GUILT OF WAR

Guilt is a crippling emotion. It comes to many veterans as a thief in the night robbing them of peace of mind. One man remembers being ordered by his superior to "waste" a boy whose raised arms clearly signaled surrender. Veterans have shared with me vivid memories of specific instances in which they were face-to-face with the enemy whom they had to kill. "I'm still mourning what I had to do there," said one veteran.

Those who served in leadership roles report they feel extremely responsible and guilty for the death of soldiers in their command. They agonize to this day over the decisions they made while leading their men in combat. Robert J. Lifton wrote of one such man in *Home from the War*:

> As platoon leader he had chosen twelve of his best men for a patrol, and for reasons not entirely clear—partly because he allowed an unfit person to lead the patrol, perhaps, partly because he had not given sufficiently precise orders himself—they were ambushed and killed in extremely violent fashion. He later came upon the scene of bodies strewn about in pieces.

The soldier explained: "I made the mistake of trusting somebody I shouldn't have trusted. I told him exactly where to set up the patrol, but he didn't do what I said. He wanted to sleep dry. Well, now he's sleeping dry.

"Some of the men we couldn't even find—they were buried under bunkers. . . . I don't know why it all happened—there was the damned fool war—and maybe I just wasn't old enough to have responsibility for so many men."[1]

Those who survived feel guilty for surviving.

Rev. John Steer reports being plagued with survivor guilt. "God, why am I alive? Why are my buddies dead and I'm alive? I asked myself that question over and over every day . . . I thought I would die from guilt," said Steer in his book, *Vietnam Curse or Blessing.*[2]

Some feel guilty for not having saved, or been able to save, the life of a fellow soldier. Some feel guilty for the killing of civilians and the atrocities performed, usually in retaliation for the death and mutilation of their friends. John Steer explains why: "I did things in Vietnam that I'm ashamed of, including watching torture, planting grenades in garbage dumps where I knew women and kids were going to dig them up, because I was so filled with hate after finding my friends tortured, hanged, or having had their skin cut off of them."[3]

"Guilt over combat experiences has played a significant role in the suicidal behavior or preoccupation with suicide of virtually all the Vietnam combat veterans with post-traumatic stress we have worked with," writes Herbert Hendin in *Wounds of War.*[4]

Some carry enormous burdens of guilt for having fired upon their own soldiers by mistake, or being asked to put a fellow soldier out of his misery. Despite their heroism, medics or corpsmen could not save everyone they treated, and they often torture themselves by blaming these deaths on their perceived incompetence. Many were made to feel even more guilty by the hostile homecomings they received, and many are still bitter about those memories. Some report having felt safer in 'Nam than in the United States.

Chuck Dean, author of *Nam Vet*, reports that another guilt men express today is "guilt for not having 'been there' because they were stationed elsewhere."

The lists of reasons for feeling guilty, whether real or imagined, is endless. Unresolved guilt is one of the major components of post-traumatic stress disorder.

You need to know that this nation bears "collective" guilt. There were those who profited during wartime economy. And there are those who sat in positions of decision making or who had powers of command indifferent to the use of soldiers' lives. Author William Mahedy in *Out of the Night* agrees:

> People like Nixon and Kissinger, for example, write about war almost without reference to the people who suffered from it. The only issues important to them are global ones; they ignore people. However much they perform a service by placing the war in a global context, our sages and leaders remain essentially amoral with respect to war because they are blind to its cost in human terms. The vets, on the other hand, never lose sight of that terrible cost.[5]

> The troops knew that individuals and corporations back in the world were making big money on the war. Body counts, the military careers of their leaders and big bucks for the folks back home—this was what the war was all about.[6]

True guilt springs from an inner sense that tells an individual he or she has done something terribly wrong—it is real and appropriate.[7] (See Notes for Lifton's explanation of guilt.) Mahedy explains the guilt typical of wartime memories:

> In the guilt that grows out of war, there is always the recognition that one's actions have had irrevocable consequences. People are now dead who would still be alive if one had not pulled the trigger of an M-16 or fired the weapons of a Cobra gunship or sprayed a village with napalm. Children are maimed and orphaned because of one's own personal actions. The consequences of these actions will last as long as the perpetrators and the survivors live. The guilt of war is the guilt of having been the bearer of death and terrible suffering to one's fellow humans.[8]

> The problem with guilt is that it remains for years, embedded in the psyche, trapped in the center of the soul.[9]

There are certain circumstances for which veterans feel no guilt. Mahedy explains:

Not surprisingly, veterans with no moral guilt—or very little—are those whose combat was against North Vietnamese troop units or VC guerrillas. Personal self-defense is indeed the major issue in combat between opposing infantry. North Vietnamese soldiers became the aggressors who endangered the lives of Americans—as the Americans did to the North Vietnamese. Killing in that kind of combat carries with it very little, if any, guilt. [10]

THE POSITIVE SIDE OF GUILT

Father Michael Mannion, author of *A Cry to Be Whole*, however, sheds a positive light on guilt:

> I see guilt as healthy and productive when it leads the [person] to coming to grips with the reality of what [he] has done. It can be a part of the way back to wholeness and inner peace through a personal relationship with a loving and forgiving God, and a commitment to embark upon the journey of that relationship. Once the commitment to the healing process is set in motion, there is no value in guilt whatsoever. [11]

> The healing process takes place in the rhythm between God and the soul of the [individual]. [12]

One has to shy away from an easy dismissal of guilt. The counselor, therapist, or pastor isn't really helping who says, "Don't worry about it. You did the best you could under the circumstances. Now get on with your life." There are times when it is necessary to feel guilty, for it is this feeling that unlocks and releases the secrets hidden or trapped in the unconscious mind. Only by feeling guilty can we be restored.

Father Mannion adds:

> Of itself, psychology can only help [you] understand the past and cope with it, but that is not enough. Knowing the whys and hows of the past do not liberate a person from the shackles of repetition and the reliving of the continuous pain of the past. Forgiveness does. That is not an invention of humankind, but a gift of God. Spiritual healing is God's seal on the human heart that the past may not just be coped with, but healed. [13]

221

GOD FORGIVES AND FORGETS—BUT WE DON'T

Native Americans have rites of purification performed by the tribe with and on behalf of the warrior. "American Indian veterans, who follow their traditional beliefs and participate in ceremonies, find spiritual help to overcome wounds to their souls from Vietnam experiences. The sweat lodge ceremony is a combination of physical, intellectual, psychological, and spiritual healing for the people in those tribes that practice it. This ceremony is seen as part of a way of life, not as a religious experience," said Harold Barse, counselor at a Vet Center in Oklahoma City, Oklahoma.

"American Indian veterans can come to terms with their Vietnam experiences if they belong to one of the organized religions, but adjustments seem to be more concrete when they follow the traditional ways," he said. Barse also claims American Indian people are much more willing than the American population to help Vietnam veterans bear their burdens. [14]

For the Christian this act of purification is both private and public: private in the sense that it is a singularly personal interaction between God and the individual; public in the sense that one often needs other persons and members of the body of Christ to move through the process. "God may use another person or a group to bring about the insights we have been unable to discover on our own," says David A. Seamands, author of *Healing of Memories*. [15] For the Christian, this purification comes through God's forgiveness. Forgiveness is the act of absolving a person of his wrongs or sins whereby the guilty person is released both from his guilt and punishment. [16]

BUT HOW DO I OBTAIN FORGIVENESS?

To work through guilt, the important first step is to recognize that violating one's conscience and breaking the Commandments has created a condition of death to the spirit. Self-respect, self-love, and innocence dies within us. The "wages of sin is death" (Rom. 6:23, KJV) is a lesson that takes on meaning for you if you feel old, dead inside, joyless, and uncaring.

It is important at this point to distinguish "spiritual death" from "psychic numbing" that also "causes a loss of capacity to feel sadness, grief, or psychological pain. Psychic numbing is done to protect oneself from death and inner death, protection without which one could not survive. It has to do with drawing oneself in to consolidate and protect oneself from external threats or assaults," said Dr. Lifton, who has become an internationally known psychiatrist and researcher on the survivors of the Holocaust and atom bomb survivors of Hiroshima.[17]

Spiritual death occurs when one violates God's laws and one's own conscience. Spiritual death results in a "hardening of one's heart" and, ultimately, despair. In spiritual terms, historically these acts have been called "sin" or "sins." There are sins of commission—things we do; and sins of omission—things we don't do. At the heart of sin is an attitude of the whole person—the attitude of turning away from God in resentment and revolt. Sin is that which separates us from God; it is being wrongly related. The state of sin—the state of being separated from God—is the climate that forms hell. It is this atmosphere that smothers and kills the soul.

Because our spirit is unseen and its dying so subtly concealed in the early stages, we do not fear that death. It is only as we begin to lose meaning to life, the will to go on, the vitality and joy, that we begin to sense this death of the spirit and its chilling consequences. Sin is the fatal spiritual disease.[18]

Mahedy expounds on the unpopularity of calling it sin:

> The notion of war as sin simply doesn't play in Peoria—or anywhere else in the United States—because a fondness for war is an essential component of the macho American god. We define deity as that supreme being who achieves his ends by force. . . . Yet the awareness of evil—in religious terms a consciousness of sin—is the underlying motif of the Vietnam War stories.

> I believe the essential failure of the chaplaincy in Vietnam was its inability to name the reality for what it was. We should have first called it sin, admitted we were in a morally ambiguous and religiously tenuous situation, and then gone on to deal with the harsh reality of the soldier's life. . . . I do not believe that a Christian chaplain can legitimately go beyond the toleration of killing in immediate self-defense. He errs if he tries in any way beyond that to supply religious motivation for the soldiers to "carry on the struggle."[19]

HOW CAN I REGAIN MY SPIRITUAL WELL-BEING?

Obstacles to faith in God for the veteran are cynicism, doubt, and feelings of unworthiness. One veteran said, "I understand the concept of forgiveness of sins, even the horrible sins I committed in Vietnam. I fear God cannot ever love me again."

To overcome these feelings, one has to recognize the fact that doubt has clouded the spirit. Jesus said, *the world's sin is unbelief in me* (John 16:9, TLB). Remember the sunflower that would no longer look at the sun. But the sun has never ceased to shine, and a compassionate God still exists. God does not come to us because of our worthiness—for absolutely none of us are worthy.

All human beings sin.

In his ministry with Vietnam veterans as he travels throughout the United States, John Steer puts it plainly:

> You're a sinner, not because you killed people in Vietnam, not because you cheat on your wife, not because you're an alcoholic and talk like a pig. You're a sinner because the Bible says, "for all have sinned and fallen short of the glory of God" (Rom. 3:10). I help them realize that they're a sinner, not because they're a Vietnam veteran, but a sinner who just happens to be a Vietnam veteran.[20]

God comes to us because of our need and his desire to be reunited with us. God took the initiative years ago to reclaim our hearts, by sending a human to earth—Jesus Christ—who could relate to us and reveal the Creator's desire to be at one with His creation. God does not desire the death of the sinner and goes to extreme lengths to reclaim our love. It would be a defeat of God's eternal purpose if not *all* were made alive in Christ—and that includes you, for you are precious to God.

HEALING AND RE-CREATION ARE POSSIBLE

For centuries, the Christian approach to spiritual healing through resolution of guilt has happened when the believer begins by accepting the responsibility for his or her actions, and has a sincere desire to be right with God by reestablishing a relationship. To be friends with ourselves requires a right relationship with God.

If it is your desire to be healed, you begin by daring to believe in the power of the Words of God as recorded in Scripture, for they are the basis of a new belief structure essential for cleansing and healing the spirit. Read the passages slowly, over and over again, paying particular attention to the progression of thought and how it leads you from tears to release. Allow your heart to hear as if God Himself were speaking only to you. It is the age-old message that has dispelled despair and given birth to hope in the hearts of countless men and women for centuries.

Return to me, and I will return to you . . . (Mal. 3:7, NASB).

As you come close to God you should be deeply sorry, you should be grieved, you should even be in tears. Your laughter will have to become mourning, your high spirits will have to become heartfelt dejection. You will have to feel very small in the sight of God before he will set you on your feet once more (James 4:9, 10, J.B. Phillips).[21]

For I am offering you my deliverance; not in the distant future, but right now! I am ready to save you (Isa. 46:12, TLB).

. . . no matter how deep the stain of your sins, I can take it out and make you as clean as freshly fallen snow. Even if you are stained as red as crimson, I can make you white like wool! (Isa. 44:22, TLB).

I've blotted out your sins; they are gone like morning mist at noon! Oh, return to me, for I have paid the price to set you free (Isa. 44:22, TLB).

I, even I, am the one who wipes out your transgressions for my own sake; and I will not remember your sins (Isa. 43:25, NASB).

I will look with pity on the man who has a humble and contrite heart, who trembles at my word (Isa. 66:2, TLB).

I solemnly declare that *any* sin of man can be forgiven, even blasphemy* against me; but blasphemy against the Holy Spirit can never be forgiven. It is an eternal sin (Mark 3:28, TLB).

---

* Blasphemy against the Holy Spirit is a sin mentioned by Jesus in Matt. 12:31; Mark 3:28–9; and Luke 12:10. It will not be forgiven, he said. It appears to be not a single act, but a continued rejection of light and truth, leading to a state in which one is unable to distinguish between the working of the Holy Spirit and that of Satan.[23]

For my thoughts are not your thoughts, neither are your ways my ways. . . . For as the heavens are higher than the earth, so are my ways higher than your ways and my thoughts than your thoughts (Isa. 55:8, 9, KJV).

I love them that love me; and those that seek me early shall find me (Prov. 8:17, KJV).

In those days when you pray I will listen. You will find me when you seek me, if you look for me in earnest (Jer. 29:12, 13, TLB).

He will again have compassion on us; he will tread our iniquities underfoot. Yes, thou wilt cast all their sins into the depths of the sea (Mic. 7:19, NASB).

THE SOUL NEEDS GOD TO LIVE

Leslie Weatherhead, noted English author and preacher of this century, elaborates on our need for God:

Just as eyes need light, just as the lungs need air, just as the ears need sound, just as the mind needs truth, so the spirit or the soul needs communion with God. Because the eyes need light, because light is the only environment in which they can function, if light is cut off they atrophy, and the same is true in the others cases I have hinted at. If you cut yourself off from God and things spiritual altogether, your soul diminishes in its power to live, so that if you are thrust suddenly by death into a spiritual world you are like a half-blind man confronted with a sunset. [22]

CONFESSION IS GOOD FOR THE SOUL—AND BODY

Certain actions on our part are essential for the God-given life force to work within us. One of those acts is the act of confession of that which troubles us. Recent studies affirm what the plain teachings of Scripture revealed centuries ago. King David declared these same truths:

"When I declared not my sin, my body wasted away through my groaning all day long. For day and night thy hand was heavy upon me; my strength was dried up as by the heat of summer" (Ps. 32:3–4, KJV).

These findings in medicine and psychology affirm King David's insights.

In the *Lexington Herald-Leader*, Lexington, Kentucky, September 23, 1984, an article appeared from the *New York Times* news service. It was entitled, "Confession May Be Good for the Body," and it went on to say, "Confession, whatever it may do for the soul, appears to be good for the body. New studies show persuasively that people who are able to confide in others about their troubled feelings or some traumatic event, rather than bear the turmoil in silence, are less vulnerable to disease." It then reported on several different experiments that confirm the "long-term health benefits" of sharing our most painful secrets with others.

Dr. James Pennebaker's research (John Hopkins School of Medicine) shows that "the act of confiding in someone else protects the body against damaging internal stresses that are the penalty for carrying around an onerous emotional burden such as unspoken remorse." Similar research conducted at Harvard University shows that those who do not share their thoughts and feelings have "less effective immune systems." Dr. Pennebaker, publishing his findings in the *Journal of Abnormal Psychology*, confirms these discoveries.[24]

Dr. Lifton, who in the early seventies met in rap groups with veterans who opposed the war after returning home, describes the relief a veteran felt after sharing in a rap group session:

> Though clearly anxious and upset, he also seemed relieved. This marked the beginning for him of a forthright exploration (over many subsequent meetings) of guilt and responsibility that left him feeling freer in all aspects of his life, and conveyed the impression of a man liberating himself from a heavy burden.[25]

FORGIVING OURSELVES

After confessing our sins and asking for God's forgiveness, we must still perform that most difficult of all spiritual disciplines— *accepting* God's forgiveness, then forgiving ourselves. Corrie ten

Boom, Dutch survivor of a Nazi concentration camp, said her father once gave her this instruction: "Throw your sins in the deepest ocean, and don't go fishing for them again."

Theologian Louis Evely believes, "God does not punish men. Men punish themselves. . . . Far from wanting to avenge himself on us, God weeps over our crimes and their consequences on us. . . ."26

In other words, one must take God's word regarding forgiveness, or else we act as a higher authority. Rely on the truth: "If our heart condemns us, God is greater than our heart" (I John 3:20, KJV). Accept God's forgiveness and don't go fishing for past deeds in your memory! Nothing is too great for God to forgive, no one too far for His hand to reach out and reclaim.

"Occasionally, a veteran will come to me and say, 'But you don't know what I did,' " says Rev. Steer. "Obviously, the enormity of the deed causes them to think what they did would be impossible for God to forgive. I inform them that they're making the Son [of God] awfully small if they think their sin is greater than Him."

According to scripture, Jesus died for the sins of all humanity—that debt has been paid. This is one of the great mysteries of faith.

Compare it to the indebtedness of having a huge debt at the bank. One day you go into the bank and say, "I want to pay on my debt," but the teller announces to you, "Your debt has already been paid." Think of how you would feel—the disbelief, the relief, the surprise, the freedom to walk out into the world and say, "My debt has been paid!"

"I have paid the price to set you free," says the Lord (Isa. 44:22, TLB).

Some veterans say they can intellectually accept the fact that God forgives, but have trouble believing because they feel no different.

Merlin Carothers, author of *Power of Praise*, writes this about feeling: "When I pray, sometimes I *feel* the presence of God's healing power and sometimes I feel absolutely nothing. The results never depend on our feelings, only on our faith, that is, our deliberate choice to believe that God is at work."27 Billy Graham claims filling [with the Holy Spirit] does not necessarily imply "feeling."28 One must *act on the fact*. Forgiveness depends on an entire surrender and an absolute faith, not emotion. Believe and trust that God's mercy includes and enfolds you.

Feeling is restored as you begin to act on that faith, especially as you relate to and help other veterans. Feeling springs from helping others and simply enjoying the quiet presence of God. It will be deep like the love and bond you felt with your brothers in 'Nam. Rely on the promises that "When someone becomes a Christian he becomes a brand new person inside. He is not the same any more. A new life has begun!" (2 Cor. 5:17, TLB). "Men can only reproduce human life, but the Holy Spirit gives new life from heaven" (John 3:6, TLB).

Again, the veteran asks: "Even if God can love me again, why do my nightmares and/or intrusive thoughts not go away?"

Weatherhead answers:

> Forgiveness restores relationship, and there is plenty of evidence of that in the Bible. At the same time . . . if clearer light on sin is granted to me, I shall still be bitterly ashamed that I ever hurt my loving Father by doing the things that I did. And although penalty is obliterated—the penalty of sin being separation from God—although I am one with Him, surely I shall still deeply regret that I ever did what I did and bear scars that can't be completely eradicated. Forgiveness does not obliterate consequences, though it alters them from resented pain to accepted discipline.[29]

FORGIVING OTHERS

One of the final steps toward purification is learning to forgive our enemies, something that seems impossible for some vets. Jane Fonda's apology for consorting with the enemy was, for many veterans, too little too late. Many are uncomfortable by the presence of Vietnamese in this country today.

After all, you were taught to hate "gooks" and think of them as nonpersons. They were the enemy who killed your friends, who used children as weapons bearers, whose women carried grenades. Once the heart and mind have been taught to hate, and kill VC!, and one's own emotions say "Retaliate!" is it any wonder those feelings still exist?

After more than six years of torture as a prisoner of war in the Hanoi Hilton, Eugene McDaniel was able to forgive his enemies. In his book, *Scars and Stripes*, Captain McDaniel tells about his response to a reporter when being asked if he was bitter about his experiences:

> With my six years in an enemy prison, I couldn't think of bitterness or the rightness or wrongness of the war that had put me there. I could think of names . . . and remembering [these men] did not bring bitterness. I saw men who cared for each other, nursed each other, took risks for each other, gave up their food for each other, and devised ways to keep hope alive in each other. I could only remember men whom I had been bound to by blood; men whose wounds I had swabbed; men who had fed me, washed me, shaved me; men who became locked with my spirit; men whose hands I held onto in our mutual pain. Six years could heap a lot of bitterness on someone for the loss of all that time, but all I could remember was the human dimension, which rose to glorious heights. And God. How could I ever look back at those years in bitterness for what Christ had done for me in suffering?[30]

God haunts us with the nagging notion that we are impure until we learn to forgive our enemies. An unforgiving spirit is like poison in one's soul. The one who cannot forgive suffers more than those against whom revenge is desired. At the heart of an unforgiving spirit is pride and an unwillingness to let go of anger. To forgive, one must do that which we resist with a passion: humbling ourselves. An unforgiving spirit is contrary to the spirit of Christ and the opposite of love.

"The only way to get rid of bitterness is to surrender it," says Corrie ten Boom, whose family members were murdered in German concentration camps. "Forgiveness is not an emotion. Forgiveness is an act of the will, and the will can function regardless of the temperature of the heart.[31] He who cannot forgive others breaks the bridge over which he must pass, for every man has the need to be forgiven."[32]

If for no other reason, it is in our own self-interest to forgive others. Fear, hate, and rage are destructive emotions. To counteract these negative emotions requires developing within our lives the healing and life-giving emotions such as trust, faith, and love.

OTHERS WHO HAVE STOOD WHERE YOU STAND

Many persons tend to think that Biblical characters were perfect individuals who lived perfect lives. Nothing could be further from the truth. Closer scrutiny of the Bible stories dispels those myths and reveals the humanity of those about whom we read.

For example, Moses—the very person through whom God chose to reveal the Ten Commandments—killed a man (Exod. 2:11–15). When he saw an Egyptian beating a Hebrew slave, he responded with force. As a result, the Egyptian died and Moses buried him in the sand. Though Moses acted selflessly, it was not God's will that he kill the man.

The Apostle Paul, the man most responsible for the spread of Christianity, was a relentless and cruel persecutor of early Christians before his conversion (Acts 9, Gal. 1:13). To overcome his guilt, he found it necessary to dwell, not on his former sins, but on the amazing miracle of God's mercy and divine forgiveness.

God chose ordinary men through whom to do his extraordinary work of redeeming humankind—men who had failed acting on their own strength and plans.

In his letter to the Ephesians, Paul writes from his own personal experience about the transforming power of God's love:

In the past you were spiritually dead because of your disobedience and sins. At that time you followed the world's evil way; you obeyed the ruler of the spiritual powers in space, the spirit who now controls the people who disobey God. Actually all of us were like them and lived according to our natural desires, doing whatever suited the wishes of our own bodies and minds. In our natural condition we, like everyone else, were destined to suffer God's anger.

But God's mercy is so abundant, and his love for us is so great, that while we were spiritually dead in our disobedience he brought us to life with Christ. It is by God's grace that you have been saved. In our union with Christ Jesus he raised us up with him to rule with him in the heavenly world. He did this to demonstrate for all time to come the extraordinary greatness of his grace in the love he showed us in Christ Jesus. For it is by God's grace that you have been saved through faith. It is not the result of your own efforts, but God's gift, so that no

231

one can boast about it. God has made us what we are, and in our union with Christ Jesus he has created us for a life of good deeds, which he has already prepared for us to do (Eph. 2:10, TEV).

STEPS THROUGH FORGIVENESS

- **Be open to God.** One cannot be cleansed and healed if there is no receptivity to God's spirit. Be sincere. (See II Chron. 15:2, Rev. 3:20, Ps. 91:15.)
- **Ask God to come into your heart and cleanse you.** God longs and waits for an invitation into our lives. Pray this simple prayer, "Create in me a clean heart, O God, and renew a right spirit within me" (Ps. 51:10, RSV).
- **Name the deed.** As the haunting memory of a past misdeed comes to mind, trust this to be the work of the Holy Spirit in bringing to your attention these areas of your life that need cleansing. (See Lam. 3:40–41.)
- **Acknowledge and accept responsibility for this deed.** Avoid assigning blame to others for your actions.
- **Be specific.** Avoid vague generalizations in trying to process guilt. Deal with a specific event about which you feel remorse.
- **Confess the deed and the feelings the deed engenders.** Allow the catharsis necessary to rid yourself of these emotions. Tears bring healing and wash away the hurt. (See James 5:16, I John 1:9, Ps. 32:1–5, Gal. 6:2–3.)
- **Ask God to forgive you.** "If we confess our sins he is faithful and just and will forgive us and purify us from all unrighteousness" (I John 1:9, RSV).
- **Surrender your anger, hate, guilt, shame, and anxious feelings.** Ask God to help you "let go" of these harmful emotions. (See James 4:7–10.)
- **Accept God's forgiveness.** Lack of acceptance and disbelief on our part discredits God's gift of pardon. (See Rom. 8:1, 8:30, 8:33, 3:24; John 8:36.)
- **Act on the fact.** Begin acting on the belief that you are forgiven. (See John 8:32.)
- **Reject doubts.** When a doubt enters your mind, say to yourself "I am free! My debt has been paid." Resist the devil, and he will flee from you. (See James 4:7, KJV.)

- **Make amends.** Though some wrongs can never be made right, you can vow to help others. You can become an effective channel through whom God can work to aid others in need. Once you are freed from guilt, you can begin to live a life that glorifies God. (See Mark 11:24, Heb. 12:1, 2 Cor. 5:19, Col. 1:20–21.)
- **Forgive others.** "When you stand to pray, forgive anyone against whom you have a grievance so that your heavenly Father may in turn forgive you your faults" (Mark 11:25). Hate in our hearts is deadly to the spirit. Ask God to help you forgive your enemies. It is an act of the will. God is the source of compassion and insight you will need in order to do what may seem to you an impossible task.
- **Remember God loves you and is overjoyed that you have taken these steps toward healing and reconciliation.** "God our Savior wants all men to be saved and to come to a knowledge of the truth" (I Tim. 2:4, NIV).
- **Seek the fellowship of other growing Christians.** For continued growth in your knowledge of God and rebuilding personal faith, fellowship with other Christians is essential. (See Ps. 32:8, I Cor. 8:3, I John 4:12.)
- **Seek comfort and gain insight for daily living from God's Word.** This keeps God's Spirit alive in your soul. (See I Pet. 2:2,3; Prov. 28:26.)

NINE STEPS FOR PERSONAL GROWTH

Step One: I recognize that I am powerless to heal the damage my wartime experiences have created in my life. I look to Jesus Christ for the power to make me whole.

Step Two: I will be willing to share my feelings with at least one other person to release myself from the secrecy and shame and allow my healing to begin.

Step Three: I understand the shame, guilt, and emotional distress I suffer is a consequence of my actions. I will acknowledge these feelings and seek to resolve them.

Step Four: I will choose to accept mourning as a part of the healing process as I grieve the loss of my friends and suffer the wartime memories. I will work through the different stages of grief with the help of God.

Step Five: I am willing to confess to God that I alone am accountable to Him for the things I did. I cannot hold resentment toward others who have assisted or pushed me into that decision.

Step Six: I accept responsibility for the loss of lives I caused, but I will choose to forgive myself and others and I will accept Christ's forgiveness.

Step Seven: I acknowledge that I am an important person and I am special in God's sight. With His help, I will develop a positive self-image and work toward my full potential.

Step Eight: With the help of God, I will use my experience to help other veterans still afflicted with wartime memories.

Step Nine: I acknowledge God's sovereignty and I will strive to learn His plan for my life. I will choose to continue the process of healing from my wartime experiences until that healing is complete, regardless of the pain and sorrow those memories might bring to the surface.[33]

ADDITIONAL READING

Jampolsky, Gerald G. *Good-bye to Guilt*. New York: Bantam Books, 1985.
_____. *Love Is Letting Go of Fear.* New York: Bantam Books, 1970.

Chapter 13

UNFINISHED BUSINESS AND
STEPS THROUGH GRIEF

In 1980 Chuck Schantag* felt that his whole life was coming apart: "I really questioned who I was and what my purpose was. I was absolutely lost. I had always held good-paying jobs, and here I was walking around in a three-piece suit and carrying a loaded pistol. I was a confirmed alcoholic and I didn't know why. One day, the gun was pointed at my head. I knew I had to do something about myself."

With help from Warren Edwards, Ph.D., a compassionate, skilled psychologist from the Veterans Administration Medical Center in Iowa City, Chuck was able to turn his life around. For months, he was counseled one-on-one. When Chuck was stable, Dr. Edwards referred him to a rap group of other combat vets. "It was like looking into a mirror and seeing others just like me. I began to think *maybe I'm not crazy*. I learned to cry again. Finally, I was able to stop drinking. It's no wonder we have all the suicides among vets,"

---

* Chuck Schantag was with the 1st Tank Battalion attached to the 3rd Battalion, 5th Marines, India Company.

Chuck added. "Life is stressful enough, but when you load it with addictions, its unbearable." He feels Dr. Edwards saved his life.

Throughout the years, Chuck had never forgotten another man who once saved his life—J. C. Carroll, his warrant officer. "He was the bravest man and the best leader I've ever met," Chuck said.

It was the night of January 30, 1968, during the Tet Offensive near Da Nang. "It was a night that lasted for years, he said. We were pinned down, outnumbered by a large company of NVA, and some of us were out of ammo. Our unit got separated by a stream. The NVA were taunting us, 'All Marines die tonight!'

"J. C. would hurl threats back at them. We all marveled at how he could be so brave when all of us were so scared. The next morning, we who survived the night were passing through a village when I met face-to-face with an NVA officer. We both fired at the same time, and I won. But my bullet set off a grenade, there was a white flash, and I was hit with flying shrapnel at close range."

He laughs about it now: "It blew most of my clothes off and I was covered with bleeding wounds. 'Where will I put my *one* bandage?' I wondered. (The marines issue each soldier only one bandage.) Jim Carroll picked me up, stayed with me, and loaded me on the helicopter. I learned later he then wrote a brief letter to my family informing them of my injuries, but assuring them I would survive."

Chuck began his search through friends in the military to find J. C. Carroll and thank him for saving his life. He learned that "J. C." lived in San Diego, California. His joy in finding his long lost friend resulted in a three-hour phone call. Chuck couldn't get plane tickets fast enough. In March, 1988, the two marines were reunited in California and reminisced about that fateful night in '68.

"After I saw Jim Carroll, I realized how much 'unfinished business' I was carrying around. Our reunion made me feel so good and helped me put so many things to rest that I wanted other veterans to have that same experience and good feeling," he said.

After having been frustrated by the military privacy laws, Chuck recognized the need for a Vet Locator Service. He began with just two names, and an investment of ten thousand dollars in computer equipment. In only three years, Chuck compiled a list of the names and current addresses and phone numbers of thirty thousand veterans. His list continues to grow as he makes new contacts. He provides the locator service to Vietnam veterans free of charge and will accept nothing for his services. Because he funds the system from his disability check, he feels no obligation to provide the list to any corporation or organization that may want to purchase or use the mailing list. His service finds about one out of every fifteen requests, Chuck says, and, as more names are added, he expects to get even better results. (His phone number and address are listed at the end of the chapter for those of you who wish to try to locate a friend.)

*   *   *

Dan Carothers* couldn't stop to grieve when his radio-telephone operator and friend, Alton Ellison, stepped on a land mine and was killed. Too many lives depended on Dan's command and his men needed his leadership. But Dan had been as close to Alton as any man could be. "There was no way to say good-bye to one of the best men I'd ever known," said Dan.

Alton had been at Dan's side constantly for four months, calling in air support when his men were pinned down. He was their squad's lifeline and was at great risk because of the easily spotted long radio antennae. But that never stopped the black soldier from Macon, Georgia, from doing his job. Race made little difference in battle; soldiers were brothers.

Alton's memory never left Dan's heart. It remained unfinished, unresolved grief. In the summer of 1987 Dan wrote a letter to Alton's family. The government passed Dan's letter on to his mother still living in Georgia. Two weeks after writing the letter, his phone rang. It was Alton's mother. Dan learned that before Alton went to Vietnam, his girlfriend had become pregnant, and she had given birth to a son, a son that Alton never knew he had. Alton's parents had adopted and reared the boy. Would Dan like to talk with him?

"She put Alton's son on the telephone," Dan said. "I told him as much as I could remember about his father. I told him he had a father any son could be proud of."

This experience helped Dan feel better about the past. "The ghosts are at rest and the living have taken their place," says Dan.[1]

* In 1969, Dan Carothers was with the army's 82nd Airborne Division as an E-5 Sergeant Infantry Squad Leader northwest of Saigon along the Cambodian border.

A HEALING JOURNEY

For David Roberts,* finishing "unfinished business" meant returning to Vietnam in 1989 along with seven other veterans, two therapists, and a film crew for the Public Broadcasting System filming of the documentary, *Two Decades and a Wakeup,* for use with other Vietnam veterans. David had been in the navy in 1968 on a cruiser offering fire support in Da Nang Harbor. In 1969–70 he served on river boats operating along the Cambodian border and throughout the Mekong Delta.

"I had carried a lot of guilt with me for twenty-one years. If any people on earth could hate, and have every reason in the world to hate us, it's the Vietnamese. And yet they were just wonderful to us. On the trip, when I finally realized that I had gone back to Vietnam to ask for forgiveness—and I received it—I was overwhelmed," he said.

David had been apprehensive about how he and his group would be received. "The Vietnamese, by their words and by their actions, forgave me," said David. He said he felt drawn to the children. Smiles and candy bridged the language barriers between the Vietnamese children and the American seeking to soothe his troubled soul. These children reminded him of other children who never had a chance to grow up.

David had been in therapy three years prior to the trip through a Veterans Administration mental hygiene clinic: "I recommend that anyone returning to Vietnam take part in formal therapy prior to making such a journey, for the emotional experience can be overwhelming."

Another healing aspect of the journey was the creation of new images of Vietnam today, rather than the wartime images that haunted him for twenty-one years. "The trouble is so many Vietnam veterans are out there running around thinking Vietnam is still like it was then, and that's a total myth," David said. He also worries about the hate some vets have locked deep within them. "It's so negative because nothing comes of it. It's a time for healing," he added.[2]

---

* David Roberts was PO-3 RivRon 13 & 15, RevDiv 132–153 in 1969–70.

MENDING RELATIONSHIPS

For Donald Saunders,* some of the war's unfinished business meant dealing with the broken relationships resulting from conflicts after returning from the war. When he returned from Vietnam, he was nervous and distant and his parents didn't understand him. No one could. In fact, Don says he didn't understand himself.

He was twenty in 1966 when he was drafted into the army, and left behind a young wife and baby. His battalion patrolled the DMZ and defended the fire bases: "There were a lot of professional people in my group, and it was hard for them to understand why they were drafted. One of the first casualties we had was a teacher. He was hit one day and there was 'nothing' left. He was simply gone."

Don says various mental images come to him today: "I have mental pictures of things like a helmet with a hole in it with a clump of hair, or I can remember feelings such as being so scared and constantly praying." He remembers one battle in particular because he thought it would be his last. Many in his platoon had been killed, but Don remembers that as the result of his praying a "calm" came over him—and somehow he survived.

Don's homecoming, however, was fraught with problems. His sister told him, "I'm glad you went to Vietnam, but I don't want my son to go. I don't think he could stand it." It hurt Don to hear his sister say she was glad he went to Vietnam, disregarding the peril he faced.

His temper flared easily and he didn't feel good about himself. He felt a year of his life had been taken away, he was frustrated with his marriage, and he had problems accepting authority. Eventually, his first marriage ended and he broke ties with his parents and family.

For five years he remained isolated from his family and did nothing but work and sleep. One day he became aware of what he was doing to himself. "I was a recluse, a loner," says Don. This self-realization prompted him to make some necessary changes in his life. He met Terry, a native of Peru, and remarried.

Don says Terry deserves a lot of credit for his healing. For exam-

* Donald Morgan Saunders was in the army's A Company, 1st Battalion, 11th Infantry, 5th Division from 1966 to 1968.

ple, while going through Don's things sometime after their marriage, she found pictures of his family.

"I'm going to meet your family and you're going with me," she told him one day.

"Terry is a strong-willed woman," says Don. With her encouragement and support, Don has mended the relationships with his parents and siblings, which has also helped to end his feelings of isolation.

Healing is in conflict resolution. Unreconciled differences within family relationships or between persons who were once friends can be a source of inner tension. If reconciliation occurs by reestablishing a relationship, it can ease tensions for all concerned. Some do this by being brave enough to talk through their past differences, sharing feelings and perceptions they had at the time these breakups occurred. Others do so by simply coming together, communicating only about the present, motivated by the knowledge that life is too short to allow differences to come between them forever. Some differences, however, are irreconcilable and that is a sad fact of life.

Today, Don feels good about himself. In 1987 he wrote to the government and asked for the medals that had been awarded to him. "I deserved them and I feel good about them. I'm starting to feel proud of myself," he admits.

Today, he works as a disabled veterans outreach-program specialist in Connecticut.

WHY CAN'T THEY GET ON WITH LIFE?

Psychiatrist Erle Fitz believes that eighty percent of Post-traumatic Stress Disorder is due to unresolved grief. My approach to an understanding of PTSD has been to separate the "grief" issues from the "guilt" issues and think of PTSD in terms of its being *compounded* grief. This observation stems from in-depth interviews with many veterans. Compounded grief more accurately describes that which has been repressed. This chapter is devoted to the "grief" issues. Chapter 12 focuses on the "guilt" issues.

One of the most frequent comments veterans hear—and this author has heard from civilians during the writing of this book—is the question: "Why don't Vietnam veterans just get on with their lives and put the war behind them?"

"I wish I could put it behind me," replied one vet.

Experts—and veterans—claim it's not that easy. There are several factors contributing to this difficulty. Society's attitude toward the veteran has been a major part of the problem. In a sense, their losses have been socially negated. Because we live in a death-denying society, few people understand the long-lasting dynamics of grief, especially complicated, unresolved, "impacted" grief. The grief and the guilt are like "lumps" of unprocessed emotions that keep pulling you back in time. The longer these feelings go untreated, the more powerful they become.

Counselor Janine Lenger-Gvist says veterans have described these "black" feelings to be "like a knife stabbing them," or "like anger being stuck in their chest and throat suffocating them." Many veterans say they feel old or as if they left a part of themselves in Vietnam. All of these phrases aptly describe the condition of being "stuck" in grief—of having one's emotions frozen in time. The following are some of the reasons that such repression occurred:

1) You could not allow yourself adequate time during combat conditions to mourn the loss of friends, most of whom died catastrophic or violent deaths. In civilian life, statistics say an individual experiences the death of a loved one on an average of every nine to thirteen years.[3] In battle, losses were frequent and devastating, sometimes senseless. But there was no time to mourn. You numbed emotionally to survive.

2) There was no time to work through your grief or "decompress" with other soldiers prior to coming home, unlike other wars when men came home in troop carriers. And once home, you were even more isolated.

3) Unlike other wars, you came home to a hostile, rejecting society that inflicted more psychological wounds. You were stigmatized and stereotyped by the very society that sent you to war. A deep sense of shame came over some—and the overwhelming feeling that they had been "used."

4) Few civilians could or would listen to your pain. You may have wanted to talk and needed to ventilate. Some of you did not want to talk about your feelings. Nonetheless, you were never

given permission to mourn for your friends in an atmosphere of warmth and caring support to do the necessary "grief work" these losses required.

5) Professional counselors were not familiar with PTSD; many of you who sought help were often misdiagnosed.

6) Loss of the war may have heightened your feelings that your sacrifices were meaningless.

All of these factors, and many more, contributed to the repression of the immense sorrow you bore *alone*.

A YEAR OF INCALCULABLE LOSSES

There were other losses that many of you incurred that were equally devastating as the death of your fellow soldiers. Some losses are more subtle, more intangible, but just as real and equally damaging, especially to self-esteem. Both men and women veterans experienced the following feelings:

—loss of innocence
—loss of youth
—loss of faith and trust in the larger human matrix of society
—loss of faith in government
—loss of religion and faith in God (although some found and deepened their faith)
—loss of job and education-related opportunities
—loss of sweethearts or spouses
—loss of the ability to care deeply or relate to loved ones
—loss of touch with civilian peers
—loss of the ability to experience more positive moods, an inability to have fun or enjoy life
—loss of self-esteem, self-worth, and belief in themselves as good persons.

Like most experiences in life, veterans admit, there were good times, too. The uniqueness of the war, however, turned even the good times into reasons for feeling a sense of loss. In almost all of the personal accounts of the war in books, and in almost every interview with veterans, there is mention of their closeness, "the bonding" with fellow soldiers. But some never again felt that closeness with anyone in civilian life.

Men (and women) report feeling "in touch with their powers." One veteran said, "You found you were capable of doing much more than you ever imagined you could do. This was a valuable thing." By comparison, many civilian jobs seemed unchallenging. Some enjoyed the exhilaration, even the "rush" of killing. War has its natural highs. But when nothing in civilian life compares with this heightened sense of awareness, life seems boring.

While serving, many of you held positions of authority and great responsibility at a very young age. As civilians you could not find good jobs when you returned home, adding to an erosion of self-esteem. Your military job experience meant nothing in most cases. "Many vets lost career opportunities due to the reduced educational and job-training benefits available to Vietnam veterans as compared to World War II vets,"[4] writes Aphrodite Matsakis.

SORROW AND THE INVISIBLE WOUNDS OF WAR

Think for a moment about your mental image of the soldier. Although fewer people today glamorize war, we still tend to envision the soldier as being strong, unfeeling, and invincible. Add to that your cultural conditioning. "Big boys don't cry" is the strong message we instill within boys at a very early age.

Reflect for a moment on a hostile society influenced by media stereotypes of "crazed" Vietnam veterans. Add to that parents and wives not knowing how to relate to you when you came home from combat. Some thought they should never ask questions about the war. This approach they believed would help you forget and go on with your life. Others were unwilling to listen when the soldier wanted to talk about the pain.

Consider the members and officials of churches who failed to recognize veterans' needs and fulfill the Church's role as the caring fellowship and Healing Body of Christ. Medical professionals, especially in the early seventies, were unfamiliar with symptoms of delayed stress, primarily because it hadn't been recognized as a legitimate mental disorder. Even today, few psychiatrists and psychologists are skilled in PTSD therapy.

Consider the discounting of the PTSD sufferer's pain, even among other veterans. "If it's not real for me, then it can't be real for them," think some. How easy it is to dismiss someone else's pain.

Combined, you have some of the reasons that Vietnam veterans—in fact, veterans of most wars—have had difficultly in processing unresolved grief. Vietnam veterans had not been given "permission to grieve" until The Wall was built in 1982. The veteran's inner wounds are not visible, and grief is buried. Lacking the proper support system to mourn these losses, you, along with many other veterans, may have attempted to deny the pain and go through the motions of living.

GRIEF'S CUMULATIVE EFFECT

If you are a veteran reading this, undoubtedly you have been able to relate to at least some of these feelings. But you ask, "How do I stop hurting? How do I deal with the rage I feel? Am I going crazy?"

"Keeping grief inside is the cause of the majority of the pain you feel," say John James and Frank Cherry in their book, *The Grief Recovery Handbook*. John W. James, coauthor and cofounder of the Grief Recovery Institute in Los Angeles, California, is a Vietnam veteran. According to these authors, "Over time the pain of unresolved grief is cumulative. Incomplete recovery can have a lifelong effect on a person's capacity for happiness."[5]

"Every grief experience not dealt with has a cumulative opposing effect on your aliveness and spontaneity. It's this accumulation of grief that has kept life from being the happy and joyous experience you want it to be," say James and Cherry. "Each time a loss is not concluded there is cumulative restriction on our aliveness. Life becomes something to endure; the world seems like a hostile place in which to live."[6]

"Only by identifying and resolving these issues will you be able to have a life filled with meaning and purpose, they add.[7] Otherwise, unresolved grief can last a lifetime."[8]

The hope James and Cherry bring to their readers is that recovery is possible. They offer a self-help, step-by-step program for resolving grief:

STEPS THROUGH GRIEF

Step One: Pain Must Be Acknowledged Before It Can Be Healed.

Pain buried in the subconscious doesn't go away on its own. Resolving and moving beyond loss requires three things:

1) a willingness on your part to do the "grief work" necessary;
2) other human beings who will *listen nonjudgmentally*, be supportive, and offer direction to you as you move through the stages of grief; and
3) belief in a Higher Power—God—who is the source of comfort and healing. The Psalmist assures us, "The Lord is close to those whose hearts are breaking" (Ps. 34:18, TLB).

How do you face your pain?

Step Two: Feel Your Feelings.

Nurse Judy O'Brien in Chapter 6 said her recovery involved "going back and feeling all the feelings she hadn't allowed herself to feel."

The answer to "how" we repress emotions is evident. Often it has been done in ways to obtain short-term relief for pain through the use of drugs or alcohol that momentarily deaden pain. Feelings are also consciously, sometimes unconsciously, denied; we withdraw emotionally, and push down our pain, denying it.

The answer to "why" we don't allow ourselves to feel may stem from fear of losing control. Grieving persons will often say, "If I start crying, I may never stop." Some persons greatly fear losing control by displaying bursts of strong emotion. Loss of control, however, does not occur when people acknowledge and express their emotions. Rather, loss of control occurs if feelings are suppressed and individuals lose touch with themselves and each other.[9]

We should not fear tearfulness. It's a sign of being a caring human being. Studies have shown that the average crying spell only lasts *seven* minutes. Dr. William Ramsey, author of *Crying: The Mystery of Tears*, a biochemist at the Psychiatry Research Laboratories in St. Paul–Ramsey Medical Center in St. Paul, Minnesota, believes tears help to relieve stress by ridding the body of potentially harmful stress-induced chemicals. One man told me that even six years after his son died, he has a biological need to cry occasionally. Mourning helps reduce internal pressures. God gave us the ability to cry to help wash away the pain deep within our hearts and minds.

"When you have an emotional reaction, let it be okay with you. You're finally experiencing the feelings you've been hiding for so long," say James and Cherry. [10]

We begin the necessary tasks of grieving by *allowing ourselves to feel—and that includes crying*. Not all people cry, however. A very caring, sensitive minister once told me that he never cries. He himself doesn't understand why this is true. The important thing to remember is that all persons mourn in their own ways.

Step Three: Take Time to Grieve.

By taking time to grieve, I mean allowing yourself to feel your feelings when the need arises and not perpetuating the pattern of denying those feelings.

Give yourself permission to feel the sadness and the pain when it comes, but don't dwell on it. Accept it, but don't invite it. Pain is an acceptable guest, but not a welcome long-term visitor. [11] Otherwise, prolonged or extreme sadness can deepen into severe depression.

Look at mementos, play music that brings back memories, look at pictures, or read letters. Laugh about the absurd and the ridiculous events that happened in-country as much and whenever possible; it's very therapeutic.

Step Four: Give Words to Your Sorrow and Ask for Help.

Grieving is a social process; we cannot do it alone. It requires relationships. Expressing feelings to someone who has shared a similar experience brings remarkable relief. "No matter how convinced you might be that no one can understand or help, it is imperative that you have support. While your pain is your own, you must find a fellow griever [veteran] so you can learn and recover together as partners," writes a noted source.[12] This is the value of support groups, rap groups, veterans' organizations, or a caring friend who will just *listen*. "The most effective way of dealing with stress and pressure is talking honestly and openly about what's going on in our lives. Not the facts, but the feelings. When we don't, we become the time bomb," say James and Cherry.[13] "Don't keep the feelings in."

Feel free to seek professional help. If severe depression persists too long or you begin to think about suicide, it's important to seek the aid of a trained professional. *Asking for help is not a sign of weakness, but a sign of courage.* By doing so, you are taking the first step toward gaining control of your life. A *good* counselor can lead you through the process. But no one can do your "grief work" for you—you must do it on your own. There should be no shame or stigma attached to two people sitting down and talking about troublesome thoughts and feelings. When psychology was in its infancy, some called this process "the talking cure." This description is especially appropriate here. Unless the past is brought to light, the power of the past will never be broken. Another method of giving sorrow expression is by keeping a journal. Recording uncensored thoughts and feelings is often therapeutic and can give you some sense of progression through the process. Furthermore, a journal can become very personal and a prized possession. Writing poetry, songs, or other means of creative self-expression can also give vent to feelings.

Should you tell your partner everything that happened or the things you did? It depends on your partner's personality, how good a listener he or she is, and if such things would be upsetting. Perhaps the answer is no, although there are some things you could share that will increase understanding. For example, you could explain why some things startle you and what the sounds remind you of. You can explain why it is uncomfortable for you to sit with your back unprotected or why it's not wise to touch you while you're asleep. Some partners do want to know and understand, but they need more information.

Reading books about the war such as those listed at the end of this chapter can be very helpful for both veterans and family members.

Step Five: Understand the Dynamics of Grief and Accept the Pain.

If you have decided you want to heal and have begun actively grieving past losses, especially those buried for many years, you need to know that there is more pain ahead.

Partners sometimes wonder why their spouses seem more agitated while attending rap sessions at the Vet Center. "Aren't they supposed to get better?" they ask. The answer to that question is: Yes and No. Yes, you will feel immediate relief after having talked about inner feelings. But no, your healing will not happen overnight. Talking may trigger the grief process, and then you will begin experiencing grief reactions. Just remember, the following are *normal* reactions:

First, it's important to know that grief is a *God-given*, natural, healthy, self-corrective, highly fluid process. [14] It is not an illness to be cured. Rather, it is an opportunity for growth as long as you avoid being trapped between the past that cannot be retrieved and the future yet to be planned. [15]

Second, some of the feelings associated with actively grieving loss—anger or rage, depression, guilt, and fear—are very intense. Grieving people often say they feel as if they are going crazy.

Third, grief can produce physical symptoms such as fatigue, headaches, irritability and restlessness, dizziness, palpitations, insomnia, and confusion. Some experience an inability to organize daily activities. The grieving person may be filled with self-blame, guilt, the feelings of not having done enough and of hostility toward those considered to be blameworthy. But repressed feelings also produce physical reactions and, over a long period of time, serious health problems that are far more serious and equally as frightening.

Step Six: Face Your Fears and Finish Unfinished Business.

The very nature of the war left soldiers with a tremendous sense of unfinished business. Dennis Osborne's good "hooch buddy" was critically injured and Dennis visited him in the hospital once before his friend left Vietnam. He remembers how tightly they squeezed each other's hands, never speaking, but saying it all. Dennis knew him only as "Pete." Soldiers often knew each other only by first names or nicknames and seldom knew addresses. Dennis doesn't know whether Pete is dead or alive and is trying to find him. This happens frequently. Some veterans fear learning the truth. Some find out whether friends are dead or alive only by going to The Wall in Washington, D.C.

Not knowing whether friends, husbands, or sons are dead or alive has made life difficult for those who have loved ones reported as missing in action or prisoners of war. It makes it almost impossible to bring closure to grief when the unknown never becomes known.

The stories at the beginning of this chapter give examples of how helpful it is to face your fears and wrap up unfinished business.

Step Seven: Accept Who You Are Now.

Anger is perhaps the most common of all emotions voiced by Vietnam veterans. Although much of it is justifiable, rage is disturbing and it disrupts lives when energies are consumed in harboring it. A woman veteran, in a statement signed only as "Linda," explained what finally helped her anger subside:

> There has been a huge amount of anger stored inside of me for a long time. Something happened that was outside of my control that changed who I am, how I act, how I react. Inside my head I still feel as I felt at nineteen or twenty years old, but outside I appear to be different. Why was I robbed of who I am? No one can go around constantly explaining that he or she isn't what they appear to be. That's ludicrous. But every time that difference showed up, the anger showed up. But only on the inside. The anger never came out. What good would it do? Nothing would change. No one person is at fault. So where did the anger go? It went deeper inside where no one would see it. The only problem is that anger stored inside over a period of years takes a hell of a lot of energy to keep it inside. Anger is a powerful force that keeps trying to get out. Sometimes little bits and pieces do get out, but then that creates more anger, because I showed that anger when it did absolutely no good. It becomes a vicious cycle that can tear a person up mentally, emotionally, and physically.

Someone has said that anger turned inward becomes depression. After having gone through that whole ordeal and deciding that suicide was not the answer, the only thing left was the anger and an emptiness that could only be filled with the unanswerable questions. Finally the anger and emptiness became so overwhelming that something had to change. Life and circumstances were never going to change, so I had to change the way of looking at them and at myself.

That conclusion wasn't immediately apparent. It was suggested by a caring friend that I am not the same person that I was at nineteen. Events and uncontrollable happenings have an impact in changing everyone, and no one remains in the same place intellectually or emotionally.

It took several months for it to soak in, but it did eventually. When I willingly gave up the nineteen-year-old reminiscence and accepted who I am now, the buried anger disappeared. I don't know where it went or what happened to it, but it's gone. Now I have more energy to concentrate on today. It's been a long time since I've felt this good, and it really does feel good. [16]

Step Eight: Keep the Faith.

Persons often commit suicide because they seek it as a means of ending pain; they have given up hope that the pain will ever end. Most suicidal persons can no longer project a future. Suicide has been defined as a "permanent solution to a temporary problem."

At a low point in my life, after the birth of our fourth child who was born with a serious birth defect, I was extremely depressed. I entertained thoughts of suicide and found this very frightening. I felt alone and isolated. Living in a small town, being the wife of a pastor, I believed there was no one in whom I could confide. That wasn't true, of course, but I believed it to be true. My despair could only be described as inner darkness. Life was joyless, emotionless. I had four beautiful children, a loving husband, but life just didn't seem worth living. But something held me back; I couldn't bring myself "to do it to them." Suicide leaves a bitter legacy. All pleasant memories of the deceased are forever tinged with sadness, or worse yet, vanish because of that one final memory of how one's life ended.

As the months passed, a line of scripture I learned long ago kept running through my mind: "Nothing will ever be able to separate us from the love of God . . ." (Rom. 8:39, TLB). Over and over again it came into my mind. It was like being at the end of the rope and hanging on by one slender thread. . . . I clung to that promise.

Eventually, I sought medical help and found that I had a thyroid deficiency causing the depression. Our son's birth defect was corrected surgically. But five years of depressed thinking left me with a lot of negative thought patterns. Recovery involved using positive self-talk, turning negative thoughts into more positive ones. My "inner dialogue" had to change for full recovery to occur.

Looking back at that five-year period of my life, I see it as being a mixed blessing. The lessons I learned "in the valley of despair" are real and profound. It would not be possible to identify with persons in pain today had I not gone through that experience. I also learned that the Holy Spirit—the Inner Voice—can and does reach us in whatever condition we find ourselves in. To survive and recover, I had to keep the faith and believe that God wanted me to be whole! I believe this experience prepared me for a writing ministry and I can truly say my life now, twenty-five years later, is good and full and worth living.

My pain was nothing compared to the extent of the pain of those of you who have wartime memories, but it consumed me and was enough to make me want to stop living. *Each person experiences his or her own pain one hundred percent.* I learned the important thing to remember is that God is in it with us. *God promised two things: to love us and be with us.* Jesus is the brother, the "Man of Sorrows," who understands our pain. Ultimately, healing comes from God and the life-giving forces within our spirit that undeniably keep saying—if we will only listen—"Choose life!"

Step Nine: Bring Closure to Grief.

Veteran nurse Lynda Van Devanter has confronted her trauma and worked through much of it. But for years she asked the same question: "One of the things I kept asking over and over while I was in Vietnam and after I came back was why, why, why, why? And it took all these years of work to finally understand *why* is not the question. The questions needs to be, 'now that it has happened, what am I going to do about it?'"

She still deals with a lot of anger . . . "anger at the war, anger at the destruction, anger at the loss, anger at the insanity," says Lynda:

> Sometimes you're able to finish dealing with it, put it up on a shelf, or put it behind a glass door so that you know that it is there, and then just go on with your life. I'm here now, and I was not here for everything before. I'm present and accounted for, and that's what I see as the goal—for an individual to be present and show up for life.[17]

Carol Troescher, Ed.D., lecturer and administrator of Realities of Life and Death Through Education, Inc., in DeKalb, Illinois, says that "a major loss, or thoughts about the loss, are never over. There is some sense of closure to grief, however, that comes when we can verbally admit to ourselves, and to others, that it has happened and a relationship [or experience] has ended."[18]

Completing or bringing closure to a relationship does not mean you'll have to *forget* your friends who died in Vietnam. Rather, it means having done the grief work necessary to heal an unhealed wound.

For Dan, that closure came by writing a letter.

For Linda, it came by accepting who she is today.

For Lynda, it came by no longer asking *Why?* Closure came for her by accepting the fact that some things cannot be changed, and asking herself, *What do I do now, now that it has happened?*

SOME WAYS TO HELP A GRIEVING PARTNER

It's often easy to recognize your loved one is experiencing intense pain, but it isn't always easy to know what to say or do as you stand by. These pointers may prove helpful:

- *Give your partner permission to grieve.* You do this by allowing him to cry in your presence, perhaps crying with him. Tears cleanse inner wounds. Avoid saying things like "be strong" or "put it behind you" or "I know how you feel."

- *Acknowledge the pain but remember that words aren't always necessary.* A sympathizing tear, a warm embrace, an arm around the shoulder, a squeeze of the hand convey you care.
- *Listen nonjudgmentally to your partner's thoughts and feelings.* Don't make statements such as "you shouldn't feel that way," or similar remarks. Convey warmth, not judgment.
- *Ask open-ended questions that invite discussion.* A question like "Would you like to talk about your friend and what happened to him?" shows you are interested and willing to listen.
- *Be patient and kind while your loved one grieves.* Lend your partner emotional support by conveying the feeling that you are *with* him and understand this special need to remember and feel sad.
- *Allow each other "space" in your relationship.* Your partner has a right to a degree of privacy with his or her feelings, including feelings of sadness.
- *Remember that nothing you can say will stop the pain.*
- *Understand that a new loss will trigger unresolved grief from the past.*

ADDITIONAL READING

Brende, Joel Osler and Erwin Randolph Parson. *Vietnam Veterans: The Road to Recovery.* New York: Plenum Press, 1985; Reprint ed., New York: Signet, 1986.

Handley, Robert and Jane with Pauline Neff. *The Life* Plus Program for Getting Unstuck.* New York: Rawson Associates (Macmillan Publishing Co.), 1989.

James, John W. and Frank Cherry. *The Grief Recovery Handbook: A Step-by-Step Program for Moving Beyond Loss.* New York: Harper & Row, 1988.

Books About the War:

Broyles, William, Jr. *Brothers in Arms: A Journey from War to Peace.* New York: Avon, 1987.

Caputo, Philip. *A Rumor of War.* New York: Holt, Rinehart and Winston, 1977; Reprint ed., New York: Ballantine, 1978.

Downs, Frederick. *The Killing Zone.* New York: W. W. Norton & Co., 1978; Reprint ed., New York: Berkley Books, 1983.

Goldman, Peter, and Tony Fuller. *Charlie Company: What Vietnam Did to Us.* New York: Ballantine, 1983.

Greene, Bob. *Homecoming: When the Soldiers Returned from Vietnam.* New York: Putnam, 1988.

MacPherson, Myra. *Long Time Passing: Vietnam and the Haunted Generation.* New York: Doubleday & Co., 1984; Reprint ed., New York: Signet Books, 1985.

Norman, Michael. *These Good Men: Friendships Forged From War.* New York: Crown Publishers, 1990.

Rogovin, Janice. *Let Me Tell You Where I've Been.* Jamaica Plains, Mass.: Stonybrook Press, 1989.

Terry, Wallace. *Bloods: An Oral History of the Vietnam War by Black Americans.* New York: Ballantine Books, 1984.

Webb, James. *Fields of Fire.* Englewood Cliffs, N.J.: Prentice Hall, 1978; Reprint ed., New York: Bantam Books, 1979.

To obtain a catalog of over four hundred books published about the Vietnam War, write:

Vietnam Bookstore
P.O. Box 469
Collinsville, CT 06022–0469

VETERAN LOCATOR SERVICES

Vietnam Veterans Locator
Chuck Schantag U.S.M.C.
7308 Volquardsen
Davenport, IA 52808
(319)388-9023

Tom Sutterfield
FIND-A-VET
P.O. Box 8518
Jackson, MS 39204–0518
(Write for form; must be registered to request a search.)

Veterans National Locator Service
David L. Daniels, Director
P.O. Box 136
Boomer, WV 25031

Publishes: *Vet Search USA.*

Larry Horn
Vietnam Veterans Registry
P.O. Box A
Bridgton, MA 04009
(Include a self-addressed stamped envelope.)

These are only a few of the Vet Locator services throughout the country.

Chapter 14

THE HEALING OF MEMORIES

In 1987, after seeing the movie *Platoon*, marine veteran Mike Hoskins* spent five weeks in the psychiatric ward of a VA Hospital in Washington State. His wife had found him curled up in the fetal position, his legs under his chin, a man filled with despair, wanting to die. A friend took Mike to the Vet Center where counselors immediately recommended hospitalization.

Today, Mike is the director of LZ Freedom, a combat recovery facility in Everett, Washington, where veterans can stay for an indefinite period of time. Here they get on their feet and connect with the social service agencies, the Vet Centers, or VA facilities that can provide the aid they need. LZ Freedom provides a Christian support base for veterans.

Mike's journey is not unlike that of many veterans. His story bears repeating because of God's healing presence in his life.

"I became very successful, ran two businesses and had all the amenities in life. I found the Lord in 1980," Mike said. "Despite that, I went downhill for seven years, losing my family and busi-

---

* Mike Hoskins was with the 1st Marine Division, Charlie Battery, 1st Battalion, 12th Marines, 71st Marine Division; and Golf Battery, 3rd Battalion, 12th Marines, 3rd Marine Division in artillery in 1967–68.

nesses in bankruptcy, not realizing it was Vietnam. If you would have said it was Vietnam, I would have called you a liar."

"Vietnam becomes an 'idol' in your life, a place you close off to everything. It's such a horrible experience, you can't find anything good in it. When you do that, you close off God. During the trauma, you've learned an alternate behavior which has become the 'new you.' In essence, the old person is gone and this is the new you created by that experience. And you begin to live under that onus. Rather than the Spirit controlling you," said Mike, "it [Vietnam] controls you."

Seeing *Platoon* triggered an emotional crisis. "I recognized the emotions in the movie as being still active in my life today, especially the fear. It put me in a state of shock for four days. I ceased to function. It just broke open. The fourth day, I curled up in front of our wood stove and pulled the curtain. My wife had allowed me to come back home at that time. I was making plans to die. I just didn't want to live any more," said Mike.

Mike had a friend who took him to the Vet Center. "I know that's how God uses the Vet Centers," Mike said. "My first night in the hospital, I was very confused. I didn't know where God had gone and what had happened to me. It was just someplace I had to go in order to work through this problem." During Mike's hospitalization, he says he was able to learn what was wrong with him and what he had to do to recover.

After hospitalization, Mike continued treatment for four and a half months as an outpatient at the VAMC, then had counseling at a Vet Center for more than a year. He claims much of his recovery was derived from helping other vets: "Through a series of miracles, LZ Freedom was made available to me and another individual. I came here and prayed, 'Lord, either I get well or I don't—it's up to You.' I wanted to get well and be a better person, but I knew it wasn't entirely up to me." Mike began to rely on strength other than his own:

"I began to heal by admitting it—facing the truth—which is very difficult to do. When you are at your worst, there is total darkness; as healing begins, light begins to penetrate that darkness. It was then that I and a co-worker started taking what we had learned about ourselves and sharing it with other vets. If God comforted us, we attempted to comfort them.

"I look at Vietnam now and ask, 'Was it a scourge in my life?' No. It was preparation. If I had not been there, I couldn't be doing what I am today. As I began to see this, I began to heal. There are still many things to work through, but the Lord will show me one thing at a time. Then I pray about it, and I'll stay after it, and it goes away. He heals me piece by piece. I believe He does that so I can comprehend and learn deeply each part of it. In doing so, I am able to share that knowledge.

"I turned a corner in August, 1988. . . . I felt free for the first time. 'Free' to me doesn't mean that I still don't associate with Vietnam. It's like a scar that's healed from a deep wound. I can look at it—I'll always remember the pain and the suffering—but it doesn't control me. It's this remembrance that allows me to extend empathy to other veterans. It was then the Lord set me free from those harmful emotions of anger and shame that are of the old nature." Mike says he has a deeper understanding of the "God of all comfort."

CAN GOD HEAL MEMORIES?

Jo Harris, a woman gifted in the art of Christian counseling and healing, claims our knowledge about the healing of memories is relatively new. "We've always known there is power in healing something that is happening now, and we've always known we could pray about the future," says Harris. "Our knowledge of praying about something that happened in the past is relatively new. *God can heal.* We now know *there is power in present prayer to heal past events.*" Harris has worked with Vietnam veterans in healing the emotional wounds of war. She finds that first she has to ascertain where the individual is in his or her spiritual life:

Most people who come to me have already had an experience with God. In the case of Vietnam veterans, one of the things that I find at the root of a lot of things is anger and rage at God. When that's true, the person nine times out of ten does not acknowledge this to himself. Because of the anger, it interferes with his whole relationship with God. One man said, "I really am very angry," and when he said that, the rage just came gushing out of him. "Why did He allow this [the war]?" he cried angrily. It's very helpful for them to verbalize that anger.[1]

Harris says she then prayerfully counsels the individual until he can find it in his heart to forgive God. (As pointed out in Chapter 11, much of our anger stems from faulty perceptions and images of God colored by our damaged emotions.) Harris explains what effect divine healing has on memories: "God doesn't take away the memory, but He takes away the pain and the guilt and the shame associated with the memory."

WHAT IS HEALING OF MEMORIES?

David A. Seamands, professor of pastoral ministries at Asbury Theological Seminary in Wilmore, Kentucky, claims that time alone cannot and will not heal the painful, haunting memories long buried in the subconscious mind that cause emotional and spiritual problems. He claims that the usual forms of counseling cannot be used successfully in treating torturous memories. These memories require, according to Seamands, a special kind of spiritual therapy known as *memory healing*. By definition, "healing of memories is a form of Christian counseling and prayer that focuses the healing power of the Spirit on certain types of emotional and spiritual problems. It is *one* and *only one* of such ministries, and should never be made the one and only one form, for such overemphasis leads to exaggeration and misuse," warns Seamands.[2]

He refers to the mysterious process we call memory as "the Incredible Giant," where our past is all stored in billions of brain cells.[3] In Scripture, memory is considered one of the most important aspects of both God's mind and ours.[4]

The value of counseling is obvious:

God may use another person or a group to bring about the insights we have been unable to discover on our own. Counseling is often necessary to uncover the hidden hurts, the unmet needs, and the repressed emotions which are preventing us from getting to the truth which will set us free. In many instances, there can be no true healing and spiritual growth until we are released from painful memories and unhealthy patterns which now interfere with our present attitudes and behavior.[5]

A time of special healing prayer with the counselor is essential to the process of healing of memories.

Seamands explains the methods he uses:

So that the Holy Spirit may actually touch the barriers to health, a full use is made of conversational prayer with emphasis on visualization, imagination, the pinpointing in time of the specific situation which produced the painful memory, and a deeply empathetic faith on the part of the praying partner. During this special prayer, we allow the Spirit to take us back in time to the actual experience and to walk through those painful memories with us. It is then, through the use of our sanctified [indwelling of the Holy Spirit] imaginations, that we pray as if we were actually there at the time it took place, allowing God to minister to us in the manner we needed at that time.

This prayer time is the very heart of the healing of memories. It is in prayer that the healing miracle begins; without it, the whole process may simply be a form of autosuggestion, catharsis, or feeling therapy. This special time of prayer cannot be bypassed, if there are to be lasting results. . . . [T]he Holy Spirit becomes our Counselor who clarifies the content and purifies the motives of the prayer itself. . . . Then, during the time of prayer, the Spirit peels away that layer and opens us up to deeper levels of our own minds and helps us to *discover what the real issue is.*[6]

BUILT-IN PROTECTION SYSTEMS

Seamands sheds light on why we bury or repress certain memories. "God in His mercy has provided a kind of mental and emotional fuse which simply blows itself when the circuits get overloaded," he says in his book, *Healing of Memories.* Accident victims, he points out, almost never remember the moment of impact:

Time by itself does not and cannot heal those memories so painful that the person's mind cannot tolerate them. The evidence shows that such experiences are as alive and as painful ten or twenty years later as they were ten or twenty minutes after they were pushed out of consciousness. What cannot be faced and borne is denied.[7]

Unhealed memories have destructive results. "The most destructive result of repressed and unhealed memories is the way in which they have distorted our perceptions and pushed us into the wrong techniques of coping with life," says Seamands.[8]

"When painful memories have not been faced, healed, and integrated into life, they often break through defenses and interfere with normal living. *One of the evidences of this is recurring mental pictures, scenes, or dreams which bring disturbance and disruption to the emotional and spiritual life.*[9]

"When people have never faced their painful memories or been loosened (unbound) from them, they are still *hung up at a certain age and stage of their development,*" he adds.[10]

GOD IS IN OUR PAIN WITH US

As Jesus Christ moved among men and women healing them during his earthly life, the very fact that faith is alive today in the hearts and minds of people the world over testifies to his unseen presence today. Through the work of the Holy Spirit, He "bears our griefs"; and with that same Spirit, He can heal us.

Jesus Christ is our eternal contemporary, the Lord of time and our healer; and His Holy Spirit is our present and available helper. . . . Christ "walks back into time" in order to minister to some hurting person, writes Seamands.[11]

Agnes Sanford, author of *The Healing Gifts of the Spirit*, says, ". . . the actual deep therapy of the Holy Spirit is not done by us at all but by Him. And it is done through the union of two souls."[12] She contrasts divine healing with psychotherapy:

In psychotherapy the doctor makes the patient relive his past life, often with pain and with many tears, over a period of months. In the healing of memories the one who prays relives it for him in the Holy Spirit of Jesus Christ, with a pain that is brief because the Lord turns it into peace, and possibly with tears of compassion but not of heartbreak. And, since the Spirit transcends time, there is no need for months of beating one's breast and reliving old sorrows.[13]

Seldom do we heal without the aid of other people in our lives. It should be said, however, that another person cannot give what only God can give—and that is healing.

In the interviews with veterans, chaplains, psychologists, counselors, and the many others who work with veterans, there has been the recurring admission of a need to deal with the moral and spiritual pain these men feel. Something is missing. The approach that Scamands is offering in his excellent book can help tap a vital Source of Healing—the supernatural power of God. This approach can set in motion those attitudes and energies that activate the God-given life force and psychological principles necessary to heal the heart and mind and soul.

With his permission, I have quoted extensively from Seamand's *Healing of Memories* to acquaint the veteran, members of the multidisciplinary team, and clergypersons with this approach. This brief introduction, however, is not sufficient. I would encourage the veteran to read the book to gain self-understanding. Counselors and the clergy so inclined may read it to learn the "how-to" approach to counseling. Counselors, says Seamands, become the *temporary assistants* through whom God works to accomplish healing.

Another author, Floyd McClung, Jr., in his book, *The Father Heart of God*, points out that God's purpose for healing is not only to free an individual from past wounds, but to set him free for growth. He says this about healing:

> If we are wounded, we should be careful not to put our focus on people as the *source* of healing in our lives. People cannot give what only God can give. *If you want people to heal you, you will easily be disappointed.* Get your attention on the heavenly Father; He is the only one capable of totally healing you. He will often do that *through people*, but He is the source and people are the channel.

> Emotional healing is almost always a process. It takes time. There is an important reason for this: *Our Heavenly Father does not merely want to free us from the pain of past wounds.* He also desires to bring us into maturity, both spiritually and emotionally. This takes time and right choices. He loves us enough to take the months and years necessary to not only heal our wounds but also build our character.

> Without growth of character we will get wounded again. We will commit foolish, selfish acts that will hurt or provoke other people to hurt us. Because God loves us, He waits for us to want this kind of character growth; He waits for us to be ready to be healed. Often our right responses to other people release healing in our own lives.[14]

A NEW LOOK AT DREAMS

Dream interpretation is becoming one of America's favorite pastimes. Throughout the history of Christianity, however, dreams have been considered a means by which God talked to His people. For the veteran, dreams and nightmares are haunting, fear-filled experiences robbing them of sleep and peace of mind. Is God speaking to the veteran through his troublesome dreams? Psychologist, Episcopalian priest, and author Morton Kelsey has done extensive research into this subject. In the introduction to his book, *Dreams: A Way to Listen to God,* he describes them as the " 'shows' that take place within our psyches each night." Kelsey comments on war dreams:

> People frequently dream about war. These dreams are commonly regarded as signifying fear of war or recalling experiences about war. This hypothesis is usually incorrect, for most war dreams indicate that the dreamer is fighting an inner enemy. . . . I have often spoken with many young people who have dreamed they were in Vietnam. They often experienced an attack or were taken prisoner. These dreams almost always had the same meaning; a destructive power was at work in these people holding them prisoner.

> The dream brings us into contact with problems in our unconscious, specifically with problems that need to be explained and worked out.[15]

Dr. Joel Brende, in giving therapy to Vietnam vets, has learned that post-traumatic dreams have unique characteristics that are different from dreams of persons who have typical traumatic experiences. He explains: "In my experience, including what I have learned in working with Vietnam veteran patients, repressed or 'split-off' traumatic memories will become accessible gradually during therapy—and this is often and only when patients began having either fragments of dreams, or entire dreams of the traumatic experience." And he adds, "It is true that post-traumatic dreams also provide information about internalized post-traumatic personality fragments representing parts of the self."[16]

Dr. Brende has found that hypnotherapy, when done in a caring way and properly timed in the therapy process, can be a useful tool in resolving painful traumatic memories. In the initial phase of psychotherapy, he says he finds it useful in helping control anxiety and symptoms [nightmares, physical symptoms]; this is aided by the veteran's learning self-hypnotic and meditative techniques as well. Brende writes in his chapter, "The Use of Hypnosis in Post-Traumatic Conditions," which appears in *Post-Traumatic Stress Disorder and the War Veteran Patient*, that hypnosis can also be useful as a means of building trust [with the therapist and/or group] and as a supportive technique. He gives this example of hypnotic suggestions used with a Vietnam veteran who suffered from chronic, severe shoulder and back pain:

> I would like to have you relax and imagine that I and the other veterans in your therapy group are all helping you with the burden that you are carrying. It's been there ever since you've returned from Vietnam and has contributed to all the pain that you are feeling in your back and shoulders. Imagine that we are right here with you now, helping you hold up the burden. As you let us share that burden with you, it will be easier for you in the future to talk about what is bothering you and to share your feelings with us.[17]

Dr. Brende says that the veteran temporarily experienced relief from pain, but more importantly felt increased support from his therapist and fellow group members. It also became easier for him to talk about emotionally charged combat experiences. Within a short time (during one of the group therapy sessions) he was able to grieve the loss of buddies who had died in Vietnam.

Hypnosis is also used, says Dr. Brende, as an abreactive technique that gives expression to the emotions of fear, guilt, and grief stored in the unconscious mind. The ultimate goal is to use it as an integrative technique during which the identity splits—the "killer-self" and the "victim-self"—are worked through and the veteran is successfully able to integrate these identities into his present personality with some acceptance.[18]

WHAT IS A DREAM?

John A. Sanford, a practicing Jungian analyst, Episcopal priest, and author of *Dreams: God's Forgotten Language*, tells us what a dream is:

> The dream is a spontaneous product of the unconscious psyche. It has the function of maintaining the psychic balance and of furthering the growth of the individual. The language of the dream seems obscure because it is not the language of the conscious mind. The dream does not speak in scientific, rational terms, but uses the language of symbol, of myth, and of parable, and expresses itself through something that resembles an inner drama, a sketch, or a cartoon. . . . [T]he unconscious realm contains within itself a certain intelligence of its own. . . .
>
> The unconscious realm which contains the refuse of our lives also contains the image of heavenly realities. Besides the effect of the past it also contains the image of the future. In spite of the chaotic multiplicity of varying tendencies, it also contains the image of wholeness and a tendency to work for the completeness of the personality. [19]

It is this "image of the future" aspect of the dream that can be helpful for the veteran. Far too often, we fail to see any good from these frightening phenomenona of the mind. Sanford lifts up for us a new and positive purpose and function for the dream:

> In our unconscious inner world we find higher and lower, heaven and hell, spirit and matter, combined in a paradoxical unity. . . . The dream expresses all of these varying aspects of unconscious psychic reality. It reveals through its sequence of images a kind of purposiveness at work which can only be described as religious, since it seeks to relate man to life and to his wholeness. When consciousness is at war with what is unconscious, when there is conflict because these two points of view have separated too far, then there is discord in the personality. But when the conscious and unconscious points of view are brought closer together, and a relationship or harmony is established, then there emerges a possibility for the wholeness which God has destined for each man. [20]

Sanford warns, "The man who hopes to deal with the things of God without dealing with his own dirty laundry is doomed to failure."[21] The author is referring, of course, to working through the guilt and grief causing the inner turmoil. I would highly recommend this book for your reading to gain new perspective and understanding of this God-given function of the human mind.

Kelsey claims he knows of no better way to achieve confrontation with God than through the dream:

> Those who take their dreams seriously often find that they are led into a deeper understanding of the spiritual world. As they bring the dreams before their inner center in meditation they often find insights into their lives and a way to come closer to their meaning, to their God. The dream, properly understood, can lead us in our inner quest because the dream reveals a part of reality that He has created. God has created the physical world and the spiritual one. God gives us the dream as one way of discovering the nature of that world and our kinship with it.

> Knowing something with the head is quite different from knowing something with the heart, knowing through experience. The latter kind of knowing gives certainty and knowledge.

> As we seriously consider our dreams, most of us can come to a relationship with the Dreamer within, the One who gives us the dream.[22]

HEALING VISIONS

Modern psychology and popular practitioners such as Bernie Siegel, M.D., author of *Love, Medicine and Miracles*, and Carl and Stephanie Simonton, authors of *Getting Well Again*, affirm the truths that have been practiced, in some degree, by people of faith for centuries. Dr. Carl Simonton uses guided imagery with his cancer patients to help them in their fight against invading cancer cells. Their successes have taught us that a positive attitude plays a significant role in recovery, and sometimes cure. *How we think and what we think—especially about ourselves—can have dramatic results in healing the body.* This is even more true for healing the mind: A change in the belief system can be used to bring healing.

A person lacking self-esteem says negative things *about himself to himself*—things like, "I'm no good" or "I can't do anything." A person who is depressed says depressing things to himself, such as, "Things are never going to be any better" or "Life isn't worth living." This *self-talk* perpetuates a negative self-image and a negative outlook on life. When we keep feeding these negative thoughts into our subconscious day in and day out, our minds accepts this as truth. After all, you've said it time after time, so it must be true. We literally do become "our own worst enemy."

Change the inner dialogue and you have a changed person. I know; I've experienced that happening in my own life. One method of changing "inner dialogue" is with an exercise called "guided or healing imagery."

Images fill our minds. We have an image of ourselves, our lover, our parent, our child, our future. The Scriptures are filled with images. Jesus gave us an image of heaven by saying, "In my Father's house are many mansions." Jesus is portrayed as the "Good Shepherd." The 23rd Psalm, probably the most often-repeated psalm of comfort in Christendom, is filled with imagery. "He maketh me to lie down in green pastures" portrays an image of one being implored by the Lord in the midst of fear and distress, to come and lie down in a place of great beauty where he can replenish his own inner strengths. To heal means *to make whole*, and that is always the intent of God—to make us whole. Scripture passages illustrate one example of healing imagery. But guided imagery is a technique anyone can find.

"Guided imagery" are exercises in using one's imagination to create new, healing images with the mind in a relaxed state so that the new messages and new healing images can replace the old, damaging, stale thoughts that have been dragging you down. The use of the tapes listed at the end of this chapter is perhaps one of the most readily available self-help tools you can find.

Psychotherapist Diana Keck defines guided imagery as a "process of creating symbols and images, while deeply relaxed, to enable the changes you want to make in your life. Engaging a powerful capacity of your mind, images can be used to facilitate deep relaxation itself, as well as creating the conditions for health and wholeness. Modern medical and scientific research is now confirming what has been known in the intuitive wisdom of the ages—*the images you hold in your mind are lived out in your body.* Guided imagery is a powerful process by which you can take charge of your life."[23]

Three things are important to remember: Be confident that when your subconscious mind accepts an idea, it immediately begins to execute it. It uses all its mighty resources to that end and mobilizes all the mental and spiritual laws of your deeper mind. This law is true for good or bad ideas. Consequently, if you use it negatively, it brings trouble, failure, and confusion. When you use it constructively, it brings guidance, freedom, and peace of mind.[21]

Second, a mistake one can make is using too much effort, or trying too hard. "Your subconscious mind does not respond to coercion; it responds to your faith or conscious mind acceptance," says Dr. Joseph Murphy, author of *The Power of the Subconscious Mind*.[24]

Third, a "once only" attempt won't do it. The mind is like the body; it needs nourishing food on a regular basis.

MANY DOORS TO HEALING

As veterans have shared their stories with me, it has been encouraging to discover that there are many approaches to healing.

Dennis Osborne, whose memories of Hill 875 are recorded in Chapter 3, said it was helpful for him to go back in time to those painful memories on the Hill and develop a new perception of himself and his role there. He helped save many lives on the many medevac flights his crew made. Being able to perceive himself in this new light has been healing. He says he found the audiocassette, *Vietnam Veteran: Let the Healing Begin* extremely helpful in rebuilding self-esteem and planting affirming thoughts in his mind. He uses the tape daily. One simply cannot expect the spiritual therapies to work without putting them into practice. This tape is free to Vietnam veterans. The address where you can obtain it is listed at the end of this chapter.

A noted psychiatrist, Dr. George G. Ritchie, said, "If a person does not like the way he feels, he has the power to change it." The feeling in the person changes as soon as he changes his thinking. When a person's feelings are changed, his perceptions change and, through the changing of perceptions, his realities will become different. St. Paul said, "God has not given us the spirit of fear but of power and of love and of a sound mind" (2 Tim. 1:7, NKJV).

The power of God is within you to change the way you feel, to change your outlook, and to change your physical and spiritual condition.[25]

HEALING COMES FROM HELPING

Healing one's self often comes through helping others.

Despite the "craziness" of the war and the killing, some soldiers continued to care and express concern for the Vietnamese people even during the fighting. That same concern continues today in the many humanitarian projects veterans are sponsoring and funding. The following are only a few of the emerging waves of veterans' movements for peace and healing. Healing one's self often comes through helping others.

In 1989, a delegation of six marine vets led by Gene Spanos from Rosemont, Illinois, went back to Vietnam to defuse a live mine field that was claiming lives and maiming Vietnamese to this day.[26]

Veteran William Kimball, founder and president of Vets with a Mission, based in South Lake Tahoe, California, organizes groups of veterans for return trips to Vietnam. "It's a place that I don't think you could ever really leave behind. You're seeing the first trickle of a flood that's going to take place in the next few years. You're not really going to find a true healing and a true reconciliation until we're able to face our former foe and to shake hands and to find a mutual understanding," said Kimball.[27]

Some of the projects Vets with a Mission funds and supports include: finding sponsors for poor children, delivering five thousand Bibles, building a Christian day-care center for children, and constructing an orthopedic ward for 350 polio orphans in Ho Chi Minh City. The Bibles were the first allowed back into the country by the Vietnamese government. "Everywhere we went, we were received with warmth and kindness because the people knew that we had not just come as tourists or curiosity seekers but as men with a heartfelt burden to show the love of God to the Vietnamese people," said Kimball.

He adds, "We set up a sponsorship program to help raise funds for these precious little children who have so little and yet are some of the most loving and joyful kids I've ever met. It was a real tearjerker to see grown men bawling their eyes out when they saw how little these children have."[28]

Conditions are worse in Vietnam than they were twenty years ago, say veterans. The inflation rate is one thousand percent. Famine plagues the North and the country has three hundred thousand disabled and sixty thousand amputees.[29]

Ralph Timperi, assistant public health commissioner of Massachusetts, says, "It's Vietnam veterans who are taking the leadership to get our country to recognize the terrible loss the Vietnamese have suffered.

"By returning and working with the people as friends rather than enemies, we can do the kind of work we thought we were doing to begin with," Timperi said. "We thought we were doing something good when we were in the war. It turned out we weren't. By returning and doing what, in our idealistic framework, we see as what Americans ought to be doing, helps us find ourselves again."[30]

A group called Veterans-Vietnam Restoration Project broke ground in early 1989 for a ten-room health clinic to be built in Vung Tau in southern Vietnam. Veterans Ruben Gomez and Gordon Smith participated along with Vietnamese medical official Dr. Nguyen van Rep, in the ceremony during which the veterans said they hoped "to deliver an olive branch of peace to the people of Vietnam. It is hoped the group's efforts may soften the hard edge of American policies toward Vietnam, and eventually lead to a better understanding and improved relationship." A dozen veterans spent about ten weeks using their skills as electricians, carpenters, and architects to build the facility that may cost as much as $100,000.[31]

Veteran Heads World Vision

Former Marine Captain Bob Seiple once flew bombers in Vietnam; now he is president of World Vision, America's largest Christian relief agency. World Vision is sending equipment and materials for making artificial limbs to aid five thousand amputees in Vietnam. The agency had been forced to leave in 1975 along with other American agencies. Now Seiple finds more openness as church leaders are allowed to deal openly and oversee operations for World Vision in Vietnam. This was made possible through the efforts of

Gen. John W. Vessey, Jr., retired Chairman of the Joint Chiefs of Staff who went as a presidential envoy in search of servicemen still missing in action.

Columnist Mike McManus asked Seiple if his actions were triggered by guilt. His answer may surprise you: "None of this is generated by guilt. I did not feel guilt in going as a marine. I went out of a sense of duty to a government which had given me everything I needed, like a relatively free education at an Ivy League school. Going was the first thing that I had been asked to do in return.

"It was not a moral issue. I didn't think I would find morality in war. But now I also feel a sense of duty. The person making the call is a little higher—God, as opposed to the U.S. government," said Seiple.[32]

Making Limbs for El Salvadorans Heals Vet

Former marine David Evans, a double amputee from Elkview, West Virginia, designs and makes artificial limbs for war victims in El Salvador under the auspices of the University of California at Los Angeles.

"Looking back, the war in Vietnam was an educational experience for me, but the cost of tuition was very high. I hope others never have this experience. Sometimes I think the war took my soul, and my work in Salvador is one way I can get it back," said Evans.

When offered the job to make prosthetics for El Salvadorans, he gave up a job that paid twice as much and was thrilled at the opportunity. Evans is an activist and speaks out against U.S. backing in Central America. He also raises funds for *Medical Aid for El Salvador.*[33]

Vets-to-Vets Delegation to USSR

David Evans was also a member of one of two teams organized by Earthstewards, a peace organization based in Bainbridge Island, Washington, that went to Russia during the fall of 1988 to help Russian "Afghansy" soldiers. Earthstewards conducts exchange programs with the Soviet Union and other countries. The Vets-to-Vets

271

two-week trip was heavily financed by the Foundation for Social Innovations, an independent Soviet organization. The delegation was comprised of a team of psychologists who are specialists in PTSD: an orthopedic surgeon, the prosthetics team, and other veterans who could afford the trip.

Russian soldiers returning from Afghanistan are experiencing much the same pain and rejection as did Vietnam veterans. Psychologist Shad Meshad, member of the team and executive director of the Vietnam Veterans Aid Foundation in El Segundo, California, explained the similarities:

> Ours was a different war, in a different country, in different circumstances politically, but what it did to us and what Afghanistan did to these men was the same. The same anger is there, in us and in them. The same residue from the stress of combat is there. They have the same difficulties—though they are just beginning to see them—in adjusting to civilian life. Similarities I expected, but the psychological impact was very nearly identical.[34]

The prosthetics team conducted demonstration fittings of temporary above- and below-knee prostheses at hospitals and clinics and shared information regarding mobility aids. The team was invited back to Russia for a second time March 25–April 1, 1989, to share an exchange of information on below-the-knee prostheses with Armenian earthquake victims. Isolated from Western technology for a number of years, Russians are eager to learn about the use of newer plastics, rubber, and vacuum systems, says Evans.[35]

The deep bonds established while talking with Russian soldiers and family members, especially mothers, was unforgettable. Steve Lohning, a member of the delegation from Missoula, Montana, summed it up this way: "We didn't understand each other's language, but the bonding and closeness among men was as great as I've ever experienced. The personal exchange made war less thinkable. I can kill a Commie, but it's hard to shoot Igor and Sergeyev."

"The planet is just too damn small to keep telling our children old lies," said Greg Burnham, another member of the team from Missoula, Montana. "If some politician says, 'The Russians are coming! The Russians are coming!' I'll say great, they can stay at my house."[36]

Veterans Assist Cambodian Tribal Orphans

They call themselves the Freedom Corps. Trav O'Hearn from Springfield, Illinois, is one of five veterans who live and work among the Nung tribesmen, postwar orphan refugees from Cambodia, now living in the Philippines.

The Nungs, a Cambodian tribe of mixed ancestry (half Chinese, half French), a result of ninety-eight years of colonization of the region by the French, once numbered almost seventy thousand persons.

From 1975 to 1979 during the "killing fields" in Cambodia, the Khmer Rouge (Communists) slaughtered most of the special people known as the Nungs. Approximately sixty-nine thousand either perished or just simply disappeared. All that remain are 829 orphaned children and a sprinkling of adults. With the leadership and assistance of O'Hearn and the Freedom Corps, the remaining orphan children and adults resettled in the Philippines in 1981.

O'Hearn and fellow (MAAG-SOG) members—Marty Flynn, Mike Ryan, Jay Stoner, and John Torrey (Eric LaForte, one of the original six, is now deceased)—had seen the devastating effects of Communism and consider their volunteer project a challenge to the failures of worldwide Communism.[37]

Voices Inc.

In the late seventies, five veterans in southern Illinois incorporated an agency that would help vets get jobs. Today, Voices Inc. serves as a model program. Bob Fowler, Director of Voices, based in Granite City, operates a low-budget agency with two full-time workers, four work-study students from Southern Illinois University, Belleville Area College, and summer youth workers paid for by JTPA.

The secret of the agency's success is having veterans ready for job placement. "We begin by having the veteran fill out a No. SF-171 application for federal employment," says Fowler. "He's one step ahead of other applicants by having done this. We assist veterans in writing and typing a resumé, and also have them fill out a CMS 100 application for state employment. We've placed as many as fifty workers at one time, and approximately 450 a year." Several large companies in the St. Louis area notify Fowler in advance of job openings.

Another secret to the agency's success is the "job match" computer program, part of a complete veterans' tracking program. Six thousand veterans are on file at the center. When the agency is notified of openings for truck drivers, for example, Fowler simply goes to the computer and checks to see which vets list this as a job skill.

Fowler and his staff also offer the veteran support and encouragement. Office equipment is made available to the vet so he can type an application or resumé. A toll-free number is open to Illinois vets. Grateful vets who benefited from the program are now in a position to hire and help other veterans get jobs. Fowler has no end to the list of ways and ideas of how he can enhance and enlarge the program. In the future, he hopes other veterans can benefit from similar programs throughout the country.[38]

* * *

These are just a few of the many programs and unique contributions to world peace and humanitarian aid that Vietnam veterans are involved in. They truly have become the "wounded healers"* of our time.

ADDITIONAL READING

Egendorf, Arthur. *Healing from the War.* Boston: Shambhala, 1986.

Evans, W. Glyn. *Practicing Peace: Spiritual Exercises That Heal.* Grand Rapids, Mich.: Daybreak Books, 1987.

Helle, Roger, as told to Ezra Coppin. *My War Beyond Vietnam.* Ventura, Calif.: Regal Books, 1985.

Kelsey, Morton. *Dreams: A Way to Listen to God.* New York: Paulist Press, 1978.

Larsen, Earnie. *Stage II Recovery: Life Beyond Addiction.* San Francisco: Harper & Row, 1985.

McClung, Floyd, Jr. *The Father Heart of God: God Loves You—Learn to Know His Compassionate Touch.* Eugene, Ore.: Harvest House, 1985.

---

* A concept of ministry introduced by Henri J. M. Nouven in his book *The Wounded Healer*, published by Image Books, 1972.

Peale, Norman Vincent. *Dynamic Imaging: The Powerful Way to Change Your Life*. Old Tappan, N.J.: Fleming H. Revell, 1982.

Sanford, Agnes. *The Healing Gifts of the Spirit*. San Francisco: Harper & Row, 1966.

Sanford, John A. *Dreams: God's Forgotten Language*. New York: Harper & Row, 1968.

_____. *Healing and Wholeness*. Mahwah, N.J.: Paulist Press, 1977.

Seamands, David A. *Healing of Memories*. Wheaton, Ill.: Victor Books, 1985.

_____. *Healing for Damaged Emotions*. Wheaton, Ill.: Victor Books, 1981.

Siegel, Bernie S. *Love, Medicine and Miracles*. New York: Harper & Row, 1986. (More for those suffering illnesses but good reading for anyone.)

Wuellner, Flora Slosson. *Healing Prayer and Our Bodies*. Nashville, Tenn.: The Upper Room, 1987.

Healing Imagery Resources

Barrie Konicov has developed an audiocassette of Healing Imagery especially for veterans called:

Vietnam Veterans: Let the Healing Begin

This tape is available at no charge to Vietnam veterans. Simply state on the order form if you are eligible to receive this tape free. (Please include shipping and handling fee of $2.25.) It can be obtained by writing:

Potentials Unlimited
4808 H Broadmore S.E.
Grand Rapids, MI 49508
(616)949–7894

LuraMedia offers excellent cassette tapes of guided imagery. (Write and ask for a catalog for each of the following for pricing information.)

Journeys to Renewal
    Spiritual Renewal—Tapping Inner Resources
    Inner Peace—Finding Serenity Within
    Healing—Drawing on God's Strength

The Spirit Series

Energy of Creation	Treehouse
Soul Room	Like a River
The Gift	Go in Peace
Journey on the Wind	Wings of the Wind

LuraMedia Books & Tapes
10227 Autumnview Lane
P.O. Box 261668
San Diego, CA 92126–0998

To order call toll free 1–800–FOR–LURA
(In California, call collect 1–619–578–1948)

More About Dreams

John Sanford, on cassettes, explains that our souls need constant attention. Our dreams articulate what kind of attention we need. Created for self-help tools, *Dreams: Your Royal Road to Healing* and *The Path to Wholeness*, are two sets of cassettes available from:

Credence Cassettes
P.O. Box 414291
Kansas City, MO 64141
To order call toll free 1–800–333–7373

Diana Keck, M.A., a psychotherapist on the faculty of Boulder College in Colorado, lectures through the U.S. and Canada and has used Guided Imagery in her practice for many years.

Topics in her series helpful for veterans are:

New Beginnings
Healing the Emotions
Awakening the Healer Within
Letting Go of Stress
On Becoming a Whole Person
Dream Recall
The Healing Light
Footprints into the Self

These audiocassette tapes are $9.95 each and can be ordered from:

Mountain Spirit Tapes, Inc.
616 Poplar
Boulder, CO 80302
(303)449–8412

Potentials Unlimited
4808 H Broadmore S.E.
Grand Rapids, MI 49508
(616)949–7894

Spiritual Healing

Clarence Thomson uses biblical images to heal negative emotions or reinforce positive ones. Biblical images are rooted deep within ourselves. When we hold these inspired images in our mind, we gradually heal ourselves with their power. His series, *Healing Emotions with Biblical Images*, provides effective meditation aid and works well as healing prayer for the following emotions:

Depression	Faith
Fear	Hope
Anger	Love
Guilt	Joy

These can be ordered from Credence Cassettes (address above).

PART IV

OTHER THERAPY

Chapter 15

DELAYED PARADES

Retired Marine Sergeant Major Walter Bussey* is a man who speaks with the authority of experience. He is a veteran of three wars— World War II, the Korean War, and the Vietnam War.

He summarizes the mood of our country following each of these wars:

"At the end of World War II," says Bussey, "everything was over and we knew the whole outcome. It had been a war of *national survival*. The country had banded together to support its fighting men.

"After Korea, it was a feeling of *complete relief*," he continued. "Generally, the mood was one of feeling that 'everything would be okay again.' For the soldiers who fought there, it was a feeling of 'I'm glad that's over.' Korea's climate is quite cold and GIs were glad to be out of there.

"Vietnam was totally different. Uppermost in the minds of the American people was the question, *'When is it going to end?'* There was no celebration when it was over. What was there to celebrate?"

---

* Walter E. Bussey enlisted in the marines in 1942. In Vietnam he served with the 3rd Battalion, Seventh Marines, a unit of the 7th Marines Regimental Landing Team, where he participated in Operation Starlite. He spent thirteen months at Chu Lai during which he was in seven major engagements against the Viet Cong.

Sergeant Major Bussey reflects on his own feelings about the war. He served in Vietnam during 1965–66. "Leaders were told we went to help protect the South Vietnamese from aggression and the Viet Cong. I believed in what we were doing and thought it was a noble cause," says Bussey. "I was optimistic we would get in and win the war and get out. In 1965, our men had 'taken the night' away from the VC.* I believed it would be over in seven months."

Following active duty in Vietnam, the Marine Corps assigned Bussey to the task of recruiting young men to serve in the Marine Corps with possible duty in Vietnam.

"I was perfect for the job. Who better than me?" he admits. Bussey's love for the Marine Corps was contagious. Besides, he thought the war would be over soon. After his two-year tour of recruiting ended, Bussey said, "No more." It had been his responsibility during that time to locate and notify families when a marine had been wounded or killed. "It was the most heartbreaking job I ever had," said Bussey. "I still weep for the ones who didn't make it." Not long ago, Bussey visited the traveling Vietnam Memorial Wall (a half-size replica 250-foot long and six feet high with names engraved on plexiglass panels) when it came to Tampa. Forty-nine men had been killed from his battalion in Vietnam. His eyes blurred with tears after locating five or six of his comrades. He stopped looking. He simply couldn't take it anymore. When Thanksgiving Day came, he was asked to give the family blessing. Bussey was again overcome with emotions. In his own words, he tells why:

After a few words, I started crying unashamedly and shook uncontrollably. . . . I could not go on! Everyone comforted me and said, "It's okay, we understand." What had happened is very simple—the more I thought of words to use for the blessing, the more I thought of my marines—not being here on *our* Thanksgiving Day. The sadness for *them* and especially knowing that *their families all* would be thinking just like me, _____ is not here. I can't erase those thoughts, ever!

Sergeant Major Bussey retired in 1968 after twenty-six-and-one-half years in the Marine Corps. He and his wife live in Florida.

* * *

* Because of the Viet Cong's familiarity with the jungle, much of their activity was at night; thus, they "owned the jungle" at night.

The mood of the country had a profound impact on soldiers return-ing from each of these wars. World War II vets were respected and treated as heroes. Though many were not given "Welcome Home Parades," there was a feeling of gratitude and respect for these fighting men. Korean vets came home and were welcomed with little or no fanfare. Vietnam veterans, as stated earlier, came home to hostile crowds or total apathy. Vietnam veterans for many years have been stereotyped as whiny cry babies, and worse yet, baby killers. These labels hurt. Each man went for his own reasons. The majority were volunteers who went in good faith because their country asked them to serve. Many believed they were going to help the Vietnamese people. Fortunately, these deep-seated civil-ian attitudes are slowly changing as the public is educated about the nature of war itself.

In the sixties and seventies, frequently the only persons welcom-ing a soldier home were family members, and sometimes these family welcomes were marred with tension.

* * *

Larry's welcome-home family gathering was a disaster. Forty-eight hours after leaving Vietnam, he was sitting in his living room. His mother and father were relieved and happy to have him home again. Aunts and uncles and other relatives were invited to join them for a family dinner and get-together to celebrate Larry's safe return.

Prior to and during military service, Larry* did not drink. But now he drank to forget . . . the killing, the noises, the smells, the fear. He had seen too much . . . done too much . . . to feel good about himself. He fought in one of the fiercest battles in the war— Dak To—and was among those who made their way to the summit of Hill 875 on South Vietnam's central highlands. For twenty-two days straight, soldiers fought without relief. He was one of ninety-three who survived without being injured; he was one of three survivors in a squadron of eight. Larry seemed invincible, for he had come through totally unscathed. Back home, nightmares began to torment him; bloody scenes seemed forever etched in his mem-ory and they surfaced in terrifying dreams.

As relatives gathered, Larry's anxieties increased. Perhaps wine

* Larry, who prefers to be identified only by his first name, served two tours in Vietnam— 1966–69—in the army as an airborne infantry elite combat rifleman.

would make it easier. He drank one quart, then a second, then a third. He felt no pain. In fact, he was ready to celebrate. His civilian clothes were confining, so he stripped down to his shorts and shoes and went out into the yard of his parent's modest home. Yes, he was glad to be home, he thought. Triumphantly, he shook his fist at the sky, and in a mocking voice, yelled, "You can't get me now, gooks!" A few short days before, he had been shot at in the jungles of Vietnam.

But his parents were embarrassed and made him apologize to the family. They could not understand the elation he felt at being away from wounded and dying men and flashing guns. To add to their embarrassment, he went to sleep, now drugged by the wine, leaving his parents even more angry and frustrated.

Larry felt ill at ease in his own home. All the things that he had once cared about now meant nothing. A few days later, in a burst of anger he tore up things that had meant something to the teenager who left home. But that was another life; now he wanted no part of it.

Larry's angry outbursts, cursing, drinking, and erratic behavior eventually caused his parents to order him to leave home. His relationship with his parents was strained and painful. The Larry who returned from the war was a different person from the one who left home when he enlisted at age seventeen. He was a Larry no one, not even himself, could understand.

Years later, Larry's uncle apologized to him for judging him so harshly. The uncle, a World War II vet, began reading about Vietnam, and was able to see for himself the major differences in the war. "I'm surprised any of you fellas made it back alive," he told Larry. He had been amazed that men were sent out in such small squadrons in Vietnam, unlike World War II.

CANADA'S INVISIBLE SOLDIERS

Canadian Robert White* was considered a mercenary and trained killer by his government when he returned from Vietnam in 1971. Canada's official political stand was against the war and it welcomed

* Petty Officer 3rd Class Robert White served in the U.S. Navy in Vietnam from 1969 to 1971. He is the only Canadian to serve as president of a VVA Chapter—Bluewater (Michigan) #284.

approximately fifty thousand young American men who chose to flee the United States to avoid being sent to Vietnam.

Robert had spent two years in the Canadian navy, but when the Canadian government decided to combine its forces, he was one of those released from duty. Robert had the desire to travel, so he decided to cross over into Michigan and join the U.S. Navy. More than thirty-seven thousand other Canadians volunteered to fight in the U.S. Armed Services and serve in Vietnam.

"It hurts to be considered a mercenary," said Robert. The Royal Canadian Legion refuses to acknowledge the service of Canadian Vietnam vets; thus they are prohibited from marching in parades and participating in various other functions.

He worries most about the thirty-seven thousand-plus potential PTSD sufferers who, like himself, have little or no access to treatment for PTSD. He and others, like Brian Campbell, VVA liaison to Canadian Vietnam veterans on a national level, are working to iron out the immigration problems that exist when Canadian vets come to the United States for treatment. U.S. immigration and naturalization rules deny entry into this country on the basis of poor health or disability. Immigration laws allow a Canadian citizen to be out of the country six months. "If a vet needs to be in a therapy program lasting more than six months," explains White, "the vet could be deported and never again be allowed to come to the United States. We're hoping to develop some treatment centers in bordering U.S. cities so that our men can commute. I don't expect our government to compensate us for service-related problems; we didn't fight for Canada. But our government could, however, ease immigration laws so these men can get treatment."

President Ronald Reagan signed a bill in May 1988 making it possible for Canadian veterans to apply for reimbursement for medical expenses for service-connected health problems. Prior to that, the only way a Canadian veteran could get benefits was to become a U.S. citizen, a long and lengthy process.

* * *

U.S. Army Major Dr. Robert Stretch is studying the effects of PTSD on Canadian vets. He describes the reception Canadian vets had when returning home. "Canadians essentially returned home to a void; they found neither rejection nor recognition. No one knew they had been in Vietnam, so they were ignored. They remain isolated, not even knowing each other," said Stretch.[1]

Duncan Spencer's article, "The Invisible Northern Veteran," in *Veteran* states that "the simple fact that there were no separate Canadian units, no return ceremonies in Canada, and no news stories tended to make the returnees an almost invisible group.

"That environment may have been even more damaging to the returning Canadians than the coolness or hostility met by their American counterparts." he adds. Stretch claims that sixty-five percent of Canadians suffer from PTSD as compared to 12.2 percent of U.S. servicemen. A study released in May 1989 reveals that Canadian vets are five times more inclined to have PTSD.

The ground swell of sympathy for Vietnam veterans, although slow to emerge in the United States, has not occurred in Canada. For many years, the government in Ottawa insisted that these veterans simply did not exist.[2]

BROTHERHOOD AND HEALING

Parades are being given new meaning and purpose by Vietnam veterans. In the past, a welcome-home parade for soldiers was done as a public celebration of a war's end, to recognize the heroics of a particular individual or group, as an expression of gratitude to soldiers for having served their country, or to remember a common event.

Parades planned for Vietnam veterans are done primarily to regain a lost sense of brotherhood and to promote healing. Unlike other wars, most of the marches or parades honoring Vietnam vets have stemmed from the veterans' own need to establish relationships, shed the old images, regain a sense of self-respect, and gain public recognition for their causes, such as the prisoners of war and those still missing in Southeast Asia. Most parades have been planned and paid for by veterans organizations, not for the purpose of glorifying war but for the purpose of healing wounds and regaining a sense of pride and brotherhood. Parades, though delayed, make it possible for veterans to experience the long-awaited welcome home—as individuals and as a group.

A National Salute

Retired Army Colonel Kelvin Hunter* was organizer of the first National Salute to Vietnam Veterans parade held in conjunction with the dedication of the Vietnam Veterans Memorial held in Washington in November 1982. *Marching Along Together Again* was the theme of one of Washington's largest parades. An estimated one hundred thousand marched in or watched the parade that had Vietnam veteran contingents from all fifty states and territories of the United States with the exception of the Marshall Islands.

It was a day participants will never forget. A police escort comprised of Vietnam vets led the parade. Three Gold Star Mothers were in the lead car. Led by the Coast Guard Band, twenty parade marshals, cadets from military academies, color guards, the Colonial Fife and Drum Corps, high school and military bands, five floats, 125 units and four divisions of men and women from all branches of the armed services, including those on active duty, were there.

General William Westmoreland, better known as "Westie" to his troops, marched at the head of the parade with the Alabama delegation and was welcomed warmly with loud applause and cheers by veterans. Some had wondered how he would be received. He told parade organizers he "wanted to lead his troops again."

"Though some veterans were reluctant to actually 'march' again," says Hunter, "when the Coast Guard Band began playing, it struck an emotional chord within them and they quickly fell into step and were soon chanting a cadence count."

Celebrities like football star Rocky Bleier marched. A World War I veteran joined the parade. World War II vets from American Legion and Veterans of Foreign Wars posts marched. Disabled veterans in wheelchairs were participants in the parade down Constitution Avenue. Entertainers such as Chris Noel, Red Cross workers, a platoon of nurses—all were represented. "The numbers became mind-boggling," claims Hunter, who worked for five months organizing the event in conjunction with the Vietnam Vet-

---

* U.S. Army Colonel Kelvin "K" Hunter (Retired) served in Vietnam in 1969–70 as a Battalion Commander in the 25th Division.

erans Memorial Fund project planners. The parade culminated at the Memorial Wall for the dedication ceremonies.

"One of our objectives was to begin the healing process," says Hunter. "It was a very memorable day for all. Vietnam veterans for the first time were being told, 'we love you,' and were embraced by bystanders. It was more than we ever expected. Despite the cold and wind, it was a great day for a parade. I felt so warm inside," says Hunter. He says he takes great pride in organizing this unique event—America's first parade honoring Vietnam veterans.

New Yorkers Honor Vets

In New York, some twenty-five thousand veterans marched down Broadway on May 8, 1985—ten years after the end of the war. The ticker-tape parade in lower Manhattan was held in conjunction with the dedication of New York's Vietnam Veterans Memorial.

This parade had its own heroes. A squad of former soldiers, some partially disabled, rescued eighteen persons from a burning building on the parade route. The eight veterans were returning from the dedication ceremonies when they saw flames shooting from the doorway of a three-story tenement. The fire escape was rusty and wouldn't lower, so the men pushed a refrigerator shell under the ladder. Jack DeFantis climbed on and made his way to the second floor. Another vet pulled a fire alarm box. As residents awakened and emerged from their apartments, the eight veterans formed a human chain handing down the children one by one. Glass fell from exploding windows.

The heroic action of Doug Paterson who is partially disabled, along with former marines Bill Worner, Billy Povano, Bill Hubell, and army veterans Regan Patrick, Jack DeFantis, Bill Giovanelli, and Doug Carlson saved three families. "It was three families—beautiful young families," said Doug Paterson.[3]

Chicago's Emotional Welcome Home

The Chicago parade was one of the largest gatherings held to honor Vietnam veterans. An estimated 200,000 men and women veterans from every state in the union started at Navy Pier and marched through the heart of downtown Chicago. Some believe as many as

300,000 spectators lined the streets on that balmy Friday morning, June 13, 1986.

William Mullen, staff writer for the *SUNDAY Chicago Tribune Magazine*, describes the scene:

> Office workers from Michigan Avenue began pouring out of sky-scrapers, joining the housewives, children and retirees who had come downtown early to line the route. Young women who must have been infants during the war, now in dress-for-success suits and jogging shoes, were sobbing and yelling to the veterans. Middle-aged men, eyes red-rimmed, stood in business suits transfixed by the spectacle marching past. At Michigan Avenue the veterans began craning their necks, wide-eyed in wonderment at the reception they were getting. The men marching with their old units . . . for the most part were strangers. It had been a long and widely scattered war, and it was hard to find anybody else who had served in the same company or regiment at the same time and place.

> No matter. As the spectators swelled in number and support, the veterans spontaneously began chanting old marching cadences and singing service songs that most of them likely hadn't sung in years.

> . . . Tears began to streak the battered faces of veterans who looked so hardened that they would rather die than show such emotion. Arms began to entwine in the ranks, to drape and hug shoulders. Wives marching with their men leaned into them, kissed them, adored them, while their children seemed bedazzled by it all. . . . [T]he air was a blizzard of shredded paper. It was a blizzard that would fall for five continuous hours, until the very last of the 200,000 veterans had marched down the street.[4]

Veteran Gary Geramanis* marched in the Chicago parade and to this day is tearful when he recalls a young woman who stood along the route. "She had been crying for a long time . . . you could see tear stains on her collar," said Gary. "She carried a sign that said, 'Welcome Home. I'm glad you boys made it. My father didn't.' Her sign read 'KIA' and gave her father's name and date of death. Her tears really got to a lot of guys. Several went over and hugged and kissed her.

"There were a lot of people there who had a direct bond [to

---

* Spec. 5 Gary Geramanis was with the army's 1st Aviation Brigade 212, Battalion 245, Surveillance Airplane Company (SAC), 1969–70.

veterans and Vietnam], but the whole audience was emotionally involved—they weren't just bystanders," said Gary.

Gary was nineteen when he went to Vietnam. He was a trained observer and flew on night missions taking infrared photographs and surveillance. He was based at Marble Mountain about eight miles south of Da Nang. Each night he had a dry bunk and mess-hall food. At times, he felt guilty about that. He was near the navy base and saw the wounded coming in daily from field hospitals.

For ten years, Gary put Vietnam behind him. "I don't think I consciously blocked it out of my mind; I was just too young and naive," said Gary.

"The most lingering effect my involvement in the war has had is the guilt I have felt for the things I saw and did that *didn't* bother me. Our involvement in the real war was clinical. Up in the air, you wouldn't even hear the noise or smell anything. The next day you would learn what the results were and get a body count."

It wasn't until a couple of years ago that he began to reach out and make contacts with friends who served in Vietnam. Associating with them and hearing them say the same things he was feeling helped Gary realize that maybe he was a victim and that was okay. "There came a point when I finally realized I had never dealt with it [my feelings about Vietnam]. In the parade, I just let my emotions come to the surface," he ended.

Gen. William Westmoreland was at the head of this parade also. Beside him were parade organizers Jim Patridge and Tom Stack. Soon, Bob Wieland joined them. Wieland lost both legs to his hips in Vietnam. Westmoreland was flanked by Patridge in a wheelchair and Wieland who sat on a specially tailored pad that fit the torso of his body. He propelled himself with muscular arms. With irrepressible spirit, he tauntingly said to those beside him, "If I go too fast for you fellas, let me know and I'll slow up."

Westmoreland replied, "My God, what guts . . . what guts." His eyes were brimming with tears.

Veteran Tom Stack had dreamed of organizing the event ever since the day he had returned and was called a "baby killer" by an antiwar protester in 1969. Stack had led a combat platoon in the army's 9th Infantry Division through the Mekong Delta in 1968–69. He felt too many men had gone to Vietnam, serving honorably and with valor, and too many had died to be dismissed by their own countrymen as unfortunate dupes caught up in an accident of history, collectively thought of as a bunch of baby killers and drug addicts.[5]

Tom Lewis had decided not to march in Chicago's parade. At the last minute, he decided someone should represent the family. Afterwards, he shared his feelings about having been there: "I can't express the pride I feel now. To see people on both sides of the street cheering us, well, it made me feel good, but it was good for the country to feel it, too."

Another veteran, Jim Hennigan, says he was staggered by his own reaction to the parade: "I wasn't prepared for all the things that happened back then to start unfolding again now. That was the surprise—the emotional release on all sides. If you've never been cheered by a half a million people before, you'd like to do it every Friday." [The parade was on a Friday.][6]

* * *

Similar parades have occurred throughout the country. One took place in my own community—the Quad Cities—on August 17, 1987, and my husband and I were privileged to attend. It stirred many emotions within us as well. Primarily it opened my eyes to the enormity of the pain that still lingers in the hearts of veterans and their families as an aftermath of America's most unpopular war. Families carried signs in remembrance of sons who died in Vietnam.

Thelma Brennan of Milan, Illinois, lost her two oldest sons in Vietnam, Marvin and Darwin Gordon. Both young men had enlisted at age eighteen. Thelma says military service was a way of life for her family. All six sons have served in the military; one is a career military man. She says she experienced a terrible "emptiness" when her sons died, Marvin in September 1967, Darwin in March 1968, but she says she is not bitter: "It's been a long time. The parade shows support [for the veterans] like I had from my family. That's what you always need."[7]

Robert Dryovl of Rock Island, Illinois, marched clutching a picture of his son. He approached one of three Medal of Honor recipients who led the parade. "My son, Donnie, died in 1968," he said, his voice trembling with emotion. Sgt. Major Kenny Stumpff of Ft. Sheridan, Illinois, gathered Mr. Dryovl in his arms and hugged him. "We're glad you came," he said quietly.

Alvino and Jane Pena of Davenport, Iowa, had called each of their nine children and asked them to bring their families. Aunts, uncles, cousins were all encouraged to attend the parade. "To me it was important that my family went," Alvino Pepe said. "I wanted the young children to see the parade. I wanted the chance for us as a family to unite and show those living that we are glad they came back." Jessie "Pepe" Pena was their son and a marine who died February 12, 1979, at Da Nang. He was twenty-one.[8]

Families who lost loved ones carried signs or pictures of their loved one. A large banner listed all the names of those killed in action from Rock Island County—seventy-four in all.

A man in a bamboo cage added a somber note to the parade. His aim was to remind spectators of the two thousand three hundred missing servicemen still unaccounted for.

Alice Varble of East Moline, Illinois, has a son among those missing: "We know he is dead, but we never got his body back. All I want to do is bring my son home to be buried."[9]

Joseph Payne wrote an editorial for a Davenport newspaper that appeared in *The Leader.* In it, he claims we all share the scar of the Vietnam war. He writes:

> . . . even those of us who imagine our families passed unscathed by Vietnam are mistaken. Even if not a single distant relation, neighbor, or acquaintance fought, was maimed, or killed in Vietnam, at the very least we share the national scar of the wound that divided our country.
>
> My first experience with the Vietnam War came via television, which brought it into our home night after night on the six o'clock news. Dinner and war footage seemed to go hand-in-hand, and with none of my brothers drafted, there was much less tension passed around the table with the bread and butter.
>
> That was until one evening at supper time, when the Vietnam War suddenly became real to me, suddenly became frightening, suddenly horrible. I was eight years old on that night in 1970 when death was introduced to me for the first time through my parents.
>
> Until then I had never even had to deal with the death of anyone I remotely knew, let alone that of a grandparent, parent or sibling. But that night I witnessed with coldness of death as my parents, with clutched hands and tear-filled eyes, learned that their best friends' son had been shot down somewhere over Laos. It might as well have

been my own brother, such was the closeness of my parents and these friends.

It was a frightening time, and I remember retreating upstairs because I couldn't stand to see my parents that way, and I couldn't understand the lump in my own throat.

After that day, the war and its television footage struck home in our household; when the war was over, I was left with vague memories of an unfinished funeral and a vivid picture of death—unexplainable, premature death at that.

Like the rest of the nation, I managed to forget those memories, to shove them far back onto a subconscious shelf. That is, until last weekend's veterans reunion brought them back up front again.

Though my own memories still sadden me, there were many at the parade whose losses were much greater than mine. . . .[10]

Parades for Vietnam veterans and those who still mourn the loss of young men and women who died there serve to remind us all of the oceans of tears created by that war. Parades for Vietnam veterans have aided the healing process. They help by allowing vets an opportunity to get in touch with their buried pain. These events create an atmosphere in which hugs and tears are appropriate. This public recognition helps restore pride so long denied Vietnam veterans. During a parade, men and women veterans regain the feeling of being closely bonded to their brothers and sisters with whom they served. The parades give civilians an opportunity to tell vets they're loved, that we appreciate their service to our country, even though we didn't agree with the war. Parades also allow relatives and friends to participate and remind us of those who didn't come home. Parades have helped heal the wounds of war for Vietnam veterans.

ADDITIONAL READING

Greene, Bob. *Homecoming: When the Soldiers Returned from Vietnam.* New York: G. P. Putnam's Sons, 1989.

Polner, Murray. *No Victory Parades: The Return of the Vietnam Veteran.* New York: Holt, Rinehart and Winston, 1971.

Chapter 16

THE WALL OF TEARS

Nearly every night after returning from Vietnam, Don Handley*
had nightmares during which he vividly saw the aircraft crashes he
had witnessed in Vietnam. As team leader of a crash recovery team,
his job was to attempt recovery of survivors on those flights. Many
times there was no one alive to rescue.

During the day, he had flashbacks: the twisted burning aircraft,
the trapped men's panicky screams for help—it all came back again
and again. Despite these problems, Don stayed on active duty in
the air force until 1974.

After he left military service, he found it difficult to settle down
and hold a job. The nightmares and flashbacks became so severe
that, in 1979, Don attempted suicide. He then opted for private
hospitalization rather than seeking assistance from VA hospitals.
Don had developed an intense mistrust of authority, including
Veterans Administration health care facilities. He found it difficult
to get along with anyone.

Don had married in 1970 and he and his wife had a son. They

* Capt. Don Handley served in the air force with the 366th Tactical Fighter Wing at Da
Nang. He was team leader of a Crash Recovery Team, 1968–69.

divorced in 1980, and, after a bitter custody battle in 1982, Don won custody of his son. He tells what happened then: "I saw my behavior from Post-traumatic Stress Disorder passed on to another generation. I watched my son develop the same hatred and mistrust of authority, including mine. His was also coupled with drug abuse and trouble at school including two expulsions."

But things began to change for Don in 1987, and the Vietnam Veterans Memorial Wall played a significant role in those changes.

"I started healing in October 1987," said Don, "when the Moving Wall, the traveling replica of The Wall in Washington, came to Big Spring, Texas. After seeing that, I developed an obsession to visit the memorial itself in D.C. This I did in April 1988.

"During the three days I was there, I must have cried enough to keep Constitution Garden watered for a month. But I was able to face old memories, and finally get the healing process started. It was also nice to get a measure of respect from people after twenty years of scorn and apathy.

"In the past few months, things have been going well for me," he continued. "My son entered a treatment program and is recovering. I've started a treatment program called *Combat Veterans Anonymous* offered through the Veterans Outreach Center. I don't feel as isolated. I'm getting along with people a little better. The nightmares aren't as devastating and I have started writing poetry, which helps to relieve the pressure. All in all, life is looking better."

For Don, his visit to The Wall was a turning point, and a time when healing began.

*   *   *

David Missavage* believed in what the United States was attempting to do in Vietnam—prevent the spread of Communism. His college classmate, Zoltan Cravas, had been a Hungarian freedom fighter who barely escaped the Russian invasion of his country in 1958. He told David many stories about the Communists' subjugation of his people and of fighting the Russian tanks that overran his people and their spirit.

In 1964 David visited Communist East Germany. The East Ger-

* Lt. David Missavage was with the 4th Psychological Operations Group in 1968–69 for which he was an Audience Analysis Officer for the 1st Corps Tactical Zone which included five northern provinces of South Vietnam.

man government, he noted, built a wall to keep people in rather than keep people out. He felt the mood of the people; life within those walls was drab and sullen. "This experience," says David, "made a lasting impression on me and taught me the evils of totalitarian states and Communist doctrines."

David was drafted into the army his senior year of college. Like his father some twenty years earlier, he graduated from the Officer Candidate School at Fort Benning, Georgia. In Vietnam, he was assigned to the intelligence section of the PsyOp Development Center, responsible for creating and disseminating propaganda. His work also involved working with prisoners of war in various settings, and proselytizing teams in VC-controlled areas. In other words, he tried to influence VC soldiers to defect and join ranks with the other side, and was successful in many cases.

He had more exposure to the Vietnamese than most soldiers; many befriended him, taking him into their homes. This exposure to Vietnamese families helped him better understand the issues they were fighting for: property rights, freedom of speech and worship, and free elections.

Late in 1968, David was promoted to captain but he declined the promotion. Accepting would have required three more years of active duty. It was only a matter of time before U.S. forces would start to withdraw, he thought. David had isolated himself during this tour of duty; personal relationships were given little time or attention.

He returned to the States and the family farm, married and had two daughters. The marriage ended and he felt as if his family was lost to him. A second marriage also ended in short order. In the mid-seventies, the bottom fell out of agriculture, and David left the family farm to seek employment. It was while working as a professional truck driver that he found himself one afternoon in December, 1985, witnessing the reenactment of the infamous "Three Days in July" at the Cyclorama Center in Gettysburg, Pennsylvania. In those three days, ten thousand soldiers had died during General Pickett's charge up Seminary Ridge in the Civil War. He listened for several hours to the roar of cannons, the rattle and cracking of rifles, and the cries of the wounded and dying.

David wasn't prepared for the emotions that swept over him.

Seventeen years after Vietnam, the emotion and feelings welled up and he cried for those dead and dying, and their families who would never see them again. He could not remember ever crying in the past for any of the losses he had endured, even the loss of his wives and two children and his business. He was crying for everything he had lost for the last forty-three years!

Nearly exhausted, he could not get Vietnam out of his mind. He knew he had to go to The Wall in Washington. It was only a short distance. He wanted to remember those who died in Vietnam.

His heart pounding, he approached The Wall. On that cold, crisp, quiet night in December, David felt as if he were gliding into another surreal space outside of time. He touched the reflective wall of black granite—and the names. The spirits of the fifty-eight thousand seemed to fill the arena and surround him. He enjoyed the solidness and permanence of its mass and density, not standing up in the air, but against the earth. He checked the index and located the names of his friends and roommate and took a rubbing of their names, like hundreds of thousands of visitors do each year.

Other visitors approached and David thought of all those who come to this special place with so much sorrow. Heartbroken mothers and fathers, widows, children who never knew their fathers, brothers and sisters, sweethearts, classmates, veterans from all of the country . . . as well as foreign countries. The Wall is a reminder of those young men and women who had been forgotten for over a decade. It is a reminder of the young people whose lives were disrupted and changed forever by the war.

The Wall touched David's pain. He felt himself letting go of the hurt, and he was able to leave some of it behind. He refers to this catharsis as a time of "purification." Like Don, it was a turning point for him. He says, "That day began a new life for me. The purification is not only a personal experience, but one for the whole nation. It is a monument that demands moral responsibility of all future U.S. government officials," says David. "My prayer is that no more of this nation's youth will be wasted on the whims of others [those in power]."

After returning home, David joined Vietnam Veterans of America Chapter #299 and he now serves on its board of directors. He attended a reunion of his 4th PsyOps Association the summer of

1989. Life is better for David than it was before visiting The Wall. He encourages all Vietnam veterans to make an effort to go there so that the healing, soul-purifying process can occur.

I would encourage all veterans to go to The Wall; it brings back pain, but it also brings healing.

HAVE YOU BEEN TO THE WALL?

"Have you been to The Wall?" is a common question veterans ask each other. Nonveterans also ask the same question. The Vietnam Veterans Memorial Wall has become the most frequently visited monument in Washington, D.C.

Ira Hamburg is president of the Friends of the Vietnam Veterans Memorial in Washington, a volunteer nonprofit, nonpolitical organization. Hamburg says he never ceases to be amazed: "I have seen pain expressed in every kind of way that you can imagine. Even though I have a background in psychology, I was not prepared for the experiences that confronted me at The Wall. I am in awe of the many forms of expressions of grief. Some stand transfixed before a panel of The Wall or the Statue. Some pace back and forth, which is telltale of the turbulence going on within them. Some are angry to the point of belligerence. Some are saddened and depressed. For many, it is the solemn stare and the scream of silence that announces their grief on this journey through the Memorial. All are deeply moved."

Ira Hamburg remembers one case in particular:

I was assisting a man in finding three names. All three were listed together, one after another. "There they are," he said, moving toward The Wall to trace each name with his finger. He looked at me, a smile of sorts on his face. He repeated, "There they are." Looking back to The Wall, he said, "Isn't that something" and back to me again, a slight smile still. He went on, "I sent them out." I was stunned, not by the words, but by the obvious paradox of his smile and the somberness of his verbal expression. He turned back to The Wall again. In a voice with a note of wonder, he said, "Isn't that something," as if he was amazed to see the names he knew were there.

And then came an experience that haunts me still. He laughed, loud enough for those within a few feet to hear, deep and low. A laugh, like none that I have ever heard, filled with pain and anguish. I remember I felt such pain from it. It was hard for me to realize the sound I heard was a laugh. Whatever it was, the visitors who heard it seemed as chilled by it as I was.

When he turned to me again, his eyes locked into mine, holding my gaze for what seemed to be forever. It is as if he were saying, "Come, look into my soul and see what it is that I have done." When he finally released me, his face saddened, he looked at me with compassion, perhaps recognizing the pain he was creating for me. "Thank you," he said, "for being here. God bless you." As he passed, he placed his hand on my shoulder and squeezed slightly. And he was gone.

I became aware of a hand stretched out toward me with a tissue in it. I looked and saw a woman who had apparently been a witness to this event. Tears were streaming down her face. She smiled tenderly, realizing that I was not aware of my own tears.

In time to come, many people, such as sociologists and psychologists, will try to explain the whys and wherefores of the phenomenal effects this memorial has on its visitors. When all is said and done, it may very well be that the Memorial will be *the* major sociological phenomenon of our day.[1]

"Grief can be so powerful, so overwhelming you cannot express it. I think that's something we see at The Wall," he said.

Hamburg believes The Wall is just as important to the nonveteran as it is to the veterans of that war: "Something that impresses me . . . something really beautiful . . . is to see the women who have supported the vets, standing in the background. They are present and they are there for them."

* * *

None of this would have been possible if it weren't for one man who wanted to honor Vietnam vets for their service and sacrifice, and the names of all those who died in Vietnam to be remembered. His name is Jan Scruggs.

In 1979, Jan Scruggs, former rifleman in the U.S. Army's 199th Light Infantry Brigade, went to see the movie, *The Deer Hunter.* The movie's war scenes weren't as disturbing to Scruggs as the apparent abandonment of the soldiers by blue-collar youth in a Pennsylvania coal town when the war went sour. The abandoned were the young men Scruggs had seen die in Vietnam. He couldn't sleep that night. He flashed back to Vietnam; faces with no names haunted him.

"No one remembers the names," he told his wife, Becky, the next morning. "I'm going to build a memorial to all the guys who served in Vietnam. It'll have the names of everyone killed," he announced.[2] The memorial would be built by private donations, not government funds. The memorial would not only recognize all those who died in Vietnam, it would bring reconciliation to a divided nation, he announced.

Scruggs shared his dream with about forty other vets at a public meeting; only one responded: attorney Bob Doubek, a former air force officer. Doubek encouraged him to form a corporation.

If he was going to build a memorial with private donations, Scruggs knew he would have to enlist the aid of the news media. His first appeal to the public on television netted $144.50. Roger Mudd reported his grand sum on *CBS Evening News*; that same night a comedian on a major network made fun of Scruggs and his wanting to build a *national* memorial. The audience laughed.

But John Wheeler wasn't laughing. Wheeler, also an attorney and Vietnam vet, was a graduate of West Point, Yale Law School, and the Harvard Business School. Wheeler contacted Scruggs.

A week later, Scruggs, Doubek, and Wheeler met for the first time. Wheeler believed it could be done and was willing to make other contacts. He called corporate lawyers, business executives, congressional aides, engineers, lobbyists . . . and they met and listened. And they, too, believed in the dream and were willing to invest time and energy into the project for no pay and little recognition.

Doubek and Scruggs incorporated and formed the Vietnam Veterans Memorial Fund (VVMF) in April 1979. The nonprofit organization was open to any vet or interested citizen and started to gain momentum. A timetable was set: 1980—obtain land for memorial; 1981—finish raising money; 1982—construct the memorial; Veterans Day 1982—dedicate the memorial.[3]

A consensus of thought emerged from the planners: The memorial would honor the veteran without making a political statement about the war. As Doubek explained on October 24, 1979, to the National Capital Memorial Advisory Committee in Washington:

The Vietnam war has been the collective experience of the generation of Americans born during and after World War II. . . . Over 2.7 million Americans served in Vietnam. More than 57,000 died and over 300,000 were wounded. . . . The Vietnam Veterans Memorial is conceived as a means to promote the healing and reconciliation of the country after the divisions caused by the war. . . . It will symbolize the experience of the Vietnam generation for the generations which follow.[4]

Like the war itself, the memorial became the subject of bitter controversy during the planning and construction phases. Acquiring the two acres of land next to the Lincoln Memorial required an act of Congress, no small feat in itself. The bipartisan co-sponsors of the bill were Senators Barry Goldwater (Rep.) and George McGovern (Dem.). Senators John W. Warner (R-Virginia) and Charles McC. Mathias, Jr., had supported the project from the very beginning and played key roles in helping with legislative issues.

A nationwide contest for a design for the memorial resulted in 1,421 entries. The winning entry was by Maya Ying Lin, a Yale architecture student from Athens, Ohio, who designed the memorial for a seminar on funerary architecture during her senior year. Prior to designing the memorial, she had visited the proposed site. Her instincts told her "that the way to build a memorial would be to cut open the earth and to have stone rise up as part of the healing—something that would be like two hands opening to embrace people."[5]

Maya perhaps was the only person who could envision the profound impact The Wall would have on its viewers. She gives her rationale for the design:

I felt a memorial should be honest about the reality of war and be for the people who gave their lives. For a strong and sobering feeling, it should carry their names. I didn't want a static object that people would just look at, but something they could relate to as on a journey, a passage that would bring each to his own conclusions. . . . I didn't visualize heavy physical objects implanted in the earth; instead it was as if the black-brown earth were polished and made into an interface between the sunny world and the quiet, dark world beyond, that we can't enter. . . . The names would become the memorial. There was no need to embellish.

301

I chose black granite to make the surface reflective and peaceful. The angle was formed solely in relation to the Lincoln Memorial and Washington Monument to create a unity between the nation's past and present.[6]

Critics called Maya's design the "black gash of shame." Most of the controversy emerged prior to the Memorial Wall's dedication. Once open to the people whose lives were dramatically touched by Vietnam, few, if any, criticisms came forth. As stated earlier, it is *the* most visited memorial in Washington. Thousands visit it daily. A year after its dedication, *U. S. News & World Report* referred to the Memorial as "the most emotional ground in the nation's capital."[7]

The Vietnam Veterans Memorial Fund, spearheaded by Scruggs, Doubek, and Wheeler, raised more than $7 million contributed by approximately 275,000 individuals, corporations, foundations, unions, veterans and civic organizations. Many others gave unlimited time and assistance to the project, and this complete story, along with all the names on The Wall, are in Scruggs and Swerdlow's book, *To Heal a Nation.*

The Memorial was dedicated as planned on November 13, 1982. Washington was filled with veterans during the week of dedication. Vietnam veterans were finally being paid the respect they deserved. They did what their country had asked them to do—serve. But it had taken nearly two decades for the country to recognize them. Vets and families came from all over the country.

WHAT'S IN A NAME?

The names of 57,939 men and the eight women who died—including those missing—in Vietnam were read at a special Candlelight Vigil of Names at the National Cathedral during the week of dedication. One mother describes what it meant to her:

When you lost a son in Vietnam, you did everything you could to never forget anything about him. You made yourself remember conversations and scenes over and over again. You studied family photographs and realized there were far too few. You climbed to the attic and opened the cedar chest in which he'd stored his things. You

302

touched the American flag that had come home with him, and you reread letters of condolence from the President.

So much had been taken from you, so you clung to the one thing they could never take away, something that had been with you since the joy of his birth: his name.

As they were read in the chapel, each name was like a bell tolling. Each ripped through the heart, into old wounds that could heal only after they were reopened.[8]

William Broyles served in Vietnam as a marine infantry lieutenant. Then editor-in-chief of *Newsweek*, he wrote this about the reading of names at the Candlelight Vigil:

"Rhythmic Spanish names. Tongue-twisting Polish names, guttural German, exotic African, homely Anglo-Saxon names . . . Chinese, Polynesian, Indian, and Russian names. They are names that run deep into the heart of America, each testimony to a family's decision, sometime in the past, to wrench itself from home and culture to test our country's promise of new opportunities and a better life. They are names drawn from the farthest corners of the world and then, in this generation, sent to another distant corner in a war America has done its best to forget. But to hear the names being read . . . is to remember. The war was about names, each name a special human being who never came home."[9]

MORE THAN JUST A VISIT

Laura Palmer in her book, *Shrapnel in the Heart*, tells the story of Chad Daugherty. His father, James, died in Vietnam in 1968 without a chance to meet his son. Chad had only one message from his father. In a letter to Chad's mother, James Daugherty wrote: "Tell Chad his Daddy loves him."

Chad says this about his visit to The Wall: "It's the only place in the world where I feel as if I am given the opportunity to communicate with my father and tell him how much I love him and respect him and wish we could have shared a life together." Its black color is appropriate, he feels, since the memorial represents to him the blank spaces the soldiers' deaths left in the lives of those who miss them. "It's a place of healing where those affected immediately by the war, and future generations, can go and see exactly what the human price of war is and understand the anguish of those left behind."[10]

The Wall was not meant by its planners to make a political statement. It was meant to bring healing to a divided nation. But it does make a statement about war, a statement that emerges from the depths of the soul of those who are emotionally and spiritually touched by the memorial. A writer for the *Patriot Ledger* in Quincy, Massachusetts, wrote: "Never mind the often-discussed public policy 'lessons of the war.' These will be recorded in history books— and kept alive in public debate. What the history books do not record, and what politicians almost always ignore, is the human sacrifice of Americans who served in Vietnam. Dedication of the Memorial closes the chapter of denial. It could end years of bitterness. It should be a balm for wounds that were too long in healing."[11]

There are also some wonderful surprises and moments of celebration that take place at The Wall. One of the marvelous stories in *To Heal a Nation* is the story of two vets, each looking for the other's name on The Wall thinking his friend had died. About to give up, the vets turned to leave—and then saw each other. They stared.

The stare continued. Then came screams. They had been looking for each other's name etched in granite.[12] Both had survived!

Most people who visit touch the names on the 492-foot-long Memorial. Names are listed in chronological, not alphabetical, order beginning with the first casualties in 1959 and ending with those casualties who died in 1975. Names have been added since its dedication in 1982; currently, there are 58,175* names on The Wall. The National Park Service has a computer to help a visitor locate the name he or she is looking for. A computer printout lists the last name, given name, rank, branch of service, birth date, casualty date, home town of record, and the panel and line on which the name appears.

At the west entrance to the Memorial site, stands a sculpture designed by Frederick Hart of Markham, Virginia. It has several names. Most call it "The Three Fighting Men"; others call it "The

* Figures obtained from Friends of the Vietnam Veterans Memorial in January, 1990.

Last Patrol." The sculpture depicts three young men in combat gear so lifelike you feel they will step off of the pedestal. This statue was dedicated November 10, 1984.

The Moving Wall, the half-size replica of the Memorial Wall, tours the country. Vietnam veteran John Devitt had attended the dedication of The Wall in Washington and was amazed at the powerful and positive feelings The Wall evoked. With the support of Vietnam Combat Veterans Ltd., based in San Jose, California, he decided to reproduce on plexiglass panels a 250-foot-long and six-feet-high replica on which the names were silk-screened using the negatives of photo stencils from the original process. Devitt sees the remarkable healing process The Wall is able to induce. After all the hate, confusion, sorrow and anger the war caused, he is happy that people see his memorial as a labor of love.[13]

Like the Wailing Wall in Jerusalem, loved ones and veterans come as if on pilgrimage. It is a journey they feel compelled to make. They bring with them reminders or messages or items that help them let go. A vast array of objects—the tangible expressions of grief and personal mementos—are collected each day and transferred to the Museum and Archaeological Regional Storage Facility (MARS) in Glen Dale, Maryland. Among the items stored there are wreaths, single flowers, medals, combat boots, photos, flags, poems, letters, a teddy bear, a bicycle fender, crosses, uniforms . . . all items that have special meaning to the person bringing them that link them to the name on The Wall.

FRIENDS OF THE VIETNAM VETERANS MEMORIAL

The memorial is now under the care of the National Park Service. Following the dedication of The Wall, however, five individuals, including Ira Hamburg, met together and discussed the need for continuing assistance to visitors. The Vietnam Veterans Memorial is not just another memorial. It has a special purpose and plays a special role in the lives of veterans and nonveterans as well. This was evidenced right from the start. Thus, the Friends of the Vietnam Veterans Memorial is made up of volunteers to meet those needs and to provide services.

Ira Hamburg explains its purpose: "The primary purpose of the

Friends is to see that the memorial continues in this healing process and to assure the historical significance and emotional legacy of the memorial are not forgotten.

"This means that we need to be able to provide the public with information," says Hamburg. "People walk through the memorial without ever knowing the kind of pain that occurs there or the kind of healing that is done there as well. Part of what we are trying to do is to help the public understand that. We do that through a series of projects."

One of the most helpful services volunteers perform at The Wall is to assist in finding names. After finding the name, a volunteer provides a form, may even climb a ladder and do the name rubbing for you. The Wall soars to ten feet at its apex so a ladder is needed. Free name rubbings can also be requested by mail. The Friends receive nearly one thousand such requests each month.

In Touch is a program designed to afford you the opportunity to be "in touch" by phone or letter with a family member, a friend, or fellow veterans of someone who died in Vietnam. This means that a child or parent or spouse can talk to someone who knew their father, son, or husband. The friend may have been with him when he died. "The emotional impact—the potential for healing and resolution—are enormous as a result of these connections," says Ira Hamburg. The Friends maintain a database, and periodically a search is made to match and connect interested parties. An application form is available upon request and the address is listed at the end of this chapter.

Other services provided by the Friends include sign language interpretation at the Memorial Day and Veterans Day ceremonies at The Wall, helping the National Park Service recruit and train volunteers who work at the memorial, making available pamphlets and books written by members of the Friends to ensure an accurate and balanced understanding of the memorial. They give assistance to special groups visiting the memorial upon request.[14]

THE NAMES SHOUT: REMEMBER US!

Scruggs and Swerdlow quote F. Scott Fitzgerald who once wrote: "Show me a hero and I will write you a tragedy."

Maybe Vietnam vets are forever condemned to be the most tragic of all heroes.

" 'No!' the Memorial shouts, 'It must not be,' " wrote the authors of *To Heal a Nation.* "The names rise from the earth. Even on the coldest days they are somehow warm. They speak. To their buddies. To their wives and children. To mothers, fathers, brothers, and sisters. To all young Americans who must prepare for future wars.

To all the politicians.

To all the generals.

To everyone who tries to understand."[15]

Jan Scruggs read the following poem at the closing of the dedication ceremony of the memorial. It is an appropriate reminder for us all to remember the young people who died in Vietnam.

THE YOUNG DEAD SOLDIERS

The young dead soldiers do not speak.
Nevertheless they are heard in the still houses.
(Who has not heard them?)

They have a silence that speaks for them at night
And when the clock counts.

They say,
We were young. We have died. Remember us.

They say,
We have done what we could
But until it is finished it is not done.

They say,
We have given our lives
But until it is finished no one can
know what our lives gave.

They say,
Our deaths are not ours,
They are yours,
They will mean what you make them.

They say,
Whether our lives and our deaths were
for peace and a new hope
Or for nothing

We cannot say.
It is you who must say this.

They say,
We leave you our deaths,
Give them their meaning,
Give them an end to the war and a true peace,
Give them a victory that ends the war
    and a peace afterwards,
Give them their meaning.

We were young, they say.
We have died.
Remember us.[16]

—ARCHIBALD MACLEISH

* * *

My husband and I visited The Wall in 1987 as part of my research for this book. It was one of the most moving experiences of my life. I felt my heart would burst. It deepened my resolve to be in touch with the pain of those living veterans whose names don't appear on The Wall, but have visions of these dead soldiers forever etched in their hearts and minds. Yes, go to The Wall and remember the dead, but also remember the living Vietnam veterans and give them your love and support. They've paid a terrible price.

ADDITIONAL READING

Fish, Lydia. *The Last Fire Base: A Guide to the Vietnam Veterans Memorial.* Available from the Friends of the Vietnam Memorial.

Grollmes, Eugene. *At the Vietnam Veterans Memorial, Washington, D.C.: Between the Lines.* A collection of thirty poems published by Friends of the Vietnam Veterans Memorial.

Katakis, Michael. *The Vietnam Veterans Memorial.* Photographs and personal statements by visitors. Available through the Friends of the Vietnam Veterans Memorial.

Lopes, Sal. *The Wall: Images and Offerings from the Vietnam Veterans Memorial.* New York: Collins, 1987.

Mayo, James M. *War Memorials as Political Landscape.* New York: Praeger, 1988.

Palmer, Laura. *Shrapnel in the Heart.* New York: Random House, 1987.

Reflections on the Wall—The Vietnam Veterans Memorial. Photographs by the Smithsonian Institution.

Scruggs, Jan C., and Joel L. Swerdlow. *To Heal a Nation: The Vietnam Veterans Memorial.* New York: Harper & Row, 1985.

Spencer, Duncan, with photographs by Lloyd Wolf. *Facing the Wall.* New York: MacMillan, 1986.

ORGANIZATION

Inquiries about the Friends' special project, In Touch, as well as items and books for sale, a fact sheet about The Wall, or a request for a name rubbing can be obtained by writing to:

Friends of the Vietnam Veterans Memorial
1350 Connecticut Ave. N.W., Suite 300
Washington, DC 20036
(202)296-1726

"All the Unsung Heroes": The National Vietnam Veterans Memorial has now been captured on video. "All the Unsung Heroes," a 30-minute video released in 1990, details the memorial's creation and features numerous touching stories of remembrance. The video is available at a cost of $19.95 through the Friends of the Vietnam Veterans Memorial, or by writing Unsung Heroes, P.O. Box 266, Lovettsville, VA 22080.

Chapter 17

Veterans Speak Out

What do veterans want? I asked a number of veterans that question, and I got some straight answers.

They want an end to stereotyping. Veterans are individuals and, as such, they resent the stereotyping perpetuated most often by the media of the long-haired, "drug-crazed" Vietnam veteran. Most consider themselves to be "ordinary guys." Some don't want to be singled out; others want to tell their story to those ready to listen.

Veterans want understanding, not pity. There are those who accuse Vietnam veterans of being "cry babies" because they have had more difficulty readjusting to society than other vets. Some do not consider PTSD a legitimate problem. Rodney Haug, Associate Manager of Region V Vet Centers, states that eighty thousand new clients seek help in the Vet Centers each year. PTSD is debilitating and it doesn't go away with time alone.

Many do not believe that veterans are dying or ill or fathering children with birth defects as a result of exposure to Agent Orange. This disbelief, lack of understanding, and caring hurts veterans, their families, and unborn generations.

Most of all, Vietnam veterans simply want the benefits coming to them. Benefits for World War II veterans have seldom been questioned. They won their war and came home as heroes. (I don't wish to take anything away from World War II vets; I'm simply stating the rationale that lies behind our acceptance of getting their full due.)

According to Seymour Leventman of Boston College whose article, "Official Neglect of Vietnam Veterans," appeared in the *Journal of Social Issues* in 1975:

> . . . fully half the entire VA budget goes to older veterans in connection with nonservice-related illness, injury, and other needs. This situation is a function of the circumstance that veterans' politics are dominated by a powerful lobby of older veterans which is capable of influencing both the Congress and the executive agency of government. Since Vietnam veterans are not really represented by this professional veterans' lobby, these younger veterans receive only about 12% to 15% of the VA budget in the areas of readjustment benefits, health services, compensation and pensions, and life insurance.[1]

These figures have undoubtedly changed since 1975. In 1988, however, the 196 Vet Centers operated on $43 million, or about 14% of the total VA budget. Vet Center closings have been threatened more than once . . . and this we dare not let happen.

In 1989, an estimated $612 million shortfall in the VA budget triggered drastic, sometimes fatal, cutbacks in medical care for all veterans. Here are some examples of how this translates into personal lives:

In Chicago, Illinois, a veteran with service-connected disabilities visited the West Side VAMC with an open, draining skin condition and was told to return in two months. The pharmacy then refused to issue two months' supply of prescribed medication.

In St. Louis, Missouri, there is a veteran who was comatose for two months and was consistently refused VA hospitalization or medical care.

In Cincinnati, Ohio, a veteran was admitted to a VA hospital pending surgical consultation. After three days of not seeing a physician and receiving what the veteran felt to be inappropriate treatment, he left the hospital and was admitted to a private facility that performed immediate surgery for cancer.

Doctors and nurses who work in VA hospitals testified to the dire conditions existing in these hospitals. Many report that no new or replacement equipment has been bought because the money was needed to pay salaries, thus drastically affecting patient care.[2]

What do veterans want? Fred Wilcox, author of *Waiting for An Army to Die*, says vets simply want the Department of Veterans Affairs to show good faith regarding the health and welfare of Vietnam veterans. Most of all, they want compensation for those veterans who are too sick to work or who are dying from cancer or other maladies related to exposure to Agent Orange.[3] They want the government to keep its promise made by Abraham Lincoln who said, *"The responsibility of the U.S. Government is . . . to care for him who shall have borne the battle, and for his widow and orphan."*

Veterans want to be heard. And rightfully so, for they have much to teach us.

It became apparent to me in my associations with veterans that they are among the prophets of our day. Their messages emerge from hearts still filled with reservoirs of deep pain. Their wisdom has been refined through the crucible of human suffering. Their thoughts and questions are profound and disturbing. And that's why we should listen.

I would hasten to add that, despite their lingering anger and feeling of being used by the government, almost without exception, I sensed each veteran's deep love for America, a renewed appreciation of living in a *free* country, and a respect for our flag that symbolizes the sacrifices they, and their friends who died, have made.

Above all else, Vietnam veterans *never again want our country to put young men and women into a war it doesn't intend to win.*

In closing, I want to let the veterans speak for themselves. The subjects about which they speak may seem unrelated. They are meant to be. Their statements—some long, some short—are simply meant to reflect the concerns and insights these individuals have gained from their experiences.

Michael Maxwell is an incarcerated vet. He served in the U.S. Navy from 1970 to 1975, serving two tours of duty in Southeast Asia from 1971 to 1973. He was a radioman third class and received numerous awards as the result of his tours in Vietnam. He made the following statement at a VVA meeting at Hill Correctional Facility in

Galesburg, Illinois, that I was privileged to attend. The Firebase Hill Chapter is the first VVA chapter for incarcerated vets in the state of Illinois.

I laid it all on the line—willing to make the ultimate sacrifice by serving my country in Vietnam. I did my job—so well, in fact, that I survived, to come back to the land of the free and home of the brave. But am I really free? Thousands of Vietnam veterans like myself arrived home to encounter an alien and hostile society that refused to recognize us as the products of its own making.

So, for one reason or another, here we are. In prison, in mental institutions, in VA hospitals, homeless on the streets, unemployed because of the lack of marketable skills and underemployed, forced to fight another war for self-respect and dignity. This time, just like the last time, we're losing. Why? Because this great Frankenstein of ours (America) cannot control the monsters it created.

Alienated warriors returning home from Vietnam faced an untold multitude of obstacles. Just like the "domino effect," one problem after another. From being rejected by a society that was raised idolizing a winner and scorning the loser, to having to suffer the long-lasting effects of our own weapons such as Agent Orange. From the "it's business-as-usual attitude" of the Veterans Administration in regards to our past due and well deserved benefits, to the debilitating disease of Post-traumatic Stress Disorder, our battles have yet to end, not to mention our long fight for the return of our brother POWs/MIAs.

I'm not offering an excuse for being here, but it has been determined that there's proven evidence pointing toward a relationship between PTSD and violent crimes and behaviors.

The present federal and state administrations have determined that we are not worthy of special concerns, so we are steadily being phased out of the medical, legislative, and judicial picture. With the VA's passé attitudes, the much-needed federally funded Vet Centers are endangered; thus one very important avenue for the treatment of PTSD, which is a mitigating factor of many incarcerated veterans, may be eliminated [sometime in the future].

With the recent formation of the cabinet-level Department of Veterans Affairs, it is our hope and prayer that these issues will be addressed and acted upon. We did not hesitate to answer when called. In fact, it was our duty to protect and serve our country in times of

313

need. We did not shy away from our responsibilities. But can we say the same about America?

The day will have to come for society to quit hiding behind the mask of indifference and denial and face up to the reality that the symptoms are not the problem, but the causes are, and by recognizing the causes, solutions can be developed.

In the meantime, we must continue to fight this new enemy: the apathetic attitudes that exist on the homefront with everything at our disposal. We must institute our own programs of self-help, petition our legislatures for support, and make our voices heard. We must say to the world, "Look at me, for I am America!"

*   *   *

Veteran Richard Rohlfs states: "Vietnam was a war about money and politics. How do you [America] justify all the killing? Everything that you do that is morally wrong, you pay for later in flashbacks, bad dreams. You don't know that till later."

*   *   *

Bill Tucker admits that he's not proud of what he did. "Every day I see in my mind the face of a man I killed. You never get over it. At the time, one part of you says, 'Thou shalt not,' and the other part of you says, 'You did a good job.' War is insanity!"

*   *   *

Veteran James Martin Davis writes in an article, "Vietnam: What It Was Really Like," which appeared in *Military Review*, January 1989:

> We went to war and shared it together—the same sights and sounds, the same feelings and fears, and the same tastes and smells. We shared love and respect, loyalty and trust, and we shared unspoken promises always to look after each other.
>
> No matter who we were, or where we were from, we learned to accept each other and count on each other for life itself. It was a relationship that transcended race, nationality, or education. While serving together, for the first time in our lives, we discovered a commitment beyond ourselves. It was the ultimate discovery for those of my generation.

Our code of conduct was never to think of ourselves, but to think about our buddies first, because they were thinking about us. Our first commandment had been to perish if we must, but to save our buddies first. In Vietnam, we discovered the cement that binds men together.

That simple, precious memory of belonging and of pride in each other is now a part of who and what we are. We are all special because of that experience, and because of that experience, we will forever be joined at the soul.

Every soldier will tell you there is nothing romantic about war and certainly there is nothing glamorous about it. Wars are lessons in excessive suffering and extreme pain, in overwhelming boredom and absolute fear, and inevitably, in unspeakable cruelty and death.

The Japanese have a saying, "You only live twice—once when you are born and once when you have looked into the face of death." War is, after all, as much about living as it is about dying.

War changes a man and combat makes him different. It can be no other way. For combat develops a person such a different way of living, of looking at life and of living with death. After witnessing our first casualties, we knew we would never be the same again. When we saw the wounded and the dead, the blood and the litters, and we heard men crying out in pain, we knew we were now combat soldiers. We had become members of a God-awful fraternity. It was a fraternity whose dues were too high. It was a fraternity that should never have been allowed to exist. But we knew it was a fraternity that would never be disbanded in our lifetime—except in the minds of dreamers.[4]

* * *

Some veterans who preferred to remain anonymous shared these thoughts:

"Wars are waged by old men too fat to fight, and fought by young men too naive to know any better."

"One wonders how many wars there would be if it was understood that the first men on the battlefield were those who failed to negotiate peace—accompanied by *their own sons*."

"Vietnam destroyed all the myths of war. I wonder when and if we have another war, will anyone show up?"

* * *

315

Veteran Joe Palmer-Litchfield of New Providence protests the manufacturing of war toys. He claims that playing with toy guns and war games as a child twisted his sense of reality when he saw combat in Indochina in 1969–70. "I was nineteen years old and had an M-16 rifle, and I couldn't understand the power associated with that and the use of it."[5]

* * *

In 1987, veteran Bill Allen, President of the Illinois State Council of Vietnam Veterans of America (1988–92) joined other veterans who voiced their concerns with the United States's involvement in the Persian Gulf and Central America, fearing that escalation of funding to the Contras could draw the United States into war. Veterans say they hope to prevent "another Vietnam."[6]

* * *

Veteran nurse Barbara Hedin wrote in an article that appeared in *MINERVA: A Quarterly Report on Women and the Military*:

> There seems to be an accepted mythology of war that goes something like: In war there is good and evil, and the two meet and the good overcomes. It is understood that whoever is making this statement is on the side of "the good." It sounds logical and clear-cut, until it is experienced. Then the reality of war becomes clear: The distinctions between good and evil become blurred as war itself unleashes an inhumanity, an evilness beyond imagination, in the name of a Higher Good, be it God, country, democracy, or whatever. The context of war legitimizes that which under any other circumstances would horrify and repulse.
>
> . . . the underlying issue . . . remains to be dealt with: the fact that war, any war, is inherently evil and necessitates such atrocious acts to be committed by those commissioned as its warriors. Admission of this truth brings us face-to-face with our myth of war. Until we confront this, we are vulnerable to repeating the debacle of inhumanity and carnage that war makes legitimate.
>
> . . . varied opportunities are within the reach and understanding of Everyman—for those wishing to inform themselves and enter into a dialogue with their own experience of the war, be it as protester, warrior, relative, friend of someone who served, or passive observer.

These offerings allow participants to engage the experience at more than an intellectual level in order to break through the myths of war to its reality and to an understanding of its devastating effects on human lives. In order for the wounds to be healed and the wounded to be reclaimed, individuals need to open themselves to the experience and allow themselves to be touched and transformed by it.[7]

* * *

Veteran Larry Tschappet says about the war:

Vietnam was a war American troops were not allowed to win. There's a difference between losing and not being allowed to win. We were winning the war in 1968 after having adapted to a style of war different from any we'd ever fought. We were winning the battles, but were not allowed to win the war. We had to fight behind borders we couldn't cross. The enemy could cross those lines but we couldn't pursue Charlie. It was like fighting a war with one hand tied behind our back.

* * *

Captain Dale Dye, forty-two, a retired Marine Corps lifer who served as technical advisor to the movie *Platoon*, says: "My hope is that it [*Platoon*] will encourage America not to waste its soldiers' lives in wars that it is not willing or able to win."[8]

* * *

Steven Tice, former Team Leader in Eugene, Oregon, now working at the VA hospital in Tacoma, Washington, was seriously injured and lost an arm in Vietnam. Steve says:

"I pray for peace for my family and yours. It's increasingly popular now for government officials, media, the public, and Vietnam vets themselves to say, 'Never again will we fight a war without going all out.' We knew that about war. That's not the lesson! The lesson of war is very simple: *No more war!* It is time to care for and nurture each other and our planet. It is time we search for and find peace within ourselves. Americans can learn a lot about this process from Vietnam veterans."*

* Taken from videotape filmed at the University of Wisconsin, *A Program for Vietnam Veterans . . . and Everyone Else Who Should Care*, hosted by Charles Haid, a production of WTTW/Chicago, Copyright 1985.

ADDITIONAL READING

Bonior, David E., et al. *The Vietnam Veteran: A History of Neglect.* New York: Praeger Publishing, 1984.

Doyle, Edward, Terrence Maitland, and the Editors of Boston Publishing Company. *The Aftermath: The Legacy of War, 1975–1985.* Boston: Boston Publishing Company, 1985.

APPENDIXES

APPENDIXES

Appendix A

THE CHURCH'S HISTORICAL APPROACH TO WAR

"Since the fourth century, Christians have killed each other in so many wars that you might think that the gospel taught war, or at least approved of it," writes Richard McSorley in *New Testament Basis of Peace Making.*[1]

Veterans, as well as others, have expressed confusion over the fact that stories of war and atrocities are recorded in the Bible.* Many of these wars were fought in God's name, which seems contradictory to the commandment, "Thou shalt not kill."

To gain some insight into this paradox of God's people killing others, it is important to understand the historical progression of thought and revelation of God's relationship to humankind.

In the beginning, God's intent was for man and woman to live in close unity with Him; peace was the ideal state of being. But Adam and Eve's disobedience introduced enmity, and later, the murder of Abel by his brother Cain saw the beginning of bloodshed in the human race. War began with the fall of man.

Around 1400 B.C., to further reveal His plan for humankind, Yahweh [God] made a special covenant with the Israelites with the intent that these

* Numbers 21:1–3; I Sam. 4:3–7, 15:1–8, 18:27, 27:8–12; Judges 7, 11:6–18.

321

"Chosen" would be faithful and rely on God alone. The covenant agreement in essence said, "You keep my laws—the Ten Commandments—and I will protect you from your enemies." God required religious purity of the Israelites, and marrying outside the tribe was forbidden. Ethnic separation was the means by which the Israelites were to remain pure and faithful to God alone.

Most wars in those days were fought for two reasons: to take slaves and to take booty. But God gave the Chosen strict orders to take neither. At times, this meant killing all prisoners and animals.

War, from the Hebrew point of view, was essentially a religious duty, begun and carried through under the highest sanctions of religion. Israel's wars of old were the wars of Yahweh. His presence was secured by the Ark of the Covenant accompanying the army in the field (I Sam. 4,5). Yahweh alone decided when and if war should be waged. No alliances were to be made with other nations; the Israelites were to be solely dependent on God. Even the kings who ruled were not free to make war or take life on their own authority. If the Israelites were disobedient, they were punished by defeat in battle or invasion by their enemies. In the Old Testament, Yahweh took part in what have been called the *Holy Wars*.

As time passed, however, God's plan for humankind was further revealed in the life of Jesus Christ. Once the promised Messiah came, and a New Covenant was made claiming *all* people as God's, war was obsolete. Wars were no longer part of the covenant agreement. Therefore, the New Testament can be viewed as a fulfillment of the Old Testament, and Old Testament wars cannot be used as an argument to justify today's wars.

Historically, there have been three attitudes toward war and peace in the Christian ethic: *Pacifism*, the *Just War*, and the *Crusade*. Today, a fourth ethic is emerging in some denominations, such as the United Church of Christ, called the *Just Peace* theology.

For the first three centuries after the death and resurrection of Christ— until the time of Constantine—the early Church fathers and mothers were called *pacifists*. They abstained or withdrew from war; this was closely related to their unwillingness to participate in idolatry. They had taken to heart Christ's teaching: "You have heard that it was said, 'An eye for an eye and a tooth for a tooth.' But I say to you, do not resist one who is evil" (Matt. 5:38). "Love your enemies and pray for those who persecute you" (Matt. 5:43–44).

During the fifth century, St. Augustine* developed the *Just War* ethic. It was an attempt to set guidelines for those initiating war, and

---

* Lived from 354 to 430, Bishop of Hippo. Both Roman Catholic and Protestant theologians think of him as founder of theology. His influence on Christianity is thought to be second only to St. Paul.

322

limit destruction once war had started. The criteria for initiation were as follows:

> Because war must serve the common good of society, it must be declared by a legitimate authority. [On the basis of this criterion, the Vietnam War and the Falkland Islands War were unjust wars.]
>
> War must be waged with good intention.
>
> War must lead to a good outcome; the situation after war must be more humane than the situation before it. War must be the last resort for conflict resolution; all peaceful means must have been exhausted.
>
> War must be waged for defensive and not offensive reasons. [Augustine did not include self-defense as a valid reason for taking another's life, but Aquinas added it eight centuries later.]

The criteria for limiting destruction are these:

> The means of war must be proportional to the ends; the methods must not be worse than the evil opposed.
>
> Combatants must be distinguished from citizens; the civil population must not be attacked. (This principle was violated by the Northern general W. T. Sherman in the American Civil War and by both sides in World War II.)[2]

The *Crusades* were a series of nine wars waged by European Christians between the years 1095 to 1272 A.D., fought in an attempt to secure a place of dominance for the Church over the world and to reclaim the Holy Land from the Muslims. The Crusaders' battle cry was: "God wills it."

During the Middle Ages, Crusaders were convinced God sanctioned their war efforts against those who represented a "great evil." The Crusades were often led by European monarchs and were comprised of noblemen as well as peasants, even children.

The first Crusade, begun in 1095 and spearheaded by Pope Urban II, was the most successful. The campaign was completed in 1099 by taking Jerusalem and killing all Muslims and Jews. The later Crusades, for the most part, were fought to assist those who were already in the Holy Land.

In the early twelfth century, lay followers of St. Francis of Assisi formed what was called the "Third Order." The Order was composed exclusively of lay membership and made an enormous impact on medieval society. St. Francis wrote in their Rule, "They are not to take up lethal weapons, or bear them about, against anybody" and "all are to refrain from formal oaths."

Part of what this meant was that members of the Third Order refused to be drafted into the armies of their feudal masters, since they were forbidden by religious vow to bear arms or to take the usual oath of loyalty. In one Italian town, Faenza, nearly every male serf eligible for the draft was a member—so there could be no army and no war, despite what the rulers wanted! In fact, the serfs' refusal to carry weapons or swear loyalty to civil rulers played a tremendous role in ending the constant wars and in the eventual collapse of the whole feudal system in southern Europe.

Today in the United States, three denominations exist that take a pacifist stance: The Mennonites, Church of the Brethren, and the Quakers. But there have always been many pacifists in mainline Protestant and Catholic churches as well.

In America today, attitudes toward war have changed—especially as a result of the Vietnam War. Susan Thistlewaite, editor of *A Just Peace Church* contends that "War is being redefined in this generation," adding:

> The war in Vietnam represented the first American conflict opposed by both religious and popular consensus, spawning a whole group of young Americans with a distaste for war in numbers unprecedented in U.S. history.[3]

In Gwynne Dyer's book, *War*, she elaborates on the factors causing these changes in beliefs:

> . . . most people all down through history have accepted killing in war as legitimate, partly because it is hallowed by tradition, but also because those who do the killing are themselves willing to sacrifice their lives. There is a heightened humanity, both good and bad, about the way soldiers behave in battle which seems to transcend ordinary morality and place them in a special category.

> Only in this century have large numbers of people begun to question the basic assumptions of civilized societies about the usefulness and inevitability of war, as two mutually reinforcing trends have gained strength. One is moral; for all the atrocities we still practice on each other, the people of the twentieth century are nevertheless more able than their ancestors to imagine that war— that is, killing foreigners for political reasons—may be simply wrong. The same great changes in society that have made war so lethal have also enabled us to see broader categories of people—even those on the far side of the nuclear palisade—as being essentially human beings like ourselves. And even if morality is no more than the rules we have made up for ourselves as we go along, one of those rules has always been that killing people is wrong.

> The other factor is severely practical; we will almost all die, and our civilization with us, if we continue to practice war. A civilization confronted with the prospect of a "nuclear winter" does not need moral incentives to reconsider the value of the institution of war; it must change or perish.[4]

The new theology emerging—the *Just Peace* theology—seeks to bring new life and meaning to the word *shalom*. For the Hebrews, this word implied far more than the absence of war. The Old Testament concept of shalom includes peace, justice, well-being, prosperity, harmony, fulfillment, and wholeness.

The Just Peace theology embraces God's vision of how human beings are to live in "covenant" relationship with God, each other, and all creation. The Just Peace theology thus picks up the Old Testament concept of "Shalom," a peace that implies right relations with God, with the human community, and with the whole creation. It is an approach to peace that has always been present in Christian theology and is perhaps more holistic than the narrower approaches of Pacifism, Just War, and Holy War (Crusade). It sees God at work in the world bringing order, reconciliation, and justice, and calls us to join in the task of creating order, reconciliation, and justice. Where the Just War theology stresses justice, and pacifism stresses reconciliation, Just Peace theology stresses justice, but insists that all three must be held in balance. Thus, it recognizes the need for governments to maintain order through police forces, and rejects "full-scale unilateral disarmament" in the current world situation. It claims that because Christ has overcome sin and death, persons and institutions can be changed. Therefore, "peace is possible" and war as a human institution can be eliminated.[5]

The yearning in the hearts of men and women for a world free of war and strife—a world filled with Shalom—is as old as time. The Prophet Micah describes a world and a time when:

> *They will beat their swords into plowshares*
> *and their spears into pruning hooks;*
> *Nations shall no longer fight each other,*
> *for all war will end.*
> *There will be universal peace, and all the military*
> *academies and training camps will be closed down.*
> *Everyone will live quietly in his own home*
> *in peace and prosperity,*
> *For there will be nothing to fear.*
> MICAH 4:3,4 (TLB)

Appendix B

DEVOTIONAL READINGS

You Survived!

I think you ought to know, dear brothers, about the hard time we went through in *Asia*. We were really crushed and overwhelmed, and feared we would never live through it. We felt we were doomed to die and saw how powerless we were to help ourselves: but that was good, for then we put everything into the hands of God, who alone could save us, for He can even raise the dead. And He did help us, and saved us from a terrible death; yes, and we expect Him to do it again. But you must help us too, by praying for us. For much thanks and praise will go to God from you who see His wonderful answers to your prayers for our safety.

> II Corinthians 1:8–11
> Paul of Tarsus,
> Point Man A.D. 65

Prayers for When You're Feeling Low

> *God*
> *hear my*
> *silent*
> *scream*
> *say*

326

peace
be still
to the storm
that rages
within me.[1]

* * *

An ex-marine who says he sought comfort in a bottle of Jim Beam whiskey for eight lost years now finds comfort in the Psalms. His favorite is Psalm 144.

PSALM 144:1–4 (NKJV)

Blessed be the Lord my Rock,
Who trains my hands for war,
And my fingers for battle—
My loving-kindness and my fortress,
My high tower and my deliverer,
My shield and the One in whom I take refuge,
Who subdues my people under me.

Lord, what is man, that You take knowledge of him?
Or the son of man, that You are mindful of him?
Man is like a breath;
His days are like a passing shadow.

* * *

PSALM 139:7–12 (NKJV)

Where can I go from Your Spirit?
Or where can I flee from Your presence?
If I ascend into heaven, You are there
If I make my bed in hell, behold, You are there.
If I take the wings of the morning,
And dwell in the uttermost parts of the sea,
Even there Your hand shall lead me,
And Your right hand shall hold me.
If I say, "Surely the darkness shall fall on me," not hide from You,
Even the night shall be light about me;
Indeed, the darkness shall be light about me;
But the night shines as the day;
The darkness and the light are both alike to You.

* * *

PSALM 83

I am so depressed tonight, O God.
I feel as if I am the sole target
of an enemy barrage—
that all the demons of hell are bent
upon damning my soul for eternity.

I remember Your precious promises,
but I do not witness their fulfillment.
I talk to people about Your love,
and they drown my zeal with scorn.
I step forth to carry out Your will,
but I feel no sense of accomplishment.
I mouth words, wave my arms,
and beat the air with fruitless endeavor.
Then I fall like a wounded warrior,
bone-weary, defeated, and lonely.
And I wonder if You are truly my God,
and if I am really Your child.

Consume, O God, these demons that depress,
these enemies that plague my soul.
May the whirlwind of Your Spirit
sweep them out of my life forever.
May I awaken with a heart full of joy,
and with the strength and the courage
to walk straight and secure
in the dangerous
and difficult paths before me.[2]

*   *   *

FEELING GUILTY

PSALM 130

O God, tonight I seek for You
out of a heart full of guilt
and a mind full of bewilderment
and frustration.
You have heard me before
and responded with grace and mercy.
Now I seek You again.

I know I am guilty, O God:
But if You kept account
of man's failings and fallings,
no one could ever face You again.
I reach for You
because You look with loving mercy
upon my wretched soul.
You will accept me and forgive me
and reinstate me in Your purposes.

It is no wonder that I return
again and again to God.
I long for His forgiveness and acceptance
more than the night watchman longs
for the dawn of day.

Thus I plead with you to focus your faith on God.
You will find love there—and salvation.
And He will cleanse you of your sin
and restore you to His loving heart.[3]

* * *

Longing For God

Psalm 42

As a desert wanderer longs for springs of cool water,
so my thirsty soul reaches out for You, O God.
How I long for a deeper sense of Your presence,
for a faith that will embrace You
without fear or doubt!
Yet while I weep in longing, people about me say,
"If God is not dead, where is He?"

I remember so well the faith of my childhood.
How real God was to me in those days
when I prayed and sang praises
and listened to His Word
in the fellowship of family and friends!
Then why am I so depressed now?
Why cannot I recapture the joy and confidence
of those years?

I remember the stories of Your love
    that I had been taught;
        how merciful and all-powerful were Your dealings
        with Your children throughout history!
Yet now my heart is empty,
    and waves of doubt flood over my soul.

I pray, but the heavens, too, are empty,
It is almost as if God had forgotten all about me.
And while I struggle with the sickness of doubt,
    people about me say,
        "If God is not dead, where is He?"

O foolish heart, why do you seethe in unrest?
God has not changed;
    His love for me is ever the same.
I must renew my faith in God;
    I must again shout His praises
        even when I don't feel His presence.
For truly He is God,
    and He is my Help and my Hope.[4]

* * *

FORGIVENESS

PSALM 32

The man who knows the meaning of forgiveness,
    whose past failures no longer plague him,
        who stands blameless and guilt-free before God—
        that man is rich indeed.

Every time I attempt to handle my own guilt—
    by ignoring it, rationalizing it,
    or just running away from it—
some unseen power or pressure
    from the depths of my being
        squeezes my life dry, leaving me empty.

But when I face up to my failures and confess them,
    when I open my guilt-ridden heart
        to you, O God,
    then I realize the blessed meaning
        of forgiveness.

Thus everyone who claims faith in a loving God
     needs to cling to God's acceptance and concern.
Times of darkness will come,
     life's storms and tempests will continue to rage,
          but he shall not be destroyed by these things.

You are, O God, a place of refuge;
     You do enable me to face my problems,
     You do keep me from being destroyed by them.
Even within the darkness about us,
     in the midst of life's turmoil,
     one can often hear the voice of God:
"Even these things serve a purpose in your life.
Don't sell them short,
     for they may be steps along My path for you.
Stop being stubborn and stupid
     like some undiscerning jackass
          that has to be driven with sticks or whips."

The faithful and the faithless both suffer
     the uncertainties and insecurities of this life,
     but the child of God can depend always
          on the love of his Father.
It is for this reason that there is
     light even in the midst of darkness
     incomprehensible joy in the midst of sorrow,
     and we can find
          a measure of happiness and well-being
               regardless of the circumstances that surround us.[5]

Appendix C

A WORD TO THE CHURCH

Far too often, pastors have counseled veterans to "put the war behind them."

"This lack of compassion that is felt by the veteran is interpreted as rejection, repulsion, and/or discrediting," says Gary Williams, former Iowa State Coordinator of ViêtNow.

Williams claims, "The veteran says 'I was abandoned. I was brought up as a Christian and served actively in support of what I believed were the basic values of our country. I came home and I found that there were conflicts in what I had been taught and what I saw.' The reality didn't match the theories taught.

"The veteran's whole philosophy of life changed. He became very distrustful," said Williams, "and this distrust carried over to those organizations that were for the betterment of all mankind. That includes the church.

"Our government truly changed this young, impressionable individual into somewhat of a machine for its purposes. The veteran felt used and thrown away. They couldn't even return into society. There's a large number of in-country men who are not adjusting, who have become self-destructive," said Williams.

"Churches are not responding to the needs of veterans. For example, in my church a Vietnam veteran, who had experience with substance abuse, approached our boards about starting a support group within the church and asked for spiritual leadership. There was no response; an apathy was there," Williams added.

He is especially concerned about the rate of suicide among Vietnam veterans. "I have been advised by my evangelical pastors to 'put it behind me and accept the rebirth and rekindling spirit to go forth in a more loving, evangelical manner preaching the Gospel,'" said Williams. "I felt like I was discredited by being told that. Part of my reluctance to put it behind me is because too many brothers out there are taking their lives. More have died after the war as the result of suicide or alcohol-related accidents than there were casualties during the war. No one knows for sure how many have taken their own lives.* My brothers and future generations can benefit if I continue to provide support to them. I never abandoned any individual who was under my command, and I still feel there's a basic good in all these individuals who are still suffering. They need outreach and other organizational shelters. That's why I work with ViêtNow. We are happening 'Now' and we are trying to curtail the loss of our brothers who were at one time responsible for our survival. We are working now for the purposes of helping one another."[1]

The invisible wounds of the warrior have never been understood by society. The civilian population, especially in America, has *no basis for comparison*. With the exception of its veterans, Americans have not experienced the ravages of war.

Talking about death and war are taboo subjects except for expounding on our own political views concerning war. And the self-imposed silence of veterans has delayed the dialogue with the church necessary for understanding the pain and needs of the veteran. Many veterans can no longer believe in the "goodness" of God, and many are "turned off" to organized religion.

These comments were made in a Vet Center by vets who expressed confusion about the churches' actions during the war. One says,

> When I was a teenager, I heard the pulpit supporting the Vietnam War and even "killing commies." This memory, when placed next to the horror of my Vietnam memories, causes me much confusion about what God and/or religion are all about.[2]

Another said:

> Some of the most horrible events in human history have occurred in the name of God or "brand-name religion." For example, the churches in the USA

* There are no accurate statistics regarding the number of suicide deaths.

333

supported Vietnam early, but condemned it late—too late—for I had already returned from doing the killing I did. I cannot belong to something like this which supports vast wars, killing, and ignorance.[3]

These comments should say something to us about the messages that should come from the pulpit in the future.

The Christian community has failed to realize how desperately the soldier needed—and still needs—our love and support. Unfortunately, many opposing the Vietnam War threw the "baby out with the bath water," and could not separate the warrior from the war.

Churches have sponsored Vietnamese refugees, providing them with temporary housing and jobs and assisting with their adjustment into this society, unaware that, in the eyes of some veterans, the church is helping the "enemy." And the veterans ask, What is the church doing to help veterans? What has the church done to assist the veteran in readjusting to his own country? What special ministries has the church implemented for those incarcerated veterans who failed to get help soon enough? What help has the church given the homeless veteran? What message of hope has the church had for those despairing veterans who take their own lives? What messages and ministries of healing has the church offered the veteran?

My hope is that this book will help Christians become sensitive to these issues. We can learn much from Vietnam veterans if we only listen to them.

Stewart Brown, team leader of the Vet Center in San Jose, California, says, "I think Vietnam combat veterans are much more in touch with important issues of the human experience than the American population in general. This is because veterans experienced life and death in a magnified, graphic form."[4]

We can listen and learn from veterans, but we can also offer them compassion and understanding they so desperately need from us. Many of them believe freedom and this country were and still are worth fighting for. Whether we agree with the war or not, I feel we owe Vietnam veterans the respect they deserve for the sacrifices they have made and love them for the persons they have become.

Appendix D

COMMUNICATION GUIDELINES FOR PASTORS

Occasionally, veterans report that they have attempted to talk with a pastor, but have been disillusioned by responses made by the clergy. The following guidelines and directives are offered to aid pastors in gaining insight into the unique needs of the veterans.

- **Read to gain an understanding of Post-traumatic Stress Disorder (PTSD).** *Out of the Night: The Spiritual Journey of Vietnam Vets* is a must. Mahedy explains why American civil religion failed the soldier. Secure a brochure called *The Etiology of Combat-Related Post-Traumatic Stress Disorders* from Disabled American Veterans, National Headquarters, P.O. Box 14301, Cincinnati, OH 45214, or a nearby Vet Center.
- **Never tell veterans to put the war behind them.** This is not helpful and it is usually resented. They need to be given permission to grieve the many losses they experienced. Vietnam will always be a part of their lives.
- **Never say you know what the veteran has been through.** Acknowledge the fact you have no basis for comparison but express a willingness to listen. Some veterans by choice do not talk about the war, and one must respect his or her defense mechanisms.

- **Listen *nonjudgmentally*.** Don't be shocked by the veteran's choice of language or graphic descriptions. Understand that the veteran needs to decompress and vent strong feelings. Allowing him to do so will aid the grief process and facilitate healing.
- **Don't rationalize guilt.** This is not helpful. A statement such as, "You did the best you could under the circumstances," is a form of rationalization. A combat veteran can never afford the luxury of a rationalization like this. What happened in the jungles and villages of Vietnam really was horrendous.[1] John Sanford offers this advice: In a case like this, the self-reproach is so great that the counselee cannot accept [himself] without the help of another human being, who sees the darkness of [his] thoughts as well as [he] does and yet himself accepts them. Only then can the healing work begin. To create this atmosphere of acceptance requires great patience and much careful, attentive listening, for the counselee will let out just a little information at a time to see how it is accepted before divulging more. All this requires a great love for the soul.[2]
- **Ask open-ended questions.** Open-ended questions like, "What was it like?" or "How did that make you feel?" invite discussion. Respect his silence if the individual chooses not to tell you. A trust relationship is essential for openness to occur.
- **Understand that whatever belief structures the individual had prior to the war may have been totally shattered as a direct result of his or her Vietnam experience.** Asking questions that will help identify what beliefs remain is essential to understanding the veteran.
- **Understand that veterans are often angry at God, the government, and authority figures.** Point out that their *beliefs* about God may be the cause of that anger, resulting from the feeling that God has abandoned them. This anger will usually pass after it has been expressed. Expressing our anger at God, without being judged, allows an individual to release those feelings. If not, this anger may become a permanent attitude and block spiritual growth. Anger at the government stems from the feelings of "being used." Anger at authority figures often results from having been under inexperienced or callous officers who abused authority or wasted lives during battle.
- **Avoid comparisons.** Each person's war experience was different. Vietnam was unlike any other war. Veterans resent being compared to other veterans who are seemingly unaffected, as well as being stereotyped and identified with the most damaged among them—the addicts, the wife killers, the sick soldier. Comparisons tend to diminish the validity of the experience, depriving the individual of its legitimate status as something unique.

- **Avoid pat answers or hurried responses.** The priest, rabbi, or minister who gives a quick sermon, a bit of hurried advice, or a nice prayer, does not know what he is doing; he is rejecting the human soul and God who loves it. The only way such a soul can be reclaimed is through the patience of the counselor, who opens the way for the healing, which comes from God.[3]
- **Unless asked, lay aside your political views about the war. Never argue.** The veteran's primary need is to be listened to. Many veterans are proud of having served their country and remain fiercely patriotic. The veteran won't explore meaningful issues with you if they sense you are judging them. You need to examine your own feelings before you try to delve into the emotions of the veteran.
- **Be supportive of families of veterans suffering from PTSD.** Long-term support is essential. Substance abuse may be a family problem that will require counseling. Some veterans with such problems often have not sought help at Vet Centers and are undiagnosed. Encourage the veteran to seek help by attending support group meetings and counseling at a Vet Center if one is available locally.
- **Be aware that women Vietnam veterans may also suffer from PTSD.** Women were often exposed to death and dying on a regular basis and experience the same readjustment problems.
- **Be familiar with veterans' readjustment services,** provided through Vet Centers available in your community, or one nearby, so that you can refer the veteran for additional counseling. The Vet Centers provide services for veterans of other wars also. To obtain information about the location of the nearest Vet Center, consult your local telephone directory under "United States Government" under Veterans Administration; call a local veterans organization; or contact the Congressman's office in your district.
- **Be supportive of veterans' organizations and, if asked, participate in functions.** Your presence means you care.
- **Encourage your church to sponsor a veteran who speaks to veterans from the pulpit or to organized groups.** Veteran evangelists are listed. Veteran speakers may sometimes be obtained from the Vietnam Veterans of America or ViêtNow organizations.
- **Encourage your church to give public recognition to veterans of all wars in some way.** Update the memorial plaques honoring veterans. By doing so, the church is recognizing the sacrifice and spiritual needs of veterans and their families, not condoning war.
- **Offer to place the POW/MIA flag in your sanctuary to remind the congregation of those men missing and their families.** Contact a local VVA chapter for more information.

Vets With a Mission
Rev. William Kimball
P.O. Box 16713
South Lake Tahoe, CA 95706
(916)544–4357

Chuck Dean, Executive Director
Point Man International
440 Mount Lake Terrace,
WA 98043
(206)486–5383

Mickey Block
Saved to Serve Ministries
4016 Longstraw Drive
Fort Worth, TX 76137

Rodney Hamilton
Jesus' People Ministry
377 South 600 West
Layton, UT 84041
(801)544–7550

Roger Helle, Executive Director
Teen Challenge of the Midlands
P.O. Box 185
Colfax, IA 50054
(515)674–3713

Mac Gober
Canaan Land Boys Home
Box 310
Prattville, AL 36067
(205)365–2200

The following resources may be helpful in preparing for ministry with Vietnam vets or for follow-up sessions about the nature of wartime memories and the Vietnam experience.

Videos and Films

"Home is Hell," video by Mickey Block ($39.95), Saved to Serve, Inc., 4016 Longstraw Drive, Fort Worth, TX 76137, (817)237–8491.
"The Mickey Block Testimony" video ($39.95); see address above.

(Both of these are recommended by Vets with a Mission to introduce the Vietnam issue.)
"Portrait of an American Hero," by Gospel Films. Film can be ordered through your local Christian bookstore or by calling Gospel Films at (300)253–0413. This film is recommended for the entire church.

Books

Vietnam: the Other Side of Glory, by William R. Kimball; hardcover— $16.95 Daring Books, P.O. Box 526, Canton, OH, 44701, 1–800–445– 6321; paperback—$3.95 Ballantine Books, 201 E. 50th St., New York, NY 10022.
Vietnam: Curse or Blessing, by John Steer; paperback, New Leaf Press, P.O. Box 311, Green Forest, AR 72638. (To obtain, write: Living Word Ministries, 75 Holmes Road, Charlotte, AR, 72522. Cost: $6.00.)

My War Beyond Vietnam, by Roger Helle; paperback. Word, Inc., 5221 North O'Connor Blvd., Suite 1000, Irving, TX 75039.

Before the Dawn, by Mickey Block; hardcover $15.00, Saved to Serve Ministries, 4016 Longstraw Drive, Fort Worth, TX 76137, (817)847-1637.

Welcome Home, Davey, by Dave Roever; hardcover $12.95, Word, Inc., address same as above.

Nam Vet: Making Peace with Your Past, by Chuck Dean; paperback $6.95. Point Man International, P.O. Box 440, Mount Lake Terrace, WA 98043.

Out of the Night: The Spiritual Journey of Vietnam Vets, by William Mahedy; hardcover and paperback. Ballantine Books, 1986. Available on videocassette from Graley Taylor, Religious Broadcasting Commission, 500 Wall St., Suite 45, Seattle, WA 98121, (206)441-6110. Write or call for pricing information.

VETERANS DAY RECOGNITION SERVICE

The following service was first presented as an afternoon service on November 5, 1989, at the Church of Peace United Church of Christ, in Rock Island, Illinois. It is included as a suggested outline for recognition services by local parishes to honor veterans. Participants addressing issues pertaining to veterans were Vietnam veterans. Each presentation was five minutes in length. Space does not allow publishing messages of each participant; this is merely an outline for you to follow.

We Remember . . . We Care . . . We Want to Understand

Prelude: "Amazing Grace"

Prayer of Invocation: (Unison)

Gracious God, we assemble today to recognize the service and sacrifices men and women veterans have made for this country and to learn about the crucial issues facing veterans today. To that end, bless our coming together. Amen.

Welcome: Local Pastor

Honor Roll Plaques

Plaques bearing the names of men and women of the local parish who served during the Korean and Vietnam era were presented.

Introduction of Guests

Hymn: "Not Alone for Mighty Empire"
Introduction of Speakers:
                Comments by Mayor of the City

"The Spiritual and Moral Aftermath of War"
(Vet Center Team Leader, Presenter)

"Post-traumatic Stress Disorder—War's Toll on Human Personality"
(Veteran shared how PTSD affected his life)

"Health Care Issues and Current Legislation"
(Representative from Congressman Lane Evans's office, presenter)

"Tribute to Women Veterans"
(Veteran told of important role women played in Vietnam)

"Missing Men in Southeast Asia"
(Veteran explained plight of unaccounted-for soldiers.)

POW/MIA Flag Presentation by local VVA Chapter
(Flag was presented to church for display in sanctuary as reminder of
POWs/MIAs.)

A Tribute to Those Who Died

Memorial Service
(For two readers)

FIRST READER: As in all wars, many innocent people and many young men
die leaving a terrible void in the lives of fellow soldiers, their families and
friends. The memory of their deaths often leave haunting memories for
those especially close.
Many of you here today have experienced such losses. Some of you lost
buddies; some lost sons, fathers, brothers, nephews, or friends.
But for those who embrace the Christian faith, those painful images are
transformed by the visions of life after death as revealed in Scripture.
Listen, as the Apostle Paul describes what he believes about a new body:
SECOND READER: "For we know that when this tent we live in now is taken
down—when we die and leave these bodies—we will have wonderful
new bodies in heaven, homes that will be ours forever, made for us by
God himself, and not by human hands" (2 Cor. 5:1).
FIRST READER: Heaven is frequently described as a realm or place far
different from this earth. It is a place where there will be no more
foxholes or hooches, no more bombs or napalm, no more death or gaping
wounds, and no more pain.

SECOND READER: "He will wipe every tear from their eyes, and death shall be no more, neither shall there be mourning nor crying nor pain any more, for the former things have passed away" (Rev. 21:4, RSV).

FIRST READER: Scripture, therefore, teaches us that death is not the end of life. Basic to our existence is that hope that one day, we will see our friends and loved ones.

SECOND READER: We live in hope that in the final day, we will see our brothers and sisters again, face to face, where they shall know us and we them, and we will not be strangers.

FIRST READER: Knowing all this, shall we pause now to remember these loved ones and all the while, envisioning them in new bodies, made by God.

(Pause for silent meditation)

SECOND READER: "I am the resurrection and the life, he that believeth in me, though he were dead, yet shall he live; and whosoever liveth and believeth in me shall never die" (John 11:25–26).

(Taps were played following these readings.)

Following these veteran presentations, a denominational official responded with appropriate comments.

Anthem: "America, the Beautiful"

Responsive Prayer:

LEADER: Lord God, this day we have assembled to build bridges of understanding between civilians and those who have served in our country's military forces.

PEOPLE: MAY YOUR SPIRIT BLESS OUR COMING TOGETHER AND BE ACTIVE AMONG US.

LEADER: We thank You for each veteran's commitment to this country, and for their idealism to make this a better and safer world in which to live.

PEOPLE: THANK YOU, LORD, FOR THEIR WILLINGNESS TO GIVE THE FULL MEASURE OF THEIR DEVOTION.

LEADER: For all who have come back physically strong and unmarked,

PEOPLE: WE GIVE YOU THANKS, O GOD.

LEADER: Many, because of their combat experiences, suffer from delayed stress. Sounds or smells bring back memories. Flashbacks come at anytime. Nightmares disturb their sleep.

PEOPLE: WE LIFT THESE MEN AND WOMEN TO YOU, O GOD.

LEADER: Some families lost loved ones in war. As a result parents, partners, children, community, and church must go on without the benefit of their presence, wisdom, and love.

PEOPLE: O GOD, HELP US TO UNDERSTAND THE WASTE OF WAR TO US ALL.

LEADER: Some have been prisoners of war and know the agony of that experience; others have been responsible for prisoners in their keeping; and still others were commanded not to take prisoners.

PEOPLE: LORD, THOSE EXPERIENCES ARE HAUNTING AND PAINFUL AND WE THANK YOU FOR THE PRIVILEGE OF LAYING THESE BURDENS AT YOUR ALTAR. WE ASK FOR HEALING.

LEADER: For people whose land has been occupied by foreign troops and all the indignities that are associated with that, as well as atrocities committed by them, and the atrocities committed to them,

PEOPLE: FOR THIS, WE LIFT THESE PEOPLE AND OURSELVES TO YOU, O GOD.

LEADER: For those spat upon when they returned to this country, and for those who did the spitting,

PEOPLE: WE ASK THE BLESSING OF YOUR GRACE, O GOD, THAT THERE MIGHT BE FORGIVENESS AND UNDERSTANDING, AND A READINESS TO LISTEN TO EACH OTHER.

LEADER: Many have turned to alcohol and to drugs to drown their grief and bury their pain.

PEOPLE: TEACH US, O GOD, TO BE SENSITIVE TO THE DEEPER NEEDS AND HURTS OF THE VETERAN, AND GRANT THEIR COUNSELORS WISDOM.

LEADER: Some vets are filled with rage and bitterness because they feel used and abandoned.

PEOPLE: LORD, HELP US TO HEAR AND UNDERSTAND AND STRIVE TO CORRECT WHAT CAN BE CORRECTED.

LEADER: Some are at the edge, almost ready to end their lives because of the despair and isolation they feel.

PEOPLE: LORD, WE CARE. MAKE US WISE BEYOND OUR KNOWING.

LEADER: For the families of those veterans who have taken their own lives to end the pain of wartime memories,

PEOPLE: WE LIFT THESE LOVED ONES TO YOU, O GOD.

LEADER: The homes of some veterans have been filled with so much anger and tension that divorces have resulted.

PEOPLE: LORD GOD, SOME OF THE PROBLEMS ARE NOT OF THEIR OWN MAKING. TEACH US HOW TO CARE. TEACH US HOW TO HELP.

LEADER: For the incarcerated veterans for whom the war never ended,

PEOPLE: WE LIFT THEM TO YOU, O GOD, AND MAY WE NOT FORGET THEM.

LEADER: Some veterans can no longer trust and are not at peace anywhere, so they roam the streets, disconnected from home, family, society, and themselves.

PEOPLE: O GOD, HELP US TO UNDERSTAND WHAT WAR DOES TO VICTOR AND VICTIM.

LEADER: Some veterans have come back with disfigurement or disabilities. Some live at home, others in nursing homes.

PEOPLE: O GOD, WE LIFT TO YOU THE FRUSTRATIONS OF THOSE WITH LIMITATIONS AND SHATTERED SELF-IMAGES.

LEADER: For veterans, their wives and family members, and those legislators who work tirelessly to correct injustices against veterans and their families,

PEOPLE: WE GIVE YOU THANKS, O GOD, AND ASK YOUR BLESSING.

LEADER: For those imprisoned in bodies that are dying from the effects of radiation or toxic herbicides,

PEOPLE: MAY WE BE SUPPORTIVE OF THEM AND THEIR FAMILIES.

LEADER: For those missing in action and for those unaccounted for,

PEOPLE: MAY WE WORK TIRELESSLY TO GET COMPLETE REPORTS AND THE RELEASE OF ANY STILL HELD AGAINST THEIR WILLS.

LEADER: For those who have had a faith crisis, but not found the church helpful,

PEOPLE: O GOD, WE PRAY FOR AN AWAKENING WITHIN THE CHURCH, THAT BOTH THE JUDGMENT AND THE HEALING OF THE GOSPEL MIGHT BE HEARD AND EXPERIENCED.

LEADER: Our government has granted Amerasian children and their families permission to come to this country to start their lives anew.

PEOPLE: O GOD, HELP US TO WELCOME THESE NEW IMMIGRANTS AS THEY STRIVE TO ADJUST TO A STRANGE NEW LAND WITH DIFFERENT CUSTOMS, A DIFFERENT LANGUAGE, AND DIFFERENT RELIGIONS.

LEADER: Some veterans are speaking at churches and schools and civic groups, making known the effects of war.

PEOPLE: WE THANK YOU FOR THEIR INSIGHTS, O GOD.

LEADER: War affects each of us differently. So now, God, in moments of silence, hear the prayers and petitions of Your people, and grant us Your peace . . . (silent prayers).

UNISON: O GOD, SCRIPTURE HAS IT THAT "FAITH IS THE EVIDENCE OF THINGS HOPED FOR AND THE CONVICTION OF THINGS NOT SEEN." MAY A PULLING TOGETHER AND SUPPORT AND RESPECT FOR ONE ANOTHER BE EXPERIENCED HERE TODAY. AMEN.

Hymn Response

Offertory
The offering was designated for and given to the Food Pantry of the local VVA chapter to assist unemployed veterans.

Doxology

Hymn: "We Yearn, O Lord, for Wholeness"

Benediction

Postlude

* * *

A reception was held following the service for refreshments and celebration.

Appendix E

HOW TO HELP POWS/MIAS

If you are interested in creating public awareness about the unresolved POW/MIA issue, the National League of Families suggests these ways in which you can help support efforts to bring back POWs/MIAs.

Write Letters:

To members of Congress, urging them to help in making the American people aware of the POW/MIA issue, to offer bipartisan support for the U.S. government's current high priority on accounting for 2,300 missing Americans (29 August 1989 League figures).

(Name of Representative)	(Name of Senator)
House of Representatives	U.S. Senate
Washington, DC 20515	Washington, DC 20510

To editors of local papers, in an effort to draw responsible public attention to the missing men and counter misinformation with facts.

To the Vietnamese and the Lao, urging them to increase efforts to fulfill their commitments to cooperate fully with the U.S. government to resolve the POW/MIA issue. Send your letters to:

SRV Mission to the UN
20 Waterside Plaza, J35
New York, NY 10010

LPDR Mission to the UN
820 Second Avenue, Suite 400
New York, NY 10017

Create Public Awareness:

Remember POWs/MIAs in ceremonies, including Veterans Day, Memorial Day, Christmas services, and National POW/MIA Recognition Week in September and other appropriate occasions. The National League can provide you with a packet of materials suggesting ways that you can create public awareness during Recognition Week.

Wear A POW/MIA Bracelet. By doing so, you can take a deeper interest in the fate of the person on your bracelet. To obtain a bracelet, write: Schilling Engraving, 202 Grand Ave., Spencer, IA 51301. Cost is $4.50. You may request a specific name or one from a specific state; if you have no preference, ask to be assigned a name.

You can write to the military branch of service that your serviceman belonged to for additional information about him. List the person's name, branch, date missing, and country where listed as missing. Be patient . . . it may take a while, but you will get a response.

NAVY: Department of the Navy
            Washington, DC 20370–5120
            (202)694–3336

ARMY: U.S. Army Military Personnel Center
            DAPC-PED/2461 Eisenhower Avenue
            Alexandria, VA 22331–0400
            (703)325–7960/5303

AF: AFMPC/DPMCB
            Randolph AFB, TX 78150–6001
            (800)531–5501

MC: HGUSMC (CODE MHP-10)
            Washington, DC 20380–0001

NOTES

INTRODUCTION

1. Jan C. Scruggs and Joel L. Swerdlow, *To Heal A Nation* (New York: Harper & Row, 1985).
2. "Unnatural Causes," A Viewer's Guide by Cultural Information Service, 10 November 1986, p. 6.
3. William P. Mahedy, *Out of the Night: The Spiritual Journey of Vietnam Vets* (New York: Ballantine, 1986), p. 6.

HOW AND WHY THE UNITED STATES GOT INVOLVED   CHAPTER 1

1. Richard F. Newcomb, *What YOU Should Know About Vietnam* (The Associated Press, 1967), p. 6.
2. Howard Zinn, "The Impossible Victory: Vietnam," in *A People's History of the United States* (New York: Harper & Row, 1980), pp. 460–461.
3. David Halberstam, *Ho* (New York: Random House, 1971), p. 92.
4. George Esper and The Associated Press, *The Eyewitness History of the Vietnam War* (New York: Ballantine, 1983), p. 6.
5. Zinn, op. cit., p. 461.
6. Jean Lacouture, *Ho Chi Minh: A Political Biography* (New York: Random House, 1968), p. 26.
7. Ibid., p. 31.
8. General Bruce Palmer, Jr., *The 25-Year War: America's Military Role in Vietnam* (New York: Simon & Schuster, 1985), p. 5.
9. Ernest Cuneo, "The Problems of Limited War," *The American Legion*, (November 1987), p. 29. The basic teaching of Sun Tzu is that the

supreme military achievement is subduing an enemy without fighting. Sun Tzu holds that the enemy's main army should never be attacked. It must be exhausted by forcing it to march to the defense of its weaknesses—never offering it battle—maneuvering it into constant effort and harassing it when it seeks rest. Sun Tzu regarded the intelligence system as the prime striking force in waging war. Under the system were five classes of agents: native country people who reported on terrain and living conditions; inside agents such as corruptible enemy officials who ascertained enemy plans, created internal dissension, and provided continuous intelligence on enemy strengths and weaknesses; "double agents," or spies who could be "turned around" by bribing or threatening them; "expendables," who functioned by furnishing false information to the enemy ("disinformation," which is a category that the KGB raised to full department status); and those who moved in and out of every territory, ostensibly on legitimate business. . . . Sun Tzu's strategy called for these agents to work from within, creating dissent and confusion in the enemy's ranks. As the enemy became exhausted, it would lose its will to resist; its forces then would collapse without a battle. Traditionally, American military have followed the teachings of Gen. Karl von Clausewitz, a nineteenth-century Prussian, who believed that grouping large armies into a great array that conquers in a great battle was the key to Napoleon's triumphs. He taught that effective war is waged by pushing violence to its utmost bounds. Its objective is to break the enemy's will to resist. Its cardinal rule is that *unlimited force* must be used.

10. *Television's Vietnam: The Real Story/The Impact of Media* © 1984 and 1985, Accuracy in Media, Inc.
11. Al Santoli, *To Bear Any Burden* (New York: Ballantine, 1986), p. 53.
12. Marc Leepson, *Veteran* (Vol. 8, No. 11/12, November/December 1988), p. 22. Book Review of *Decision Against War* by Melania Billings-Yun.
13. Palmer, op. cit., p. 9.
14. James Lawton Collins, Jr., *Development and Training of the South Vietnamese Army, 1950–1972*, Vietnamese Studies (Washington, D.C.: U.S. Department of the Army, 1975), pp. 2–4.
15. Zinn, op. cit., p. 465.
16. William S. Turley, *The Second Indochina War: A Short Political and Military History, 1954–1975* (Boulder, Colo.: Westview Press, 1986), p. 16.
17. Palmer, op. cit., p. 7.
18. Frances FitzGerald, *Fire in the Lake* (Boston: Little, Brown & Co., 1972).

19. Maxwell D. Taylor, *Swords and Plowshares* (New York: W. W. Norton, 1972), pp. 222–26, 245–47.
20. Thomas D. Boettcher, *Vietnam: The Valor and the Sorrow* (Boston: Little, Brown & Co., 1985), p. 190.
21. Tim Wells, "The Assassination of Ngo Dinh Diem," *Veteran* (Vol. 8, No. 10, October 1988), pp. 15–19.
22. Stanley Karnow, *Vietnam: A History* (New York: Viking Press, 1983), p. 22.
23. Phillip B. Davidson, *Vietnam at War: The History 1946–1975* (Novato, Calif.: Presidio, 1988), pp. 318–19.
24. Stockdale, Jim and Sybil, *In Love and War* (New York: Harper & Row, 1984), p. 25.
25. Stockdale, op. cit., p. 454.
26. Newcomb, op. cit., p. 9.
27. Palmer, op. cit., pp. 12–13.
28. *Television's History: The Real Story/The Impact of Media.*
29. Ibid.
30. *Dictionary of American History*, Vol. VIII (New York: Charles Scribner's Sons, 1976, 1961, 1940), p. 237.
31. Palmer, op. cit., p. ii.
32. Tom Riddell, "The Inflationary Impact of the Vietnam War," *Vietnam Generation* (Vol. 1, No. 1), p. 45, as quoted from the U.S. Department of Defense (Comptroller), *The Economics of Defense Spending* (Washington, D.C.: US Government Printing Office, 1972), p. 149.
33. Doyle et. al, *The Aftermath: The Legacy of War, 1975–1985* (Boston: Boston Publishing Company, 1985), p. 106.
34. Zinn, op. cit., p. 469.
35. VVA Staff Report, "POW/MIA Fact-Finding Mission in Indochina," *Veteran* (Vol. 9, No. 7, July 1989), p. 9.
36. Karnow, op. cit., p. 11.
37. Betty Sue Flowers, ed. *Bill Moyers: A World of Ideas* (New York: Doubleday, 1989), p. 12.

WHY VIETNAM WAS A DIFFERENT WAR   CHAPTER 2

1. Joel Brende, M.D., edited by Gary Sorenson, Vet Center *Voice* (Fargo, N.D.: Vol. VI, No. 11, December 1985), p. 10.
2. Tom Williams, Psy.D., *Post-Traumatic Stress Disorder: A Handbook for Clinicians* (Cincinnati, Ohio: Disabled American Veterans, 1987), p. 86.
3. L. Fiedler, "Who Really Died in Vietnam?" *Saturday Review* (18 November 1972), pp. 44–49.

4. Mark Shields, " 'Volunteers' For America," *Washington Post* (4 August 1987), p. A15.
5. Marc Pilisuk, "The Legacy of the Vietnam Veteran," *Journal of Social Issues* (Vol. 31, No. 4, 1975), p. 4.
6. Irving M. Allen, M.D., "Post-traumatic Stress Disorder Among Black Vietnam Veterans," *Hospital and Community Psychiatry* (Vol. 37, No. 1, January 1986), p. 55.
7. Kolb, Richard K., Chairman, Houston Vietnam Veterans' Leadership Programs of Houston, "Vietnam Veteran Statistics" (20 March 1985), p. 3.
8. Laura Palmer, *Shrapnel in the Heart* (New York: Random House, 1987), p. 57.
9. Marc Leepson, "Going After Tim O'Brien," *Veteran* (Vol. 7, No. 5, May 1987), p. 31.
10. Jim Goodwin, Psy.D., "Readjustment Problems Among Vietnam Veterans," a brochure published by Disabled American Veterans, pp. 6–7.
11. Byron Coghlan is a psychiatric social worker. Since earning his master's degree from the University of Iowa in 1978, he worked in Veterans Administration's Readjustment Counseling Services until 1989. He presently serves as Staff Assistant to the director at Mountain Home VAMC in Johnson City, Tennessee.
12. Goodwin, op. cit., p. 8.
13. Private interview with Byron Coghlan, M.S.W., 16 June 1987.
14. Dr. Robert J. Lifton, Congressional Hearing, *The Vietnam Veteran in Contemporary Society* (Washington, D.C.: Veterans Administration, May 1972), pp. iv–28.
15. William Kimball, *Vietnam: The Other Side of Glory* (Canton, Ohio: Daring Books, 1987), p. 213.
16. Joel Osler Brende, M.D., and Erwin Randolph Parson, Ph.D., *Vietnam Veterans: The Road to Recovery* (New York: Plenum Press, 1985), p. 65.
17. Peter Goldman and Tony Fuller, *Charlie Company: What Vietnam Did to Us* (New York: Ballantine, 1983), p. 1. (A *Newsweek* book.)
18. As cited in Gerard Caplan, M.D., Congressional Testimony, *The Vietnam Veteran in Contemporary Society* (Washington: Veterans Administration, May, 1972), pp. iv–22.
19. James William Gibson, *The Perfect War: The War We Couldn't Lose and How We Did* (New York: Random House), p. 209.
20. Ibid., p. 472.
21. Philip Caputo, *A Rumor of War* (New York: Ballantine, 1977), p. xix.
22. Lifton, p. 48.

23. Caputo, pp. *xviii–xiv*.
24. Charles Moskos, "The American Combat Soldier in Vietnam," *Journal of Social Issues* (Vol. 31, No. 4, 1975), p. 25.
25. Jerry L. and Sandra S. Straight, *Vietnam War Memorials: An Illustrated Reference to Veterans Tributes Throughout the United States* (Jefferson, N.C.: McFarland & Company, Inc., 1988).
26. Coglan interview, 16 June 1987.
27. Wallace Terry, *Bloods: An Oral History of the Vietnam War by Black Americans* (New York: Ballantine, 1984), p. *xv*.

THEY CAME HOME CHANGED—WHAT IS
POST-TRAUMATIC STRESS DISORDER?   CHAPTER 3

1. VVA Staff Report, "War and Memory: Picking Up the Pieces After PTSD," *Veteran* (Vol. 8, No. 9, September 1988), p. 13.
2. Tom Williams, Psy.D., ed., *Post-Traumatic Stress Disorders: A Handbook for Clinicians* (Cincinnati, Ohio: Disabled American Veterans National Headquarters), p. 206.
3. Interview with Richard A. Kulka, 4 January 1989. It should be noted that the "Contractual Report of Findings from the National Vietnam Veterans Readjustment Study" done by the Research Triangle Institute (7 November 1988) identified nine other postwar psychological problems (in addition to PTSD) suffered by veterans. They are: *Affective Disorders* such as Major Depressive Episode, Manic Episode, and Dysthymia; *Anxiety Disorders* such as Panic Disorder, Obsessive Compulsive Disorder, and Generalized Anxiety Disorder; and *Substance Abuse Disorders* such as Alcohol Abuse or Dependence, Drug Abuse or Dependence, and Antisocial Personality Disorder.
4. Studies: Frye and Stockton (1982); Foy, Sipprelle, Rueger and Carroll (1984); Wilson and Krauss (1981); Card (1983); Keane, Scott, Chavoya, Lamparski, and Fairbank (1985); authors Solkoff, Gray, and Keill (1986) as cited in "Which Vietnam Veterans Develop Post-traumatic Stress Disorders?" *Journal of Clinical Psychology* (Vol. 42, No. 5, September 1986).
5. David Holzman, "Peace Is Elusive for Some Veterans," *Insight* (12 August 1988), p. 50.
6. Daniel Goleman, "A Key to Post-Traumatic Stress Lies in Brain Chemistry, Scientists Find," *New York Times*, 12 June 1990, C1.
7. Ibid.
8. *Quad-City Times*, 27 June 1988, p. 6.
9. Chuck Dean with Bob Putnam, *Nam Vet: Making Peace with Your Past* (Mountlake Terrace, Wash.: Point Man International, 1988), p. 94.

10. VVA Staff Report, op. cit., pp. 11–13.
11. Richard Restak, M.D., *The Brain* (New York: Bantam, 1984), pp. 211–12.
12. Private interview with Phil Ross, R.N., 20 August 1987.
13. Private interview with Jan Scruggs, 21 July 1988.
14. Holzman, op. cit., p. 50.
15. Goleman, op. cit.
16. In Holzman, op. cit., p. 51.
17. Private interview with Fred Gusman, 10 August 1989.
18. Gregory Bittle, "Posttraumatic Stress Disorder—A Conversation with Charles Figley," *Vocational Rehabilitation and Counseling Professional Review* (Fall 1988), p. 10.
19. Joel Brende, M.D., "Twelve Steps to PTSD Treatment Prove Successful," ed. by Gary Sorenson, Vet Center *Voice* (Vol. VI, No. 11, December 1985), pp. 10–12.
20. Telephone interview with Robert Erikson, Ph.D., 16 November 1988.
21. Kim Heron, "The Long Road Back," *New York Times Magazine*, 6 March 1988, p. 33.
22. Dean, op. cit., p. 36.
23. Mickey Block and William Kimball, *Before the Dawn* (Canton, Ohio: Daring Books, 1988), pp. 187–88.
24. John Steer with Cliff Dudley, *Vietnam: Curse or Blessing* (Green Forest, Ark.: New Leaf Press, 1982), pp. 190–91.
25. Brende, in Vet Center *Voice*, pp. 10–12. Reproduced by permission of author.

WOMEN—THE FORGOTTEN VETERANS   CHAPTER 4

1. Triage is a method of sorting casualties according to priority of need determined by the chances of survival. The priorities of a military casualty situation are the reverse of the natural inclination: the most seriously wounded are relegated to the lowest treatment priority. Since those patients are expected to die, they receive the least care and resources so as to allow personnel to treat more casualties with less severe injuries, according to Linda Spoonster Schwartz, R.N., M.S.N., in "Women and the Vietnam Experience," *IMAGE: Journal of Nursing Scholarship* (Vol. 19, No. 4, Winter 1987), p. 171.
2. Lynda Van Devanter with Christopher Morgan, *Home Before Morning* (New York: Beaufort Books, 1983; Reprint ed. New York: Warner Books, 1984).
3. Schwartz, op. cit.
4. Doreen Spelts, "Nurses Who Served—And Did Not Return," *Ameri-*

can Journal of Nursing (September 1986), pp. 1037–39. Their names were: 2nd Lt. Carol Ann Drazba; 2nd Lt. Elizabeth Ann Jones; 1st Lt. Hedwig Diane Orlowski; Capt. Eleanor Grace Alexander; 1st Lt. Kenneth R. Shoemaker, Jr.; 1st Lt. Jerome Edwin Olmsted; 2nd Lt. Pamela Dorothy Donovan; Lt. Col. Annie Ruth Graham; 1st Lt. Sharon Ann Lane; and Capt. Mary Therese Klinker.

5. Rose Sandecki, "Women Veterans," *Post-Traumatic Stress Disorders: A Handbook for Clinicians* (Cincinnati, Ohio: Disabled American Veterans, 1987), p. 164.
6. Ibid, pp. 160–61.
7. Keith Walker, *A Piece of My Heart* (New York: Ballantine, 1985), p. 2.
8. "Invisible Veterans: A Legacy of Healing and Hope," Washington, D.C.: The Vietnam Women's Memorial Project, Inc.
9. O'Neill, Jacquelyn S., and Elizabeth A. Paul, *The Psychological Milieu of Nursing in Vietnam and Its Effects on Vietnam Nurse Veterans* (College of Nursing, Northwestern State University of Louisiana, Shreveport, LA, January 1984), p. 85–88.
10. Schwartz, op. cit., p. 169.
11. Vincent Coppola, "They Also Served," *Newsweek* (12 November 1984), p. 36.
12. Schwartz, op. cit., p. 169.
13. Ibid.
14. Rita K. Tamerius, "Vietnam—A Legacy of Healing," *California Nursing Review* (September/October 1988), p. 45.
15. O'Neill and Paul Study, pp. 89–90.
16. Tamerius, op. cit., p. 38.
17. Ibid., p. 16.
18. Sandecki, op. cit., p. 165.
19. In Coppola, op. cit., p. 35.
20. Kulka, et al., *Executive Summary NVVR Study* (7 November 1988), p. 31.
21. *Veteran* (November/December 1988), p. 32.
22. "Communication from the Women's Advisory Committee of the New Jersey Agent Orange Commission to Women Who Served in the Republic of Vietnam Between 1960 and 1973 (Military, Red Cross, Missionaries, and Other Civilians)," 1988.
23. *Veteran* (September 1988), p. 14.
24. In Coppola, op. cit., p. 36.
25. In Cliff Borden, "Vietnam Nurse," *Veterans Affairs in Wisconsin* (January 1985), p. 13.
26. Invisible Veterans, op. cit.
27. *Congressional Record*, 23 September 1988, H 8104–09.

OVERCOMING THE EMOTIONAL SCARS OF
PHYSICAL WOUNDS   CHAPTER 5

1. In Ken Carlson, Rock Island *Argus* (19 September 1976), pp. 1–2.
2. Rita K. Tamerius, "Vietnam—A Legacy of Healing," *California Nursing Review* (September/October 1988), p. 16.
3. "Report on the Working Group on Physically Disabled Vietnam Veterans, Submitted to Readjustment Counseling Service Department of Veterans Affairs," Washington, D.C., April, 1988, p. 8.
4. Disabled American Veterans Fact Sheet, p. 4.
5. Ibid.
6. Ibid.
7. Ibid.
8. Telephone interview with Frederick Downs, 29 September 1989.
9. Frederick Downs, *The Killing Zone* (New York: Berkley, 1978), preface.
10. Dave Roever with Harold Fickett, *Welcome Home, Davey* (Waco, Tex.: Word Books, 1986), pp. 128–29.
11. Delores A. Kuenning, *Helping People Through Grief* (Minneapolis, Minn.: Bethany House, 1987), pp. 165–67.

WARRIORS' WOMEN—LIVING WITH A VIETNAM VETERAN   CHAPTER 6

1. "No More Tears," anonymous Vietnam wife, unpublished manuscript.
2. Idem, telephone interview, 2 November 1987.
3. Maryln March, telephone interview, 9 November 1988.
4. Candice Williams, "The Veteran System with A Focus on Women Partners," *Post-Traumatic Stress Disorders: A Handbook for Clinicians*, ed. by Tom Williams (Cincinnati, Ohio: Disabled American Veterans National Headquarters, 1987), p. 185.
5. Kulka et al., *Executive Summary: Contractual Report of Findings from the National Vietnam Veterans Readjustment Study* (Research Triangle Park, N.C.: Research Triangle Institute, 1988), p. 13.
6. Ibid., p. 25.
7. Ibid., p. 20.
8. Williams, op. cit., p. 184.
9. Ibid., p. 183.
10. Janine Lenger-Gvist, private interview, 26 August 1987.
11. Judy O'Brien, R.N., public lecture, 1987 Illinois ViêtNow State Convention, Bloomington, Illinois, 21 May 1987.
12. Interview with Dr. Erle Fitz in Des Moines, Iowa, 28 September 1987.

13. Aphrodite Matsakis, *Vietnam Wives* (Kensington, Md.: Woodbine House, 1988), p. 130.
14. Ibid, p. 354.
15. Stark, E. et al., "Wife Abuse in the Medical Setting: An Introduction for Health Personnel," Monograph Series No. 7, National Clearinghouse on Domestic Violence, Washington, D.C.: U.S. Government Printing Office, April 1981.
16. Robert Marrs, *Post-Traumatic Stress Disorder and the War Veteran Patient*, ed. William E. Kelly (Larchmont, N.Y.: Brunner/Mazel, 1985), pp. 93–94.

THE ENDURING WOUNDS OF AGENT ORANGE   CHAPTER 7

1. Letter dated 24 March 1987 written by B. S. Ajaikumar, M.D., Burlington, Iowa, submitted as testimony in Congressional Hearings before the U.S. House and Senate Veterans Affairs Committee on 12 May 1988.
2. Medical record/autopsy report and postmortem laboratory results on Wayne Barton, VAMC Iowa City, Iowa, 2 April 1987, pp. 3, 9.
3. Steven D. Stellman, Jeanne M. Stellman, and John F. Sommer, Jr., "Combat and Herbicide Exposures in Vietnam Among a Sample of American Legionnaires," Department of Epidemiology and Statistics, American Cancer Society, New York, New York; School of Public Health, Columbia University; and National Veterans Affairs and Rehabilitation Commission, The American Legion, Washington, D.C.
4. Letter to Senator Tom Harkin from Daniel H. Winship, M.D., dated 25 May 1988.
5. Veterans Administration 38 CFR Ch. 1 (7–1–85 Edition), Subpart A— General Policy in Rating, 4.3 Resolution of reasonable doubt (40 FR 42535, Sept. 15, 1975), p. 157.
6. Telephone interview with Wayne Wilson, Executive Director of the New Jersey Commission on Agent Orange 24 August 1988.
7. Letter to Mary Barton from Peter C. Kahn, Ph.D., dated 23 January 1989.
8. Rappe, C., G. Choudhary, and L. Keith, eds., *Chlorinated Dioxins and Dibenzofurans in Perspective* (Chelsea, Mich.: Lewis Publishers, 1986), p. 46.
9. Testimony of the National Association of Agent Orange Survivors in Congress, Veterans Affairs Committee, 12 May 1988.
10. Breslin et al., "Proportionate Mortality Study of Army and Marine Corps Veterans of the Vietnam War" (Washington, D.C.: Veterans Administration, 1987), p. 15.

11. Transcript of Hearing, Board of Veterans Appeals, Washington, D.C., 16 November 1988.
12. National Veterans Law Center, "The Veteran's Self-Help Guide on Agent Orange," February, 1983, p. 2.
13. Unpublished paper of Mark Thoman, M.D., former president of the American Academy of Clinical Toxicology, 1980, Des Moines, Iowa.
14. For further study of occupational or environmental incidents of exposure to dioxin, refer to studies on Seveso, Italy, ICMESA plant explosion; Kansas farmers; Alsea, Oregon; Yusho, Japan, contaminated rice oil; Pigeon River, Tenn.; Love Canal, Hooker chemical wastes. Contact George Claxton for more information.
15. "Self-Help Guide," op. cit., p. 2.
16. John Pilger, *The Last Day* (New York: Vantage, 1975), 9:00 A.M. entry.
17. Proceedings, Conference on the Effects of the Use of Herbicides in War, 1983, Vietnam Health Ministry Publications, 1983.
18. Drs. Ton That Tung, Ton Duc Lang, and Do Duc Van (Viet Duc Hospital, Hanoi, Vietnam), "The Mutagenecity of Dioxin and Its Effects on Reproduction among Exposed War Veterans," unpublished paper.
19. "Vietnam Veterans' Risks for Fathering Babies with Birth Defects," Centers for Disease Control, 17 August 1984.
20. Anthony L. Kimery, "Focus: New VA Study Connects Dioxins to Birth Defects," *Veteran* (Vol. 8, No. 1 January 1988), p. 9.
21. As cited by Admiral E. R. Zumwalt, Jr., "Report to the Secretary of the Department of Veterans Affairs on the Association Between Adverse Health Effects and Exposure to Agent Orange," 5 May 1990, p. 44.
22. Telephone interview with Professor Ken Ruder, 13 May 1988.
23. Agent Orange Product Liability Litigation, MDL No. 381.
24. Taken from: World Health Organization, International Agency for Research on Cancer, Monographs on the Evaluation of the Carcinogenic Risk of Chemicals to Man, Vol. 15 (Lyon, France: August 1977).
25. Lewis, Judy, ed., "National Association of Agent Orange Survivors Newsletter," p. 4. Legislation referred to is H.B. 4479 (Hochbrueckner) and S.B. 1805 (Mitchell).
26. VVA *Veteran*, Agent Orange Issue, December 1986, pp. 5–6, 14–15.
27. *For Veterans Only*, airdate 12 November 1988.
28. *Congressional Record*, 14 October 1987, Vol. 133, No. 160, p. 2.
29. In Tom Fruehling, "Agent Orange—Viet Vets Can Help Unravel Mystery That Affects Us All," *Cedar Rapids Gazette*, 19 February 1989.
30. Ibid.

31. Personal interview with Congressman Lane Evans, 29 January 1988, Moline, Illinois.
32. Zumwalt, op cit., p. 54.

WHEN LOVED ONES DID NOT COME HOME   CHAPTER 8

1. Mock, Herb, "Fullback 6" in *Everything We Had* by Al Santoli (New York: Ballantine, 1981), pp. 179–84.
2. Palmer, Laura. "Welcome Home," Rock Island *ARGUS*, 23 April 1989, A10.
3. Idem., 19 February 1989, p. A12.

POWs/MIAs—THEN AND NOW   CHAPTER 9

1. "POWs Tell the Inside Story," *U.S. News & World Report* (9 April 1973), p. 33.
2. Edna J. Hunter, Ph.D., "The Vietnam POW Veteran: Immediate and Long-Term Effects of Captivity," Charles Figley, ed., *Stress Disorders Among Vietnam Veterans: Theory, Research, and Treatment Implications*. (New York: Brunner/Mazel, 1978), p. 188.
3. Ibid., p. 194.
4. John G. Hubbell, *P.O.W.: A Definitive History of the American Prisoner-of-War Experience in Vietnam, 1964–1973* (New York: Reader's Digest Press, 1976), p. 410.
5. "Playboy Interview: Robert Garwood," *Playboy* (July 1981), p. 88.
6. Ibid., p. 188.
7. In Mike Blair, "Witness Says He's Positive," *The Spotlight* (10 July 1989), pp. 1, 2.
8. Telephone interview with Lt. Com. Edward Lundquist, 7 August 1989.
9. Margaret Shipro, "Freed Vietnam Captive Reports Seeing U.S. POWs," *Washington Post*, 9 June 1989.
10. U.S. Senator Charles Grassley personal correspondence to Charles Schantag, 10 July 1989.
11. Victoria Butler/Bangkok and Ross M. Munro/Washington, "Colonel Gritz's Dubious Mission," *Time* (4 April 1983), p. 31.
12. "MIA Families Are Hoping Reward Offers Reach Laos," Rock Island *Argus*, 18 September 1987, p. D1.
13. *Concerned Citizen Newsletter*, op. cit., 30 June 1989, p. 2.
14. Personal interview with Colleen Shine, 21 July 1988.
15. In Karen Cook, "Mary Comes Marching Home," *SAVVY* (March 1988), p. 102.

16. Department of Defense, *POW-MIA Fact Book*, July, 1989, p. 19.
17. "Vietnamese Plight To Be Examined," Rock Island *Argus*, 11 August 1987, p. C6.
18. VVA Staff Report, "Fact-Finding Mission in Indochina," *Veteran* (Vol. 9, No. 7, July 1989), p. 18.
19. "The Search for Missing Service Men," *Newsweek* (10 November 1980), p. 16.
20. M.S. Enkoll, "Mixup Leaves Mother Only a Dream to Bury," *USA Today*, 4 March 1988, p. 3A.

AMERASIANS—A LEGACY OF WAR   CHAPTER 10

1. Private interview with Betty Anderson, 4 October 1989.
2. Donald A. Ranard and Douglas F. Gilzow, "The Amerasians," *In America—Perspectives on Refugee Resettlement* (Number 4, June 1989), p. 6.
3. Stephen D. Goose and R. Kyle Horst, "Amerasians in Vietnam: Still Waiting," *Indochina Issues 83* (August 1988), p. 3.
4. Telephone interview with Marta Brenden, 11 November 1989.
5. Op. cit. Ranard and Gilzow, p. 2.
6. Ibid., p. 1.
7. Ibid., p. 4.
8. Op. cit. Ranard and Gilzow, p. 3.
9. Ibid., p. 2.
10. In Julia Lawlor, *USA Today*, 31 December 1987, p. 2A.
11. In Anne Keegan, "Three Fathers Struggle to Reclaim Past in Vietnam," *Chicago Tribune*, 3 May 1988, Section 1, p. 16.
12. Ibid.
13. Holly Fletcher, "San Jose Vet Center Staff Member Helps Locate Amerasian Children," *Scan* (Vol. 8, No. 2, February 1988), pp. 1, 4.
14. J. Kirk Felsman, "Vietnamese Amerasians: Practical Implications of Current Research," Office of Refugee Resettlement, 1989.
15. *The Oprah Winfrey Show*, 27 January 1988, transcripts by Journal Graphics, p. 3.
16. In Anne Keegan, "Amerasians Find Unlikely Allies in U.S. Women," *Chicago Tribune*, 8 November 1987.
17. Ibid.
18. *International Number Notice #22*, June 21, 1989. Courtesy of the American Red Cross.
19. "Amerasian Children in Vietnam," *International Number Notice #15*, March, 1988. As circulated 20 June 1989 by American Red Cross National Headquarters, p. 8.

WHERE WAS GOD IN VIETNAM?   CHAPTER 11

1. William Kimball, *Vietnam: The Other Side of Glory* (Canton, Ohio: Daring Books, 1987), p. 271.
2. In William E. Kelly, M.D., ed., *Post-Traumatic Stress Disorder and the War Veteran Patient* (New York: Brunner/Mazel, 1985), p. 89.
3. Kimball, op. cit., p. 321.
4. Ibid., p. 323.
5. A term first used by G. K. Chesterton; also used as a title by Sydney E. Mead and published in *Church History*, Vol. 36, No. 3, and reprinted in *American Civil Religion*.
6. Ron Kovic, *Born on the Fourth of July* (New York: Pocket Books, 1976), pp. 205–7.
7. William P. Mahedy, *Out of the Night: The Spiritual Journey of Vietnam Vets* (New York: Ballantine, 1986), p. 29.
8. Ibid, p. 153.
9. Gavin Reid, *Living the New Life* (Nashville, Tenn.: Abingdon, 1977), pp. 33, 34.
10. In Kimball, op. cit., pp. 271–72.
11. Mahedy, op. cit., pp. 224, 225.
12. Iona Henry with Frank S. Mead, *Triumph Over Tragedy* (New York: Fleming H. Revell Company, 1957), pp. 110, 111.
13. Chuck Dean with Bob Putnam, *Nam Vet: Making Peace with Your Past* (Mountlake Terrace, Wash.: Point Man International, 1988), p. 63.
14. John A. Sanford, *Dreams: God's Forgotten Language* (New York: Harper & Row, 1968), pp. 52–53.
15. Rev. Kenneth J. Zanca, *Mourning: The Healing Journey* (Locust Valley, N.Y.: Living Flame Press, 1980), p. 46.
16. Warren W. Wiersbe, *Why Us? When Bad Things Happen to God's People* (Old Tappan, N.J.: Fleming H. Revell Company, 1984), p. 96.
17. Richard Rice, *God's Foreknowledge and Man's Free Will* (Minneapolis, Minn.: Bethany House, 1985), p. 67.
18. Ibid., p. 103.
19. Ibid., p. 104.
20. W. Robert McClelland, *God Our Loving Enemy* (Nashville, Tenn.: Abingdon, 1982) p. 36.
21. Ibid., p. 34.
22. Ibid., p. 51.
23. Ibid., p. 35.
24. Ibid., pp. 59–60.
25. Pierre Wolff, *May I Hate God?* (New York: Paulist Press, 1979), pp. 16, 17.

26. Zanca, op. cit., 47–48.
27. Don Baker, *Heaven: A Glimpse of Your Future Home* (Portland, Ore.: Multnomah Press, 1983), p. 10.

COMING TO TERMS WITH THE GUILT OF WAR   CHAPTER 12

1. Robert J. Lifton, *Home from the War* (New York: Simon and Schuster, 1973), p. 113.
2. John Steer with Cliff Dudley, *Vietnam Curse or Blessing?* (Green Forest, Ark.: New Leaf Press, 1982), pp. 100, 156.
3. Private interview with Rev. John Steer, 15 September 1988.
4. Herbert Hendin and Ann P. Haas, *Wounds of War: The Psychological Aftermath of Combat in Vietnam* (New York: Basic Books, 1984), p. 161.
5. William P. Mahedy, *Out of the Night: The Spiritual Journey of Vietnam Vets* (New York: Ballantine, 1986), p. 29.
6. Ibid., p. 27.
7. Psychiatrist Robert J. Lifton in his book *Home from the War* (pp. 126–28) describes two forms of guilt typical of the veteran: static and animating. *Static guilt* is characterized by a closed universe of transgression and expected punishment, in which one is unable to extricate oneself from a death-like individual condition, a form of which is *numbed guilt*, in which one's "deadened state" seems to be a literal form of retribution for one's own act of "killing": the "punishment fits the crime." . . . the entire being is frozen or desensitized, in order to avoid feeling the "wound" (or "death") one has caused (or thinks one has caused), leaving one anesthetized from much of life itself. Numbed guilt includes a vague feeling of badness. . . . Unable to confront what one has done, or even to feel clearly guilty, one is plagued by an unformed, free-floating discomfort with oneself, which is likely to be associated with touchiness, suspiciousness, and withdrawal. *Self-lacerating guilt* is another form of static guilt, in which, rather than a sustained "deadening," one performs a perpetual "killing" of self. Guilt accompanying clinical forms of depression, and what we speak of more generally as "neurotic guilt," tends to be of this self-lacerating variety. In both of these forms of static guilt one is cut off from the life process—held in a state of separation and inner disintegration as well as stasis—that is, in a death-dominated condition. *Animating guilt*, in contrast, is characterized by bringing oneself to life around one's guilt. Animating guilt propels one toward connection, integrity, and move-

ment. Animating guilt engenders an energy of aspiration emanating from a sustained and formative dissatisfaction with both self and world. It presses beyond toward new images and possibilities, toward transformation. It is inseparable from the idea of being responsible for one's actions—so much so that we may define it as the anxiety of responsibility.

8. Mahedy, op. cit., p. 103.
9. Ibid., p. 14.
10. Ibid., p. 98.
11. Michael T. Mannion, *A Cry to Be Whole* (Kansas City, Mo.: Sheed & Ward, 1986), p. 73.
12. Ibid., p. 47.
13. Ibid., p. 21.
14. In John Cruden, Assistant Editor, "Veterans' Spiritual Needs Arising in Counseling Sessions," Vet Center *Voice* (Fargo, N.D.: December 1985), pp. 8–9.
15. David A. Seamands, *Healing of Memories* (Wheaton, Ill.: Victor Books, 1986), p. 24.
16. Colin Brown, ed, *The New International Dictionary of New Testament Theology* (Grand Rapids, Mich.: Zondervan Publishing House, 1975), Vol. 1: A–F, p. 698.
17. In Michael S. Kimmel, "Prophet of Survival," *Psychology Today* (June 1988), p. 47.
18. Daily Family Devotions, P.O. Box 1246, Palisades, CA 90272, Monday, 27 April 1987.
19. Mahedy, op. cit., p. 135.
20. Steer private interview, op. cit.
21. J. B. Phillips, *The New Testament in Modern English* (Great Britain: Cox & Wyman Ltd., 1959), p. 483.
22. Leslie D. Weatherhead, *Life Begins at Death* (Nashville, Tenn.: Abingdon, 1969), p. 73.
23. Millard J. Erickson, *Concise Dictionary of Christian Theology* (Grand Rapids, Mich.: Baker Book House, 1986), p. 22.
24. Seamands, op. cit., pp. 76–77.
25. Lifton, op. cit., p. 113.
26. In Sister Corita Dickinson, "The Search for Spiritual Meaning," *American Journal of Nursing* (Vol. 75, No. 10, October 1975), p. 1793.
27. Merlin R. Carothers, *Power in Praise* (Plainfield, N.J.: Logos International, 1972), p. 52.
28. Billy Graham, *The Holy Spirit* (Waco, Tex.: Word Books, 1978), p. 150.
29. Weatherhead, op. cit., p. 67.

30. Eugene B. McDaniel with James Johnson, *Scars and Stripes* (New York: A. J. Holman/Harvest House, 1975), pp. 168–69.
31. Corrie ten Boom and Jamie Buckingham, *Tramp for the Lord* (Old Tappan, N.J.: Christian Literature Crusade and Fleming H. Revell Company, 1974), pp. 41, 47.
32. Corrie ten Boom, *Each New Day* (Minneapolis, Minn.: World Wide Publications, 1977), April 25.
33. Adapted from and used by permission of Conquerors Post Abortion Support Group, a ministry of New Life Homes & Family Services, 3361 Republic Avenue, Suite 201, Minneapolis, Minn. 55436.

UNFINISHED BUSINESS AND STEPS THROUGH GRIEF   CHAPTER 13

1. In Susan Scott, "Vietnam Veteran Celebrates Peace," *Rock Island Argus*, 22 November 1988, A2.
2. David Roberts, telephone interview, 15 February 1989.
3. John W. James and Frank Cherry, *The Grief Recovery Handbook: A Step-by-Step Program for Moving Beyond Loss* (New York: Harper & Row, 1988), p. 33.
4. Aphrodite Matsakis, *Vietnam Wives* (Kensington, Md.: Woodbine House, 1988), p. 84.
5. James and Cherry, op. cit., pp. 4, 5.
6. Ibid., p. 44.
7. Ibid., p. 123.
8. Ibid., p. 60.
9. Barbara Giaquinta, "Helping Families Face the Crisis of Cancer," *American Journal of Nursing* (Vol. 77, No. 10, October 1977), p. 1587.
10. James and Cherry, op. cit., p. 91.
11. Colgrove et al., *How to Survive the Loss of a Love* (New York: Bantam Books, 1976).
12. Ibid., p. 59.
13. James and Cherry, p. 118.
14. Kenneth Moses, Ph.D., lecture at Western Illinois University, Macomb, Illinois, 1980.
15. Sister Teresa M. McIntier and Nan R. Kenton, "From the Valley of Grief to the Mountain of Renewal: A Journey of Loving Pain," *Thanatos* (Winter 1988), p. 18.
16. Personal statement signed only as "Linda" from a Vet Center in Chicago, Illinois, undated.
17. *Veteran* (Vol. 8, No. 9, September 1988), p. 14.
18. Private interview with Carol Troescher, Ed.D., 8 October 1988.

1. Private interview with Jo Harris, 11 March 1988.
2. David A. Seamands, *Healing of Memories* (Wheaton, Ill.: Victor Books, 1985), p. 24.
3. Ibid., p. 13.
4. Ibid., p. 12.
5. Ibid., p. 24.
6. Ibid., p. 27.
7. Ibid., pp. 34–35.
8. Ibid., p. 181.
9. Ibid., p. 79.
10. Ibid., pp. 63–64.
11. Ibid., pp. 66–67.
12. Agnes Sanford, *The Healing Gifts of the Spirit* (San Francisco: Harper & Row, 1966) p. 137.
13. Ibid., pp. 139–140.
14. Floyd McClung, Jr., *The Father Heart of God* (Eugene, Ore.: Harvest House, 1985), p. 78.
15. Morton Kelsey, *Dreams: A Way to Listen to God* (New York: Paulist Press, 1978), p. 47.
16. Personal correspondence with Joel Osler Brende, M.D., dated 2 January 1990.
17. Joel Osler Brende, M.D., "The Use of Hypnosis in Post-traumatic Conditions," *Post-Traumatic Stress Disorder and the War Veteran Patient*, ed. William E. Kelly, M.D. (New York: Brunner/Mazel, 1985), pp. 193–210.
18. Brende Correspondence op. cit.
19. John A. Sanford, *Dreams: God's Forgotten Language* (New York: Harper & Row, 1968), pp. 151–152.
20. Ibid., pp. 152–153.
21. Ibid., p. 151.
22. Kelsey, op. cit., pp. 100–101.
23. Mountain Spirit Tapes Catalog, Diana Keck, M.A.
24. Dr. Joseph Murphy, *The Power of the Subsconscious Mind* (Englewood Cliffs, N.J.: Prentice-Hall, 1963), p. 98.
25. In the Rev. Rufus J. Womble, D. D., "With God All Things Are Possible," *Sharing: A Journal of Christian Healing* (April 1989), p. 10.
26. George Esper "Vets Finding Warm Welcome," *Daily Courier-News*, Elgin, Ill., 30 January 1989, p. 3.
27. William Kimball, "Vets With a Mission," *Update Letter*, March Issue, 1989.

28. Ibid.
29. General John W. Vessey, "The Problem of the Disabled in Vietnam," U.S. Department of State (Washington, D.C., 13 October 1987).
30. In Esper, op. cit.
31. *Rock Island Argus*, 9 February 1989, p. C11.
32. In Mike McManus (Washington), "Wartime Killer Becomes a Healer," *Daily Dispatch*, 25 February 1989, p. B9.
33. Personal correspondence from David Evans, 24 March, 1989.
34. In Michael Parks, "U.S., Soviet Vets Share Grief of War," *Los Angeles Times*, 18 October 1988, Part I.
35. Telephone interview with David Evans, 11 March 1989.
36. In Don Baty, "Wounds of War," *Missoulian*, 3 January 1989, p. 10.
37. Personal interview and correspondence with Trav O'Hearn, 1 January 1989.
38. Telephone interview with Bob Fowler, 4 April 1989.

DELAYED PARADES   CHAPTER 15

1. In Duncan Spencer, "The Invisible Northern Veteran," *Veteran* (Vol. 9, No. 11, November 1989), p. 7.
2. Ibid.
3. "Veterans Rescue 18 from Fire," United Press International, 8 May 1985.
4. William Mullen, "Chicago's Vietnam Veterans Parade—How One Weekend Healed a Million Old Wounds," *SUNDAY Chicago Tribune Magazine*, 17 August 1986, p. 16.
5. Ibid., p. 13.
6. Ibid., p. 16.
7. In Brett Brune, "Mom of Two Killed in Vietnam Celebrates Recognition," *Quad City Times*, 8 August 1987.
8. In Susan Scott, "Penas Will Make Parade," *The Daily Dispatch*, p. 1.
9. In Joseph Payne, "We All Share the Scar of the Vietnam War," *The Leader*, 12 August 1987, p. A4.
10. Ibid.

THE WALL OF TEARS   CHAPTER 16

1. From private interview with Ira Hamburg, 21 July 1988, and personal correspondence, 31 December 1989.
2. Jan C. Scruggs and Joel L. Swerdlow, *To Heal a Nation: The Vietnam Veterans Memorial* (New York: Harper & Row, 1985), p. 7.
3. Ibid., p. 12.

4. Ibid., p. 16.
5. Ibid., p. 54.
6. Statement by Maya Ying Lin appeared in *National Geographic* (Vol. 67, No. 5, May 1985), p. 557.
7. Scruggs and Swerdlow, op. cit., p. 160.
8. Ibid., p. 142.
9. Ibid.
10. Laura Palmer, *Shrapnel in the Heart* (New York: Random House, 1987), p. 95.
11. In Scruggs and Swerdlow, op. cit., pp. 154, 155.
12. Ibid., p. 154.
13. Taken from a brochure on "The Moving Wall," produced by the McDonough County Chapter of ViêtNow, Macomb, Illinois.
14. Taken from a brochure published by Friends of the Vietnam Veterans Memorial.
15. Scruggs and Swerdlow, op. cit., p. 160.
16. Taken from *New and Collected Poems, 1917–1976* by Archibald Mac-Leish (Boston: Houghton Mifflin, 1976).

VETERANS SPEAK OUT   CHAPTER 17

1. Seymour Leventman, "Official Neglect of Vietnam Veterans," *Journal of Social Issues* (Vol. 31, No. 1, 1975), p. 172.
2. Michelle Lewis, "Veterans Denied Health Care Because of Budget Shortfall," *The Stars and Stripes—The National Tribune*, 3 April 1989, pp. 1, 9.
3. Fred A. Wilcox, *Waiting for An Army to Die: The Tragedy of Agent Orange* (New York: Vintage, 1983), p. *xv*.
4. James Martin Davis, "Vietnam: What It Was Really Like," *Military Review* (January 1989), pp. 39, 40, 44.
5. Argus staff/wire report, "Peace Activists Protest War Toys," *Rock Island Argus*, 30 November 1987.
6. Patrick Seitz, "Vietnam Vets Want Aid to Contras Stopped," *Rock Island Argus*, 1 October 1987, p. A3.
7. Barbara A. Hedin, R.N., Ph.D., "Through a Glass Darkly: Vietnam, Alienation, and Passion," *MINERVA: Quarterly Report on Women and the Military* (Vol. VI, No. 4, Winter 1988), pp. 56–64.
8. In Dan Goodgame/Los Angeles, "How the War Was Won," *Time* (26 January 1987), p. 58.

APPENDIX A

1. Richard McSorley, *New Testament Basis of Peace Making* (Scottdale, Pa.: Herald Press, 1979, 1985), p. 13.
2. Susan Thistlewaite, ed., *A Just Peace Church* (New York: United Church Press, 1986), p. 17.
3. Ibid., p. 24.
4. Gwynne Dyer. *War* (New York: Crown, 1985), pp. *xi, xii.*
5. "Affirming Illinois Conference United Church of Christ A Just Peace Conference," Pronouncement and Call to Action, Prepared by the Peace, Poverty, Hunger Network, with additions by Jay Lintner, Director, Office for Church in Society, in personal correspondence dated 19 October 1989.

APPENDIX B

1. Joseph Bayly, *A Psalm of Suffering* (Elgin, Ill.: David C. Cook, 1987), p. 20.
2. Leslie F. Brandt, *Psalms/Now* (St. Louis, Mo.: Concordia, 1973), p. 131.
3. Ibid., p. 199.
4. Ibid., pp. 68–69.
5. Ibid., pp. 51–52.

APPENDIX C

1. Private interview with Gary Williams, 21 February 1988.
2. McFarland, Tolstedt, and Meyer, comps., "Moral and Spiritual Issues with Vietnam Veterans," The Chicago Area Consortium for Veteran Providers, 24 October 1985.
3. Ibid.
4. Vet Center *Voice* (Fargo, N.D.: December, 1985), p. 9.

APPENDIX D

1. William P. Mahedy, *Out of the Night: The Spiritual Journey of Vietnam Vets.* (New York: Ballantine, 1986), p. 14.
2. John A. Sanford, *Dreams: God's Forgotten Language* (New York: Harper & Row, 1968), pp. 160–61.
3. Ibid., p. 161.

SELECTED BIBLIOGRAPHY

Austin, Anthony. *The President's War: The Story of the Tonkin Gulf Resolution and How the Nation was Trapped in Vietnam.* New York: J.B. Lippincott Co., 1971.

Bainton, Roland H. *Christian Attitudes Toward War and Peace.* Nashville, Tenn.: Abingdon, 1960.

Baker, Mark. *Nam.* New York: William Morrow, 1980; Reprint ed. New York: Berkley, 1981.

Beattie, Melody. *Codependent No More.* New York: Harper/Hazelden, 1987.

Blakey, Scott. *Prisoner at War: The Survival of Commander Richard A. Stratton.* Garden City, N.Y.: Anchor Press, 1978.

Brende, Joel Osler and Erwin Randolph Parson. *Vietnam Veterans: The Road to Recovery.* New York: Plenum Press, 1985; Reprint ed. New York: Signet, 1986.

Broyles, William, Jr. *Brothers in Arms: A Journey From War to Peace.* New York: Alfred A. Knopf, 1986; Reprint ed. New York: Avon, 1987.

Carothers, Merlin R. *Power in Praise.* Plainfield, N.J.: Logos International, 1972.

Cleland, Max. *Strong at the Broken Places.* New York: Chosen Books, Fleming H. Revell Co., 1980; Reprint ed. New York: Berkley, 1982.

Davidson, Lt. Gen. Phillip B. (Ret.). *Vietnam at War: The History 1946–1975.* Novato, Calif.: Presidio, 1988.

Davis, Ron Lee with James C. Denney. *The Healing Choice.* Waco, Tex.: Word Books, 1986.

Dean, Chuck with Bob Putman. *Nam Vet: Making Peace with Your Past.* Mountlake Terrace, Wash.: Point Man International, 1988.

Del Vecchio, John M. *The 13th Valley*. New York: Bantam, 1982.

Denton, Jeremiah A., Jr., with Ed Brandt. *When Hell Was in Session*. New York: Readers Digest Press, 1976.

Downs, Frederick, Jr. *Aftermath*. New York: W. W. Norton, 1984; Reprint ed. New York: Berkley, 1985.

Doyle, Edward, Terrence Maitland, and the Editors of Boston Publishing Co. *The Aftermath. The Legacy of War, 1975–1985*. Boston: Boston Publishing Co., 1985.

Droege, Thomas A. *Guided Grief Imagery*. Mahwah, N.J.: Paulist Press, 1987.

Duncan, David Douglas. *War Without Heroes*. New York: Harper & Row, 1974.

Dyer, Gwynne. *War*. New York: Crown, 1985.

Edelman, Bernard, ed. *Dear America: Letters Home from Vietnam*. New York: Pocket Books, 1985.

Egendorf, Arthur. *Winning the War We Lost*. Miami, Fl.: New Age, 1985.

———. *Healing from the War*. Boston: Shambhala, 1985.

Ellsberg, Daniel. *Papers on the War*. New York: Simon & Schuster, 1972.

Emerson, Gloria. *Winners and Losers*. New York: Random House, 1972.

Erickson, Millard J. *Concise Dictionary of Christian Theology*. Grand Rapids, Mich.: Baker Book House, 1986.

Esper, George, and The Associated Press. *The Eyewitness History of the Vietnam War*. New York: Ballantine, 1983.

Figley, Charles R., ed. *Stress Disorders Among Vietnam Veterans*. New York: Brunner/Mazel, 1978.

FitzGerald, Frances. *Fire in the Lake*. Boston: Little, Brown and Co., 1972.

Flowers, A. R. *De Mojo Blues*. New York: Ballantine, 1985.

Frey, William H., with Muriel Langseth. *Crying: The Mystery of Tears*. New York: Harper & Row, 1987.

Gentz, William H., ed. *The Dictionary of Bible and Religion*. Nashville, Tenn.: Abingdon, 1986.

Gibson, James W. *The Perfect War: The War We Couldn't Lose and How We Did*. New York: Random House, 1986.

Glick, Allen. *The Winter Marines*. Austin, Tex.: Eakin Press, 1984 (formerly titled, *Winter's Coming, Winter's Gone*); Reprint ed. New York: Bantam, 1987.

Goldman, Peter, and Tony Fuller. *Charlie Company: What Vietnam Did to Us*. New York: Ballantine, 1983.

Hackworth, Col. David. *About Face*. New York: Simon & Schuster, 1989.

Halberstam, David. *The Best and the Brightest*. New York: Random House, 1969, 1971, 1972.

_____. *Ho*. New York: Random House, 1971.

Harris, William H., and Judith S. Levey, eds. *The New Columbia Encyclopedia*. New York: Columbia University Press, 1975.

Helle, Roger, as told to Ezra Coppin. *My War Beyond Vietnam*. Ventura, Calif.: Regal Books, 1985.

Helm, Eric. *The Iron Triangle*. Ontario, Can.: Worldwide, 1988.

Hendin, Herbert, and Ann P. Haas. *Wounds of War: The Psychological Aftermath of Combat in Vietnam*. New York: Basic Books, 1984.

Herrington, Stuart A. *Silence Was a Weapon*. New York: Presidio Press, 1982; Reprint ed. New York: Ballantine, 1982.

Hubbell, John G. *P. O.W.: A Definitive History of the American Prisoner-of-War Experience in Vietnam, 1964–1973*. New York: Reader's Digest Press, 1976.

James, John W., and Frank Cherry. *The Grief Recovery Handbook: A Step-by-Step Program for Moving Beyond Loss*. New York: Harper & Row, 1988.

Jampolsky, Gerald G. *Good-bye to Guilt*. New York: Bantam, 1985.

_____. *Love Is Letting Go of Fear*. Berkeley, Calif.: Celestial Arts, 1979; Reprint ed. New York: Bantam, 1981.

Jennings, Patrick. *Battles of the Vietnam War*. New York: Bison Books, 1985.

Jury, Mary. *The Vietnam Photo Book*. New York: Grossman, 1971.

Karnow, Stanley. *Vietnam: A History*. New York: Viking Penguin, 1983.

Kelly, William E., ed. *Post-Traumatic Stress Disorder and the War Veteran Patient*. New York: Brunner/Mazel, 1985.

Kelsey, Morton. *Dreams: A Way to Listen to God*. New York: Paulist Press, 1978.

Kimball, William R. *Vietnam: The Other Side of Glory*. Canton, Ohio: Daring Books, 1987; Reprint ed. New York: Ballantine, 1988.

Krause, Patricia, A., ed., *Anatomy of An Undeclared War: Congressional Conference on The Pentagon Papers*. New York: International Universities Press, 1972.

Kubey et al. *The Viet Vet Survival Guide*. New York: Ballantine, 1985.

Lacouture, Jean. *Ho Chi Minh: A Political Biography*. New York: Random House, 1968.

Larsen, Earnie. *Stage II Recovery: Life Beyond Addiction*. San Francisco: Harper & Row, 1985.

Leventhal, Albert R., and Jerry Mason, eds. *War*. A Ridge Press Book/A & W Visual Library, 1973.

Lifton, Robert J. *Home From the War*. New York: Simon & Schuster, 1973.

_____. *The Broken Connection*. New York: Simon & Schuster, 1979.

Ligon, Ernest M. *The Psychology of Christian Personality*. New York: Macmillan, 1961.

Lind, Millard C. *Yahweh Is a Warrior*. Scottsdale, Pa.: Herald Press, 1980.

Linedecker, Clifford. *Kerry: Agent Orange and an American Family*. New York: St. Martin's Press, 1982.

Lowry, Timothy S. *And Brave Men, Too*. New York: Crown Publishers, 1985; Reprint ed. New York: Berkley, 1986.

McClelland, Robert W. *God Our Loving Enemy*. Nashville, Tenn.: Abingdon, 1982.

McClung, Floyd, Jr. *The Father Heart of God: God Loves You—Learn to Know His Compassionate Touch*. Eugene, Ore.: Harvest House, 1985.

McDaniel, Eugene B., with James Johnson. *Scars and Stripes*. (Formerly *Before Honor*). New York: A. J. Holman/Harvest House, 1975.

McLaughlin, Iona Henry, with Frank S. Mead. *Triumph Over Tragedy*. Nashville, Tenn.: Abingdon, 1957.

MacNutt, Francis. *Healing*. Notre Dame, Ind.: Ave Maria Press, 1974.

MacPherson, Myra. *Long Time Passing: Vietnam and the Haunted Generation*. Garden City, N.Y.: Doubleday & Co., 1984; Reprint ed. New York: Signet, 1985.

McSorley, Richard. *New Testament Basis of Peacemaking*. Scottdale, Pa.: Herald Press, 1979, 1985.

Mahedy, William P. *Out of the Night: The Spiritual Journey of Vietnam Vets*. New York: Ballantine, 1986.

Mangold, Tom, and John Penycate. *The Tunnels of Cu Chi*. New York: Random House, 1985; Reprint ed. New York: Berkley, 1986.

Mason, Robert. *Chickenhawk*. New York: Viking Press, 1983; Reprint ed. New York: Penguin, 1984.

Matsakis, Aphrodite. *Vietnam Wives*. Kensington, Md.: Woodbine House, 1988.

Mills, Nick. *The Vietnam Experience: Combat Photographer*. Boston: Boston Publishing Co., 1983.

Murphy, Joseph. *The Power of the Subconscious Mind*. Englewood Cliffs, N.J.: Prentice-Hall, 1963.

Neilands, J. B., et al. *Harvest of Death: Chemical Warfare in Vietnam and Cambodia*. New York: Free Press, 1972.

Nixon, Richard. *No More Vietnams*. New York: Arbor House, 1985; Reprint ed. New York: Avon, 1986.

Nolan, Keith W. *Battle for Hue: Tet Offensive 1968*. New York: Presidio, 1983; Reprint ed. New York: Dell, 1983.

Norwood, Robin. *Women Who Love Too Much: When You Keep Wishing and Hoping He'll Change*. New York: St. Martin's Press, 1985; Reprint ed. New York: Pocket Books, 1986.

Ogden, Richard E. *Green Knight, Red Mourning*. New York: Zebra Books, 1985.

Palmer, General Bruce, Jr. *The 25-Year War: America's Military Role in Vietnam*. Lexington, Ky.: University Press of Kentucky, 1984; Reprint ed. New York: Simon & Schuster, 1985.

Palmer, Laura. *Shrapnel in the Heart*. New York: Random House, 1987.

Parrish, John A. *12, 20, and 5: A Doctor's Year in Vietnam*. New York: E. P. Dutton & Co., 1972.

Pilger, John. *The Last Day*. New York: Vantage, 1975.

Pollock, J. C. *Mission M.I.A.* New York: Dell, 1982.

Polner, Murray. *No Victory Parades: The Return of the Vietnam Veteran*. New York: Holt, Rinehart and Winston, 1971.

Reflections on the Wall. Smithsonian Institution's Office of Printing & Photographic Services, 1987.

Reid, Gavin. *Living the New Life*. Nashville, Tenn.: Abingdon, 1977.

Restak, Richard M. *The Brain*. New York: Bantam, 1984.

Roever, Dave, and Harold Fickett. *Welcome Home, Davey*. Waco, Tex.: Word Books, 1986.

Rowe, James N. *Five Years to Freedom*. New York: Ballantine, 1971.

Sanford, Agnes. *The Healing Light*. St. Paul, Minn.: Macalester Park Publishing Co., 1947.

————. *The Healing Gifts of the Spirit*. San Francisco: Harper & Row, 1966.

Sanford, John A. *Dreams: God's Forgotten Language*. New York: Harper & Row, 1968.

Sanford, John and Paula. *Healing the Wounded Spirit*. South Plainfield, N.J.: Bridge Publishing, 1985.

Santoli, Al. *Everything We Had*. New York: Ballantine, 1981.

————. *To Bear Any Burden*. New York: E. P. Dutton, 1985; Reprint ed. New York: Ballantine, 1986.

Scruggs, Jan C. and Joel L. Swerdlow. *To Heal A Nation: The Vietnam Veterans Memorial*. New York: Harper & Row, 1985.

Seamands, David A. *Healing of Memories*. Wheaton, Ill.: Victor Brooks, 1986.

Segal, Julius. *Winning Life's Toughest Battles: Roots of Human Resilience*. New York: McGraw-Hill, 1986.

Sheehan, Neil. *A Bright Shining Lie: John Paul Vann and America in Vietnam*. New York: Random House, 1988.

Siegel, Bernie S. *Love, Medicine and Miracles*. New York: Harper & Row, 1986.

Smith, George E. *P.O.W.: Two Years With the Vietcong*. Berkeley, Calif.: Ramparts Press, 1971.

Selected Bibliography

Spencer, Duncan. *Facing the Wall*. New York: Macmillan, 1986.

Stanton, Shelby L. *The Rise and Fall of an American Army: U.S. Ground Forces in Vietnam, 1965–1973*. New York: Dell, 1985.

Steer, John, with Clifford Dudley. *Vietnam: Curse or Blessing*. Green Forest, Ark.: New Leaf Press, 1982.

Stein, Jeff. *The Vietnam Fact Book*. New York: Dell, 1987.

Summers, Harry G., Jr. *Vietnam War Almanac*. New York: New York Facts on File Publication, 1985.

————. *On Strategy: A Critical Analysis of the Vietnam War*. Novato, Calif.: Presidio, 1982.

Terry, Wallace. *Bloods: An Oral History of the Vietnam War by Black Americans*. New York: Ballantine, 1984.

Thistlewaite, Susan, ed. *A Just Peace Church*. New York: United Church Press, 1986.

Turley, William S. *The Second Indochina War: A Short Political and Military History, 1954–1975*. New York: New American Library, 1986.

Van Blair, Bruce. *A Year to Remember: 52 Contemplative Messages on 12 Step Recovery and Christianity*. Seattle: Glen Abbey Books, 1988.

Vance, Samuel. *The Courageous and the Proud: A Black Man in the White Man's Army*. New York: W. W. Norton, 1970.

Van Devanter, Lynda, with Christopher Morgan. *Home Before Morning*. New York: Beaufort Books, 1983; Reprint ed. New York: Warner Books, 1984.

Veninga, James, and Harry A. Wilmer, eds. *Vietnam in Remission*. College Station, Texas: University Press, 1985.

Walker, Keith. *A Piece of My Heart. The Stories of Twenty-Six American Women Who Served in Vietnam*. New York: Ballantine Books, 1985.

Weatherhead, Leslie D. *Life Begins at Death*. Nashville, Tenn.: Abingdon, 1969.

Wells, John M., comp. and ed. *The People vs. Presidential War*. New York: Dunellen Company, 1970.

Wiersbe, Warren W. *Why Us? When Bad Things Happen to God's People*. Old Tappan, N.J.: Fleming H. Revell Co., 1984.

Wilcox, Fred A. *Waiting for An Army to Die: The Tragedy of Agent Orange*. New York: Vintage, 1983.

Williams, Tom, ed. *Post-Traumatic Stress Disorders: A Handbook for Clinicians*. Cincinnati, Ohio: Disabled American Veterans National Headquarters, 1987.

Wolff, Pierre. *May I Hate God?* New York: Paulist Press, 1979.

World Book Encyclopedia, "Vietnam," Vol. 20. Chicago: World Books, 1987.

Selected Bibliography

Zinn, Howard. *A People's History of the United States*. New York: Harper & Row, 1980.

Zumwalt, Admiral Elmo, Jr., and Lt. Elmo III, with John Pekkanen. *My Father, My Son*. New York: Macmillan, 1986.

STUDIES/SPECIAL REPORTS

CDC Vietnam Experience Study. "Health Status of Vietnam Veterans, I. Psychosocial Characteristics, II. Physical Health, III. Reproductive Outcomes and Child Health," *Journal of the American Medical Association*, Vol. 359 No. 18 (13 May 1988), pp. 2701–19.

Columbia University and American Legion Study of Vietnam Veterans, No. 27–85 (19–6), 29 July 1985.

Kulka et al. *National Vietnam Veterans Readjustment Study*, "Executive Summary: Contractual Report of Findings from the National Vietnam Veterans Readjustment Study" Research Triangle Park, N.C.: Research Triangle Institute, 7 November 1988.

Mollison, Fr. Roger. "A Cry From the Heart: A Paper about the Dilemma and Sufferings of the Vietnam Veteran," 4 March 1982.

O'Neill, Jacquelyn, and Elizabeth A. Paul. "The Psychosocial Milieu of Nursing in Vietnam and Its Effects on Vietnam Nurse Veterans." Study done by the College of Nursing, State University of Louisiana, Shreveport, La., January 1984.

Physically Disabled Vietnam Veterans, Report of the Working Group, Submitted to Readjustment Counseling Service Department of Veterans Affairs, Washington, D.C., April 1988.

Postservice Mortality Among Vietnam Veterans, U.S. Department of Health and Human Services Public Health Service. Centers for Disease Control, Atlanta, GA, 1987.

Problem of the Disabled in Vietnam, The. A Report to Nongovernment Organizations Stemming From the Mission to Hanoi by Presidential Emmissary, General John W. Vessey, U.S. Department of State, Washington, D.C., 13 October 1987.

Texas Department of Health, *Texas Veterans Agent Orange Assistance Program*, Austin, Tex., August, 1985.

Vietnam Veteran in Contemporary Society. Veterans Administration, May 1972.

Wheeler, John P. "Theological Reflections upon the Vietnam War," *Anglican Theological Review*, Vol. 61 No. 4, 1982.

Zumwalt, Admiral Elmo, Jr. "A Statement before the Human Resources and Intergovernmental Relations Subcommittee of the Committee on

Government Operations" made before the House of Representatives, 26 June 1990.

————. "Report to the Secretary of the Department of Veterans Affairs on the Association Between Adverse Health Effects and Exposure to Agent Orange," 5 May 1990.

VIDEOTAPES

Facing Evil: With Bill Moyers, A Co-Production of Public Affairs Television, Inc., and KERA/Dallas; A Co-Presentation of WNET/New York, WTTW/Chicago, and KERA/Dallas, air date 28 March 1988.

A Program for Vietnam Veterans . . . and Everyone Else Who Should Care, filmed at the University of Wisconsin, hosted by Charles Haid, a production of WTTW/Chicago, Copyright 1985.

Television's Vietnam: The Real Story/The Impact of Media, narrated by Charlton Heston and produced by Accuracy in Media, Inc., Copyright 1984 and 1985.

Wolff, Perry. "The Wall Within," *CBS Reports*, 2 June 1988.

INDEX

Index